(45)

GLIMPSES OF THE DIVINE

by

Bishop Cyril Bulley

Special note

All the author's Royalties in respect of this book
will be paid direct to Helen House, Oxford
for the sustenance of its work for seriously ill
children and their parents.

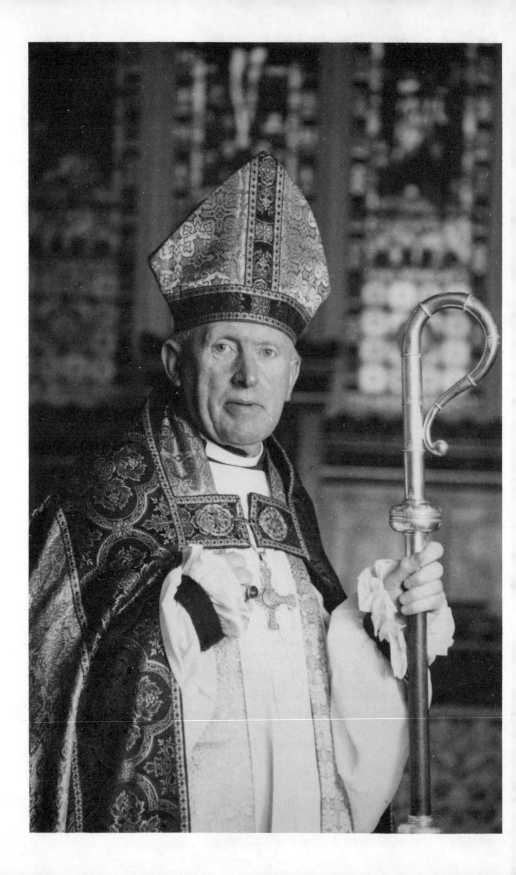

GLIMPSES OF THE DIVINE

A Spiritual Anthology for Use on Every Day of the Year

ঔ

Compiled by

CYRIL BULLEY D.D.

Formerly Bishop of Carlisle

With a Foreword by

HER ROYAL HIGHNESS THE DUCHESS OF KENT

ঔ

CHURCHMAN PUBLISHING: 1987

©1987

The copyright of the arrangement of this anthology
belongs to Sydney Cyril Bulley

GLIMPSES OF THE DIVINE
A SPIRITUAL ANTHOLOGY
compiled by
Cyril Bulley
was first published in Great Britain
in 1987 by
CHURCHMAN PUBLISHING LIMITED
117 Broomfield Avenue
Worthing BN14 7SF
West Sussex

Publisher: E. Peter Smith

Churchman are represented in Sydney, Wellington
and Kingston, Ontario, and
distributed to the book trade by
Bailey Book Distribution Limited
Warner House
Wear Bay Road
Folkestone CT19 6PH
Kent

ISBN 1 85093 081 3

Designed and typeset by
Electronic Village Editorial Services Limited, Richmond, Surrey
Made and Printed by Biddles Limited of Guildford, Surrey

H.R.H. The Duchess of Kent

ᛞ

YORK HOUSE

ST. JAMES'S PALACE

LONDON S.W.1

　　　Bishop Bulley, will earn the gratitude of many
people for writing this book which is such a help in
reminding us that God's love is for us just as we are,
for all the days of our years and for all the moments
of our days. His choice of readings and prayers is not
only beautiful but practical in guiding and encouraging
us on our journey. It helps us to remember that we are
not alone as we journey; there is One who walks beside
us and we can put our hand into the hand of God.

Katharine .

Introduction

This book is designed to help Christians to have a rule of life which demands that some time every day should be set aside for prayer. Prayer is dedication, it is self-forgetting and God directed. It is not invariably compassed in words. Whenever we fix our minds on anything which helps our spirits to soar, we are indeed praying. When I set out upon the task of writing this book some friends, clerical and lay, exhorted me to 'write it for the people in the pews, and remember that we are not all theologians'.

The book offers for every day of the year – following the Church's calendar – something from the works of poets, philosophers, saints, theologians, mystics, and writers who would claim no such titles, something to help our spirits to soar. Following each quotation is a comment which, as necessary, explains, expounds, amplifies or applies, and a prayer which lifts our thoughts, be they aspirations, intercessions, adorations or petitions, to the Living God. But let us remember that 'Prayer', as opposed to 'the prayer' at the foot of each page, is that communion with God which can be ours throughout the ten or fifteen minutes which we give to the reading of, and the pondering upon, the day's offering.

John Keble, the nineteenth century priest, pastor and poet, who in his ministry exercised as profound an influence on the life of the nation as on the lives of individuals, was severely practical in his advice to the Christians of his day. He told them that they must live by rule if they aspired to make progress in the Christian life. 'We must walk orderly before our God', he said. 'We must set ourselves rules and examine ourselves regularly as to how we have kept them and are keeping them'. He added this salutary warning: 'Be quite sure of this, that if you are not really trying to live by rule you have no right to think that you are led by the Spirit'.

Those are stern words but wise because they take account of human frailty. We may well have made our commitment to Christ long since and, maybe, have sealed it in Confirmation. We know well what that commitment demands of us in terms of personal holiness, and in our hearts and minds we have resolved never to renounce it. But, as for Peter, James and John in Gethsemane, so for us: 'The spirit indeed is willing, but the body is weak'. Conscious as we are of the reality of evil, and of its power to shackle our consciences and corrupt our minds, we need to heed Keble's stern warning meticulously.

As we live physically by rule, so we must live spiritually by rule. That rule must embrace personal prayer as well as public worship. To this end many great and good men and women have written words of enlightenment, of encouragement and of direction. Their writings – some profound, some equally valuable for their simplicity – all point, as Keble did, to our need for a rule of life. The basis of that rule is prayer. 'When my spirit soars', said a German theologian, 'my body falls on its knees'.

+ CYRIL BULLEY

East Hagbourne
Summer, 1987

The Naming of Jesus

'Still glides the stream'

I thought of Thee my partner and my guide
As being past away. Vain sympathies!
For backward, Duddon! as I cast my eyes;
I see what was, and is, and will abide;
Still glides the stream, and shall for ever glide;
The Form remains; the Function never dies;
Whilst we, the brave, the mighty, and the wise
We Men who in our morn of youth defied
The elements, must vanish; be it so!
Enough if something from our hands have power
To live, and act, and serve the future hour;
And if, as toward the silent tomb we go,
Through love, through hope, and faith's transcendent dower,
We feel that we are greater than we know.

WILLIAM WORDSWORTH (1779–1850)

Comment

Like the River Duddon, still glides the stream of time. The first day of a new year is also Christ's naming day – 'He shall be called Jesus'. Jesus is the Lord of Time since he unfolded in time God's eternal purpose, and lives ever in the hearts of those who turn to him to unfold that purpose in the stream of time. As Frederick Faber said, 'Each hour comes with some little faggot of God's will fastened upon its back'. The moment offered to take up this opportunity is the moment which resembles eternity. We must therefore take –

Time to work which is the path of service.
Time to play which is the secret of eternal youth,
Time to think which can give birth to wisdom
Time to care which is the road to fulfilment,
Time to repent which is the way to renewal,
Time to forgive which is the path to reconciliation,
Time to love which is the road to heaven,
Time to be silent which is the secret of being,
Time to be still which is to know of God's being,
Time to worship which is the highway to reverence.

Prayer   *O Almighty God, who hast given unto thy Son Jesus Christ the name which is above every name, and hast taught us that there is none other whereby we may be saved. Mercifully grant that as thy faithful people have comfort and peace in his name, so they may ever labour to publish it unto all nations; through Jesus Christ our Lord.*

SCOTTISH PRAYER BOOK

Grant, O Lord, that as the years change we may find rest in thine eternal changelessness. May we meet this new year bravely, sure in the faith that while men come and go, and life changes around us, thou art ever the same, guiding us with thy wisdom, and protecting us with thy love; through Jesus Christ our Lord.

WILLIAM TEMPLE

Religion

And an old priest said (to the Prophet of God): 'Speak to us of Religion'. And he said: 'Have I spoken this day of aught else? Is not religion all deeds and all reflection, and that which is neither deed or reflection but a wonder and a surprise ever springing in the soul, even while the hands hew the stone or tend the loom? Who can separate his faith from his actions, or his belief from his occupations? Who can spread his hours before him saying, "This for God and this for myself; this for my soul and this other for my body"'?

Your daily life is your temple and your religion. Whenever you enter into it take with you your all. Take the plough and the forge and the mallet and the lute. The things you have fashioned in necessity and for delight. And take with you all men. For in adoration you cannot fly higher than their hopes nor humble yourself lower than their despair.

And if you would know God, be not therefore a solver of riddles. Rather look about you and you shall see Him walking in the cloud, outstretching his arms in the lightning and descending in rain. You shall see Him smiling in flowers, then waving His hands in trees'.

KAHLIL GIBRAN (1883–1931)
FROM THE PROPHET

Comment

Poets, theologians, essayists, statesmen, philosophers, historians—they have all in their turn sought to define religion. None has done it more simply yet more profoundly than Kahlil Gibran, and no one has made the Karl Marx definition 'religion is the opium of the people' so plainly absurd. Religion, as defined by The Prophet, does not 'anaesthetise' a person so that he puts up patiently with whatever life brings, however bad, or lies quiescent and content in a busy world which demands response from thinking and caring people. Religion confronts a man with God and, so confronted he is impelled to adore and to serve Him in his daily life, in his leisure as in his work. Religion is that which turns a man's eyes upward to God, inward to himself and outward to his brother man. Whenever the religious man sees a manifestation of goodness, of beauty, of truth—there he sees God. Whenever he loves his neighbour as himself, at that moment God works in him.

Prayer   *Eternal God, giver of light and life, impart to me thoughts higher than my own thoughts and powers beyond my own powers that I may spend and be spent in the ways of love and goodness after your perfect image, through Jesus Christ our Lord.*

Reaching God

But now you will ask me, 'How am I to think of God himself, and what is He?' and I cannot answer you except to say 'I do not know!'. For with this question you have brought me into the same darkness, the same cloud of unknowing where I want you to be! For though we, through the grace of God, can know fully about all other matters, and think about them–yes, even the very works of God himself–yet of God himself can no man think . . . God may well be loved but not thought. By love God can be caught and held, but by thinking never. Therefore though it may be good sometimes to think particularly about God's kindness and worth, and though it may be enlightening too, and a part of contemplation, yet in the work before us it must be put down and covered with a cloud of forgetting. And you are to step over it resolutely and eagerly, with a devout and kindling love, and try to penetrate that darkness about you. Strike that thick cloud of unknowing with the sharp dart of longing love, and on no account whatever think of giving it up.

THE CLOUD OF UNKNOWING (14TH C.)

Comment

Whoever he was who wrote *The Cloud of Unknowing*–and his identity is a mystery–had clearly drawn on the works of great saints who lived before him, men and women who, like himself, had concluded that God cannot be apprehended by the human intellect. So much we must accept. But it does not mean that God cannot be reached by Man. God can be comprehended in the context of love. In this book of contemplation the reader is encouraged to reach out to God not with his mind as one who sees God, but with his heart as one who feels him. It might be said that the author reminds us that there is a rhythm in the Christian life, and that an essential part of that rhythm is contemplation. Reaching through the cloud of unknowing in contemplation, we expose our hearts and minds and wills to the love of God out of His love for us. So will our Christian activity be kindled, informed, sustained and secured.

Prayer   **An Act of Love**

O my God, I desire to love Thee
With all my heart,
With all my soul,
And with all my strength:
Because Thou alone art perfectly good
And worthy of Love
And because Jesus Christ died for me upon the Cross
Help me by thy grace
To continue ever in my love for Thee
And to love my neighbour as Thou dost love me.

ANONYMOUS

Joy in the Morning

When Adam and Eve were driven out of the Garden of Eden they wandered over the face of the earth. The sun began to set and they looked with fear at the lessening of the light, and felt horror like death steal over their hearts. The light of heaven grew paler and the wretched ones clasped each other in an agony of despair. Then all grew dark. The luckless ones fell on the earth, silent, and thought that God had withdrawn from them the light for ever; and they spent the night in tears. But a beam of light began to rise over the eastern hills, after many hours of darknesss, and the golden sun came back and dried the tears of Adam and Eve and then they cried with joy and said, 'Heaviness may endure for the night but joy cometh in the morning.'

THE TALMUD

Comment

'A quotation from the *Talmud* in a Christian devotional book?' perhaps you ask. In fact, Jewish book though it is the *Talmud* embraces so much that is spiritually uplifting that Christians could find in it gems of spiritual counsel. Here was a physical darkness which struck terror in the hearts of Adam and Eve. In the pilgrimage of life, Christians are often impeded and indeed frightened by a spiritual darkness which Robert Browning identified as 'a darkness quenched by hope'. The Psalmist made this discovery and sings of it in his poem (Psalm 139. 'If I say surely the darkness is no darkness with you, but the night is as clear as the day; the darkness and light are both alike'. All of us have periods of darkness – of spirit, of suffering, of sorrow, of disappointment or of failure. There is no promise that we shall be providentially shielded from them. But that we shall be sustained and guided through them is an assurance which the psalmist recognised and experienced and which is confirmed in Our Lord's promise, 'Lo, I am with you always'.

Prayer   *Look down, Lord, from they heavenly throne, illuminate the darkness of this night with thy celestial brightness and from the sons of light banish the deeds of darkness; through Jesus Christ our Lord.*

ORDER OF COMPLINE

God, whose blessed Son promised that all who followed him should not walk in darkness but should have the light of life, grant that when the darkness of disappointment, doubt or despair closes upon me, I may have the wisdom to lift up my heart and eyes to you, and the courage to follow that Light which no darkness can quench, even the Light of your Son our Saviour Jesus Christ.

Divinity Within Us

Now, for my life, it is a miracle of thirty years, which to relate were not a history but a piece of poetry, and would sound to common ears like a fable.

For the world, I count it not an inn but a hospital, and a place not to live in but to die in. The world that I regard is myself; it is the microcosm of my own frame that I cast mine eye on; for the other, I use it but like my globe, and turn it round sometimes for my recreation. That mass of flesh which circumscribes me limits not my mind. That surface that tells the heavens it hath an end cannot persuade me that I have any . . . Whilst I study to find how I am a microcosm, or little world, I find myself something more than the great. There is surely a piece of divinity in us – something that was before the elements, and owes no homage to the Sun.

SIR THOMAS BROWNE (1605–1682)

Comment

Those are the words not of a theologian but of a physician who practised in Norwich, but at the same time wrote a number of books on various aspects of the Christian faith, the quotation being from his most celebrated book *Religio Medici*. Here is a physician who makes a clear distinction between himself and the body in which he lived. For the body there would be an end, for himself there would be no end. For him God was no external power who occasionally interfered with his private life. He was indeed the great transcendent Reality who made himself known through the natural world and through the history of mankind, but he was too that 'piece of divinity' within – the Living God of whom he was ever aware. As for that physician, so for us. There is a 'divinity within', a gentle 'pressure' whom we call the Holy Spirit who seeks from us a response to the transcendent beauty and goodness and truth of the Living God. 'There's a divinity which shapes our ends, rough-hew them how we will', said Shakespeare, but that does not mean that man becomes what God desires him to be even though a man rejects him. God takes the initiative, but he does not impel response. Man may not hear or hearing may not heed, but God does not withdraw nor cease to stir within.

Prayer *Spirit of the Living God, who dwellest in us; who art holy, who art good. Come thou, and fill the hearts of thy people and kindle within them the fire of thy love; through Jesus Christ our Lord.*

LITURGY OF THE CATHOLIC APOSTOLIC CHURCH

Epiphany of Our Lord

The Star

Star of the East, how sweet art Thou.
  Seen in Life's early morning sky,
E're yet a cloud has dimm'd the brow,
  While yet we gaze with childish eye;

What matter? if in calm old age
  Our childhood's star again arise,
Crowning our lonely pilgrimage
  With all that cheers a wanderer's eyes.

Ne'er may we lose it from our sight,
  Till all our hopes and thoughts are led
To Where it stays its lucid light
  Over our Saviour's lowly bed.

There, swathed in humblest poverty,
  On Chastity's meek lap enshrined,
With breathless Reverence waiting by
  When we our sovereign Master find.

Look on us, Lord, and take our parts
  E'en on Thy throne of purity!
From these our proud yet grovelling
  hearts
  Hide not Thy mild forgiving eye.

JOHN KEBLE (1792–1866)

Comment

Keble's Epiphany verses, extracted from his *Christian Year*, make no mention of the Wise Men. It is to the star and the Christ over whom it shone that his words direct our thoughts. Innumerable legends have been woven around this incident of Christ's 'showing forth' to the Gentiles – that those who came were three in number, that they were kings, that their names were Caspar, Melchior and Balthasar, that Melchior was an old man, Caspar young, Balthasar middle-aged, that Melchior brought the gold, young Caspar the frankincense and Balthasar the myrrh. Professor Barclay warns us not 'to turn this lovely poetry into crude and lifeless prose'. Nor must we. The story of the Magi is itself no legend. Whoever these visitors were they came from the East, they were looking for a King, they found him and they worshipped him. 'The Adoration of the Magi' became a subject for Christian art as early as the second century. Therein we find, as they found, the pointer to our response to Christ – adoration.

Prayer

Almighty God, you made known the incarnation of your Son by the bright shining of a star, grant that the star of your righteousness may always shine in our hearts, and that for our treasure we may give to your service ourselves and all that we have; through the same Jesus Christ our Lord.

ADAPTED FROM GELASIAN SACRAMENTS

Eternal God, who by the shining of a star led the wise men to the worship of your Son; guide by his light the actions of the earth that the whole world may behold your glory: through Jesus Christ our Lord.

A.S.B. COLLECT

God in Everything

In the market, in the cloister – only God I saw
In the valley and on the mountain – only God I saw
Him I have seen beside me oft in tribulation;
In favour and in fortune – only God I saw.
In prayer and fasting, in praise and contemplation,
In the religion of the Prophet – only God I saw.
Neither soul nor body, accident nor substance,
Qualities nor causes – only God I saw.
I opened mine eyes and by the light of His face around me
In all the eye discovered – only God I saw.
Like a candle I was melting in his fire:
Amidst the flames outflanking – only God I saw
Myself with mine own eyes I saw most clearly,
But when I looked with God's own eyes – only God I saw.
I passed away into nothingness, I vanished,
And lo, I was the All-living – only God I saw.

Baba Kubi of Shiraz
trans. R.A. Nicholson
from The Sufi Path of Love

Comment

Here is a vision of one who was so far advanced in the spiritual life – in what we call mysticism – that he felt himself ever to be in the conscious presence of the living God. Wherever he went, whatever he saw, in whatever circumstances he found himself, he was aware of God's presence. He was not a pantheist – that is he did not hold the belief that God is omnipresent, that no part of the universe which God created, and certainly Man who is the crown of God's creation, no part of God's handiwork lacks the imprint of God's hand upon it, that God is indeed in everything. This he held to be true through Time and into Eternity. Here he would see God 'through a glass darkly' but beyond death he would pass through gradations of glory to see God face to face. It is not given to mystics alone to sense God's omnipresence. The nineteenth century poet John Clare expresses his own experience in beautiful lines:

> *I feel a presence of delight and fear,*
> *Of love and majesty, far off and near;*
> *Go where I will its absence cannot be,*
> *And solitude and God are one with me;*
> *A presence that one's gloomiest cares caress*
> *And fills up every place to guard and bless.*

Prayer *Give us, O God, a sense of the majesty of your presence; you whom we now seek, you whom we now confess, you whom we adore in faith, you whom we worship in spirit – Holy, Holy, Holy God, come into our home and into our hearts and dwell there, through Jesus Christ our Lord.*

Man begins to wonder

Man saw around him the world with its great silent hills and green valleys; its rugged ridges of purple-tinted mountains and miles of barren flat; its trees and fragrant flowers; the graceful forms of men, the soaring bird, the swift deer and kingly lion, the big ungainly shaped mammoth; the wide scene which came forth with the bidding touch of the sunlight, or bathed in the shadows cast by passing clouds. He saw the sun rise and travel to the west, carrying its light away; the moon at regular times growing from sickle-shape to full round orb; then each night the stars few or many, bursting out like sparks struck off the wheels of the Sun-God's chariot, or like the glittering sprays of water cast out by a ship as she ploughs the sea. His ears listened to the different sounds of Nature; the music of the flowing river; the roar of the never-silent sea; the rustle of the leaves as they were swept by the unseen fingers of the breeze; the patter of the rain as it dripped from the great black clouds. These and a hundred other sounds, now harsh, now sweet, all made him ask, 'What am I? Whence came I?'

EDWARD CLODD

Comment

'What is man that thou art mindful of him?' Ask that question of the chemist and he might list man's constituent parts – fat, iron, water, phosphorus, etc. Ask the physicist and he will add to your knowledge, so too the philosopher, the psychologist and learned men of other disciplines. Add their answers together and you have the truth, nothing but the truth, but not the whole truth. Samuel Butler covered all in his answer: 'Man is God's highest present development. He is the latest thing in God' - by which he declares that man is more than the sum total of the scientists' answers. Man is made in the image of God. The scientists were not in fact defining man. They were defining the body in which a man lives. Edward Clodd is enthralled by the majesty and beauty and power of the natural world. It is from his own seeming smallness in comparison that he asks, 'What am I? Whence came I?'. The answer is, 'I am the child of God, made in his image, I came from God. I belong to God, I go to God.'.

Prayer   *O Thou in whom we live and move and have our being, grant us Thy grace in rich measure, that we may rise to our full stature and dignity as those who are made in Thine image. Renew in us day by day faith and hope and love that we may bear our witness in thought and word and deed that we are thine. We ask this for thy glory and to the welfare of all who are one with us in your family.*

Perfection

All perfection in this life hath some imperfection mixed with it; and no knowledge of ours is without some darkness.

All humble knowledge of thyself is a surer way to God than a deep search after learning.

Yet learning is not to be blamed, nor the mere knowledge of anything whatsoever to be disliked, it being good in itself, and ordained of God; but a good conscience and a virtuous life is always to be preferred before it...

Truly, at the day of judgement we shall not be examined on what we have read, but on what we have done; not how well we have spoken, but how religiously we have lived.

THOMAS À KEMPIS (1379–1471)
THE IMITATION OF CHRIST

The pursuit of perfection, then, is the pursuit of sweetness and light...he who works for sweetness and light united, works to make reason and the will of God prevail.

MATTHEW ARNOLD (1822–1888)

Lord of the loving heart,
May mine be loving too;
Lord of the gentle hands,
May mine be gentle too;
Lord of the willing feet,
May mine be willing too;
So may I grow more like to Thee
In all I say or do.

ANONYMOUS

Comment

The words of St Thomas à Kempis above are salutary, but they do not deny our Lord's command to us: 'You therefore must be perfect as your heavenly Father is perfect'. That commandment strikes us as a commandment to achieve the impossible. In fact the perfection towards which the Christian is directed is perfection in performance. Our Lord is telling his disciples that their function in life is to be Godlike because they were made in the image of God. The moment we forgive one who has wronged us, in that moment we reach perfection. God is love and when we love in the way God loves – forgiving, caring, consoling, reconciling – we are in those moments Christlike – momentarily we have reached perfection, for God lives in us and his perfection shines through us. Our anonymous poet recognised just that in the verse which is, in fact, a prayer for that perfection which is in Christ.

Prayer   *Almighty and Eternal God, who in your Son Jesus Christ has revealed your nature as Love: help me to radiate that love day by day in thought and word and deed, help me to forgive as I am forgiven; help me to care for others as you care for me; help me to comfort, to console, to reconcile, that in my words and my actions others may see something of your great love for all your children that the glory may be yours for ever.*

Confidence

Lord, what is my confidence that I have in this life? Or what is the greatest comfort I can derive from anything under heaven? Is it not Thou, O Lord, whose mercies are without number? Where hath it ever been well with me without Thee? Or when could it be ill with me when Thou wert present? I had rather be poor for Thee, than rich without Thee. I rather choose to be a pilgrim on earth with Thee than without Thee to possess heaven. Where Thou art, there is heaven, and where Thou art not there is death and hell . . . Thou therefore art the End of all that is good, the Height of Life, the Depth of all that can be spoken; and to hope in Thee above all things is the strongest comfort of Thy servants. To Thee therefore do I lift up mine eyes; in Thee, my God, the Father of mercies do I put my trust . . . Protect and keep the soul of me the meanest of Thy servants amidst so many dangers of this corruptible life, and by Thy grace accompanying me, direct it along the way of peace to its home of everlasting brightness.

THOMAS À KEMPIS (1379–1471)
THE IMITATION OF CHRIST

Comment

The mystic Thomas à Kempis knew by personal experience that putting his trust in the Living God, even when he could not trace him in the ups and downs of his own spiritual experience, had never been misplaced. He had the implicit confidence which the Psalmist enjoyed: 'In God have I put my trust: I will not be afraid what man can do unto me'. (Psalm 56, v.11). But both psalmist and saint knew that this confidence in the caring God does not supersede prudence on our part. The dedicated will ensures the directed way and finding that, the Christian goes forward with confidence. The evangelist Charles Spurgeon expressed it in some such words as these: 'When you have no helpers see all your helpers in God. When you have many helpers, see God in all your helpers. When you have nothing but God see all in God'.

Prayer

Most Loving Father, who willest us to give thanks for all things, to dread nothing but the loss of thee, and to cast all our care on thee who carest for us, preserve us from faithless fears and worldly anxieties, and grant that no clouds of this mortal life may hide from us the light of that love which is immortal, and which thou hast manifested unto us by thy Son Jesus Christ our Lord.

A WAR PRIMER

Creation

I have learned
To look on Nature, not as in the hour
Of thoughtless youth; but hearing often-times
The still, sad music of humanity,
Not harsh nor grating, though of ample power
To chasten and subdue. And I have felt
A presence that disturbs me with the joy
Of elevated thoughts; a sense sublime
Of something far more deeply interfused,
Whose dwelling is the light of setting suns,
And the round ocean and the living air,
And the blue sky and in the mind of man;
A motion and a spirit, that impels
All thinking things, all objects of all thought
And rolls through all things.

WILLIAM WORDSWORTH (1770–1850)
TINTERN ABBEY

Comment

The psalmist said it all before: 'The heavens declare the glory of God: and the firmament proclaims his handiwork', and Darwin in his *Origin of Species*, published a year after Wordsworth's death, said it all again: 'There is grandeur in this view of life, with its several powers having been originally breathed by the Creator into a few forms or into one; and that, while this planet has gone cycling on according to the fixed law of gravity, from so simple a beginning, endless forms most beautiful and wonderful have been and are being evolved.'

Prayer

Almighty God, whose glory the heavens are telling, the earth thy power and the sea thy might, and whose greatness all feeling creatures everywhere herald: To thee belongeth glory, honour, might, greatness and magnificence, now and for ever, to the ages of ages.

FROM THE LITURGY OF ST JAMES

All things bright and beautiful,
All creatures great and small,
All things wise and wonderful
The Lord God made them all.

MRS C.F. ALEXANDER

Sic transit gloria mundi

I have employed myself of late pretty much in the study of history and have
been reading the stories of the great men of past ages: Alexander the Great,
Julius Caesar, the great Augustus and many more down, down, down... and
'hic jacet' is the finishing part of their history. Such is the end of human
glory and so little is their world able to do for the greatest of men that come
into it and for the greatest merit those men can arrive to... What then is
the work of life? What the business of great men, that pass the stage of the
world in seeming triumph as these men, we call heroes, have done? Is it
to grow great in the mouth of fame and take up many pages in history?
Alas! that is no more than making a tale for the reading of posterity till
it turns into fable and romance. Is it to furnish subject to the poets and live
in their immortal rhymes, as they call them?... Or is their business rather
to add virtue and piety to their glory which alone will pass them into eternity and make them truly immortal? What is glory without virtue? A great
man without religion is no more that a great beast without a soul. What
is honour without merit? And what can be called true merit but that which
makes a person be a good man as well as a great man?

DANIEL DEFOE (1659–1731)

Comment

So, Daniel Defoe, butcher's son, great man of letters, on the instability of human
glory. The world may accord man many accolades. It may put him on the path
to wealth and fame and greatness. It can indeed make him all those things – famous,
wealthy, great – but it cannot make him a good man and it is goodness which outlasts
all. For the Christian it is always 'To God be the glory', but the giving is not merely in worship, corporate or private. Concluding an address on the life of St Ignatius, Gerard Manley Hopkins sent home those who heard him with this message:
'To lift up the hands in prayer gives God glory, but a man with a dungfork in
his hand, a woman with a slop-pail, gives him glory too. He is so great that all
things give him glory if you mean they should. So brethren live!'

Prayer *God, Whose glory fills the heavens and who for us men and our salvation has unveiled that same glory in the person of your Son our Lord,
enable me by your grace to reflect that glory day be day in my leisure
as in my work. Help me to do all that I have to do cheerfully and willingly, so that, confirmed in your service, all that I do may be done to
the glory of your holy name, through the same Christ our Lord.*

Hilary, Bishop of Poitiers, Teacher of the Faith, 367

The Spirit Comes

Hail, this joyful day's return,
Hail, the pentecostal morn,
Morn when our ascended Head
On his church his spirit shed!
Like to cloven tongues of flame
On the twelve the Spirit came –
Tongues, that earth may hear their calls,
Fire, that love may burn in all.

Hear thy speech before unknown;
Trembling crowds the wonder own;
What though hardened some abide,
And the holy work deride?
Mystic hour, when Easter's sun
Seven times seven its course hath run;
Church of Christ from debt made free,
Hail thy day of jubilee.

Lord, to thee thy people bend;
Unto us thy Spirit send;
Blessings of this sacred day
Grant us, dearest Lord, we pray.
Thou who didst our fathers guide,
With their children still abide;
Grant us pardon, grant us peace,
Till our earthly wanderings cease.

ST HILARY (D.367)
TRANS. R. CAMPBELL (1814–1868)

Comment

Hilary, a child of pagan parents, embraced the Christian Faith in early manhood. He became Bishop of Poitiers in 353 and soon began to attract attention by his vigorous opposition to the Arians who denied the true divinity of Christ. The Arians, however, won the confidence of the Emperor Constantinus who in turn banished Hilary. This did not silence the bishop who in his four years exile in Phrygia defended the orthodox Faith in many treatises, his most famous being *De Trinitate*. In these days too, he wrote many hymns though few of these have found their way into our hymn books. His unswerving defence of the Catholic Faith sealed for him a place among the greatest theologians and in 1851 he was duly proclaimed a 'Doctor of the Church'.

Read verse 3 of Hilary's hymn once more but this time as a prayer. Here is a further prayer based on Hilary's own words:

Prayer   *Lord, you have taught us that you will give to those who ask, that those who seek will find and that to those who knock it shall be opened, impart to us the meaning of the words of Holy Scripture, give us light to understand and confidence to proclaim the truth as you have given it, that by our words and by our example, others may be won to the Faith, to God's glory and to their own salvation, through Jesus Christ our Lord.*

Reverence

O London town has many moods
And mingles 'mongst its many broods
A leavening of saints.
And ever up and down its streets,
If one has eyes to see one meets
Stuff that an artist paints.

I've seen a back street bathed in blue,
Such as the soul of Whistler knew:
A smudge of amber light,
Where some fried fish-shop plied its trade
A perfect note of colour made –
Oh, it was exquisite.

I once came through St James's Park
Betwixt the sunset and the dark,
And of the mystery
Of grey and green and violet
I would I never might forget
That evening harmony.

I hold it true that God is there
If beauty breaks through anywhere;
And His most blessed feet
Who once life's roughest roadway trod,
Who came as man to show us God
Still pass along the street.

FATHER ANDREW S.D.C. (1869–1946)

Comment

It can escape no one's notice that the Lord's Prayer, which was the prayer which Jesus gave to his disciples at their request, begins with an act of reverence: 'Hallowed be Thy Name'. Reverence is the foundation-stone of religion. It is the humble acknowledgement of God's Being and of His nature – that He is our Father and we are His children made in His image and therefore able to communicate with Him. It is, too, an indication of our readiness to submit to His will. But reverence is not something which is practised only when we are engaged in corporate worship or saying our prayers at home. It is, too, an indication of our readiness to treat the whole of God's creation as holy. In the eye of his soul Father Andrew, who was a priest of the Religious Order known as the Society of the Divine Compassion, saw God in Man, in the beauty of the natural world and even in a fried-fish shop!

Prayer

O God most holy, most loving, infinite in wisdom and power: teach us to reverence you in all the works of your hands and to hallow your name both in worship and in daily life that in the things of the temporal we may ever sense the vision of the Eternal: through Jesus Christ our Lord.

Aridity

My heart is empty. All the fountains that should run
With longing, are in me
Dried up. In all my countryside there is not one
That drips to find the sea.
I have no care for anything thy love can grant
Except the moment's vain
And hardly noticed filling of the moment's want
And to be free from pain.
Oh, thou that art unwearying, that didst neither sleep
Nor slumber, who didst take
All care for Lazarus in the careless tomb, oh keep
Watch for me while I wake.
If thou think for me what I cannot think, if thou
Desire for me what I
Cannot desire, my soul's interior Form, though now
Deep buried, will not die,
– No more than the insensible dropp'd seed which grows
Through winter ripe for birth
Because, while it forgets, the heaven remembering throws
Sweet influence still on earth
– Because the heaven, moved mothlike by thy beauty, goes
Still turning round the earth.

C.S. LEWIS (1898–1963)
THE PILGRIM'S REGRESS

Comment

There are moments, even periods, when the most dedicated pilgrim feels that he has come to a dead end. Spiritual resources appear to him to have been exhausted; church going is motivated by convention rather than constraint: prayers have become formal. The pilgrim's progress has been arrested abruptly or retarded by a spiritual dryness or laziness from which he seems to be incapable of bestirring himself. The condition is one which demands treatment. The psalmist reminds us that 'man never continues in one stay'. In the pilgrimage of life there is progress or regress. There is no 'stand still' period. Maybe what is needed is the spiritual counsel and advice of a man of God, or a new assessment of the place in our lives of the ties of sacrament and prayer which are the means of grace. For many this is afforded by attendance at a Retreat or Quiet Day.

Prayer *Help me Lord, to remember that one thing is needful and that 'he that hath the Son hath life'. Lord, you have given your children this one thing, this life – freely, fully and wonderfully. Grant me purity, a heart to accept it, spiritual understanding to apprehend it, courage to follow where it leads and steadfastness to hold fast to it day by day.*

There was I found

I was a stricken deer, that left the herd
Long since; with many an arrow deep infix'd
My panting side was charged, when I withdrew
To seek a tranquil death in distant shades.
There was I found by One who had himself
Been hurt by th'archers. In his side he bore
And in his hands and feet, the cruel scars,
With gentle force soliciting the darts,
He drew them forth, and heal'd, and bade me live.
Since then, with few associates, in remote
And silent woods, I wander, far from those
My former partners of the peopled scene;
With few associates, and not wishing more.

WILLIAM COWPER (1731–1800)

Comment

William Cowper, whose contribution to poetry and hymnody is notable, wrote the lines above in a period of mental illness. In a moment of despair he pleads for release by death, but suddenly, indicting himself for his depression, he discovers that he is not alone. In his moment of bodily, mental and spiritual weakness he is found 'by One who had himself been hurt'. Christ's 'Lo, I am with you always' – that is 'there is not a day when I will not be with you' – is a promise to all his disciples. In every circumstance we shall be 'found by One who had himself been hurt'. The caring love of Christ is ever at hand. The same poet expressed the same truth in his much loved hymn, 'Hark, my soul...'

> *Mine is an unchanging love,*
> *Higher than the heights above,*
> *Deeper than the depths beneath,*
> *Free and faithful, strong as death*

Prayer

Lift up our souls, O Lord, to the pure, serene light of thy presence; that there we may breathe freely, there repose in thy love, there may be at rest from ourselves, and from thence return arrayed in thy peace, to do and bear what shall please thee; for thy holy name's sake.

E.B. PUSEY

Heavenly Father, you know the anxieties and fears of all your children, I bring before you... in his/her sickness. Help all who are ill in body or in mind to cast their care upon you, to be found by Him who was himself hurt and, with serenity and unshaken trust, to find peace in His abiding presence and caring love.

Anthony of Egypt, Abbot, 356

In omnibus unitas

We are all one, whatever we may say.
The warp-minded beggar, wending her weak way
Across the garden, is part of me
And will be throughout all eternity.
What e'er I do or say is part of them
And must concern all these, my fellow-men.
We cannot live unto ourselves alone
If God upon the throne of our frail hearts is reigning.
For if we love Him and He made all,
Than we are one, and follow, at His call
To live out here, on earth, our puny lives
According to His way. And whosover strives
With peace towards all men, just to do His will
Will find Him in them, e'en through good or ill,
He the true end of all our feeble striving.

SISTER MARY ANSELM, C.S.M.V.

Comment

Those lines would have appealed to Anthony of Egypt for he saw all God's children as one and for his part he would have a special concern for the 'warp-minded beggar'. Anthony inherited from his parents vast properties. But he inherited something infinitely more precious than that, namely a strong and virile faith expressing itself in devotion to Our Lord and His Way. The words of the Gospel 'If thou wouldst be perfect, sell all that thou hast, and give to the poor' so impressed him that he sold his vast possessions, gave the money to the poor, saving a proportion to care for his own sister, and lived the life of a hermit, earning his daily bread by working for it. Later he created cells in the desert which were inhabited by monks who spent their days in prayer and worship and in working in order to be able to help the poor. These monks looked to Anthony as their Father Abbot and he is thus regarded as the greatest of the hermits and as the founder of monasticism. Athanasius described him as 'a physician given by God to Egypt', and he posed the question, 'Who met him grieving, and did not go away rejoicing? Who came full of anger, and was not turned to kindness? Who came troubled by doubts and failed to gain peace of mind?' Anthony saw all God's children as equally precious in the sight of God. Is there not here a lesson for all Christians touching their attitudes to people of other races and cultures and beliefs?

Prayer   *Almighty God, you have taught us through your Son our Lord to pray to you as our Father, grant that so doing we may ever remember that we are all members of one family. Give us a lively concern for our fellows especially those in special need, and help us, as you helped your servant Anthony, to live not to ourselves alone but to all your children throughout your world. This we ask for the sake of him who bade us love one another, even your Son, our Saviour, Jesus Christ.*

Christian influence

There is something mysteriously impressive about the Gulf Stream, a warm river rushing through the ocean, and bringing fertility and comfort to every coast it washes. One of our great writers compares Christianity to the Gulf Stream and, if you think it over, it is not unsuitable. All the activities and interests of the world's life are enriched and exalted when they become Christian. There are no such homes as Christian homes; no such friendship as Christian friendship; no such justice as Christian justice, and so on... St Chrysostom somewhere says that the Christian home is 'a little Church'.

BISHOP HENSLEY HENSON (1859–1943)

Six things are necessary to create a happy home. Integrity must be the architect, and tidiness the upholsterer. It must be warmed by affection, lighted up with cheerfulness; and industry must be the ventilator, renewing the atmosphere and bring in fresh salubrity day by day; while over all, as a protecting canopy and glory, nothing will suffice except the blessing of God.

JAMES HAMILTON (1814–1867)

True to Thyself

Think truly and thy thoughts
  Shall the world's famine feed;
Speak truly, and each word of thine
  Shall be a fruitful seed;
Live truly and thy life shall be
  A great and noble creed.

HORATIUS BONAR (1808–1889)

Comment

'You are the salt of the earth', said Jesus to his disciples and there was nothing enigmatic in that utterance to disturb them. In the ancient world salt was a symbol of purity; it was too a common preservative which stemmed putrefaction and decay. Furthermore it turns things insipid into things tasty. It is part of the mission of the Christian to be the 'salt of the earth', the person who brings to his home and to the world in which he moves, the standard of purity in speech and in behaviour which can serve as a prophylactic against the putrefaction which threatens our moral standards. Nor must we forget that no one should know more about a true *joie de vivre* than the Christian and he should radiate that joy which has been described as the echo of God's life within us. The first two of the quotations point the Christian in the right direction if he is to be 'the salt of the earth'. Horatius Bonar's verse tells him where he must begin. He must be true to himself – that is, his real self. His soul must overflow if he 'another's soul would reach'.

Prayer   *Help me, good Lord, to be the salt of the earth – in my home, in my work, in my leisure. Give me joy in my heart and help me to share it with those with whom I live and work day by day. So may I obey your command to be the salt of the earth.*

Living in calm

Life appears to me to be too short to be spent in nursing animosity or register-ing wrongs. We are one and all burdened with faults in this world, but the time will come when, I trust, we shall put them off in putting off our cor-ruptible bodies; when debasement and sin will fall from us and only the spark will remain, the impalpable principle of life and thought, pure as when it left the Creator to inspire the creature. Whence it came, it will return, perhaps to pass through gradations of glory.

This is a creed, in which I delight, to which I cling. It makes Eternity a rest, a home; not a terror and an abyss. With this creed, revenge never worries my heart, degradation never too deeply disgusts me, injustice never crushes me too low. I live in calm, looking to the end.

CHARLOTTE BRONTË (1816–1855)

Comment

Charlotte Brontë is saying what Our Lord said, 'Make friends with your enemy quickly'. It may well be that we have been maligned, that our reputation has been unjustly blackened by slander or misrepresentation. Such a situation is certainly not helped nor healed by adopting an 'eye for an eye' approach nor will good rela-tions be restored by engendering bitterness which itself breeds bitterness in return. Our Lord advises us to sort out our troubles, bitter differences and resentments quickly. It is not always easy to admit that we were wrong, or to seek an understan-ding with one who shows no willingness to seek reconciliation. The wound which festers by neglect, has to be lanced and the final treatment is the harder. To seek to reconcile, is a step towards holiness and this, for our own sakes and for God's glory, is the way for Christians even if we are rebuffed.

Prayer   *Lord, make me an instrument of thy peace*
Where there is hatred, let me sow love;
Where there is injury, pardon;
Where there is discord, union;
Where there is doubt, faith;
Where there is despair, hope;
Where there is darkness, light;
Where there is sadness, joy,
For thy mercy and for thy truth's sake.

ANONYMOUS
THOUGH FREQUENTLY ATTRIBUTED IN ERROR
TO ST FRANCIS OF ASSISI

'Thy sleepless ministers move on'

One lesson, Nature, let me learn of thee,
One lesson which in every wind is blown;
One lesson of two duties kept as one
Though the loud world proclaim their enmity.

Of toil unsevered from tranquillity!
Of labour, that in lasting fruit outgrows
Far noisier schemes, accomplished in repose,
Too great for haste, too high for rivalry!

Yes, while on earth a thousand discords ring,
Man's fitful uproar mingling with his toil,
Still do thy sleepless ministers move on.

Their glorious tasks in silence perfecting;
Still working, blaming still our vain turmoil,
Labourers that shall not fail when man is gone.

MATTHEW ARNOLD (1822–1888)

Comment

I suppose that, in plain language, Arnold is saying, 'Get on with your job in life and make no undue fuss about it'. He is also making it clear that certain qualities are needed to that end. There are two divine ministers which take the drudgery out of toil and the boredom out of labour, and which inject into both a serenity which at its highest ensures perfection. But such qualities are not imbibed from the air. Opportunities for their development have to be created – moments of quiet reflection, of prayer, of reading the Bible, of reading poetry and other inspirational writing. Tranquillity and repose are not easily come by. The world does not offer them freely. They have to be won by conscious effort. St Augustine summed it up thus: 'Thou hast created us for thyself, and our heart cannot be quieted till it find repose in Thee'. Dag Hammarskjöld, one time secretary of the United Nations, carried with him wherever he went in his many travels a small devotional book which he read as he travelled from place to place. Thus did he create for himself the tranquillity and repose which sustained him for a task of unique difficulty and importance.

Prayer   *Lord Jesus, grant me thy tranquillity. Be my life hid in thine; let thy*
fearless and imperturbable spirit come to dwell in mine. So let me be
still; and inwardly worship, in private, in public, everywhere, always.
Be thou the rock of my repose, the moving pillar before and behind my
pilgrimage, thus to serve faithfully in the work which is mine.

ADAPTED FROM JOHN DONNE

Agnes, Virgin, Martyr, 304

'My childhood's faith'

How do I love thee? Let me count the ways.
I love thee to the depth and breadth and height
My soul can reach, when feeling out of sight
For the ends of being and of ideal Grace.
I love thee to the level of every day's
Most quiet need, by sun and candle-light.
I love thee freely as men strive for Right.
I love thee purely as they turn from Praise.
I love thee with the passion put to use
In my old griefs, and with my childhood's faith.
I love thee with a love I seemed to lose
With my lost saints − I love thee with the breath,
Smiles, tears, of all my life! − and, if God choose,
I shall but love thee better after death.

ELIZABETH BARRETT BROWNING (1806–1861)

Comment

'I may be a child, but faith dwells not in years, but in the heart'. So said 13-year-old Agnes to the Prefect who tried to persuade her to recant to save her life. She saw in the advances of that Prefect's son a challenge to her virginity and her faith. The manner of her martyrdom is not clear from the legends which surround her, but the certainty of it − probably in the year 303 − is sealed in, for example, the writings of St Ambrose (339–397) and by the building in the year 350 of a basilica over her remains. It is good that among our commemorations there is a place for one child martyr. There have been others, not least the martyr boys of Uganda who, like Agnes, were thrown to the flames for refusing to deny their faith. Elizabeth Barrett Browing set her 'childhood's faith' high in her list of ways in which she loved the Lord, who warned 'Unless you turn and become like children, you will never enter the kingdom of Heaven'. 'Childhood's faith' is a faith which helps us to stand in humility before God, to trust Him implicitly, recognising our utter dependence upon Him.

Prayer *Grant, O Lord, that we who commemorate the martyrdom of thy child Agnes, may be strengthened to bear witness before the world to the redeeming love of your Son Jesus, who for us endured the Cross and now lives and reigns in the unity of the Spirit, one God world without end.*
Almighty God and Heavenly Father, we thank thee for the children whom thou hast given to us; give us also grace to train them in thy faith, fear and love; that as they advance in years they may grow in grace, and be found hereafter in the number of thine elect children; through Jesus Christ our Lord.

'To be a pilgrim'

'On this road you are called to be least of all and not master:
To carry other men's burdens, and not to lay your own on them;
To give freedom in stead of taking it;
To grow poor in order to make others rich;
To take the cross upon yourself; Then bring joy to other men;
To die in order that others may live.
This is the mystery of the Gospel and there is no purpose in endless talk about it.
Be silent for it will be true and genuine only if you practise it.
Set out on the road together with your brother,
Together with the numberless people of God,
All pilgrims travelling to the Father's house.
Go on your way singing a song of hope on your lips,
And your heart burning within you.
Now we have the alleluias of the journey. . .
Set out on the road, brother, and peace be with you forever'.

SOURCE NOT KNOWN, QUOTED FROM
TRAVELLING LIGHT BY BISHOP OLIVER ALLISON

Comment

The quotation, from an unknown hand, is addressed apparently to one joining some missionary enterprise, or maybe entering a Religious Order concerned with caring work. But there is a message in it for all Christian pilgrims. Disciples of Christ are also apostles – people sent. Because we are the Body of Christ we are one with our fellow travellers including the blind, the lame and the halt. We may find ourselves on a road to Jericho where the wounded traveller must not be passed by on the other side. It may be a Damascus road where some flashing light of God's purpose bids us pause to ask, 'Lord what will you have me do?' The road may be upwards to a mount where we catch a new vision of Christ – an experience so exhilarating that, like Peter at Christ's transfiguration, we are tempted to withdraw from the people on the plain. Be it any of these we are always our 'brother's keeper'. If we meet him on the way, we cannot pass without sharing with him 'the peace of the Lord' which could be more than a verbal greeting however sincere.

Prayer   *Teach us, good Lord, to serve thee as thou deservest: to give and not to count the cost; to fight and not to heed the wounds: to toil and not to seek for rest; to labour and not to ask for any reward, save that of knowing that we do thy will; through Jesus Christ our Lord.*

ST IGNATIUS LOYOLA

Inasmuch as you have done it . . .

Abou Ben Adhem (may his tribe increase!)
Awoke one night from a deep dream of peace
And saw, within the moonlight in his room,
Making it rich, and like a lily in bloom,
An angel writing in a book of gold, –
Exceeding peace had made Ben Adhem bold,
And to the presence in the room he said,
'What writest thou?' – the vision raised its head,
And with look made of all sweet accord,
Answered 'The names of those who love the Lord'.
'And mine is one?' said Abu. 'Nay, not so',
Replied the angel. Abu spoke more low,
But cheerly still; and said, 'I pray thee, then,
Write me as one that loves his fellow men'.
The angel wrote and vanished. The next night
It came again with a great awakening light,
And showed the names whom love of God had blest,
And lo! Ben Adhem's name led all the rest.

LEIGH HUNT (1784–1859)

Comment

The Angel was clearly not in possession of all the necessary facts on the first night! Abou's love of his fellow men qualifies him for entry into the angel's book of gold. In his first letter St John, himself a mystic but one whose feet were firmly on the ground, boldly asserts that the final proof that man has 'passed from death to life', that is, that he is in fellowship with God, is 'love of the brethren'. Love of God and fellowship with God will reveal themselves to the world in acts of love towards our fellow men. If those acts of love are lacking, the claim to love God is called into question. If those acts of love are manifest, they themselves are proof of love of God. 'Inasmuch as you have done it, you have done it unto Me'.

Prayer *O God, fountain of love, pour thy soul into our souls, that we may love those whom thou lovest with the love thou givest us, and think and speak of them tenderly, meekly, lovingly: and so loving our brethren and sisters for thy sake, may grow in thy love, and dwelling in love may dwell in thee; for Jesus Christ's sake.*

E.B. PUSEY

Heavenly Father, who by thy blessed Son has taught us to ask of Thee our daily bread: help us to remember that the poor and the hungry of the world are our brethren and give us grace to show our love for them by acts of love which may relieve their poverty and serve to meet their needs; this we ask for the sake of our Lord Jesus Christ.

Frances de Sales, Bishop, Teacher of the Faith, 1622

Little with love

Great works do not always lie in our way, but every moment we may do little ones excellently, that is, with great love. I beg you to remark the saint who gives a cup of water for God's sake to a poor thirsty traveller; he seems to do a small thing; but the intention, the sweetness, the love with which he animates his action, is so excellent that it turns this simple water into the water of life, and of eternal life. Bees gather honey from the lily, the iris and the rose; but they get as much booty from the little minute rosemary flowers and thyme; they not only draw more honey from these, but even better honey, because in these little vessels the honey being more closely locked up is much better preserved. Truly in small and insignificant exercises of devotion, charity is practised not only more frequently, but also as a rule more humbly too, and consequently more holily and usefully. Those condescensions to the humours of others, that bearing with the troublesome actions and ways of our neighbour, those victories over our own tempers and passions – all this is more profitable to our souls than we can conceive, if heavenly love only have the management of them.

ST FRANCIS DE SALES (1567–1622)

Comment

In the early seventeenth century St Francis de Sales was famous as a teacher of the Faith, as a spiritual director and organiser of the catechism. His best-known writings are *The Introduction to the Devout Life* and *Treatise on the Love of God*. As Provost of Geneva he was regarded by everyone, except his father, as a powerful and popular preacher since, as in the extract above he was able to embrace profound thoughts in simple language. His father told him he preached too often and too simply. Speaking of his early experiences he rebuked his son saying that in his younger days, 'Sermons were much rarer and those were something like sermons, full of learning and with more Latin and Greek in one than you put in a dozen!'. But the Provost fortunately did not heed his father's advice, continuing as he did to preach in his own way which was his Lord's way too – by parables. He became Bishop of Geneva in 1602 and whilst his zeal for preaching in no way diminished, he cared for his diocese lovingly – for clergy, laity and the little children, with great devotion. The extract above mirrors the writer – a great man of God but a humble one, prepared to present the Gospel in terms which everyone could understand. There is here a lesson not only for those who preach that Gospel, but for all who try to bring others into the fellowship of God's Church.

Prayer

Lord, thy will be done in father, mother, child, in everything and everywhere, without a reserve, without a 'but', or an 'if' or a limit.

ST FRANCIS DE SALES (1567–1622)

The conversion of Saint Paul

Mystic and Man of Action

Among all the great men of antiquity there is none, with the exception of Cicero, whom we may know so intimately as Saul of Tarsus. He is a saint without a luminous halo. His personal characteristics are too distinct and too human to make idealisation easy. For this reason he has never been the object of popular devotion. No fairy tales are attached to his cult; he remains for us what he was in the flesh. . . The dominant impression that he makes upon us is that he was cast in an heroic mould. He is serenely indifferent to criticism and calumny; no power on earth can turn him from his purpose. He has set his face to achieve, almost single-handed, the conquest of the Roman Empire. . . He is absolutely indifferent whether his mission will cost him his life, or only involve a continuation of almost intolerable hardship. It is this indomitable courage, complete self-sacrifice and single-minded devotion to a magnificently audacious but not impracticable idea, which constitute the greatness of St Paul's character. He was, for all this, a warm-hearted and affectionate man, as he proves abundantly by the tone of his letters. His personal religion was in essence, a pure mysticism; he worships a Christ whom he has experienced as a living presence in his soul. The mystic who is also a man of action, and a man of action because he is a mystic, wields a tremendous power over other men. He is like an invulnerable knight, fighting in magic armour.

DEAN INGE (1860–1954)
QUOTED FROM ESSAY ON ST PAUL

Comment

Of all the Apostles it was Paul who, under God, established Christianity as a religion for the world, as Christ meant it to be. In the history of the Church he stands out, indubitably as the most powerful human personality. He himself was converted about 36 A.D. and from then for twenty years or more he was caught up in his momentous missionary journeys, in the course of which, though he suffered the most cruel persecution, he continued to expose himself to all kinds of dangers for the cause of Christ. It was whilst he was in prison in Rome that he wrote many of the letters which became the foundation stones of Christian theology and which have come down to us. Clement of Rome, writing fifty years or so after Paul's martyrdom, describes him as 'herald both in the East and the West' and notes too that he came 'to the limit of the West' by which he means Spain. God does not call us all to suffer in the same way or to the same extent; but he does call us to be willing to do so. Paul did not go around seeking suffering, but when it was meted out to him he accepted it as the price of fidelity to his discipleship.

Prayer   *Almighty God, who caused the light of the Gospel to shine throughout the world through the preaching of your servant Saint Paul: grant that we who celebrate his wonderful conversion may follow him in bearing witness to your truth; through Jesus Christ our Lord.*

A.S.B COLLECT

Timothy and Titus, Companions of St Paul

Employment

If as a flower doth spread and die,
Thou would'st extend to me some good,
Before I were by frost's extremity
Nipt in the bud;

Let me now languish then, and spend
A life as barren to Thy praise
As is the dust to that which life doth tend,
But with delays.

The sweetness and the praise were Thine;
But the extension and the room,
Which in Thy garland I should fill, were mine
At Thy great doom.

All things are busy; only I
Neither bring honey with the bees,
Nor flowers to make that, nor the husbandry
To water these.

For as Thou dost impart Thy grace
The greater shall our glory be.
The measure of our joys is in this place,
The stuff with Thee.

I am no link of Thy great chain,
But all my company is a weed,
Lord! place me in Thy concert; give one strain
To my poor reed.

GEORGE HERBERT (1593–1633)

Comment

George Herbert had his dark days when it seemed that health and lack of confidence conspired against the work he was trying to do. But he was ever a man of prayer and here in the last verse of this prayer-poem he suddenly sees himself as just one person in God's great concert and in his humility prays that he may be worthy of a place in the orchestra of employment for God and His Church. Sometimes we lack confidence in ourselves. We need to see ourselves as part of the orchestra of employment for God and His Church. In 'God's great concert' there is always a place for the soloist. No one can play the part which is peculiarly ours. The great St Paul set himself a task for the accomplishment of which he desperately needed companions. Two of these, Timothy and Titus, were his 'spiritual sons' – young men who helped him fulfil his ministry in God's 'concert', young men too for whom he had great affection and in whose fidelity to Christ he had great confidence.

Prayer   *O Lord, without whom our labour is lost, and with whom thy little ones go forth as the mighty; be present in all works in thy Church which are undertaken according to thy will and grant to thy labourers a pure intention, perfect faith, sufficient success upon earth, and the bliss of serving thee in heaven. Through Jesus Christ our Lord.*

WILLIAM BRIGHT

John Chrysostom, Bishop of Constantinople, Teacher of the Faith, 407

Long-suffering

A certain wise man said – 'A man that is long-suffering is abundant in understanding'; and comparing it with a strong city he said it was stronger than that; for it is both an invincible weapon and a sort of impregnable tower, easily beating off all annoyances: and as a spark falling into the keep doth it no injury, but is itself easily quenched, so whatever unexpected thing falls upon a long suffering soul speedily vanishes, but the soul it disturbs not; for of a truth there is nothing so impenetrable as long-suffering. You may talk of armies, horses, walls, arms, or anything else, you will name nothing like long-suffering; for he that is surrounded by these, being overcome by anger, is upset, like a worthless child, and fills all with confusion and tempest; but the long-suffering man, settled as it were in a harbour, enjoys a profound calm. The possessor of this passive virtue hath a kind of long and noble soul, whose great strength is love.

ST JOHN CHRYSOSTOM (347–407)

Comment

John, called Chrysostom, which means 'golden-mouthed', was born in Antioch in 347. Although brought up in a Christian home he was not baptized until he was 23. Sixteen years later he became a priest and quickly attained fame as a preacher. In the year 397 he became Bishop of Constantinople. There he discovered that the way of life of many of his clergy, and even more of the gentry of his day, was wholly inconsistent with the Christian vocation or profession. He dealt severely with those who were doing harm to the cause of Christ and His Church and for his pains he was hounded out of the country. At his death in 407 his body was taken back to Constantinople and there received with great pomp and pride, in a manner which suggested that the city which had exiled him had recognised its grave error. The passage quoted above on long-suffering, which means in effect bearing insult and injury without complaint, or as Chrysostom himself defined it, 'the spirit which has the power to take revenge but which never does', was doubtless written from the depths of a soul frequently tortured by the unjust treatment meted out against him. How do we re-act to what to us seems to be unjust treatment?

Prayer   *Almighty God, who hast given us grace at this time with one accord to make our common supplications unto thee: and dost promise, that when two or three are gathered together in thy name thou wilt grant their requests: Fulfil now, O Lord, the desires and petitions of thy servants, as may be most expedient for them: granting us in this world knowledge of thy truth, and in the world to come life everlasting.*

CRANMER, BASED ON THE LITURGY
OF ST JOHN CHRYSOSTOM

Thomas Aquinas, Priest, Teacher of the Faith, 1274

Adoration

Godhead here in hiding, whom I do adore
Masked by these bare shadows, shape and nothing more.
See, Lord, at thy service low lies here a heart
Lost, all lost in wonder at the God thou art.

Seeing, touching, tasting are in thee deceived;
Who says trust hearing? that shall be believed;
What God's Son has told me, take for true I do;
Truth himself speaks truly or there's nothing true.

On thy cross thy godhead made no signs to men;
Here the very manhood steals from human ken;
Both are my confession, both are my belief,
And I pray the prayer of the dying thief.

Jesu, whom I look at shrouded here below,
I beseech thee send me what I thirst for so,
Some day to gaze on thee face to face in light,
And be blest for ever with thy glory's sight.

St Thomas Aquinas (1227–1274)
trans. G.M. Hopkins

Comment

Thomas Aquinas has been described as the most learned of the saints and the most saintly of the learned. His claim to learning is indisputable and his mantle of saintship has been recognised throughout the ages and by the whole Church. He became a Dominican friar and at the age of 22 was appointed to a professorship in their Cologne College. As a lecturer, a writer and a powerful preacher he was universally recognised by theologians and philosophers alike. His most famous writing was his *Summa Theologica* which occupied the last nine years of his life, and although unfinished, concerns the whole realm of the Christian religion from belief in the existence of God to the fundamental Christian verities and the precepts of morality which derive from them. Shortly before he died he experienced a vision whilst he was saying Mass. From that moment he wrote no more and on being asked for a reason he replied, 'Everything I have written seems worthless by the side of what I have seen'. Here is a prayer of his which we can make our own.

Prayer

Give us, O Lord, a steadfast heart, which no tribulation can wear out; give us an unconquered heart which no unworthy purpose may tempt aside. Bestow upon us also, O Lord our God, understanding to know thee, diligence to seek thee, wisdom to find thee, and a faithfulness that may finally embrace thee: through Jesus Christ our Lord.

The angels' questions

When God made the Earth it shook to and fro till He put mountains on it to keep it firm. Then the angels asked, 'O God, is there anything in Thy creation stronger than the mountains?' And God replied, 'Iron is stronger than the mountains, for it breaks them'.

And is there anything in thy creation stonger than iron?

Yes, fire is stronger than iron for it melts them.

And is there anything stronger than fire?

Yes, water is for it quenches fire.

Is there anything stronger than water?

Yes, wind for it puts water in motion.

Is there anything stronger than wind?

Yes, a good man giving alms. If he give it with his right hand and conceal it from his left he overcomes all things. Every good act is charity. Your smiling in your brother's face, your putting a wanderer on the right road, your giving water to the thirsty, is charity. A man's true wealth hereafter is the good he has done to his fellow-men. When he dies people will ask, 'What property has he left behind him?' But the angels will ask, 'What good deeds has he sent before him?'

MAHOMET (570–632)

Comment

Wisdom from Mahomet's pen, but culled, as it were, from the New Testament itself from which he derived the truth that 'a good man giving' is greater than all else in God's creation. 'Every good act is charity', he says, clearly following St Paul who, looking at charity through the prism of his inspired intellect, saw charity broken down in all its different 'colours' – patience, kindness, modesty, truthfulness, affability, hope, courtesy, humility among them – all of which we see supremely potrayed in the life and teaching of Jesus himself. St Paul teaches us that these 'colours' are the gift of the spirit – fruits which will grow in us if we let the spirit of Jesus live in us. Read again 1 Corinthians Ch.13.

Prayer   *O Lord, grant us to love thee; grant that we may love those that love thee; grant that we may do the deeds that win thy love.*

MAHOMET (570–632)

Heavenly Father, help us ever to remember the words of the Lord Jesus, how he said 'It is more blessed to give than to receive'. Grant that we who have received much, may in our turn give freely to those who are in need. We ask this in the name of him who gave himself, even thy Son, our Saviour, Jesus Christ.

Charles the First, King and Martyr, 1649

Martyrdom

'That then the Royal actor borne
The tragic scaffold might adorn
*   While round the armed bands*
*   Did clap their bloody hands.*

He nothing common did or mean
Upon that memorable scene,
*   But with his keener eye*
*   The axe's edge did try;*

Nor called the gods with vulgar spite
To vindicate his helpless right,
*   But Bow'd his comely head*
*   Down, as upon a bed.'*

Comment

Charles the First of England had been in the Calendar of the Church's saints and heroes long before the appearance of the Alternative Services Book. At the Restoration, the church of England gave him his rightful place as one of its martyrs, and January 30th was assigned as the day for his commemoration. A special form of service for use on the day was drawn up and continued to be in use until the middle of the nineteenth century when it was decided to withdraw the service but to leave his name in the Kalendar. However, the printers decided otherwise and omitted the name. Hence restoration of a different kind was called for. Andrew Marvell's well-known lines tell but half the tale of this saintly man's character. Perrinchef's *Royal Martyr* gives more. He describes him as 'devout and punctilious in the performance of his religious duties', living his life 'in the sight and fear of God and with a single eye to His glory'. Like all the saints 'he sinned as have all other men; but unlike most other men, he repented deeply and sincerely of his sins'. It was said of him by Keble and others that had he been willing to abandon the church and give up episcopacy he might have saved his throne and his life. Charles was not willing to do that and his defence of the Church led him to his execution. 'I die a Christian according to the profession of the Church of England, as I found it left me by my Father, and that honest man I think will witness it'. The prayer below has been attributed to Charles.

Prayer   *Close thine eyes and sleep secure,*
Thy soul is safe, thy body sure;
He that guards thee, He that keeps,
Never slumbers, never sleeps.
A quiet conscience in the breast
Has only peace, has only rest.
The music and the mirth of kings
Are out of tune unless she sings.
Th.. ...

Serving God

God has created me to do Him some definite service; He has committed some work to me which He has not committed to another. I have my mission – I may never know it in this life, but I shall be told it in the next.

I am a link in a chain, a bond of connection between persons. He has not created me for naught. I shall do good, I shall do His work, I shall be an angel of peace, a preacher of truth in my own place, while not intending it, if I do but keep His commandments.

Therefore I will trust Him. Whatever, wherever I am, I can never be thrown away. If I am in sickness, my sickness may serve Him; if I am in sorrow, my sorrow may serve Him. He does nothing in vain. He knows what He is about. He may take away my friends. He may throw me among strangers. He may make me feel desolate, make my spirit sink, hide my future from me – still He knows what He is about.

CARDINAL NEWMAN (1801-1890)

Comment

John Henry Newman, author of great literary and theological works and of many hymns, among them *Lead Kindly Light* affirms here a belief that everyone has a particular service or piece of work to do, which is specifically his and which only he can do. Certainly each of us is a member, that is a limb, of the Body of Christ, and just as every part of a living body has a function to discharge, without which the body cannot fulfil its total function, so within the Church every member has his part and lot. The Cardinal goes beyond that by suggesting that there is some special duty which is assigned to each of us. We may never know what it is. We may never know whether we have in fact already discharged it. What we do know is that in close communion with God, in ties of sacrament and prayer, we shall not fail him. As the Cardinal says, God knows what he is about, and, if our wills are dedicated, our ways will be directed and that in every circumstance. If we breathe in God in prayer, in contemplation, in public worship, we shall breathe out God in the ways he wants in our daily lives.

Prayer   *Almighty God, who didst ordain that thy Son, Jesus Christ, should labour with his hands to supply his own needs and the needs of others; teach us, we beseech thee, that no labour is mean, and all labour is divine. Help us so to approach our daily work that it may redound to the service of our fellows and to the glory of thy holy name.*

Desiderata

Go placidly amid the noise and haste and remember what peace there may be in silence. As far as possible be on good terms with all persons. Speak your truth quietly and clearly and listen to others, even the dull and ignorant; they too have their story. Avoid loud and aggressive persons, they are vexatious to the spirit. If you compare yourselves with others you may become vain and bitter, for always there will be greater and lesser persons than yourself. Be yourself. Especially do not feign affection. Neither be cynical about love, for in the face of all avidity and disenchantment, it is perennial as the grass. Take kindly the counsel of the years, gracefully surrendering the things of youth. Nurture strength of spirit to shield you in sudden misfortune. But do not distress yourself with imaginings. Many fears are born of fatigue and loneliness. Beyond a wholesome discipline, be gentle with yourself. You are a child of the universe no less than the trees and the stars. You have a right to be here. And whether or not it is clear to you, no doubt the universe is unfolding as it should. Therefore be at peace with God whatever you conceive Him to be, and whatever your labours and aspirations in the noisy confusion of life, keep peace with your soul. With all its sham and drudgery and broken dreams, it is still a beautiful world. Be cheerful. Strive to be happy.

MAX EHRMANN ( )

Comment

The author of this list of *Desiderata* – desirable attitudes to life – is an Indiana poet. Note that it starts and ends with an exhortation to peace; the peace there is in silence, being at peace with God and keeping peace with your soul. The peace of which the author is thinking is not an exterior peace which the world may or may not afford us. It is an interior peace – not, of course, imbibed from the air without any conscious effort on our part, but actively sought. The prophet Isaiah gives us the clue to its possession and enjoyment: 'Thou will keep him in perfect peace whose mind is stayed on thee'. The 'staying', which needs to be constant not fitful, is secured by a day to day communion with God sought in prayer and in quiet reflection upon God's word and God's love.

Prayer   *O God, my God, make your way plain before my face. In the thoughts I think, in the words I speak, in the decisions I make and in the meetings I have day by day with others of your family, may your will be done in me through the power of your Holy Spirit, and your peace reign in my heart through Jesus Christ our Lord.*

The Presentation of Christ in the Temple

Lighten our Darkness

Lighten our darkness, Lord! in bygone years
Oft have I prayed and thought on childish fears,
Glad in my heart that, when the day was dead,
God's four white angels watched about my bed.
Lighten our darkness, Lord! Kneeling in the mud
My hands still wet and warm with human blood.
Oft have I prayed it! Perils of this night!
Sorrow of soldiers! Mercy! give us light.
Lighten our darkness! Black upon the mind
Questions and doubts. So many paths that wind,
Worlds of blind sorrow crying out for light.
Peace, where is Peace? Lord Jesus, give us light.
Lighten our darkness! Stumbling to the end,
Millions of mortals feeling for a friend,
Shall not the Judge of all the earth do right?
Flame through the darkness, Lord, and give us light.

G.A. STUDDERT-KENNEDY (1883–1929)

Comment

The Feast commemorates the time when Jesus was presented in the Temple as the Jewish Law required (St Luke Ch.2, vv 22–39). Its popular name is Candlemas – a name which derives from the very early custom of carrying lighted candles in procession in church symbolising the entrance into the world of Christ, the True Light. It was in the fourth century that the Emperor Constantine initiated the Feast in thanksgiving for the cessation of the Plague – a 'darkness' as deep as that which Studdert-Kennedy experienced as a padre in the First World War. Not for nothing do candles play such a prominent part in our worship and devotion. 'The True Light shines in the darkness and the darkness does not put it out', says St John's Gospel. The darkness of the world cannot extinguish the Light of Christ, and when, through us, that Light shines in a darkness, that darkness is dispelled. But the Light of Christ can be reflected in a dark world only if we expose ourselves to Him; that demands sacrifice of time and concentration of mind and heart. The candle gives its light by giving itself – by burning itself out. So the Christian who would bring the Light of Christ to the dark places of the world must give himself sacrificially. He is, however, never burnt out, for the Light which shines through him is the True Light of the Living Lord.

Prayer   *Almighty God, the brightness of faithful souls, we thank Thee that Thou didst give Thy Son Jesus Christ to be the light of the world, and that in Him Thou hast revealed Thy glory and the wonder of Thy saving love; grant that His light may so shine throughout the world that everywhere His children may be drawn to Him who is the Saviour and Lord of all, and the whole earth shall be filled with Thy glory.*

Saints and Martyrs of Europe

Glorious the sun in mid-career;
Glorious the assembled fires appear;
Glorious the comet's train:
Glorious the trumpet and alarm;
Glorious the almighty stretched out arm;
Glorious the enraptured main:

Glorious the northern lights astream;
Glorious the song, when God's the theme
Glorious the thunder's roar:
Glorious hosanna from the den
Glorious the catholic amen:
Glorious the martyr's gore.
Glorious – more glorious is the crown
Of him that brought salvation down
By meekness, called thy Son;
Thou that stupendous truth believed,
And now the matchless deed's achieved.
DETERMINED, DARED, and DONE.

CHRISTOPHER SMART (1722–1771)

Comment

The poet in his *Song to David* moves in his crescendo of things glorious from the inanimate wonders of the universe to man who utters his Amen to the song of praise. He sees in man's willingness to offer his very life, something most splendid, but discerns that his song must move on from that height to a point yet higher: 'More glorious is the crown that brought salvation down by meekness, called thy Son'. There have been many great saints and martyrs in Europe who have lived and died for that same faith, but who are not remembered by name. There were many holy men and women who would not have held back at that point had the sacrifice of their lives been the alternative to a renunciation of their faith. 'For some', said John Donne, 'not to be martyred was a martyrdom'. It is appropriate that those of our own land and continent, the stories of whose witness are familiar though they have no memorial in the shape of a day assigned to them, should thus be commemorated.

Prayer

O God, whom the glorious companies of the redeemed adore, we praise thee for the Saints and Martyrs of our own land and continent who in their day and generation bore faithful witness to their faith. Inspired by their example, may we strive by thy grace to hold fast to the faith by which they lived and in which they died, that we may be numbered among those who see thee face to face; through Jesus Christ our Lord.

Anxiety

It is not possible to make a simple separation between the creative and de-structive elements in anxiety... Man may be anxious because he has not become what he ought to be... The philosopher is anxious to arrive at the truth; but he is also anxious to prove that his particular truth is the truth. He is never completely in the possession of the truth as he imagines. That may be the error of being ignorant of one's ignorance. But it is never sim-ply that. The pretensions of final truth are always partly an effort to ob-scure a darkly felt consciousness of the limits of human knowledge. Man is afraid to face the problem of his limited knowledge lest he fall into the abyss of meaninglessness. Thus fanaticism is always a partly conscious, part-ly unconscious, attempt to hide the fact of ignorance and to obscure the problem of scepticism.

REINHOLD NIEBUHR (1892–1971)
QUOTED FROM *The Nature and Destiny of Man*

Comment

But does not Our Lord deal with this vexed question of anxiety much more sim-ply? Reading the Authorised Version of the Bible, one could be forgiven for think-ing that Jesus had nothing to say about anxiety or worry. 'Take no thought for your life', seems to suggest that his disciples should adopt an improvident attitude to life. Earlier translations of the New Testament conveyed Our Lord's meaning more accurately: 'Be not careful (i.e. full of care) for your life'. In other words, don't worry, don't be anxious. All the modern versions of the New Testament give this more accurate translation of the Greek word *merimna* – worry or anxiety. It was against this that Jesus warned his disciples, telling them that if their first concern was always to seek the will of God and to trust him implicitly, and their second was to live a day at a time they would soon discover the secret of tranquil-lity. There is everything to be said for a provident approach to life in the areas cited by Reinhold Niebuhr as well as in the daily round of life, but there is nothing to be said for anxiety or worry. God knows what is best for us. He wants for each of us what is best and He is able to bring it about.

Prayer   *Most Loving Father, who willest us to give thanks for all things, to dread nothing but the loss of thee, and to cast all our care on thee who carest for us, preserve us from faithless fears and worldly anxieties, and grant that no clouds of this mortal life may hide from us the light of that love which is immortal, and which thou has manifested unto us through Jesus Christ our Lord.*

Union with God

Behold I call my creature, even thee
The poor, the frail, the sinful and the sad;
And with My glory, I will make thee glad;
Come unto Me, my friend, come unto Me!
Even so the voice from heaven I heard, and came
And veiled my face and plunged into the flame.
Last night I lived a mean and abject thing
Content in bondage, glad and prison-bound,
With greedy fingers, blindly groping round
For such brief comfort as the hour might bring.
To-day I am the North wind on the wing
And the wild roaring of the clamorous sea,
And the huge heaven's calm immensity.
And all the bloom and music of the spring
I lived and loved. How is it life or death
Here in this vast world wherein I move?
How when the winds of heaven are my breath,
And the great sun whereby I see?
I live not in myself, only in Thee.
Last night I loved. This morning I am love.

TRANSLATION BY SIR CECIL SPRING-RICE
OF AN ARABIAN MYSTIC'S POEM

Comment

The mystic describes a never-to-be-forgotten experience when he felt himself to
be one with God. 'I live not in myself, only in Thee'. There are moments, and
normally they are fleeting, when some such sense possesses less experienced pilgrims on the Christian Way. There are moments when, maybe in solitude, prompted by something ineffably beautiful, in nature, in ordinary human love, in
music, in art, in worship, we are lifted out of ourselves into Reality, into God himself. Separateness fades, and union with God is for that moment complete. If we
ask whether we can do anything to extend such experiences or to make them more
frequent, the answer is probably 'No!' – if we set out to 'fix' the experience. Whilst
most of us may never be able to realise experiences such as the great mystics describe, we can certainly do something about creating the conditions which favour
their occurrence. The Christian contemplative shows us the way to what Evelyn
Underhill calls the 'profound inward peace' which opens the way to the rich mystical experience. Stillness, silence and solitude are essentials to that end. Read tomorrow what one of the great mystics of our day tells us about her experiences.

Prayer   *Holy and Eternal God, I see the wonder of the stars in the silence of*
the night. Help me in the silence of my soul so to be possessed of thee
that I shall be one with thee in love and that through my words, my
thought, my deeds, others may be brought to sense thy wonder and be
drawn to thee by the magnet of thy love.

Mysticism

I beheld the ineffable fullness of God; but I can recall nothing of it save
that I have seen the fullness of Divine Wisdom, wherein is all goodness. . .
The eyes of my soul were opened and I beheld the plenitude of God, by
which I understood the whole world both here and beyond the sea, the abyss
and all other things. In this I beheld nothing but the Divine Power in a
way that is utterly indescribable, so that through the greatness of its wonder the soul cried with a loud voice: 'The whole world is full of God'. Wherefore I understood that the world is but a little thing; and I saw that the power
of God is above all things, and the whole world was filled with it. After I
had seen the power of God, His will and His justice, I was lifted higher
still; and then I no longer beheld the power and will as before. . . If thou
seekest to know what I beheld, I can tell thee nothing save that I beheld
a Fullness and a Clearness. . . a beauty so great that I can say nothing of
it save that I saw the Supreme Beauty which contains in itself all goodness.

EVELYN UNDERHILL (1875–1941)

Comment

So wrote Evelyn Underhill in *The Essentials of Mysticism*. Of all the quotations in
this book so far, the above is undoubtedly the most difficult to understand. It is
not given to many to rise to such heights of spiritual perception but to aspire to
do so is not to lose touch with reality, but to reach out to Reality. The lives of
such mystics as St John of the Cross, St Teresa and Mother Julian of Norwich,
demonstrate beyond question that mystics are not people who become so heavenly
minded as to be of no earthly use to society. These and many other holy men and
women have found, in this deep contemplation and mysticism, a sure path to such
union with God that they have lived lives which were overflowing with the love
of God expressed in their love of God's people. Mother Teresa is a living example.
Expressed as above we may find it difficult to understand, but seeing its effect in
a human life lets us into the secret. 'Just looking at God and loving Him' was how
a labourer described contemplation to the great French Curé d'Ars. Simply defined, mysticism is growing into ever closer and closer communion with God until
the soul senses the gift of union with ultimate Reality. The way through to this,
whether it be finally accomplished in this life or not, is the way of prayer and meditation, of worship and of the sacraments.

Prayer *O Lord, my heart is ready; my mind awake, attent, alert; my spirit,
open and ardent, abandoning all else, holding itself in leash, straining
the eye of faith, hearkening for thy step, leaping with love, throbbing
loudly yet lying still. Speak Lord, for they servant heareth.*

ERIC MILNER-WHITE

Except the Love of God

All things that are on earth shall wholly pass away,
Except the love of God, which shall live and last for aye.
The forms of men shall be as they had never been,
The blasted groves shall lose their fresh and tender green,
The birds of the thicket shall end their pleasant song,
And the nightingale shall cease to chant the evening long;
The kine of the pasture shall feel the dart that kills,
And all the fair white flocks shall perish from the hills.
The goat and antlered stag, the wolf and the fox,
The wild boar of the wood, and the chamois of the rocks,
And the strong and fearless bear in the trodden dust shall lie;
And the dolphin of the sea and the mighty whale shall die,
And realms shall be dissolved, and empires be no more,
And they shall bow to Death who ruled from shore to shore;
And the great globe itself, so the holy writings tell,
And the rolling firmament where the starry armies dwell
Shall melt with fervent heat – they shall all pass away,
Except the love of God, which shall live and last for aye.

WILLIAM C. BRYANT (1794–1878)

Comment

There is mysticism in these simple lines from the pen of an American poet. In another of his poems he affirms his conviction that the same love of God which shall 'live and last for aye', is not some powerful impersonal force but a Person who 'in the way that I must tread, will guide my steps aright'. In one of her revelations of divine love, Mother Julian of Norwich enjoyed the same rich experience: 'I saw for certain, both here and elsewhere, that before ever he made us, God loved us; and that his love has never slackened, nor ever shall. In this love all his works have been done, and in this love he has made everything serve us, and in this love our life is everlasting'. Love is not merely a characteristic of God but the character of God Himself. Therein lies our hope, for since God's love for us lives and lasts for ever, his forgiveness of our sins is for ever – awaiting only our penitence. As our poet exhorts us elsewhere:

> *So live that when thy summons comes to join*
> *The innumerable caravan that moves*
> *To the pale realms of shade, where each shall take*
> *His chamber in the silent halls of death,*
> *Thou go not, like the quarry slave at night,*
> *Scourged to his dungeon; but, sustained and soothed*
> *by an unfaltering trust.*

Prayer   *Dear Lord, help me to radiate your love among all whom I meet day by day, that whether in sin or sorrow or suffering they may be conscious of your unchanging love for them, forgiving, freeing and fortifying.*

Life's Weaving

My life is but a weaving
  Between my God and me;
I may not choose the colours
He knows what they should be;
For He can view the pattern
  On His the upper side,
While I can see it only
  On this, the under side.
Sometimes He allows sorrow
  Which seems so strange to me;
But I will trust His judgement
And work on faithfully;
'Tis He who fills the shuttle,
He knows just what is best;
So I shall weave in earnest,
  And leave with Him the rest.
At last, when life is ended,
  With Him I shall abide,
Then I may view the pattern
On His the upper side;
Then I shall know the reason
Why pain with joy entwined
  Was woven in the fabric
  Of life that God designed.

Comment

The anonymous author had perhaps gone through one of those periods not uncommon to Christians, of being utterly bewildered by the changes and chances of life. Successes, failures, disappointments, sorrows, sufferings, seemingly insoluble problems, pressures, doubts, ecstatic joys – all intermingling in a higgledypiggledy mixture which suggests that life in its totality is an insoluble enigma without pattern or progressive purpose. The author's answer is a familiar one but it is none the less true for that. The Christian commitment offers no easy or straightforward path through life – no immunity from suffering, sorrow, disappointments and all the trials of life, no advance warnings of opportunities or responsibilities. But it does promise Our Lord's abiding presence and His assurance that all things work together for good to them that love God.

Prayer   *Teach us, good Lord, to serve thee as thou deservest: to give and not to count the cost, to fight and not to heed the wounds, to toil and not to seek for rest, to labour and not to ask for any reward save that of knowing that we do thy will, through Jesus Christ our Lord.*

IGNATIUS LOYALA

Ozymandias

I met a traveller from an antique land
Who said: 'Two vast and trunkless legs of stone
Stand in the desert... Near them, on the sand,
Half sunk, a shattered visage lies, whose frown
And wrinkled lip, and sneer of cold command,
Tell that its sculptor well those passions read,
Which yet survive, stamped on these lifeless things,
The hand that mocked them, and the heart that fed:
And on the pedestal, these words appear:
"My name is Ozymandias, king of kings,
Look on my works ye mighty and despair!"
Nothing beside remains. Round the decay
Of that colossal wreck, boundless and bare
The lone and level sands stretch far away'.

P.B. SHELLEY (1792–1822)

Comment

This is one of the greatest sonnets in English literature written indeed by a poet who was not a believer, yet it serves to remind us of the transitoriness of worldly empires, compared with the durability of Christ's empire of love. We know nothing of Ozymandias save what the sonnet tells us – a king of kings, yet all that is left of him is a broken statue in a desert. 'I know men,' said Napoleon Bonaparte, 'and I tell you that Jesus Christ is more than man. Between him and every other person in the world there is no possible term of comparison'. How does he sustain that view? 'Alexander, Caesar, Charlemagne and I have founded empires. But on what did we rest the creation of our genius? Upon force! Jesus Christ founded his empire upon love; and at this hour millions of men would die for him'. Jesus said, 'I will build my church and the gates of hell shall not prevail against it'. (St Matthew Ch.16 v.18). Even his closest friends must have recalled those words rather sadly as they went to their homes on the first Good Friday. But the gates of hell did not prevail then, and have not prevailed against the Church. Despite infidelity from within and persecution from without – Nero, Hitler, Stalin and countless others – the Church lives, and ever will. We must never forget that as the Church is the Body of Christ, divinely founded and divinely inspired, its impact upon the world depends upon us, its members, as limbs of the Body.

Prayer   *O Lord God, we pray for thy whole Church throughout the world. May we and all its members be faithful in witness, vigorous in service and sincere in worship, that as thy Son our Lord has promised that no evil power may prevail against it, so through its life may Thy will be done and Thy kingdom come, through the same Jesus Christ our Lord.*

Eyes to see

When I consider how my light is spent
Ere half my days, in this dark world and wide,
And that one talent which is death to hide
Lodged with me useless, though my soul more bent
To serve therewith my Maker, and present
My true account, lest He returning chide –
'Doth God exact day-labour, light denied?'
I fondly ask – but Patience, to prevent
That murmur, soon replies: 'God doth not need
Either man's work, or his own gifts: who best
Bear his mild yoke, they serve him best. His state
Is kingly; thousands at His bidding speed
And post o'er land and ocean without rest:
They also serve who only stand and wait'.

JOHN MILTON (1608–1674)

I have walked with people whose eyes are full of light, but who see nothing in wood, sea or sky, nothing in the city streets, nothing in books. What a witless masquerade is this seeing! It were far better to sail for ever in the night of blindness, with sense and feeling and mind, than to be thus content with the mere act of seeing. They have the sunset, the morning skies, the purple distant hills, yet their souls voyage through this enchanted world in a barren state... I believe that God is in me as the sun is in the colour and fragrance of a flower – the Light in my darkness, the Voice in my silence.

HELEN KELLER (1880-1968)

Comment

Two who were blind yet light shines from each, for each had eyes to see beyond the physical and the material. They could not look 'at', but they could look 'into', and looking 'into' they saw something of God's beauty and God's purpose. They were physically blind but spiritually sighted. Each is saying in effect that the spiritually blind are in worse state than they. Where do we stand?

Prayer   *O God, who art the Father of Lights and with whom there is no darkness at all, we thank thee for the good gift of sight which thou hast bestowed upon us and we pray thee to fill us with thine own compassion for those who have it not. Direct and prosper all that is done for their welfare. Reveal to them by thy Spirit the things which eye hath not seen. Comfort them with the hope everlasting, to which, of thy great mercy, we beseech thee to bring us all, through Jesus Christ our Lord.*

Hope

We must not disguise from ourselves that God's dealings with this world are still a very difficult problem... There is a great deal of shallow optimism which 'heals too lightly' the wounds which experience inflicts upon Faith and Hope. It is useless to say, 'God's in His Heaven; All's right with the world' when many things are obviously all wrong in the world... Eminent literary men in the last century were too secure and comfortable to see what a rough place the world is for the majority of those who live in it. It was only after long travail of soul that the Jews learned their lesson; we shall not learn ours by turning epigrams. Remember that complacent optimism, no less than pessimism, is treason against Hope. The world, as it is, is not good enough to be true. We ought not to be satisfied with it. 'God has prepared some better thing'... This world exists for the realisation in time of God's eternal purposes. Some of these are bound up with individual lives, for God intended each one of us to do and to be something; others have a far wider scope and require far more time for their fulfilment. The manifold evils in the world are allowed to exist because only through them can the greater good be brought into activity. This greater good is not any external achievement, but the love and heroism and self-sacrifice which the great conflict calls into play. We must try to return to the dauntless spirit of the early Christians.

DEAN INGE (1860–1954)
QUOTED FROM *Personal Religion*

Comment

Hope is one of the so-named theological virtues. That says at once that it goes deep, that it is something more than the casual 'I hope that...' which frequently passes our lips. It is not escapism nor wishful thinking. Certainly it touches our lives in the here and now; it has an earthly content. To hope for some good end without dedicating or bending our wills towards achieving it, whether it be to pass an examination or to see the world at peace – is to slam the door in God's face. But hope has its heavenly content too. The poor dispirited Job bewailed, 'My days are swifter than a weaver's shuttle, and are spent without hope' (Job Ch7, v.6). The confident Christian on the other hand can, as Paul reminded Titus, look forward to 'the hope of eternal life which God who never lies promised ages ago'. Here, in the darkness of this world, Christians can be and must be beacons of hope.

Prayer   *God, who has prepared for them that love thee such good things as pass man's understanding, pour into our hearts such love towards thee, that we, loving thee above all things, may obtain thy promises which exceed all that we can desire; through Jesus Christ our Lord.*

Hope no more to me

Fire and the windows bright glittered on the moorland;
  Song, tuneful song, built a palace in the wild.
Now, when day dawns on the brow of the moorland,
  Lone stands the house and the chimney-stone is cold.
Lone let it stand now the friends are all departed,
  The kind hearts, the true hearts, that loved the place of old.
Spring shall come, come again, calling up the moor-fowl,
  Spring shall bring the sun and rain, bring the bees and flowers;
Red shall the heather bloom over hill and valley,
  Soft flow the stream through the ever-flowing hours;
Fair the day shine as it shone on my childhood –
  Fair shine the day on the house with open door;
Birds come and cry there and twitter in the chimney –
  But I go for ever and come again no more.

R.L. STEVENSON (1850–1894)

Comment

The transience of earthly things is a theme upon which many poets have dwelt – Wordsworth, Yeats, Tennyson and Kipling are among those who have left us poignant and melancholy lines – albeit lines of great beauty, lines which have dwelt on what was and is no more. Here Stevenson sees again the home of his childhood and is conscious of much that has changed and so much that is changeless. The word 'nostalgia' began its life as a medical term – a disease in fact! – but as we advance in years it is a disease we tend to enjoy. But the Christian must never forget that Time is Eternity begun, that amidst the changing there is ever the changeless. He can look back on his past and praise God for all that was good and lovely in it, but he must never forget that his past was – indeed the whole created world in all its splendour and beauty is – but a parenthesis in Eternity. Eternity does not begin when Time ends. Eternity is now and we are wise if we learn its language – the language of worship – which alone outlasts Time.

Prayer   *Lord God of Time and Eternity, who makest us creatures of Time that when Time is over, we may attain thy blessed Eternity. With Time thy gift, give us also wisdom to redeem the Time, lest our day of grace be lost.*

CHRISTINA ROSSETTI (1830–1894)

Friendship

After the two noble gifts of friendship – peace in the affections and support of the judgement – followeth the last fruit, which is like the pomegranate, full of many kernels: I mean aid, and bearing a part in all actions and occasions. Here the best way to represent to life the manifold use of friendship is to cast and see how many things there are which a man cannot do himself: and then it will appear that it was a sparing speech of the ancient to say 'that a friend is another himself': for that a friend is far more than himself. Men have their time and die many times in desire of some things which they principally take to heart; the bestowing of a child, the finishing of a work or the like. If a man have a true friend he may rest almost secure that the care of those things will continue after him; so that a man hath, as it were, two lives in his desires... How many things are there which a man cannot, with any face or comeliness, say or do himself. A man can scarce allege his own merits with modesty, much less extol them; a man cannot sometimes brook to supplicate or beg, and a number of the like; but all these things are graceful in a friend's mouth, which are blushing in a man's own. A man cannot speak to his son but as a father; to his wife but as a husband; to his enemy but upon terms; whereas a friend may speak as the case requires, and not as it sorteth with the person: but to enumerate these things were endless. I have given the rule, where a man cannot fitly play his own part, if he have not a friend, he may quit the stage.

FRANCIS BACON (1561–1626)

Comment

Francis Bacon dwells here on the 'income' derived from friendship rather than the 'expenditure' involved in winning it. The gift of making friends is undoubtedly one of God's best, because it is an aspect of loving our neighbours. It is not given to the self-centred to make friends. It involves getting out of oneself and into the mind and heart of another, sharing – as Jeremy Taylor defined it – 'the greatest usefulness, the most open communications, the noblest sufferings, the severest truth, the heartiest counsels and the greatest union of minds of which brave men and women are capable.' It is worth reflecting from time to time: How many friends have I and how deep are my friendships? To how many do I offer friendship?

Prayer   *O Heavenly Father, I thank you for my loved ones and for all my friends. Give me the grace both of offering and receiving friendship. Draw us all ever nearer to you that we may be bound together in your love and by the power of the Holy Spirit live our lives according to your will through Jesus Christ Our Lord.*

Trust

'My Lord God, I have no idea where I am going. I do not see the road ahead of me. I cannot know for certain where it will end. Nor do I really know myself, and the fact that I think I am following your will does not mean that I am actually doing so. But I believe that the desire to please you does in fact please you, and I hope that I will never do anything apart from that desire. I know that if I do this you will lead me by the right road though I may know nothing about it. Therefore will I trust you always though I may seem to be lost and in the shadow of death. I will not fear for you are ever with me, and you will never leave me to face my perils alone'.

ANONYMOUS

Comment

The thoughts of the anonymous writer correspond with those of the writer of Psalm 139. Like the Psalmist there were times when he was bewildered, perplexed, 'lost', in the ups and downs and twists and turns of daily life. But they share a common approach to life in at least two ways. Each is conscious that he is a person in his own right. (Note how frequently the 'I' comes both into the prayer and into the psalm.) Each is conscious that whatever the circumstances of the moment he is not alone. Our author says to God: 'I trust you always...' The psalmist says: 'If I climb up into heaven thou art there; if I go down to hell thou are there also'. Our author will trust, even though he may 'seem to be lost'. The psalmist, feeling lost, bewails 'peradventure the darkness shall cover me', and immediately expresses his confidence in God's care – 'the darkness is no darkness in thee, but the night is as clear as the day; the darkness and light to thee are both alike'. Each recognises that God is inescapable, and each recognises that whatever the circumstances of the moment, God is at hand. Trust in God does not, of course, supersede the need for prudence in the affairs of daily life but it does afford the assurance that if the will is dedicated the way will be directed. A nineteenth century American poet, Mary Frances Butts, sums up the lesson in a simple verse:

> Build a little fence of trust
> Around to-day;
> Fill the space with loving work
> And therein stay;
> Look not through the sheltering bars
> Upon tomorrow;
> God will help thee bear what comes
> Of joy or sorrow.

And the psalmist said the same even more succinctly: 'In God have I put my trust: I will not be afraid what men can do unto me' (Psalm 56).

Prayer *Into your loving hands, O God, I commit myself and all those near and dear to me. In you is our trust whether we wake or sleep, whether we work or play, whether we laugh or weep. In you is our trust for ever.*

Hope

'Youth's beauty fades and manhood's glory fades,
Faith dies and unfaith blossoms as a flower;
Nor ever wilt thou find upon the open streets of men,
Or secret places of the heart's own love,
One wind blows true for ever'.

SOPHOCLES (490–406 BC)

We did not dare to breathe a prayer
Or to give our anguish scope!
Something was dead in each of us,
And what was dead was Hope!

OSCAR WILDE (1854–1900)

Hope like the gleaming taper's light
Adorns and cheers our way
And still as darker grows the night
Emits a brighter ray.

OLIVER GOLDSMITH (1728–1774)

Hope, child, tomorrow and tomorrow still,
And every tomorrow hope; trust while you live
Hope, each time the dawn doth heaven fill,
Be there to ask, as God is there to give.

VICTOR HUGO (1802–1885)

Comment

First, the melancholy despair of Sophocles, writer of Greek tragedies 500 years before Christ; then four lines from Oscar Wilde's poem *The Ballad of Reading Gaol* – the pathetic cry of sick men. Then Oliver Goldsmith, in his *The Captivity, an Oratio*, affirms his confidence that true hope loses nothing of its brightness when 'darkness grows the night'. on the contrary it 'emits a bright ray'. Finally Victor Hugo reminds us of the Source of that hope – God himself – and counsels communion with him 'each time the dawn doth heaven fill'. The psalmist declared that his belief in the caring God was such that he would 'hope continually' and would praise God more and more. So too the writer of the Epistle to the Hebrews who exhorts his readers to 'lay hold upon the hope set before us, which hope we have as an anchor of the soul both sure and steadfast'. Situations arise within families, within societies, within nations, which we tend to write off as 'hopeless'. In the eyes of God there are none such. Of all people Christians should be what Matthew Arnold called 'beacons of hope' in a dark world. So will they, in the darkest hour, reflect the light of him who said, 'I am the Light of the world' and who bade his disciples to be themselves lights of the world.

Prayer

Lord God, help us to lay hold upon the hope before us which hope we have as an anchor of the soul, both sure and steadfast.

EPISTLE TO THE HEBREWS

Nobility

There was very lately a lad in the University of Oxford who was by his poverty forced to leave his studies there; and at last to join himself to a company of vagabond gypsies. Among these vagrant people, by the insinuating subtilty of his carriage, he quickly got so much of their love and esteem as that they discovered to him their mystery. After he had been a pretty while exercised in the trade, there chanced to ride by a couple of scholars, who had formerly been of his acquaintance. They quickly spied out their old friend among the gypsies; and he gave them an account of the necessity which drove him to that kind of life, and told them that the people he went with were not such impostors as they were taken for, but that they had a traditional kind of learning among them and could do wonders by the power of imagination, their fancy blinding that of others; that himself had learned much of their art, and when he had compassed the whole secret, he intended, he said to leave their company, and give the world an account of what he had learned.

FROM GLANVIL'S VANITY OF DOGMATIZING, 1661

Comment

This was the story which inspired Matthew Arnold to write *The Scholar Gypsy*, in which he speaks:

> *this strange disease of modern life*
> *with its sick hurry, its divided aims,*
> *its head o'er taxed, its palsied hearts –*

It is a picture with which we are not unfamiliar, and that a hundred years after Arnold put pen to paper – save that the scholar now would find help at hand enabling him to pursue his academic ambitions. But the lesson lies not there. Poverty had driven the scholar into an environment which he would not have chosen for himself. But humility has preserved him from bitterness and magnanimity had prompted him to live among simple people without any sense of superiority. Indeed he was ready to confess that he had learnt much from them and what he had learnt he would gladly give to the world. We can learn from the scholar who mingled easily with the gypsies that our approach to people must be for what they are in themselves, not for the position they occupy, nor for their social status. Thomas à Kempis gives wise advice when he says: 'Do not consider yourself to have made any spiritual progress, unless you account yourself the least of men. God walks with the humble; he reveals himself to the lowly; he gives understanding to the little ones; he discloses his meaning to pure minds, but hides his grace from the proud'.

Prayer   *Take from us, O Lord God, all pride and vanity, all boasting and self-assertion and give us the true courage which shows itself in gentleness, the true wisdom which shows itself in simplicity and the true power which shows itself in modesty; through Jesus Christ our Lord.*

Love in action

Give me thine eyes to see in each
With whom I have to do,
All that those eyes of thine would see,
All that is good and true.
Give me a mind which has no will
To judge and criticise,
Which strives to think the best of all
And from all gossip flies.
Give me a heart so kind and good
To everyone I meet,
That each may know that here is one
Who sitteth at thy feet.
Give me a humble spirit, Lord,
Which seeks not place nor power,
Which looks to thee in every need
For guidance hour by hour.
Give me thy love, that I may love
As thou hast loved me.
Give me a heart humble and meek
That I may learn of thee.
Give me thyself, beloved Lord,
Oh, how I long for thee!
Take and make me all thine own,
Naught else sufficeth me.

SISTER LILIAN AILSA, C.S.M.V. (1882–1967)

Comment

'See how these Christians love one another' has frequently been the taunt of the cynics, of those who see Christians so called at bitter variance with one another – hating, despising, uncaring. When Jesus proclaimed his 'new commandment that ye love one another' he proclaimed a new charter of human relationships which shook the accepted standards of his day and mocked the existing social system. Those who dubbed Christians as 'these that have turned the world upside down' were in fact speaking the truth. Citizens of an empire in which pride was exalted as a virtue to be cultivated and humility a vice to be stunned, where 'old and sickly slaves' should be thrown on to a human rubbish heap was the world in which Christ's was indeed a new commandment. Tenderness, gentleness, kindness, generosity, modesty, compassion – all these and more were the strands of the love of which he spoke, and which he declared to be the attitudes of those who followed him to all other of God's children of whatever race, colour or station. Christianity is love in action. We are not enjoined to like our neighbour, though even that makes for easier relationships. We are, however, bidden to love him and to do that, we have ever to strive to be what C.S. Lewis indicated as our aim, that we should be 'little Christs'.

Prayer *Add an 'amen' to Sister Lilian Ailsa's poem and you will make it your own prayer.*

Self-scrutiny

The Christian cannot elude ethics on his way to the sanctuary of God. Over against the contrite acknowledgement of our own faultiness, our ingrained egotism and turbulent desires, the Church sets the acknowledgement of our responsibility, and the bracing appeal to the moral will. Humility does not mean an easy acquiescence in our own shabbiness. The human nature which is to be offered a the altar for God's purpose, must be ordered and purified, in so far as man is able to do it. He must at least set his life in order as well as he can, submit thought, word and deed to the judgement of Love before he goes further. 'Let a man examine himself', says St Paul to those who come to the Christian mysteries. Not as to whether he is good enough; but as to whether he is able to take trouble enough, whether his face is set towards Eternity, and whether the demands and interests of self-will. . .

A purely mystical religion, leaving the sense-world and its conflicts behind in its flight towards God, might elude all this; but an incarnational religion never can. 'Look well if there be any way of wickedness in me and lead me in the way everlasting, says the Psalmist. That kind of interanl examination may be very painful, very shaming, very searching, but only those willing to submit to it can hope for the full healing of Christ.

EVELYN UNDERHILL (1875–1961)

Comment

Evelyn Underhill would not have claimed for herself the title 'mystic' but her own definition of a mystic, as one who knows for certain the presence and activity of the Love of God', indubitably puts her among the great mystics of the Church. Yet here she is making it crystal clear that the Love of God is not merely something which we sense. It is something which makes demands of us in the sphere of our activity in the world. Self-examination is, for the Christian, nt an optional extra in his commitment to Christ but an essential element in it. We have frequently to look into our hearts and minds and souls and consciences, to discover whether we can claim what in another place Evelyn Underhill calls 'a clean bill of health'. Unless and until we do just that there is not likely to be in our hearts that penitence which is both th prerequisite for and the assurance of God's forgiveness and our own spiritual progress.

Why not do just that, just now, and then pray this:

Prayer *Lord, for thy tender mercies' sake, lay not my sins to my charge, but forgive all that is past; and give me grace to amend my life, to decline from sin, and incline to virtue, that I may walk with a perfect heart before thee now and ever.*

The Shepherd Psalm

The Lord is my Pace-setter, I shall not rush,
He makes me stop and rest for quiet intervals,
He provides me with images of stillness, which restores my serenity.
He leads me in ways of efficiency; through calmness of mind,
And his guidance is peace.
Even though I have a great many things to accomplish each day
I will not fret for his presence is here.
His timelessness, His all importance will keep me in balance.
He prepares refreshment and renewal in the midst of my activity
By anointing my mind with His oils of tranquillity.
My cup of joyous energy overflows.
Surely harmony and effectiveness shall be the fruits of my hours,
For I shall walk in the peace of my Lord, and dwell in his house for ever.

TOKI MIYASHINA, A JAPANESE WOMAN

Comment

The much-loved 23rd psalm has been the basis of many familiar hymns – George Herbert's *The God of love my shepherd is*, Addison's *The Lord my pasture shall prepare* and Henry Baker's *The King of love my shepherd is* are favourites among them. Other writers have adapted the psalm using picture-language more suited to people's experience and understanding. (There are some countries where sheep are unknown!') The Japanese author has caught the essence of the Psalmist's thoughts – confidence that God leads and guides, that he restores the balance of life and in such a manner that, come what may in tasks, in troubles, in the difficulty of decisions, he is at hand to clear the path enabling us to go forward with confidence. There is no promise that Christians shall be immune from the possibility of finding themselves in the dark places of life (i.e. in the valley of the shadow), but there is the assurance that God is ever at hand to sustain those who are in fellowship with him and that through life and death. Note that the Japanese author has used almost the same words as the Psalmist in her conclusion: 'dwell in his house for ever'. We need, as the Psalmist needed, not only fellowship with God but fellowship with other worshippers. That says something not only about private prayer but also about public worship and our need to make time in our lives for both.

Prayer   *Read the Japanese author's version again and add to the last line –*
AMEN, a Hebrew word which means 'firmly' and which Christians
use as an expression of assent.

The World

I have not loved the world, nor the world me;
I have not flatter'd its rank breath, nor bow'd
To its idolatries a patient knee,
Nor coin'd my cheek to smiles, – nor cried aloud
In worship of an echo; in the crowd
They could not deem me one of such; I stood
Among them, but not of them; in a shroud
Of thoughts which were not their thoughts, and still could,
Had I not filled my mind, which thus itself subdued.
I have not loved the world, nor the world me, –
But let us part fair foes; I do believe,
Though I have found them not, that there may be
Words which are things, – hopes which will not deceive
And virtues which are merciful, nor weave
Snares for the failing; I would also deem
O'er others' griefs that some sincerely grieve;
That two, or one, are almost what they seem, –
That goodness is no name, and happiness no dream.

LORD BYRON (1788–1824)

Comment

Here is something of a confession of faith by a poet 'who awoke one morning to find himself famous'. His first literary effort was a dismal failure but *Childe Harold* lifted him immediately to a place among the most distinguished poets of his day. Nevertheless, his way of life was wayward and turbulent, ending in his involvement with revolutionary movements in Italy and Greece. But the man who could write lines such as the above could well be one to whom Our Lord would say 'Thou art not far from the kingdom of God'. 'No one can be in love with the world and in love with God at one and the same time' (1 John, Ch.2). The world which Byron claims not to have loved was the world against which the writer of the epistle warned his readers – not the world of God's creation which not even Solomon in all his glory could match, not the 'cosmos', but the world which turned its back on God, the society of false standards and values, the world which though it believes in God, dismisses him to the periphery of life. The Christian must not conform to this world nor compromise with it.

Prayer

O God, have mercy on all who live without faith, on all who forget thee amid their worldly business and on all who are hardened by the deceitfulness of sin, and convert them to thy service, for the merits of Jesus Christ our Lord.

WILLIAM BRIGHT

Saints and Martyrs of Africa

Martyrdom

We do not think of a martyr simply as a good Christian who has been killed because he is a Christian: for that would be solely to mourn. We do not think of him as a good Christian who has been elevated to the company of the saints; for that would be simply to rejoice; and neither our mourning nor our rejoicing is as the world's. A Christian martyrdom is no accident. Still less is a Christian martyrdom the effect of a man's will to become a saint, as a man by willing and contriving may become a ruler of men. A martyr is never the design of man; for the true martyr is he who has become the instrument of God, who has lost his will in the will of God – not lost it but found it, for he has found freedom in submission to God. The martyr no longer desires anything for himself not even the glory of martyrdom.

T.S. ELIOT (1888–1965)

Comment

Of such are those we remember in the *Te Deum* as 'the noble army of martyrs' – there remembered with the Apostles, the Prophets and the 'holy church throughout the world'. They are not all remembered by name in the church's calendar; they are so many that if but one were cited for every day of the year there would be hundreds more from every continent, whose martyrdom or holy life would be unsung. Not one of the martyrs sought martyrdom, but martyrdom sought many. Nor is our own day lacking in that bold and determined witness to the faith which has led many to sacrifice their lives, and may yet demand more men and women who, despite all the threats which confront them steadfastly refuse to deny the Christ to whom they have sworn their allegiance. We must pray for these of the present as we remember those of the past. 'The blood of the martyrs' is the seed of the church', said Tertullian and if, like Erasmus, we 'have no inclination to risk life for the truth' we may still not be immune, for it may call for higher energies of the soul to live for martyrdom than to die for it. It falls to some Christians to face contempt and persecution for the faith that is in them. Others may be denied human or civic rights. To stand firm in any such circumstance is to bear a witness which is noble in the sight of God.

Prayer   *Heavenly Father, as we remember all those who held fast to their faith even unto death and praise you for their witness and courage, grant that in our own struggles against indifference, opposition and cynicism, we may stand firm in the power of your Holy Spirit and for the sake of our Lord and Saviour Jesus Christ.*

Before Sleep

The toil of day is ebbing,
  The quiet comes again,
In slumber deep relaxing
  The limbs of tired men.
And minds with anguish taken,
  And spirits racked with grief,
The cup of all forgetting
  Have drunk and found relief.
The still Lethean waters
  Now steal through every vein
And men no more remember
  The meaning of the pain.
Let, let the body weary
  Lie sunk in slumber deep,
The heart shall still remember
  Christ in its very sleep.

PRUDENTIUS (348–419)
TRANS. HELEN WADDELL

Comment

'Lethean Waters' is a reference to the River of Oblivion in ancient mythology. Its waters were said to have the power of making those who drank from it forget the past. So often the day's concerns become the night's last thoughts. Joyous, anxious, happy, sad – these race through the mind, sometimes impeding sleep. One of the most beautiful acts of devotion of the Western Church is Compline, which in its present form we owe to St Benedict (480–550) who developed it as a form of corporate prayer and dedication to be offered just before going to bed. It is, in effect, a quiet commendation of the self – body, mind and spirit – to God's care whilst we sleep. The service as we know it would not have been known to Prudentius who was a fourth century Latin poet but it could be said that, prolific verse and hymn writer that he was, he must have devised a nightly commendation such as the above gentle poem. Here are three night prayers each worth memorising.

Prayers *Look down, O Lord, from thy heavenly throne, illuminate the darkness of this night with thy celestial brightness, and from the sons of light banish the deeds of darkness: through Jesus Christ our Lord.*

ORDER OF COMPLINE

Be present, O merciful God, and protect us through the silent hours of this night, so that we who are wearied by the changes and chances of this fleeting world may repose upon thy eternal changelessness; through Jesus Christ our Lord.

LEONINE SACRAMENTARY

Watch thou, dear Lord, with those who wake, or watch, or weep to-night, and give thine angels charge over those who sleep. Tend thy sick ones, O Lord Christ. Rest thy weary ones. Bless thy dying ones. Soothe thy suffering ones. Pity thine afflicted ones. And all for thy love's sake.

ST AUGUSTINE

Polycarp, Bishop of Smyrna, Martyr c.155

'What is to come'

What is to come we know not. But we know
That what has been was good – was good to show,
Better to hide, and best of all to bear.
We are the masters of the days that were:
We have lived, we have loved, we have suffered. . .
      even so.
Shall we not take the ebb who had the flow?
Life was our friend. Now, if it had been our foe –
Dear, though it spoil and break us! – need we care
      What is to come?

Let the great winds their worst and wildest blow,
Or the gold weather round us mellow show:
We have fulfilled ourselves, and we can dare,
And we can conquer, though we may not share,
In the rich quiet of the after-glow
      What is to come.

WILLIAM ERNEST HENLEY (1849–1905)

Comment

Unlike our poet, the saint whom we commemorate today knew what was to come both in the immediate and in the future. Polycarp, Bishop of Smyrna in the second century experienced in his long ministry both the ebb and flow of life. He had lived and loved and suffered but it was not until he was well over 80 that the 'worst and wildest' winds were to blow. Returning to his See city he found it caught up in a pagan festival in the course of which he was arrested and ordered to declare Caesar as Lord. Ever a stalwart defender of the Faith, against heresies and paganism alike, he refused and yielded to none of the persuasions of the pro-consul or the judge before whom he stood. 'Eighty and six years have I served my Christ and he never did me wrong. How can I blaspheme my King and my Saviour?' Unmoved by further threats against his life the aged bishop shouted, 'You threaten fire that burns for a moment, for you know nothing of the judgement to come'. Polycarp went to his martyrdom with this prayer on his lips, 'Father, I bless thee that thou hast thought me worthy of the present day and hour to have a share in the number of martyrs and in the cup of Christ unto the resurrection to eternal life. Wherefore on this account and for all things, I bless thee, I glorify thee through the Eternal High Priest Jesus Christ, thy well-beloved Son'. In the prayer which follows, the words 'thy Church' could be replaced by the word 'we' – for we *are* the Church.

Prayer   *O God, who dost inspire us to confess thy holy name by the witness of*
thy martyrs, grant that thy Church, encouraged by their example, may
be ready to suffer fearlessly for thy cause, and to strive for the reward
of thy heavenly glory; through Jesus Christ our Lord.

What is Man?

If we think that our nature is limited by the little wave of our being which is our conscious waking self, we are ignorant of our true being. The relation of our life to a larger spiritual world betrays itself even in the waking consciousness through our intellectual ideals, our moral aspirations, our cravings for beauty, and our longing for perfection. Behind our conscious self is our secret being, without which the superficial consciousness cannot exist or act. Consciousness in us is partly manifest and partly hidden. We can enlarge the waking part of it, by bringing into play ranges of our being which are now hidden. It is our duty to become aware of ourselves as spiritual beings, instead of falsely identifying ourselves with the body, life or mind. ·

S. RADHAKRISHNAN

Comment

'Man is the measure of all things' said Protagoras 400 years before Christ. 'Glory to Man in the highest, for Man is the master of things', wrote the nineteenth-century poet Swinburne. Poetic licence must be allowed to each, but taken at their face value each assertion could at the least be gravely misleading, suggesting that Man is not only self-sufficient but also in supreme control. Radhakrishnan in *Eastern Religion and Western Thought* has a more penetrating definition of Man's structure and place in the universe. Man must become conscious of himself as a spiritual being, and not until he has so become is he competent either to be the measure or the master of things. In each of the synoptic Gospels there is recorded our Lord's warning, 'What does it profit a man to gain the whole world and forfeit his life'. Man has to know himself as made in the image of God – a spiritual being living for a span in a material body, and so ordering his life as one conscious that – as Wordsworth puts it – his 'destiny is with infinitude'. He came from God. He shares the image of God. He belongs to God. He goes to God. The author of the *Wisdom of Solomon*, who wrote his book when the devout people of God were suffering persecution, encouraged them by reminding them where they stood in God's sight. He said, in Chapter 2, verse 25, 'God made man to be immortal, and to be an image of his own eternity'.

Prayer   *Almighty God, who didst wonderfully create man in thine own image, and didst yet more wonderfully restore him. Grant we beseech thee, that as thy Son our Lord Jesus Christ was made in the likeness of men, so we may be made partakers of the divine nature, through the same thy Son, Jesus Christ our Lord.*

1928 PRAYER BOOK

Doomed by God

Hatred and vengeance – my eternal portion
Scarce can endure delay of execution –
Wait with impatient readiness to seize my
      Soul in a moment

Damned below Judas; more abhorred than he was,
Who for a few pence sold his holy Master!
Twice betrayed Jesus me, the last delinquent,
      Deems the profanest.
Man disavows, and Deity disowns me,
Hell might afford my miseries a shelter;
Therefore, Hell keeps her ever hungry mouths all
      Bolted against me.
Hard lot! encompassed with a thousand dangers;
Weary, faint, trembling with a thousand terrors,
I'm called, if vanquished! to receive a sentence
      Worse than Abiram's

Him the vindictive rod of angry Justice
Sent quick and howling to the centre headlong;
I fed with judgement, in a fleshly tomb am
      Buried above ground.

WILLIAM COWPER (1731–1800)

Comment

Wonderful though terrible lines from the hand of the man who wrote such lovely hymns as 'O for a closer walk with God'. 'Jesus, where'er Thy people meet' and 'Hark my soul it is the Lord'. Cowper suffered periods of intense depression and it was from the depths of this that these lines of doom emerged. These are the thoughts which filled the mind of a man with a sound intellect and a broken spirit. In that state he could think only that salvation would be denied him from all eternity, which was Calvinism at its worst. Such fits of depression seized this godly man from time to time, but it is significant that the days he spent as a lay assistant to John Newton, the incumbent of the parish of Olney in Buckinghamshire, were not only his happiest but the most productive of lines of exquisite beauty and feeling. Maybe that the 'blessed assurance' which the evangelical incumbent – the writer of *Amazing Grace* – pressed in his preaching, exercised a spiritual therapy on a man whose life, 'blameless as the water lilies he loved' was clouded so often by a seemingly impenetrable despair. From all this we can draw two truths. The first: no sickness of the spirit is ever beyond the healing power of God, and no sin beyond the scope of his forgiveness. The second, ours may well be the voice, the touch, the prayer, which mends the broken heart and heals the broken spirit of another child of God.

Prayer   *Lord, lift me when I am down-hearted, dispirited or in despair and make of me the instrument in your hand to lift another in distress.*

In the Beginning

It is interesting to contemplate a tangled bank, clothed with many plants of many kinds, with birds singing in the bushes, with various insects flitting about, with worms crawling through the damp earth, and reflect that these constructed forms, so different from each other, and dependent upon each other in so complex a manner, have all been produced by laws acting around us. These laws, taken in the largest sense, being Growth and Reproduction, Inheritance which is almost implied by Reproduction, Variability from the indirect actions of the conditions of life, and from use and disuse; a ratio of increase so high as to lead to a struggle for Life, and as a consequence to Natural Selection, entailing Divergence of character, and the extinction of less improved forms. Thus, from the war of Nature, from famine and death, the most exalted object which we are capable of achieving, namely, the production of the higher animals, directly follows. There is a grandeur in this view of life, with its several powers, having been originally breathed by the Creator into a few forms or into one; and that, whilst this planet has gone cycling on according to the fixed laws of gravity, from so simple a beginning endless forms most beautiful and most wonderful have been and are being evolved.

CHARLES DARWIN (1809–1882)

Comment

Darwin undoubtedly suffered what might now be called unfair treatment by the media of his day – not least the religious media. His *Origin of Species* and his *The Descent of Man* were seen by some to be impious. But his theory of evolution was not his only or his last word. Agnostic he claimed to be, but a man who could conceive ideas and write words such as the above – the closing words of his *Origin of Species* – cannot be dubbed an atheist. His researches afforded him such a sense of the wonders of the universe and the grandeur of life that he was impelled to set 'the Creator' at the beginning. In other words he begins where the Book of Genesis begins: 'In the beginning God. . . '. Genesis offers us a beautiful poem of Creation. Darwin offers us a learned and reverent study of Creation. The two are not mutually exclusive. Genesis points us to the Creator, as Darwin does. The psalmist looks at Creation and senses the wonder of it all (see Psalm 19) – and the people of God, through the ages, have been moved to reverence for all things living. From wonder, to reverence, to worship.

Prayer

Almighty God, whose glory the heavens are telling, the earth thy power and the sea thy might, and whose greatness all feeling and thinking creators everywhere herald; to Thee belongeth glory, honour, might, greatness, and magnificence, now and for ever, to the ages of ages.

LITURGY OF ST JAMES

George Herbert, Priest, Poet, Pastor, 1633

Love

Love bade me welcome; yet my soul drew back,
*   Guilty of dust and sin.*
But quick-eyed Love, observing me grow slack
*   From my first entrance in,*
Drew nearer to me, sweetly questioning,
*   If I lacked anything.*
'A guest', I answered, 'Worthy to be here',
*   Love said, 'You shall be he',*
'I, the unkind, ungrateful? Ah, my dear,
*   I cannot look on thee'.*
Love took my hand, and smiling did reply,
*   'Who made the eyes, but I?'*

'Truth, Lord, but I have marred them; let my shame
*   Go where it doth deserve;*
'And know you not', says Love, 'who bore the blame?'
*   'My dear, then I will serve'.*
'You must sit down', says Love, 'and taste my meat'.
*   So I did sit and eat.*

GEORGE HERBERT (1593–1633)

Comment

Here shines the modesty of a great man of God who in his short life made such an impact as poet, priest and pastor that his words and his work have earned for him a secure place in the history of the Church. A gentle piety breathes through his poetry and through his much loved hymns. In the three years of his work in the tiny Wiltshire parish of Bemerton he exercised a priestly and pastoral ministry which became a model for others to follow. The poem above is from *The Temple*, which in his will he passed to Nicholas Farrar – a fellow priest and friend who had founded a religious community at Little Gidding. He told Farrar that he would find in the poem 'a picture of the many spiritual conflicts which have passed between God and my soul, before I could subject my will to the will of Jesus my Master'. In any list of commemorations of holy men, and more explicity a list drawn up by the Church of England, the name of George Herbert could not be omitted. Nicholas Farrar's judgement that his life and his work for God and his Church were such as to make him 'a companion to the primitive saints' is one which cannot but win universal acclaim.

Prayer

Thou hast given so much to us, give us one more thing, a grateful heart;
for Christ's sake.

GEORGE HERBERT (1593–1633)

A Seventeenth Century Nun's Prayer

Lord, Thou knowest better than I know myself that I am growing older and will some day be old. Keep me from the fatal habit of thinking that I must say something on every subject and on every occasion. Release me from craving to straighten out everybody's affairs. Make me thoughtful but not moody; helpful but not bossy. With my vast store of wisdom, it seems a pity not to use it all, but thou knowest, Lord, that I want a few friends at the end.

Keep my mind free from the recital of endless details: give me wings to get to the point quickly. Seal my lips on my aches and pains, for love of rehearsing them will become sweeter as the years go by. I dare not ask for grace enough to enjoy the tales of others' pains, for a growing humility, and a lessening cocksureness when my memory seems to clash with the memories of others. Teach me the glorious lesson that occasionally I may be wrong.

Keep me reasonably sweet; I do not want to be a Saint – some of them are so hard to live with – but a sour old person is one of the crowning works of the devil. Give me the ability to see good things in unexpected places, and talents in unexpected people. And give me, O Lord, the grace to tell them so.

Comment

The origin of this prayer is unknown. Its attribution to a Nun is questionable and its alleged date possibly belied by the use within it of words which can hardly be regarded as seventeenth-century English. Nevertheless it embraces sentiments with which we are all familiar and seeks preservation from weaknesses which beset not merely the aged. But surely 'I do not want to be a Saint' is a request which a Christian cannot make, despite the reason which is given to sustain it. Christians are 'called to be saints', called to be dedicated, called to be holy. That does not mean, of course, that Christians should adopt a 'holier than thou' attitude. Far from being 'hard to live with' they should, of all people, be good companions, conspicuous in any company for their readiness to mingle easily with others bringing with them not a presence which repels, but one which, for its sincerity and warmth, attracts a friendly response. People who – as the Nun puts it – are so hard to live with cannot be called saints!

Prayer   *Lord, help me to be true to my calling and in my striving to that end help me to make goodness attractive.*

Divinity in Man

Poetry is indeed something divine. It is at once the centre and circumference of knowledge... It is the perfect and consummate surface and bloom of all things; it is as the odour and the colour of the rose to the texture of the elements which compose it, as the form and splendour of unfaded beauty to the secrets of anatomy and corruption. What were virtue, love, patriotism, friendship – what were the scenery of this beautiful universe which we inhabit; what were our aspirations beyond it – if poetry did not ascend to bring light and fire from those eternal regions where the owl-winged faculty of calculation dare not ever soar?... Poetry thus makes immortal all that is best and most beautiful in the world. Poetry redeems from decay the visitations of the divinity in man... Poetry turns all things to loveliness; it exalts the beauty of that which is most beautiful, and it adds beauty to that which is most deformed; it marries exultation and horror, grief and pleasure, eternity and change; it subdues to union under its light yoke all irreconcilable things. It transmutes all that it touches, and every form moving within the radiance of its presence is changed by wondrous sympathy to an incarnation of the spirit which it breathes... It strips the veil of familiarity from the world, and lays bare the naked and sleeping beauty which is the spirit of its forms.

PERCY BYSSHE SHELLEY (1792–1822)

Comment

Leap Year! Perhaps the right occasion for the intrusion into a religious anthology of beautiful words written by one whose first literary effort, entitled *The Necessity of Atheism*, resulted in his expulsion from Oxford where he nursed an implacable enmity towards Christ Church and all that happened within it. He remained a rebel almost to the end of his days, yet in his short life, marred though it was by lack of self-control, he wrote many poems in which there are indeed glimpses of the divine. *Prometheus Unbound* stands high among the most splendid of the lyrical dramas in the whole realm of literature and his simple lyrics, such as *Ode to a Skylark* are works of exquisite beauty. Beauty is indeed a reflection of the Infinite. For those with eyes to see, it is a revelation of God himself. To reflect beauty – in literature, in art, in music, in daily life – is to reflect the divinity in Man.

Prayer   *I pray Thee, O God, that I may be beautiful within.*

SOCRATES (B. 469 BC)

Commemorating David, Bishop
Patron Saint of Wales, 601

Batter my heart, three-person'd God; for you
As yet but knock, breathe, shine, and seek to mend;
That I may rise, and stand, o'erthrow me, and bend
Your force, to break, blow, burn and make me new.
I, like a usurp'd town, to another due,
Labour to admit you, but Oh, to no end;
Reason, your viceroy in me, me should defend,
But is captiv'd, and proves weak or untrue.
Yet dearly I love you, and would be loved fain,
But am betroth'd unto your enemy:
Divorce me, untie, or break that knot again,
Take me to you, imprison me, for I
Except you enthral me, never shall be free,
Nor ever chaste, except you ravish me.

JOHN DONNE (1573–1631)

Comment

The sonnet is from the pen of a troubled soul. John Donne was Dean of St Paul's for the last years of his life. The world knew him as a great preacher. He knew himself as one who was ever torn between earthy desires and heavenly aspirations. The little that we know about David, the patron saint of Wales, suggests that he too struggled in the same way. Certainly the monasteries which he founded in the southern part of Wales were conducted on severely ascetic lines comparable with those of the Egyptian monks. Legend has it that he died at Menevia – now St David's – in or about the year 601. 'Kings mourned him as a judge, the older people mourned him as a brother, the younger as a father', and one and all asked, 'Who will teach us? Who will pray for us? Who will be a father to us as David was?' Legend aside, here clearly was a holy man, as was Donne, and a man who so loved God that he could plead 'Batter my heart... imprison me... take me to you'. As for them, so for us. There is ever the battle between the lower and the higher nature, between the lust of the flesh and the fruits of the Spirit. For St David, for John Donne, for St Paul and for Christ's disciples, that was a battle which each had to face. For each it was either abject surrender or triumphs in the Spirit. They fought. They won. What of us?

Prayer *O God, our Judge and Saviour, set before us the vision of thy purity,*
and let us see our sins in the light of thy holiness. Pierce our self-contentment
with the shafts of thy burning love, and let that love consume in us,
all that hinders us from perfect service of thy cause; for as thy holiness
is our judgement, so are thy wounds our salvation.

WILLIAM TEMPLE (1881–1944)

Commemorating Chad, Bishop of Lichfield
Missionary, died 672

To feel the universe as a sea, and oneself as a wave in it – that is humility. But there is a false humility and a true humility. For a man to feel scorn of himself and to forget that by his works and behaviour he can bless the whole world – this is false humility. 'The greatest evil is to forget that you are the son of a king'. The truly humble feel others as they feel themselves, they feel themselves in others. To be proud is not to know one's own value, but to contrast oneself with others, to measure up and make judgement on others. True humility is not a virtue you can will yourself to practise; it is a state of mind, an expression of your whole personality. The truly humble man lives in every being; he knows the nature and virtue of each. Because everyone is as himself to him, he knows from within him that everyone has some hidden value, that everyone has his hour. Every soul stands bright and clear for him in the splendour of its own existence. He can condemn no one, for 'he who judges another has judged himself'. To live with understanding of others is mere justice; to live *in* others as in oneself, is love.

MARTIN BUBER (1878–1965)

Comment

Chad and his three brothers were all priests, members of the monastic community of Lastingham of which Chad's brother Cedd was Abbot. Chad became Bishop of York at the instigation of the King who became impatient at the failure of Wilfrid, who had been appointed Bishop of York, to return from his consecration in France. However, Theodore, the new Archbishop of Canterbury, decided that Wilfrid was the lawful Bishop of York and consequently Chad was translated to the see of Lichfield. His humble submission to this action on the part of Theodore was typical of his humility, 'If you know that I have not duly received episcopal ordination, I willingly resign the office for I never thought myself worthy of it: but though unworthy I submitted out of obedience to undertake it'. Bede tells us that Chad insisted on going around his diocese on foot until, that is, Theodore both provided him with a horse and hoisted him on it for his first episcopal visitation. Chad was a humble and pious man, tireless in his ministry of preaching the Word and administration of the sacraments. His body rests in Lichfield Cathedral. As we reflect on St Chad's humility and Martin Buber's definition of true humility each of us can make Charles Kingsley's prayer his own – 'Take from me, . . . give out me . . . '.

Prayer   *Take from me, O Lord God, all pride and vanity, all boasting and self-assertion, and give me the true courage that shows itself in gentleness; the true vision that shows itself in simplicity; and the true power that shows itself in modesty: through Jesus Christ our Lord.*

CHARLES KINGSLEY (1819–1875)

Temptation

There are but two things we can do about temptations. The first is to be faithful to the light within us in avoiding all exposure to temptation which we are at liberty to avoid... The other is to turn our eyes to God in the moment of temptation, to throw ourselves immediately upon the protection of heaven, as a child when in danger flies to the arms of its parent.

The habitual conviction of the presence of God is the sovereign remedy; it supports, it consoles, it calms us. We must not be surprised that we are tempted. We are placed here to be proved by temptation. Everything is temptation to us. Crosses irritate our pride and prosperity flatters it; our life is a continual warfare but Jesus Christ combats with us. We must let temptation, like a tempest, beat upon our heads, and still move on; like a traveller surprised on the way by a storm, who wraps his cloak around him, and goes on his journey in spite of the opposing elements... It is not the multitude of hard duties, it is not the constraint and contention, or our wills without restriction to tread cheerfully every day in the path in which Providence leads us; to seek nothing; to be discouraged by nothing, to see our duty in the present moment, to trust all else without reserve to the will and power of God.

FRANCOIS FENELON (1651–1715)

Comment

March comes and with it many of Lent's forty days, and Lent speaks of abstinence, of discipline, of temptation, of evil, of repentance, of forgiveness and of the Cross. Thus our thoughts during this month can be so directed, save when some Feast Day or Commemoration turns them momentarily aside. François Fenelon, a seventeenth-century French archbishop and notable theologian and philosopher, concerned himself in particular with the education of the young and had the ability, great scholar though he was, of writing in such a way that young people and non-scholars could understand. Every Christian, however deeply dedicated, is vulnerable when temptation comes, as it does to us all, but temptation is not of itself evil. It is the free man's choice between good and evil, and in the Lord's Prayer we ask that we may be led through it safely, and be preserved from the evil into which we are trapped if we yield. Temptation comes from outside us – from the circumstances of the moment, even at times from friends – and it comes from inside us by reason of our lower nature. Sometimes it prods us subtly, sometimes it batters us fiercely. Self-respect may come to our aid and so too may the counsel of those whom we love. But the surest defence is 'to throw ourselves upon the protection of heaven' and that we can do in the confidence of the inescapable presence of Christ, ever at our side to see us through if we turn to him.

Prayer   *O Lord, shield of our help, who wilt not suffer us to be tempted above that we are able, help us we entreat thee, in all our straits and wrestlings, to lift up our eyes unto thee and stay our hearts on thee.*

CHRISTINA ROSSETTI (1830–1894)

Uphill

Does the road wind uphill all the way?
Yes, to the very end.
Will the day's journey take the whole long day?
From morn to night my friend.

But is there for the night a resting-place?
A roof for when the slow dark hours begin:
May not the darkness hide it from my face?
You cannot miss that inn.

Shall I meet other wayfarers at night?
Those who have gone before.
Then must I knock or call when just in sight?
They will not keep you standing at the door.

Shall I find comfort, travel-sore and weak?
Of labour you shall find the sum.
Will there be beds for me and all who seek?
Yes, beds for all who come.

CHRISTINA ROSSETTI (1830–1894)

Comment

This very familiar poem speaks of the striving which is of the essence of the Christian pilgrimage through the world of time – a striving, ultimately rewarded with 'beds for all who come'. Yet it is ever 'uphill'. The fierce temptations which assail Christians in different ways are rarely set aside with ease. It was Thomas à Kempis who reminded the Christian, striving against temptation and often discouraged, 'You are a man, not God. How can you expect to remain always in a constant state of virtue, when this was not possible even for an angel of heaven, nor for the first man in the Garden?' But this is not a recipe for relaxation in the struggle against evil. Evil is in the world. It cannot be explained away. It is, as it were, one of the facts of life which we have to accept, not in any sense that we have merely to put up with it, but in the sense that it represents a continuing challenge to our courage, which in its turn is sustained by waiting upon God. There are times for us all when evil seems attractive. Those are times when we must turn with determination to Christ as did his disciples 'Lord save us we perish' (Matthew Ch.6, verse 5). We shall find ourselves drawn irresistibly to him by the magnet of his love.

Prayer *Blessed Lord, who was tempted in all things like as we are, have mercy upon our frailty. Out of weakness, give us strength. Grant to us thy fear, that we may fear thee only. Support us in time of temptation. Embolden us in time of danger. Help us to do thy work with good courage, and to continue thy faithful soldiers and servants unto our life's end: through Jesus Christ our Lord.*

BISHOP WESTCOTT (1825–1901)

The world? Or Eternal Life?

The generality of persons do more willingly listen to the world than to God; they sooner follow the desires of their own flesh, than God's good pleasure. The world promises things temporal and mean and is served with great eagerness; I promise things more high and eternal, and yet the hearts of men remain torpid and insensible.

Who is there that in all things serveth and obeyeth Me with so great care as the world and its lords are served withal? . . . For a small income, a long journey is undertaken; for everlasting life many will scarce lift a foot from the ground. The most pitiful reward is sought after; for a single bit of money sometimes there is shameful contention; for a vain matter and slight promise, men fear not to toil day and night.

But alas! For an unchangeable good, for an inestimable reward, for the highest honour, and glory without end, they grudge even the least fatigue. Be ashamed therefore, thou slothful and complaining servant, that they are found to be more ready to destruction than thou to life. They rejoice more in vanity, than thou dost in the truth. Sometimes, indeed, they are frustrated of their hope; but My promise deceiveth none, nor sendeth him away empty that trusteth in Me. What I have promised, I will give; what I have said I will fulfil; if only any man remain faithful in My love even to the end.

THOMAS À KEMPIS (1380–1471)

Comment

This is an extract from one of the greatest books in the whole realm of Christian literature – *The Imitation of Christ*. Thomas à Kempis had no doubt that the Christian commitment was a commitment to perfection – 'Be ye therefore perfect' was Our Lord's injunction to his disciples. For Thomas à Kempis, the great spiritual counsellor, that meant nothing less than taking Christ as our model. His book is in four parts – two of them setting out advice to Christians touching the demands which their commitment to Christ's Way makes upon them; and two of them dealing with the spiritual exercises he regarded as essential for the strengthening of the soul and, in particular, the essential place in the life of every Christian of prayer and the Sacrament of Holy Communion. The call to accept Christ's promise – 'I promise things more high and eternal' – as opposed to 'things temporal and mean' is still ours. To accept it is to choose eternal life.

Prayer *Who can tell what a day may bring forth? Cause us, therefore, gracious God, to live every day as if it were to be our last, for that we know not for that it may be such. Cause us to live so at present as we shall wish we had done when we come to die. Grant that we may not die with any guilt upon our consciences, or any known sin unrepented of, but that we may be found in Christ, Who is our only Saviour and Redeemer.*

THOMAS À KEMPIS

To strive, to seek, to find and not to yield

There lies the port; the vessel puffs her sail;
There gloom the dark broad seas. My mariners,
Souls that have toiled, and wrought and thought with me –
That ever with a frolic welcome took
The thunder and the sunshine, and opposed
Free hearts, free foreheads, you and I are old;
Old age hath yet his honour and his toil.
Death closes all; but something ere the end,
Some work of noble note, may yet be done,
Not unbecoming men that strove with gods.
The lights begin to twinkle from the rocks:
The long day wanes; the slow moon climbs: the deep
Moans round with many voices. Come, my friends
'Tis not too late to seek a newer world.
Push off, and sitting well in order smite
The sounding furrows; for my purpose holds
To sail beyond the sunset, and the paths
Of all the western stars, until I die,
It maybe that the gulfs will wash us down:
It maybe we shall touch the Happy Isles,
And see the great Achilles, whom we knew.
Tho' much is taken, much abides; and tho'
We are not now that strength which in old days
Moved earth and heaven; that which we are, we are;
One equal temper of heroic hearts,
Made weak by time and fate, but strong in will
To strive, to seek, to find, and not to yield.

ALFRED TENNYSON (1809–1892)

Comment

There is a deep emotional quality in these dramatic lines from Tennyson's poem about the adventures and wanderings of Ulysses, the Greek hero King of the Island of Ithaca, who was engaged in the war against Troy. The poem tells of the King's varying adventures and trials and of his ultimate re-union with his country and his wife. But the poet is not merely relating historical facts. He is betraying something of his own disillusionments and his own pilgrimage – 'I am a part of all that I have met'. He sees in the wanderings of Ulysses a picture of the destiny of Man who himself moves forward on his pilgrimage faced by temptations which impede, obstacles which deter, moods which betray, and failures which prompt surrender. The last line can be an exhortation to the Christian in the hazardous journey through life to which he is committed: 'To strive, to seek, to find and not to yield'. Have a look at St Paul's advice to the Christians in Philippi (Philippians Ch.3, vv 7–14).

Prayer   *Most Gracious God, to know and love Whose will is righteousness, enlighten our souls with the brightness of Thy presence, that we may both know Thy will and be enabled to perform it: through Jesus Christ our Lord.*

(ROMAN BREVIARY)

Commemorating Perpetua and Her Companions
Martyrs at Carthage 202

Mounting eternally

Foiled by our fellowmen, depressed, outworn,
We leave the brutal world to take its way,
And Patience! In another life we say,
The world shall be thrust down, and we upborne.
And will not, then, the immortal armies scorn
The world's poor, routed leavings? Or will they,
Who failed under the heat of this life's day
Support the fervours of the heavenly morn?
No, no! The energy of life may be
Kept on after the grave, but not begun:
And he who flagged not in the earthly strife,
From strength to strength advancing – only he,
His soul well knit and all his battles won,
Mounts, and that hardly, to eternal life.

MATTHEW ARNOLD (1822–1888)

Comment

Arnold entitled his sonnet *He who mounts eternally*. Changing the pronoun to 'they', the sonnet could cover Perpetua and her Companions – Perpetua that is to say, with Felicity a slave girl and four Christian men, whose martyrdom under the Emperor Severus in 202 A.D. is one of the most moving in the annals of Christian martyrs. Perpetua was born of pagan parents but she, along with many, turned to Christ. When the Emperor forbade all conversions to Christianity, all who had been baptized were thrown into prison, condemned to execution. Perpetua and her companions refused to recant and, according to a contemporary account, were thrown to wild beasts in the arena at Carthage. *The Holy Martyrs of Carthage* chronicles the grim proceedings, how the Christians were led to the middle of the amphitheatre, how they completed their witness with the customary kiss of peace, and how, following their goring by wild beasts, a sword was thrust through each. 'Bravest and happiest martyrs!' concludes the grim account. 'You were called and chosen for the glory of our Lord Jesus Christ'. They indeed mounted eternally. Many today bear their witness to Our Lord against virulent opposition and often cruel persecution. They evoke our admiration. They need our prayers.

Prayer

Be with all who suffer for thee, O Christ, and give them thy steadfast strength, that as they suffer for thee thou mayest bear them, and carry them and their cross to victory and life.

BISHOP GEORGE APPLETON (CONTEMPORARY)

Be merciful, O Father of all mercies, to thy Church universal dispersed throughout the whole world, that all thy faithful people may have grace to confess thy holy name; and especially be merciful to such as are under persecution for their testimony, and their profession of the gospel; that as they stand fast for thy holy Word, so they may be upheld by it; through Jesus Christ our Lord.

AFTER PRAYER OF 1585

Commemorating Edward King, Bishop of Lincoln
Teacher, Pastor, died 1910

The quality of mercy is not strained,
It droppeth as the gentle rain from heaven
Upon the place beneath; it is twice blest;
It blesseth him that gives, and him that takes:
'Tis mightiest in the mightiest: it becomes
The thronéd monarch better than his crown;
His sceptre shows the force of temporal power,
The attribute to awe and majesty,
Wherein doth sit the dread and fear of kings;
But mercy is above this sceptred sway:
It is enthroned in the hearts of kings,
It is an attribute to God Himself:
And earthly power doth then show likest God's
When mercy seasons justice. Therefore, Jew,
Though justice be thy plea consider this,
That, in the course of justice, none of us
Should see salvation: we do pray for mercy;
And that same prayer doth teach us all to render
The deeds of mercy.

WILLIAM SHAKESPEARE (1564–1616)

Comment

Edward King, Bishop of Lincoln from 1885 to 1910 knew those words and lived out their truth in a ministry marked by gentleness, tenderness and mercy. He has been described as 'a saint, simple, sane, sensible, strong, and a saint who made saintliness infinitely attractive'. He was a pastor of great holiness and sensitivity. An incident recalled by John A. Newton in *Christian* exemplifies this. It is that 'two years after he became bishop, a young Grimsby fisherman was sentenced to death for murder. He was apparently a poor, ignorant fellow, scarcely knowing the difference between right and wrong. King visited him in Lincoln Prison, talked with him gently about the Prodigal Son, about Our Lord, about repentance and forgiveness. No one will ever know precisely what transpired between the two save that before the bishop left he confirmed the young man and administered the Holy Sacrament to him first saying, 'Let us say a prayer to consecrate the hand which did the sad deed'. In a later letter to a friend, King wrote: 'His end was beautiful; I felt utterly unworthy of him'. Mercy certainly 'becomes the throned monarch better than his crown'. It became the enthroned bishop better than his mitre! It becomes every Christian.

Prayer

Father of all mercies, teach us to be merciful, as thou art merciful. Father of all forgiveness, help us to forgive others, as thou hast forgiven us; knowing that, with what measure we meet, it shall be measured to us again; through Jesus Christ our Lord.

Inside Man

Once upon a time, or rather at the birth of Time, when the gods were so new that they had no names, and Man was still damp from the clay of the pit whence he had been digged, Man claimed that he, too, was in some sort a god. The gods weighed his evidence, and decided that Man's claim was good.

Having conceded Man's claim, the legend goes that they came by stealth and stole away this godhead, with intent to hide it where Man should never find it again. But this was not so easy. If they hid it anywhere on Earth the gods foresaw that Man would leave no stone unturned till he had recovered it. If they concealed it among themselves they feared Man might batter his way up even to the skies.

While they were all thus at a standstill the wisest of the gods said, 'I know, Give it to me!' He closed his hand upon the tiny unstable light of Man's stolen godhead, and when that great hand opened again the light was gone. 'All is well', said Brahm. 'I have hidden it where Man will never dream of looking for it. I have hidden it inside Man himself'.

RUDYARD KIPLING (1865–1936)

Comment

Poets, philosophers, theologians, historians – even politicians have fashioned their definitions of Man and the legend above starts, as it were, from the standpoint that there is more in Man than meets the eye and ends with more than a hint that he has a divinity within him. Turn to the Bible and we find the psalmist declaring that Man 'is fearfully and wonderfully made' – that he is but 'a little lower than the angels'. Turn to Thomas Carlyle and Man is 'the great inscrutable mystery of God', and to the seventeenth-century satirical poet Samuel Butler, Man is 'God's highest present development. He is the latest thing in God'. And that is where we stand. Made as we are in the image of God we cherish immortal longings which are satisfied only as we reach towards God in the good life. But in that struggle we have to remember that evil is endemic in Man too. Man is a 'wobbler' twixt the good and the evil. Choosing the evil when temptation comes Man demeans himself; he belies his essential dignity. He stands in need of re-instatement. God in Christ comes to his aid so that, 'wobbler' though he is, he is enabled to stand upright – but only after contrition and repentance.

Prayer   *We confess to thee, O Lord most holy, all the sins which hinder thy purpose for our lives and do harm to the lives of others. Forgive us, Lord, we humbly beseech thee, and turn our hearts to seek thee more sincerely, and to serve thee and our fellow men more faithfully. We ask this through our Saviour Jesus Christ.*

WILLIAM TEMPLE (1881–1944)

Holy Sonnet

Thou hast made me, and shall thy work decay?
Repair me now, for now mine end doth haste,
I run to death, and death meets me as fast.
And all my pleasures are like yesterday;
I dare not move my dim eyes any way,
Despair behind, and death before doth cast
Such terror, and my feeble flesh doth waste
By sin in it, which it t'wards hell doth weigh;
Only thou art above, and when towards thee
By thy leave I can look, I rise again;
But our old subtle foe so tempteth me
But our old subtle foe so tempteth me,
Thy Grace may wing me to prevent his art,
And thou like adamant draw mine iron heart.

JOHN DONNE (1573–1631)

Comment

John Donne, who became Dean of St Paul's in 1621, led a turbulent life before his Ordination in 1615. Quite clearly the memories of those reckless and wasted years haunted him throughout his life and notes of penitence and fear are sounded in much of his poetry and many of his sermons. The awfulness of sin and the seeming proximity of death made of him a poet and a preacher of great spiritual fervour. Torn as he ever was between the sensual delights of earth and the spiritual joys of heaven, his poems reflect the conflict within his own soul and at the same time the conviction of ultimate victory which could be his in Christ. The sonnet above is one of a series which are entitled *Holy Sonnets*, each concerned with sin and/or death. For long years they were all but unknown and unrecognised either for their poetic grandeur or spiritual power. Now they can help many a similarly troubled soul to rise again, as Donne did, to find that peace and serenity which communion with God in Christ offers to us all. Such peace and serenity of spirit is something for which all of us yearn, for which all of us pray, and which all of us can experience if we follow John Donne's example. Turning to Christ he found himself able to say with conviction: 'When towards thee by leave I can look, I rise again'.

Prayer *Heavenly Father, I pray that you may so increase my faith that when I ask forgiveness for my sins, and release from uncertainty and anxiety, I may rise again resolved to stand fast, believing in the power of your love to pardon my offences, and to banish the darkness from the sanctuary of my soul, through Jesus Christ, my Lord and Saviour.*

Waiting upon God

Coming nearer to God is always a discovery both of the beauty of God and of the distance there is between Him and us. 'Distance' is an inadequate word, because it is not determined by the fact that God is holy and that we are sinful. Distance is determined by the attitude of the sinner to God. We can approach God only if we do so with a sense of coming to judgement. If we come having condemned ourselves; if we come because we love Him, in spite of the fact that we are unfaithful; if we come to Him loving Him more than a godless security, then we are open to Him and He is open to us, and there is no distance; the Lord comes close to us in an act of compassionate love. But if we stand before God wrapped in our pride, in our assertiveness; if we stand before Him as if we had a right to stand there, if we stand and question Him, the distance that separates the creature and the creator becomes infinite.

Whenever we approach God the contrast that exists between what He is and what we are becomes dreadfully clear. We may not be aware of this so long as we live at a distance from God, so to speak, as long as His presence or His image is dimmed in our thoughts and in our perceptions; but the nearer we come to God, the sharper the contrast appears. It is not the constant thought of their sins but the vision of the holiness of God, that makes the saints aware of their own sinfulness. When we consider ourselves without the fragrant background of God's presence, sins and virtues become small and somewhat irrelevant matters; it is against the background of the divine presence that they stand out in full relief and acquire their depth and tragedy.

METROPOLITAN ANTHONY BLOOM (CONTEMPORARY)

Comment

It must always be against the holiness of God himself that we measure our own spiritual condition – and whilst this task is particularly relevant to the season of Lent, it is one which the Christian pilgrim must regularly make his own. We are so prone to think ourselves better than we are – perhaps to measure ourselves against a neighbour and take some pride in the contrast. Contrition, which is a prelude to receiving God's forgiveness, does not come easily. A newly washed white handkerchief appears to be whiter than white until it is thrown down upon a lawn covered with new-fallen and untrodden snow. I have never forgotten the sermon preached at my ordination to the priesthood, when the preacher – Bishop Vernon Smith – announced his text and then stood in silence for a moment and then repeated it in order, I am sure, that the young ordinands should appreciate the special significance of that solemn text to them at that moment in their lives. The text had but three words: 'Holy, holy, holy'.

Prayer   *Holy, holy, holy God, let me see my life against your holiness. Forgive my sins, help me to wait upon you that I may glorify your name in all I say and do.*

The Pilgrimage

Give me my scallop-shell of quiet,
My staff of faith to walk upon,
My scrip of joy, immortal diet,
My bottle of salvation.
My gown of glory, hope's true gauge,
And thus I'll make my pilgrimage.

And by the happy blissful way
More peaceful pilgrims I shall see,
They have shook off their gowns of clay,
And go apparelled fresh like me
From thence to heaven's bribeless hall,
Where no corrupted voices brawl
No conscience molted into gold,
Nor forged accusers bought and sold,
No cause deferred, nor vain-spent journey,
For there Christ is the King's Attorney,
Who pleads for all without degrees,
And he had angels, but no fees.

And when the grand twelve million jury
Of our sins with sinful fury
'Gainst our souls black verdicts give,
Christ pleads his death, and then we live.

SIR WALTER RALEIGH (1552–1618)

Comment

Sir Walter Raleigh is known to every schoolboy for his gallantry to his queen and for his services against the Spanish Armada rather than for his writings. He wrote this and other poems during his sixteen years of imprisonment in the Tower. A pilgrim in the Middle Ages was distinguished by his badge – a scallop shell. Raleigh's hold upon the things of God was such that, in his adverse circumstance, he could still call upon God that in the quietness of his enforced solitude he might remain confident that his pilgrimage could be sustained by his faith. He was convinced that whatever sins he had committed he could plead forgiveness through Christ's death. He was released from the Tower in 1616 but two years later was executed by order of King James. After his death friends found between the pages of his Bible lines clearly written just before his death:

> *And from which earth and grave and dust*
> *The Lord shall raise me up I trust.*

As for him, so for us, it is not the nature or extent of our sins which Christ measures. It is the depth of our conviction, the earnestness of our repentance, and the sincerity of our confession, which earns for us the forgiveness which sends us on our way again, clothed with the 'gown of glory'.

Prayer   *Lord, I beseech you in your forgiving love, that as I come in sorrow for my sins, I may by your mercy go on my pilgrimage again, released from the burden of sin, clothed with the gown of forgiveness and renewed by that divine grace which comes alone from you.*

Temptation and Consent

The world, the flesh and the devil send tempting suggestions to a soul espoused to Christ. First the sin is proposed; secondly the soul is either pleased or displeased; thirdly the soul either consents or refuses. These three steps to sin – temptation, pleasure in the temptation, consent – are not always easy to distinguish but they are clear enough in the case of grave sin.

Temptation of any sort, no matter how long it endures, cannot make us displeasing to God so long as we take no pleasure in it and do not yield; to be tempted is something passive, not active, and no blame attaches to us while we are opposed to it. St Paul suffered temptations to the flesh for years without being displeasing to God, on the contrary, they were a means of promoting God's glory . . . St Francis and St Benedict suffered such great temptations that one cast himself naked upon thorns, and the other into the snow to overcome them, gaining instead of losing grace.

Have great courage in the midst of temptations, knowing that your displeasure is the sign of your victory, for it is one thing to experience temptations and another to consent to them; we may still feel them even though they displease us, but we can consent to them only if they please us, this pleasure being the first step to consent.

Let the enemies of the soul lay their alluring snares before us as often as they like; let them knock for admittance at the door of our heart as long as they like; so long as we are resolved to take no pleasure in such things . . . no matter how long the temptation lasts, it can do us no harm unless we take pleasure in it.

St Francis de Sales (1567–1622)

Comment

'Lead us not into temptation'. To Christians the world over those words are among the most frequently uttered. Are any of those who say that prayer prompted sometimes to think: 'As though God would!'? Yet the Gospel tells us that 'Jesus was led up into the wilderness to be tempted by the devil' (Matthew Ch.4 v.1). This cannot possibly mean that the Spirit was seducing Jesus to sin. It means rather that the Spirit was subjecting Jesus to a testing and that, in fact, better reflects the meaning of the Greek word. The Lord's Prayer petition, expressed colloquially might read 'Lead us safely through temptation'.

Prayer   *O Lord, Shield of our help, Who wilt not suffer us to be tempted above that we are able, help us in all our straits and wrestlings, to lift up our eyes unto Thee, and stay our hearts on Thee; through Jesus Christ.*

Christina Rossetti (1830–1894)

Gethsemane

In golden youth when seems the earth
A summer-land of singing mirth,
When souls are glad and hearts are light,
And not a shadow lurks in sight,
We do not know it, but there lies,
Veiled somewhere under evening skies
A garden which we all must see –
The garden of Gethsemane.

With joyous steps we go our ways,
Love lends a halo to our days;
Light sorrows sail like clouds afar,
We laugh, and say how strong we are,
We hurry on; and hurrying go
Close to the borderland of woe,
That waits for you and waits for me –
Forever waits Gethsemane.

Down shadowy lanes, across strange
    streams,
Bridged over by our broken dreams;
Behind the misty gaps of years,
Beyond the great salt fount of tears,
The garden lies. Strive as you may,
You cannot miss it in your way,
All paths that have been, or shall be,
Pass somewhere through Gethsemane.

All those who journey, soon or late,
Must pass within the garden's gate;
Must kneel alone in darkness there,
And battle with some fierce despair.
God pity those who cannot say
'Not mine but thine', who only pray,
'Let this cup pass', and cannot see
The purpose of Gethsemane.

ELLA WHEELER WILCOX (1855–1919)

Comment

Christ fought and won his soul's battle in the garden of Gethsemane. He chose to die because he knew that to be the way in which God's purpose would ultimately triumph. A violent reaction to the treatment being meted out to him would contribute nothing to the divine purpose. Violence begets violence. Only when it is challenged by love can it be defeated. That was what might be described as the purpose of the Garden, taking Christ a step nearer to his 'It is finished'. Jesus took three of the disciples with him because he needed the fellowship of others. They let him down. There are times when, desperately needing the fellowship of others, we may find ourselves alone. Christ's 'aloneness' in Gethsemane prompted his cry 'Abba' – 'Father' – and he was thus fortified. There are times when others need our fellowship. Whatever may be our own experience when we pass through our lesser 'Gethsemanes', we should never forget that we ourselves can be instruments in the hand of God to minister to others as they pass through theirs.

Prayer Blessed Lord, may thy spirit hallow and thy Grace fortify all who are in deep distress, especially . . . Give them thy pardon to reassure them, thy guidance to see them on their way, thy peace to comfort them.

Kyrie Eleison

The devil will make thee believe as soon as thou fallest into any fault, that thou walkest in error, and therefore art out of God and his favour, and herewith would he make thee distrust of the divine grace, telling thee of thy misery, and making a giant of it; and putting it into thy head that every day thy soul grows worse instead of better, whilst it so often repeats these failings.

O Blessed Soul, open thine eyes; and shut the gate against these diabolical suggestions, knowing thy misery and trusting in the mercy divine. Would not he be a mere fool who, running at tournament with others, and falling in the best of the career, should lie weeping on the ground and afflicting himself with discourses upon his fall? Man (they would tell him), lose no time, get up and take the course again, for he that rises again quickly and continues his race is as if he had never fallen. If thou seest thyself fallen once and a thousand times, thou oughtest to make use of the remedy which I have given thee, that is a loving confidence in the divine mercy. These are the weapons with which thou must fight and conquer cowardice and vain thoughts. This is the means thou oughtest to use – not to lose time, not to disturb thyself and reap no good.

MIGUEL DE MOLINOS 1640–1697)

Comment

The author of this exhortation to trust in God's mercy and God's grace was a Spanish mystic who in his day was one of the Church's most able and sought after spiritual directors. In this passage he urges Christians never to despair into whatever depths of sin they might fall for none can ever be beyond the reach of God's mercy. In one of Faber's hymns we sing

There's a wideness in God's mercy, like the wideness of the sea;
There's a kindness in his justice which is more than liberty.

Faber sets God's mercy above God's justice, as indeed did the Spanish novelist and dramatist Miguel de Cervantes, who wrote that 'although the attributes of God are all equal, mercy shines with even more brilliance than justice'. no wonder then that we begin every Eucharist pleading 'Lord have mercy'. Molinos reminds us of another truth. Not only can we be confident in God's mercy, we can also avail ourselves, for the asking, of his abounding grace to help us to the good life.

Prayer   *God, of thy mercy grant unto us that the fire of thy love may burn up in us all things that displease thee and make us meet for thy heavenly kingdom, for the sake of Jesus Christ, our Saviour.*

(ROMAN BREVIARY)

The Power of Grace

View me, Lord, a work of thine;
Shall I then lie drowned in night?
Might thy grace in me but shine,
I should seem made all of light.
But my soul still surfeits so
On the poisoned baits of sin,
That I strange and ugly grow,
All in dark and foul within.
Cleanse me, Lord, that I may kneel,
At thine altar, pure and white;
They that once thy mercies feel,
Gaze no more on earth's delight.
Worldly joys like shadows fade,
When the heavenly light appears;
But the cov'nants thou hast made,
Endless, know not days nor years.
In thy word, Lord, is my trust,
To thy mercies fast I fly;
Though I am but clay and dust,
Yet thy grace can lift me high.

THOMAS CAMPION (1567–1620)

Comment

One of the hymns which has captured the imagination of the young in recent years – and that largely because of its tune – is *Amazing Grace*, which tells something of the life of its author John Newton. The adjective 'amazing' is not too strong for it means 'overwhelming with wonder'. Asked to define Grace, St Augustine answered: 'I know until you ask me; when you ask me I do not know'. So wonderful a gift of God that he dare not wrap it up in a few words! But the Bible helps us to define it, though not in a word. It means the mercy and active love of God by which He helps us to overcome whatever temptations assail us. It means the strength by which He enables us to rise above vices and embrace virtues. Grace is, quite simply, God's help to do right. Grace is ours for the asking, but asking there must be. Its channels are prayer, meditation and sacraments.

Prayer   *O Lord, may thy all-powerful grace make us perfect as thou hast commanded us to be: through Jesus Christ, Our Lord.*

BISHOP WILSON (A.D. 1663)

Commemorating Patrick, Bishop, Patron Saint of Ireland, d.460

As Patrick approached the palace of Loegaire, the High King of Ireland, he chanted the brave song which is called St Patrick's Breastplate, or the Deer's Cry. For the king had caused men to lie in ambush on Patrick's road to destroy him and his followers, and Patrick, aware of danger, sought strength and courage from the thought of Christ's nearness. 'If Christ be with me', he thought to himself, 'of whom shall I be afraid?' Tradition says that when Patrick and his monks pased by, they appeared to men in ambush as wild deer with a fawn following in the mist. And this was the brave and noble song which Patrick chanted as he went bravely to preach Christ in the royal palace of Tara:

> Christ with me, Christ before me, Christ behind me
> Christ in me, Christ beneath me, Christ above me,
> Christ on my right, Christ on my left,
> Christ in breadth, Christ in length, Christ in height,
> Christ in the heart of every man who thinks of me,
> Christ in the mouth of everyone who speaks of me,
> Christ in the eye that sees me,
> Christ in every ear that hears me.

Patrick failed to persuade the king to become a Christian, but received his permission to preach the Gospel in his country.

PHYLLIS GARLICK ( )

Comment

The story of Patrick and his mission to Ireland is too well-known to call for expansion here but some of his prayers have a special poignance about them as we reflect upon the cruelties, the oppression and the sufferings being inflicted on that unhappy country today. 'Our God is the God of all things', he prayed. 'He hath a dwelling in heaven and earth and sea and all that are therein.. He inspires all things; He quickens all things. He kindles the light of the sun and the light of the moon. He hath a Son co-eternal with Himself, and like unto Him. And the Holy Spirit breathes in them. Father, Son and Holy Spirit are not divided. I desire to unite you to the Son of our heavenly King'.

A Prayer – for ourselves and for all the people of Ireland:

> May the strength of God pilot us.
> May the power of God preserve us.
> May the wisdom of God instruct us.
> May the hand of God protect us.
> May the way of God direct us.
> May the shield of God defend us.
> May the host of God guard us against the snares
>   of evil and the temptations of the world.
> May Christ be with us.
> Christ before us. Christ in us. Christ over us.
> May Thy salvation, O Lord, be always ours this day and
>   for evermore.

ST PATRICK (389–461)

The greater Wonder

Why are we by all creatures waited on?
Why do the prodigal elements supply
Life and food to me, being more pure than I,
Simple, and further from corruption?
Why brook'st thou, ignorant horse, subjection?
Why dost thou bull, and boar, so slyly
Dissemble weakness, and by one man's stroke die,
Whose whole kind, you might swallow and feed upon?
Weaker I am, woe is me, and worse than you,
You have not sinned, nor need be timorous.
But wonder at a greater wonder, for to us
Created nature doth these things subdue,
But their Creator, whom sin, nor nature tied,
For us, his Creatures and his foes, hath died.

JOHN DONNE (1573–1631)

Comment

Here is Donne, still demeaning himself (see note on March 10th), so conscious of his spiritual and moral failures, even suggesting that among God's creatures, the lower animals, the horse, the bull and the boar are stronger and 'purer' than he, for they had not sinned. But, as ever in his sonnets, this one ends with a great affirmation of faith. The marvels of the natural world, the powers of the lower animals, evoke man's wonder. A greater wonder still to us is that their and his creator died for man's salvation. It was G.K. Chesterton who put in a nutshell the truth which doubtless lurked in Donne's mind as he wrote this. 'You often address a man with words which challenge his behaviour: 'Be a man!' you say. But you never say to a dog 'Be a dog!'. A dog can never be less than a dog, but a man can behave like a beast. Man is an animal too – but he is an 'animal plus'. He is the crowning wonder of God's creation, made in the image and likeness of God. So long as his life is 'God orientated' – and only so long – he retains his 'plus'. The eighteenth-century poet and philosopher Samuel Taylor Coleridge says in the *Table Talk:* 'If a man is not rising upwards to be an angel, he is sinking downwards. He cannot stop at the beast. He becomes a devil'. That is man's predicament. Donne knew the answer. Remind yourself of it by reading Paul's words to Titus (Ch.2 vv 11–14).

Prayer   *O Christ, give us patience, and a faith and hope as we kneel at the foot of Thy cross and hold fast to it. Teach us by Thy cross that however ill the world may go, the Father so loved us that he spared not Thee.*

CHARLES KINGSLEY (1819–1875)

St Joseph of Nazareth, Husband of the Blessed Virgin Mary

Remember the Workman

When the dust of the workshop is still
The dust of the workman at rest,
May some generous heart find a will
To seek and to treasure the best.

From the splendour of hopes that deceived
From the wonders he planned to do;
From the glories so nearly achieved;
From the dreams that so nearly came true.

From his struggle to rise above earth
On the pinions that could not fly;
From his sorrows; Oh, seek for some worth
To remember the workman by.

If in vain; if Time sweeps all away
And no laurel from that dust springs;
'Tis enough that a loyal heart says
'He tried to make beautiful things'.

EDEN PHILLPOTTS (1862–1960)

Comment

After figuring in the infancy narratives in the Gospels Joseph all but disappears from the story, though two facts about him are clear. We learn that he was a carpenter; we learn that he was a just man. But more may safely be surmised. Jesus grew up in his home and about his workshop, which latter must have differed little from that described by Eden Phillpotts above, until he was at least 12 years of age. It was then that Mary and Joseph took him to Jerusalem and he became 'a son of the law'. The end of that story of his being lost and found reveals something of the attitude of Jesus to his parents, 'He was obedient unto them', but, more than that, it tells us with what care Joseph, the hard-working carpenter and the gentle Mary cared for and guided him in what would now be called his teenage years. We are told that he grew 'in wisdom and stature, and in favour with God and man'. Joseph the workman who kept his home together by making beautiful things, achieved with Mary something much greater. Together they ensured for Jesus his balanced growth – mentally, physically, spiritually and socially. It is worth reflecting how much we owe to our parents and to others who have nurtured us in God's family in the Church.

Prayer   *Almighty God, who called Joseph to be the husband of the virgin Mary, and the guardian of your only Son; open our eyes and our ears to the messages of your holy will, and give us the courage to act upon them, through Jesus Christ our Lord.*

O God our Father, who hast made men to live together in families: Preserve to us the sanctities of family life; unite parents and children in true affection to one another in thy holy fear; and give wisdom to all Christian parents and teachers, that they may bring up children in true faith and in obedience to thy Word; through Jesus Christ our Lord.

Commemorating
Cuthbert, Bishop of Lindisfarne, died 687
Thomas Ken, Bishop of Bath and Wells, died 1711

Give me the priest, these graces shall possess:
Of an Ambassador the just address,
A Father's tenderness, a Shepherds's care,
A Leader's courage which the cross can bear,
A ruler's arm, a Watchman's wakeful eye,
A pilot's skill, the helm in storms to ply,
A Fisher's patience and a Labourer's toil,
A guide's dexterity to disembroil,
A Prophet's inspiration from above,
A Preacher's knowledge and a Saviour's love.
Give me a priest, a light upon a hill,
Whose rays his whole circumference can fill,
In God's own Word and Sacred learning versed,
Deep in the study of the heart immersed,
Who in such souls can the disease descry,
And wisely fair restoratives supply.

THOMAS KEN (1637–1711)

Comment

Today commemorates the lives and work of two holy men with much in common – in vocation, in dedication, in piety and in zeal for the proclamation of the Gospel. Of Cuthbert, Bede wrote: 'He protected the people committed to him with frequent prayers, and incited them to heavenly desires by wholesome counsels, enforcing his teaching by the example of his life. He saved the poor and needy from the hand of the oppressor, comforted the weak and sorrowful, and endeavoured to bring the sinful to godly sorrow'. From his monastery in Melrose, he frequently went out to teach the peasants in the mountains about the things of God. He became Bishop of Lindisfarne in A.D. 685 but held the office for only a short time, for he died in 687. In his dying charge he bade his brethren: 'Have peace and divine charity among yourselves and be at peace with other Christian communities'.

Thomas Ken was a parish priest after the pattern of George Herbert whose treatise *Country Parson* was one of his most cherished books. He became Bishop of Bath and Wells in 1685 but as a non-juror was later deprived of his See. He is best known as the author of several of our popular hymns. Many of us are called today, whether priests or not, to be counsellors in one way or another and Ken's 'prescription' is relevant to us.

Prayer   *Almighty God, as you called your servant Cuthbert to leave his sheep to become a shepherd of souls, be present with all who shepherd your people today. Make them sure and steadfast in their faith and zealous in their calling to your glory and the welfare of all your people, through Jesus Christ our Lord.*

O my God, my love, let Thine unwearied and tender love for me make my love unwearied and tender to my neighbour, zealous to procure, promote and preserve his health, safety, happiness and life, that he may be the better able to serve Thee and love thee.

THOMAS KEN (1637–1711)

Commemorating Thomas Cranmer
Archbishop of Canterbury, Martyr 1556

He sung of God – the mighty source
Of all things – the stupendous source
On which all strength depends,
From whose right arm, beneath whose eyes,
All period, power and enterprise
Commences, reigns and ends.

Glorious the sun in mid-career;
Glorious th'assembled fires appear;
Glorious the comet's train;
Glorious the trumpet and alarm;
Glorious th'almighty stretched-out arm;
Glorious th'enraptur'd main.

Glorious the northern lights astream;
Glorious the song, when God's the theme;
Glorious the thunder's roar:
Glorious hosanna from the den;
Glorious the catholic amen;
Glorious the martyr's gore.

Glorious – more glorious is the crown
Of Him that brought salvation down
By meekness call'd thy Son;
Thou that stupendous truth believe'd,
And now the matchless deed's achieve'd
Determined, dared, and done.

CHRISTOPHER SMART (1722–1771)

Comment

Thomas Cranmer was Archbishop of Canterbury 1533–1556. He was a great man of God and if he had done no more for the Church than produce the 1549 Prayer Book, which has influenced every Anglican Prayer Book since, his name could not but be honoured for ever in the history of the Church. The story of his trial for heresy is too well known to need repetition. Before St Mary's Church, Oxford, a crowd waited anticipating a re-affirmation of the doctrines he had denied. Their expectations were perhaps heightened as he began his last utterance: 'And now I come to the great thing that so much troubleth my conscience, more than anything that I ever did or said in my whole life; and this is the setting abroad of a writing contrary to the Truth; which now here I renounce and refuse, as things written with my hand, contrary to the truth which I thought in my heart, and written for fear of death, and to save my life, if it might be... Now forasmuch as my hand offended, writing contrary to my heart, my hand shall first be punished therefore; for, may I come to the fire, it shall be first burned'. As the flames caught his hand he prayed, 'Lord, receive my spirit'. 'Glorious the martyr's gore'. We may pray that we may have courage to bear our witness in the face of opposition to the Faith.

Prayer   *Praise be to Thee, O God, for the noble army of martyrs all through the ages and for all converts to the faith who have sealed their witness with their blood: for the mighty company who now praise thy name, out of every kindred and nation and tongue. All praise be to thee thou king of saints.*

BISHOP GEORGE APPLETON

God – ever around!

God, in all that is most living and incarnate in Him, is not far away from us, altogether apart from the world we see, touch, hear, smell and taste about us. Rather He awaits us every instant in our action, in the work of the moment. There is a sense in which He is at the tip of my pen, my spade, my brush, my needle – of my heart and of my thought. By pressing the stroke, the line or the stitch, on which I am engaged, to its ultimate natural finish, I shall lay hold of the last end towards which my innermost will tends. Try with God's help to perceive the connection – even physical and natural – which binds your labour with the building of the Kingdom of Heaven; try to realise that heaven itself smiles upon you, and throughout your works, draws you to itself; then, as you leave church for the noisy streets, you will remain with only one feeling, that of continuing to immerse yourself in God. Never consent to do anything without first of all realising its significance and constructive value in Jesus Christ, and pursuing it with all your might. This is the very path to sanctity for each man according to his state and calling.

PIERRE TEILHARD DE CHARDIN (1881–1955)
EXTRACT FROM : LE MILIEU DIVIN

Comment

A salutary reminder to us all not to leave God behind when we 'leave church for the noisy streets'. Pierre de Chardin's writings are not easy reading but here, in one of his potent works, is a simple message for us all. The testing ground for our fidelity to Christ, the seas where we become most vulnerable to temptations, are not when we are saying our prayers, meditating on the scriptures, or worshipping God in church, but when we fail to carry those rich experiences of the reality and presence of God out into the world of work and leisure where God is always around waiting to care, to guide, to strengthen, to sustain. Note that de Chardin assumes that his reader will join in public worship: 'when you leave church'. Note too that he enjoins them to 'immerse themselves in God' – so that their daily activities become their path to sanctity.

Prayers   *Lord Jesus, grant us daily grace for daily needs; daily patience for a daily cross; daily, hourly, incessant love of Thee to take up our cross daily and bear it after Thee.*

CHRISTINA ROSSETTI (1830–1894)

My Father, light up the small duties of my daily life. May they shine with the beauty of your countenance. Let me never forget that glory may dwell in the commonest task. Grant me your grace, that in the midst of my work I may be conscious of your presence and find joy in all that ministers to your service, through Jesus Christ Our Lord.

Happiness

If I have faltered more or less
In my great task of happiness;
If I have moved among my race
And shown no glorious morning face;
If beams from happy human eyes
Have moved me not; if morning skies
Books, and my food, and summer rain
Knocked on my sullen heart in vain: –
Lord, thy most pointed pleasure take
And stab my spirit broad awake;
Or, Lord, if too obdurate I,
Choose thou, before that spirit die,
A piercing pain, a killing sin,
And to my dead heart, run them in!

R.L. STEVENSON (1850–1894)

Comment

In his poem *The Celestial Surgeon* the poet is indicting himself for his failure to respond to the gifts of God and the joys of life with a happiness which in his heart of hearts he believes to be due. Kierkegaard somewhere writes of an Arab who, desperate for water and unable to find any in his wanderings, suddenly discovers a spring in his desert tent and responds with a joy and happiness which he had not known before. The Danish philosopher draws the conclusion that it is when a person who is always seeking happiness outside himself, suddenly realises that its source lies within himself and finally in his relationship to God, that he experiences happiness in abundance. Joy and happiness are not, as it were, 'for sale'. They come from within. To shop around looking for them, for example in a search for wealth or the plaudits of the world, may prove to be like looking for water in the desert. 'Set your heart on things that are above' and there is discovered within a tranquillity which expresses itself in a joy and happiness which the world can neither give nor take away. It is then too, that we recognise things around us which awaken the 'sullen heart' to God's glory and the happiness of those about us.

Prayer   *O God, who hast made the heaven and the earth and all that is good and lovely therein, and hast shown us through Jesus our Lord that the secret of all happiness and joy is a heart set free from selfish desires, help me to respond with happiness and joy to everything which is good and beautiful in the world.*

The Pilgrim's Way

And therefore, good Christian, come a little way with me, and I will teach thee the way thou must go. Look before thee; dost thou see this narrow way? That is the way you must go. It was cast up by the patriarchs, prophets, Christ and his Apostles; and it is as straight as a rule can make it. But, said Christian, are there no turnings or windings by which a stranger may lose his way? Yes, answered Good-Will, there are many ways but down upon this, and they are crooked and wide. But thou mayest distinguish the right from the wrong, the right only being straight and narrow.

Then I saw in my dream, that Christian asked him further what was upon his back; for as yet he had not got rid thereof, nor could he by means get it off without help. He told him, As to thy burden, be content to bear it, until thou comest to the place of deliverance; for there it will fall from thy back itself.

Then Christian began to gird up his loins, and to address himself to his journey. So the other told him that by that he was gone some distance from the gate, he would come at the house of the Interpreter, at whose door he should knock, and he would show him excellent things. Then Christian took his leave of his friend, and he again bid him God-speed.

JOHN BUNYAN (1628–1688)

Comment

Poor simple John Bunyan whose only school and teacher was the Holy Bible little thought that his homely tale, hammered out in prison, would come to be regarded as a masterpiece. Spurned at first by all but the uneducated, it has now gone around the world in a hundred or more languages, and Mr Worldly-Wiseman, Mr Facing-both-ways, not to mention the Slough of Despond and the Hill of Difficulty, are characters or states with which all pilgrims are familiar. Bunyan saw 'the world' – society organised apart from God – for the dangerous place that it is. He saw the pilgrim way as uphill and fraught with many obstacles. But concerned as he was with the salvation of the soul, and convinced as he was of the power of God in Christ to save, his simple story ends with grandeur. 'It was glorious to see how the open region was filled with trumpets and pipers, with singers, with players in stringed instruments, to welcome the pilgrims as they went up and followed one another in at the beautiful gate of the city'.

Prayer   *O Lord God, when thou givest to thy servants to endeavour any great matter, grant us to know that it is not the beginning, but the continuing of the same, until it be thoroughly finished, which yieldeth the true glory; through him who for the finishing of thy work laid down his life, our Redeemer, Jesus Christ.*

SIR FRANCIS DRAKE (1545–1596)

The Annunciation of Our Lord to the Blessed Virgin

Annunciation

' I will your will', said Mary. So shining clouds
Enclosed her wholly, and she received the future
Into herself. And the Spirit moved in her as wind
Stirring the silken grass in waves,
And joy was formed in her, and grew and shone
Like candles in her eyes, and sparkled where she trod,
Skimming the mountain tops like waves; on airy heights
She danced in safety on the sword-point peaks.
And all the sword-flames seared and pierced,
They could not shake her calm accepting will
Because the point of central stillness was in her
And she was at the centre. The active Word
From her took living bones and marrow. He cried
First breathing frosty air in the starlit quiet night.

SISTER PHOEBE MARGARET, C.S.M.V. (1902–1979)

Comment

In these fourteen lines, Sister Phoebe Margaret expresses beautifully Mary's sublime submission to the Divine Will: 'I am the Lord's servant. Whatever He says, I accept'. But there is also the echo of the aged Simeon's warning to her. With the Infant Jesus in his arms he tells Mary that such was the mission of Jesus in God's plan that he would meet fierce opposition, adding, 'A sword shall pierce through your own soul also'. She cannot but have felt the point of that sword even as he spoke. But there was no question to Simeon of 'How?' of 'Where?' or 'Why?'. No fears were expressed. Her soul still magnified the Lord. Here is what someone has called the paradox of blessedness. It confronted Mary; and in lesser measure it has confronted many servants of God since. Men and women who have felt themselves called by God to some high privilege of mission or work have responded eagerly, only to discover later that it involved a piercing of the soul. Mary appears prominently in the Gospel story on only three occasions – in the birth stories, at the time Jesus became a son of the Law, and at the Cross. But she is there throughout, from the cradle to the grave and beyond. Our own Bishop Ken, Bishop of Bath and Wells in the seventeenth century, makes clear in one of his hymns that Mary's place is unique among the saints of God. He says

Heaven with transcendent joys her entrance graced,
Next to his throne, her Son his Mother placed;
And here below, now she's of Heaven possessed.
All generations shall call her blest.

Prayer   *We beseech Thee, O Lord, make us subject unto Thee with a ready will,*
and evermore stir up our wills to make supplication unto Thee: through
Jesus Christ our Lord.

GELASIAN SACRAMENTARY

Discovery

I don't know Who – or What – put the question, and I don't know When it was put. I don't even remember answering. But at some moment I did answer Yes to Someone – or Something – and from that hour I was certain that existence is meaningful and that, therefore, my life, in self-surrender, had a goal. From that moment I have known what it means 'not to look back', and 'to take no thought for the morrow'. Led by the Ariadne's thread of my answer through the labyrinth of Life, I came to a time and place where I realised that the Way leads to a triumph which is a catastrophe, and to a catastrophe which is a triumph; that the price for committing one's life would be reproach, and that the only elevation possible to man lies in the depths of humiliation. After that the word 'courage' lost its meaning, since nothing could be taken from me.

As I continued along the Way, I learned, step by step, word by word, that behind every saying in the Gospels, stands one man and one man's experience. Also the prayer that the cup might pass from him and his promise to drink it. Also behind each of the words from the Cross.

DAG HAMMARSKJÖLD (1905–1961)

Comment

Dag Hammarskjöld's devotional writings give no inkling as to the important part he played in the world's affairs as Secretary General of the United Nations. Nevertheless all who met him in the course of his time in that high office sensed in him the man of God. He left behind him a series of what might best be called 'meditations', in prose and verse, entitled *Markings*. We cannot tell at what point in his life Hammarskjöld said 'Yes' to God, but we know that once commitment followed discovery, he sustained the massive burden imposed upon him by his unique position in the world – he once jokingly described himself as the 'secular Pope of the world' – by prayer and quiet contemplation of God's being, God's Holiness and God's power. Travelling around constantly among his personal luggage there would be a devotional book. 'The road to holiness necessarily passes through the world of action' he said, and since all of us are willy-nilly caught up in the world of action that affords us something to think about. Reading *Markings* it would certainly appear that the great man had learnt the lesson which Jesus taught Martha when she appeared to down-grade the contemplative side of life with which Mary was engaged.

Prayer *We offer to Thee, O Lord our God, our daily work. Help us to do it heartily and faithfully, as in thy sight and for thy glory, that all who are touched by our service may be blest by it and by thy grace may respond to thy love in service to others through Jesus Christ our Lord.*

Commitment

Thou who art over us,
Thou who art one of us,
Thou who art –
Also within us,
May all see Thee – in me also,
May I prepare the way for Thee.
May I thank Thee for all that shall fall to my lot.
May I also not forget the needs of others.
Keep me in Thy love
As Thou wouldst that all should be kept in mine.
May everything in this my being be directed to Thy glory
And may I never despair
For I am under Thy hand
And in Thee in all power and goodness.
Give me a pure heart that I may see Thee.
A humble heart – that I may hear Thee,
A heart of love – that I may serve Thee,
A heart of faith – that I may abide in Thee.

DAG HAMMARSKJÖLD (1905–1961)

Comment

Hammarskjöld's reference to 'Ariadne's thread of my answer through the labyrinth of Life' which appeared in yesterday's reading, calls for an explanation. In Greek mythology Ariadne, who was a daughter of the King of Crete, gave Theseus a clue of thread to conduct him safely out of the labyrinth after his defeat of the Minotaur. Once Hammarskjöld had said 'Yes' to God he experienced the sense of being led or drawn by God through the labyrinth of his own life. Most of his verses, which betray a serenity not always apparent in his earlier writings, were written in the three or four years before his life and work were suddenly brought to an end in the crash of a plane in which he was going in pursuit of the vocation of reconciliation of nation with nation to which he had dedicated himself. His poems were, of course, written in Swedish, and not all of them are patient of translation in a way which preserves their beauty of expression and rhythm. The poem quoted above, probably written in 1954, years before his death, is a prayer which breathes a supreme confidence and a deep commitment, which all of us must admire and for which all of us long and should pray.

Prayer   *Read Dag Hammarskjöld's prayer again, but this time as a prayer of your own concluding with your own 'Amen'.*

The Cross

Far too often the Cross is presented for our adoration, not so much as a sublime end to be attained by our transcending ourselves, but as a symbol of sadness, of limitation and repression... This manner of speech ends by conveying the impression that the kingdom of God can only be established in mourning, and by thwarting and going against the current of man's aspirations and energies.

In its highest and most general sense, the doctrine of the Cross is that to which all men adhere who believe that the vast movement and agitations of human life opens on to a road which leads somewhere, and that that road climbs upward. Life has a term: therefore it imposes a particular direction, orientated, in fact, towards the highest possible spiritualisation by means of the greatest possible effort. To admit that group of fundamental principles is already to range oneself among the disciples – distant perhaps, and implicit, but nevertheless real – of Christ crucified.

TEILHARD DE CHARDIN (1881–1955)

Comment

Mighty tomes have been written by eminent scholars throughout Christian history about the doctrine of the Atonement and the meaning of the Cross. Most of them have been by scholars for scholars as indeed is this quotation. Happily their work has been distilled in many of our finest hymns so that the humblest Christian knows what Our Lord accomplished by his death on the Cross. Isaac Watts' 'When I survey the wondrous cross' and Mrs Alexander's 'There is a green hill', summarise in memorable language both the truth and the appeal of the Cross. The enemies of Jesus shouted 'Come down from the Cross and we will believe'. To have come down would have nullified all that he had ever taught about the Love of God. In contrast, his 'It is finished' was his cry of triumph that man's redemption was sealed. The Cross is at once the measure of man's sin and the measure of God's love. It assures us that however gravely we may sin against God, His love for us is not shaken and His forgiveness awaits only our repentance and confession.

Prayer *O Christ, give us patience, and faith, and hope as we kneel at the foot of thy Cross, and hold fast to it. Teach us by thy Cross that however ill the world may go, the Father still loves us that He spared not Thee.*

CHARLES KINGSLEY (1819–1875)

Commemorating John Keble,
Priest, Pastor, Poet, died 1866

We must be continually sacrificing our own wills, as opportunity serves, to the will of others; bearing, without notice, sights and sound that annoy us; setting about this or that task, when we had far rather be doing something very different; persevering in it, often, when we are thoroughly tired of it; keeping company for duty's sake, when it would be a great joy to us to be by ourselves; besides all the trifling untoward accidents of life; bodily pain and weakness long continued, and perplexing us often when it does not amount to illness; losing what we value, missing what we desire; disappointments in other persons, wilfulness, unkindness, ingratitude, folly, in cases where we least expect it.

> *The trivial round, the common task*
> *Would furnish all we ought to ask, –*
> *Room to deny ourselves, a road*
> *To bring us daily nearer God.*

JOHN KEBLE (1792–1866)

Comment

John Keble was ordained priest in 1816 and from then until 1823 he was a college tutor in Oxford. His years as a parish priest – 1823 to 1831 – were also the years in which he wrote many of his hymns and poems which were subsequently gathered together in the *Christian Year*. These verses for the Sundays and holy days throughout the year reveal something of their author – the depth of his personal religion, his spirituality, his tenderness and his ability to expound the Christian Faith. Insofar as any one man can be called the leader of the Oxford Movement that title belongs to Keble who by his sermon on National Apostasy delivered in the pulpit of the University Church in Oxford in 1833, launched a movement which was to lift the Church of England from its doldrums and wrest it from the dangers of an Erastian utilitarianism. It was Keble and his friends in the Oxford Movement who summoned the members of the Church to remember its divine credentials as the Holy Catholic Church and of its place and purpose in the life of the nation and in the lives of Christians. The Church of England cannot but count John Keble as among its saints. He understood what sacrifice means, as the quotation above shows. We in our lives have similar experiences, and what he says must help us to face and offer them creatively.

Prayer

O God, as we thank you for the life and witness of your servant John Keble, for his devotion to your Church and for the gifts he bestowed upon it, help us in our turn to hold fast to the Faith of our Fathers and to show forth in our lives day by day a like steadfastness to the Way, the Truth and the Life of him who is the Church's Lord, even thy Son Jesus Christ.

A Hymn to God the Father

Wilt thou forgive that sin where I begun,
* Which was my sin though it were done before?*
Wilt though forgive that sin; through which I run,
* And do run still: though still I do deplore?*
*   When thou hast done, thou hast not done,*
*   For, I have more.*
Wilt thou forgive that sin which I have won
* Others to sin? and, made my sins their door?*
Wilt thou forgive that sin which I did shun
* A year or two: but wallowed in, a score?*
*   When thou hast done, thou hast not done,*
*   For I have more.*
I have a sin of fear, that when I have spun
* My last thread, I shall perish on the shore;*
But swear by thyself, that at my death thy Son
* Shall shine as he shines now, and heretofore;*
*   And, having done that, Thou hast done,*
*   I fear no more.*

JOHN DONNE (1573–1631)

Comment

This is one of a number of the *Divine Poems* which Donne wrote at the time he was Dean of St Paul's – a period of his life when his religious fervour prompted not only powerful sermons but much more pious verse. Here he touches on a human weakness of which Christians generally are all too aware, that is recidivism – the habitual relapse into sins which we are particularly prone to commit. He reflects too how his own sinful behaviour may well have led others astray. And we may be sure that he is thinking of the whole gamut of sin of which St Paul wrote in what was probably his first letter – that to the Galatians. In that letter he warns Christians against the kind of things for which the lower part of our nature is responsible, things like 'fornication, impurity, blatant immorality; idolatry and sorcery; enmity, strife and jealousy; outbursts of explosive temper; selfish ambition, divisions, the party spirit, envy; drunkenness and revelling (Galatians Ch5.) Donne was conscious of his own grave failures and concerned for those whose spiritual welfare he felt himself responsible. But he states his last sin to be 'fear' – ungodly fear – but he is confident that God's love will ultimately burn up all that is evil in him. That is a confidence which we may share.

Prayer

O Thou that beholdest all things, I have sinned against Thee in thought and word and deed, especially... , be merciful to me a sinner, blot our my transgressions and grant that my name may be found written in the book of life, for Jesus Christ's sake.

AFTER A 14TH CENTURY PRAYER

Indifference

When Jesus came to Golgotha they hanged him on a tree,
They drave great nails through hand and foot, and made a Calvary;
They crowned him with a crown of thorns, red were his wounds and deep,
For those were crude and cruel days, and human flesh was cheap.

When Jesus came to Birmingham they simply passed him by,
They never hurt a hair of him, they only let him die;
For men had grown more tender, and they would not give him pain;
They only just passed down the street, and left him in the rain.

Still Jesus cried, 'forgive them for they know not what they do',
And still it rained –a wintry rain that drenched him through and through.
The crowds went home and left the streets without a soul to see,
And Jesus crouched against a wall and cried for Calvary.

G.A. STUDDERT KENNEDY (1883–1929)

Comment

Confronted with the person of Jesus there are two attitudes which can be rationally adopted. One is the acceptance of him as the Christ of God; the other is – if a man can sustain it – to reject him. The attitude which is irrational is to ignore Christ. Such is the impact he has made on the world's history, such is his infusion of the gospel of love into the affairs of mankind, both in the past and in the present, that he cannot be ignored. Henry Fosdick sums up the evidence which indicts men's indifference succinctly, when he writes: 'Christ has given us the most glorious interpretation of life's meaning that man has ever had. The fatherhood of God, the fellowship of the Spirit, the sovereignty of righteousness, the law of love, the glory of service, the coming of the Kingdom, the eternal hope – there never was an interpretation of life to compare with that.'

Christ demands an answer. It is for Christians to give that answer to an indifferent world, bearing witness by word and action as individuals and working within the fellowship of Christ's body the Church. 'Let the redeemed of the Lord say so!', pleads the psalmist. In a day when millions have no sense of a spiritual dimension of life, the Christian's 'say so' must be loud and clear – in his mind, on his lips and from his heart.

Prayer *Grant, O blessed Lord, that thy Church in this our day may hear anew thy call to launch out into the deep in the service of thy glorious gospel; that the souls for whom thou hast died may be won for thee, to the increase of thy Kingdom and the glory of thy holy name.*

CANON FRANK COLQUHOUN (CONTEMPORARY)

New Life

Out in the rain a world is growing green,
On half the trees quick buds are seen
   Where glued-up buds have been.
Out in the rain God's acre stretches green,
Its harvest quick though still unseen
   For there the Life hath been.

If Christ hath died His brethren well may die,
Sing in the gates of death, lay by
   This life without a sigh:
For Christ hath died and good it is to die;
To sleep when so He lays us by,
   Then wake without a sigh.

Yes, Christ hath died, yea, Christ is risen again;
Wherefore both life and death grow plain
   To us who wax and wane;
For Christ who rose shall die no more again:
Amen: till He makes all things plain
   Let us wax and wane.

CHRISTINA ROSSETTI (1830–1894)

Comment

There is no fixed calendar date for the celebration of Christ's victory over death for Easter Day is determined by the behaviour of the moon. Since, however, it falls far more frequently in April than in March – between now and the year 2000, March will claim but three Easter Sundays against April's ten – maybe we can regard April as 'the resurrection month' – Christ's resurrection, nature's resurrection, man's resurrection to the new life – and turn our thoughts in those directions. The Divine assurance is 'Behold, I make all things new' (Revelation ch.21 v.5). 'New', mark you, not 'better', but new!

    Christina Rossetti's thoughts about the resurrection of Christ are prompted here by the resurrection she sees about her in nature. In her second verse she declares that death hold out no fears for her, nor should it for us, for Christ's passage through death to resurrection represents not only a triumph for Christ – but also an assurance for us that death never has the last word. Man may die unto sin but because of Christ's redemptive work, he may rise again unto righteousness. The day comes when his body dies. He lives still.

Prayer   *O Lord Jesus Christ, raise up our souls unto newness of life, granting us repentance from dead works, and planting in us the likeness of thy resurrection. Thou who didst give Thy most Holy Spirit, grant to all thy servants who ask of Thee that they may be daily renewed and more plentifully enriched in the same, for Thine own mercies' sake; who livest and reignest with the Father and the Holy Spirit, ever one God, world without end.*

BISHOP ANDREWES (1555–1626)

Birth of the Church

The resurrection of Christ was what called the Church into being, and turned a group of shattered, demoralised men into evangelists who, against all odds, gave a new direction to history. The whole proclamation of the Gospel is centred in Christ risen from the dead. The four Gospels obviously presupposed it. If the Crucifixion had been the end, nobody would have bothered to write down the story of a discredited Messiah... They would have done their best to forget about that and would surely have tried, if they could, to hush it up. Why have Christians always met together to break the bread on the first day of the week? Why is Sunday observed as a day of rest? To commemorate a twenty-four hours' nightmare? All Christian faith, worship, and experience, all the Church's teaching and missionary activity, all our hopes in this world and the next are irrevocably bound up with the conviction that Christ is risen, and He, the conqueror of death, has 'opened the gate of everlasting life', and is with us always, 'even unto the end of the world'... Christian faith does not rest only, if ultimately at all, on the discovery of the Empty Tomb... the real ground is what happened in people's lives – the creation of the Christian society in its depth, and the transformed quality of living – 'risen with Christ', as they said, 'unto newness of life'.

BISHOP RUSSELL BARRY (1890–1976)

Comment

Russell Barry, who for 23 years was Bishop of Southwell, was undoubtedly one of the Church's 20th century prophets. Having himself an enquiring mind, he was able to help many to find their way through difficulties to an active membership of the Church. He seldom spoke of 'God'. For him it was always 'the Living God'. For him too it was always 'the Risen Christ' who was raised from the dead by an act of 'the Living God'. If anyone were to ask him why he was so sure of that, he would point to the Church which, despite its chequered history, lived still because it was founded by, and indwelt by the Risen Christ who had assured its ultimate triumph over evil. More than once I heard him say, 'Never fear! The church is not fighting some desperate rearguard action which presages an inglorious defeat'. The Church means all who have committed themselves to the Risen Christ. Would that all Christians could share that confidence! Fidelity to Christ's Church on our part, to its fellowship, its teaching and its witness, could be instruments in the hand of the Risen Christ to transform the quality of living for all God's family. Surely we are prompted to ask, 'How faithful am I?'

Prayer *Make me, O Lord, a lively member of your Church, constant in worship, bold in witness, and resolute in spirit.*

Easter

Oh! day of days! shall hearts set free
No 'minstrel rapture' find for Thee?
Thou art the Sun of other days.
They shine by giving back Thy rays;
Enthronèd in the sovereign sphere
Thou shedd'st Thy light on all the year;
Sundays by Thee more glorious break,
An Easter day in every week.
And week-days following in their train
The fullness of Thy blessing gain,
Till all, both resting and employ
Be one Lord's day of holy joy.

Then wake, my soul, to high desires,
And earlier light thine altar fires:
The world some hours is on her way,
Nor thinks of thee, thou blesssed day!
Oh! joy to Mary first allowed,
When roused from weeping o'er the shroud
By His own calm, soul-soothing tone,
Breathing her name as still His own.
So is it still: to holy tears,
In lonely hours, Christ risen appears;
In social hours, who Christ would see,
Must turn all tasks to Charity.

JOHN KEBLE (1792–1866)

Comment

The quotation is part of the Easter Day poem in John Keble's *The Christian Year* – a massive tome published in 1827, in which he sets out his 'thought in verse for the Sundays and Holy Days throughout the year'. The copy from which I quote is beautifully illustrated and has on its first page what is described as an 'Advertisement' in which Keble outlines his purpose. 'Next to a sound rule of faith', he writes, 'there is nothing of so much consequence as a sober standard of feeling in matters of practical religion'. He suggests that his object in writing his book of verses will have been attained 'if any person find assistance from it in bringing his own thoughts and feelings into more entire union with those recommended and exemplified in the Prayer Book'. There are no less than 60 lines in his Easter Day poem, and the note of joy which he strikes at the outset rings through to the end. He sees joy as God's Easter gift, the echo of God's life within us, and something we can all possess if we 'turn all tasks to Charity'.

Prayer   *Let us serve God joyfully for His honour and glory.*

BISHOP HACKETT (XVI CENTURY)

New Life

'I came to believe in Christ's teaching and my life suddenly changed'. . . It happened to me as it happens to a man who goes out on some business, and on the way suddenly decides that the business is unnecessary, and returns home. The direction of my life and my desires became different, and good and evil changed places. . . I, like the thief on the Cross, have believed Christ's teaching and been saved. . . I was unhappy and suffering. . . I was nailed by some force to that life of suffering and evil. And as, after the suffering and evils of life, the thief awaited the terrible darkness of death, so did I await the same. In all this I was exactly like the thief. But the difference was that the thief was already dying while I was still living. The thief might believe that his salvation lay beyond the grave, but I could not be satisfied with that because, besides a life beyond the grave, life still awaited me here. But I did not understand that life. It seemed to me terrible. But suddenly I heard the words of Christ and understood them, and life and death ceased to seem to me evil, and instead of despair I experienced happiness and the joy of life undisturbed by death.

COUNT LEO TOLSTOY (1828–1910)

Comment

The quotation is from the pen of a man with a brilliant intellect, a man who fought with distinction in the Crimean War, a man who had to his credit a number of substantial literary works, *War and Peace* being among the best known. Tolstoy was, however, 50 years of age before he reached the conclusion that he had not begun to penetrate the sense and meaning of life. He turned to philosophy, he turned to science, but neither gave him the answer to the questions which haunted him. At long last he found his answer in Christ and His teaching. From that day he poured out a number of books setting out his religious, moral and social ideas and ideals. These called for a new look at moral standards, a new estimate of social responsibilities and international relationships. Changes there must be, but they must come about not by violence but by the vigorous proclamation of Christ's law of love. He would not have it that what he was now teaching was something new which he had conceived. 'There is no such thing as Tolstoyism and never will be; all I have said has already been said eighteen centuries ago, and much better, in the Gospels'. We know the sort of answer which he would give to the person who says, 'the Church should keep out of politics'. Christians cannot 'keep out' of anything which concerns people, and that because of Christ's New Commandment – 'that you love one another'.

Prayer   *O Thou who hast ordained love to be the bond and basis of true life, so fill thy Church with love towards mankind, that by thy light all men and nations may walk in sacred fellowship, and in secure and righteous peace, through Jesus Christ our Lord.*

A Better Resurrection

I have no time, no words, no tears:
  My heart within me like a stone
Is numbed too much for hopes or fears;
  Look right, look left, I dwell alone;
I lift mine eyes, but dimmed with grief
  No everlasting hills I see;
My life is as the falling leaf:
  O Jesus, quicken me.

My life is like a faded leaf,
  My harvest dwindled to a husk;
Truly my life is void and brief,
  And tedious in the barren dusk;
My life is like a frozen thing,
  No bud nor greatness can I see;
Yet rise it shall – the sap of Spring;
  O Jesus, rise in me.

My life is like a broken bowl,
  A broken bowl that cannot hold
One drop of water for my soul,
  Or cordial in the searching cold;
Cast in the fire the perished thing,
  Melt and remould it, till it be
A royal cup for Him my King;
  O Jesus, drink of me.

CHRISTINA ROSSETTI (1830–1894)

Comment

Christina Rossetti, who in another poem posed the question: 'Does the road wind uphill all the way?', and answered it with an emphatic 'Yes' – clearly had her moments of spiritual dryness, even of despair. In expressing them frankly she speaks for many a Christian. Maybe she speaks for us. But we can take heart. Jesus was a realist, and when he found his disciples in that condition, he warned them that the world – the 'world' within them and the 'world' about them – would often leave them downcast, bewildered and frightened. But he exhorted them, 'Be of good cheer, I have overcome the world'. That assurance must have sounded rather hollow to the disciples on the first Good Friday evening. Their eyes would be 'dimmed with grief', and they would suddenly have become 'faded leaves' or 'broken bowls'. But the assurance which Good Friday seemed to mock was upheld by Easter Day. There are times when we sink very low – in doubt, in sorrow, in despair, in disappointment, in sin. Those are times, not for surrender, but for a prayer such as the poet's: 'O Jesus, quicken me rise in me, drink of me'.

Prayer   *Into thy hands, O Lord, we commend ourselves, for thou hast redeemed us. Raise us up. Sanctify us and save us, good Lord.*

Out of Heaven from God

The achievement of Christ, in founding by His single will and power a structure so durable and so universal, is like no other achievement which history records. The masterpieces of the men of action are coarse and common in comparison with it, and the masterpieces of speculation flimsy and unsubstantial. When we speak of it, the common phrases of admiration fail us altogether.

The creative effort which produced that against which, it is said, the gates of hell shall not prevail, cannot be analysed. No architect's designs were furnished for the new Jerusalem. No committee drew up rules for the Universal Commonwealth. The inconceivable work was done in calmness; before the eyes of men it was noiselessly accomplished, attracting little attention.

No man saw the building of the New Jerusalem, the workmen crowded together, the unfinished walls and unpaved streets; no man heard the clink of trowel and pick-axe. It descended out of heaven from God.

SIR J.R. SEELEY (1834–1895)

Comment

'Out of Heaven from God'. That is a conclusion about the Church's origin which came, not from the pen of a professional theologian, but from one who for a time was a Professor of Latin and later a Professor of History. He wrote a notable book entitled *Ecce Homo! (Behold the Man!)* – at first published anonymously, but which won him fame when once it became known that he was its author. His concern was to paint a vivid picture of the historic Jesus. So compelling was this that he soon found himself under criticism from some scholars who complained that he left no room for, or at least failed to emphasise, Christ's divinity. Nevertheless he clearly sets Jesus above all others in the unique power which he attributes to him. He makes it clear that in his judgment the Church itself is a phenomenon which cannot be explained if Good Friday had eliminated Jesus from the stage of history. The Church may have its critics, but it has no rivals. 'Like a mighty army moves the Church of God'. We sing those words frequently. Each of us can pose the question to himself: 'Am I in it, of it, moving with it, alert to its purpose and to my responsibility to join actively in its worship, its fellowship and its witness, as one who has joined it of his own freewill?'

Prayer *Gracious Father, we humbly beseech thee for thy universal Church. Fill it with all truth, in all truth with all peace; where it is corrupt, purge it; where it is in error, direct it; where it is superstitious, rectify it; where anything is amiss, reform it; where it is right, strengthen and confirm it; where it is in want, furnish it; where it is divided and rent asunder, make up the breaches of it, O Thou Holy One of Israel: for Jesus Christ's sake.*

ARCHBISHOP LAUD (1573–1645)

Life's Purpose

I live for those who love me,
  Whose hearts are kind and true;
For the heaven that smiles above me,
  And awaits my spirit too;
For all human ties that bind me,
For the task my God assigned me,
For the bright hopes left behind me,
  And the good that I can do.

I love to hold communion
  With all that is divine;
To feel there is a union
  'Twixt Nature's heart and mine;
To profit by affliction,
Reap truths from field of friction,
Grow wiser from conviction,
  And fulfil each great design.
I live for those who love me,
  For those who know me true;
For the heaven that smiles above me,
  And awaits my spirit too;
For the cause that lacks assistance,
For the wrong that needs resistance,
For the future in the distance,
  And the good that I can do.

GEORGE LINNAEUS BANKS (1821–1881)

Comment

Beautiful sentiments indeed and from the pen of a little-known nineteenth-century poet. He discerns the purpose of life wisely and sees God's 'grand design' as one in which he has his special place and part. Sometimes that great design would call for his help in its furtherance; sometimes it would demand his resistance to things which would impede its progress. Throughout his life he must never be a mere spectator, for God achieves His purpose for his people through his people. Our poet sees that clearly and, setting the fulfilment of God's purpose at the centre of his verses, he sees himself involved in every aspect of its implementation, and twice reminds himself that the good which he could do was an essential part of the 'grand design'. One can imagine that our Lord's response to his poem would be the same as his response to the scribe who asked him which was the first commandment. Read the story in St Mark, chapter 12, verses 28–35. Our Lord's ready response to the scribe who grasped so readily the tenet of life's priorities was the response he will make to us if we do the same, namely 'You are not far from the Kingdom of God'.

Prayer *What better prayer than the poem itself? Read it again as an affirmation of resolve and seal it with your own 'Amen'.*

Our Influence on Mankind

We cannot, like Beethoven or Handel, lift the soul by the magic of divine melody into the seventh heaven of ineffable vision and hope; we cannot, like Newton, weigh the far-off stars in a balance, and measure the heavings of the eternal flood; nor, like Milton or Burke, awaken men's hearts with the note of an organ trumpet; we cannot, like the great saints of the Church and the great sages of the Schools, add to those acquisitions of spiritual beauty and intellectual mastery which have, one by one and little by little, raised men from being no higher than the brute to be only a little lower than the angels. But what we can do – even the humblest of us – is to help to swell the common tide on the force and set of whose currents depends the prosperous voyaging of humanity... The thought that this is so may well lighten the poor perplexities of our daily life, and even soothe the pang of its calamities. It lifts us from our feet as on wings, opening a larger meaning to our private toil and a higher purpose to our public endeavour... It nerves our arm with boldness against oppression and injustice, and strengthens our voice with deeper accents against falsehood, while we are yet to the full noon of our days; yes, and perhaps it will shed some ray of consolation when our eyes are growing dim to it all, and we go down to the Valley of the Dark Shadow.

JOHN MORLEY (1838–1923)

Comment

The first Viscount Morley was an author of distinction, and a politician who began his political career as M.P. for Newcastle and finished it as Lord President of the Council. He resigned from the Cabinet when Great Britain decided to enter the European War in 1914. He wrote a number of books and in his *Recollections* he dwells on the easy way in which the world falls for hero-worship, and tends to overlook the contributions to its well-being of the little man of average ability. As Christians we believe in and must work for a Christ-like world. We can conceive of nothing more splendid. We can be satisfied with nothing less. But such a world is not one which can be built merely by those accounted as 'great men' or 'great women'. (Read 1 Corinthians ch.1 vv.26–29). To say that we can exercise no influence at all on the world and its affairs – its sufferings, its sorrows, its strifes, its starvation – is to deny our responsibility for stewardship of time, of talents, of money. These are all gifts we hold in trust for God's service to his people in his world. It is good from time to time to examine ourselves to this end, remembering that, 'It is required of stewards, that a man be found faithful'. (1 Cor.ch.4 v.2).

Prayer   *Teach us, good Lord, to serve Thee as Thou deservest, to give and not to count the cost, to fight and not to heed the wounds, to toil and not to seek for rest, to labour and not to ask for any reward, save that of knowing that we do Thy will.*

ST IGNATIUS LOYOLA (1491–1556)

Commemorating William Law, Mystic, Non-Juror 1761

As therefore when we think of God himself, we are to have no sentiments but of praise and thanksgiving; so when we look at those things which are under the direction of God's hand and governed by his Providence, we are to receive them with the same tempers of praise and gratitude. And although we are not to think all things right, and just, and lawful, which the Providence of God permits; for then, nothing could be unjust because nothing happens without his permission; yet we must adore God in the greatest public calamities, the most grievous persecutions, as things suffered by God, like plagues and famines, for ends suitable to his wisdom and glory in the government of the world.

There is nothing more suitable to the piety of a reasonable creature, or the spirit of a Christian, than thus to approve, admire and glorify God in all the acts of his general Providence: considering the whole world as his particular family and all events as directed by his wisdom.

WILLIAM LAW (1686–1761)

Comment

William Law, who was the son of a grocer, was ordained and became a Fellow of Emmanuel College, Cambridge. He became a non-juror, that is he refused to take the Oath of Allegiance to George 1 since that would have meant breaking his oath to James 2. That refusal resulted in his being deprived of his Fellowship. He gave himself to various works of charity, and for the rest of his life lived simply and with great concern for others. He wrote a number of books designed to help people towards Christian perfection. One of these , indeed the greatest, was *A Serious Call to the Devout and Holy Life*, from which the quotation comes. When it appeared in 1729 it exercised a profound influence on the nation, comparable, it was said, with Bunyan's *Pilgrim's Progress*. It was the *Serious Call* which earned for him the title of Mystic, but that title does not mean that his book was written only for people far advanced in the spiritual life. He had the ability and the insight to write simply about the virtues which should mark the life of a Christian and which should be practised to the glory of God. All things to the glory of God!

Prayer   *O Thou in whom all things live, who commandest us to seek thee and art ever ready to be found: to know thee in life, to serve thee in freedom, to praise thee in our soul's joy. We bless thee and adore thee, we worship thee and magnify thee, we give thanks to thee for thy great glory; through Jesus Christ our Lord.*

ST AUGUSTINE (354-430)

Virtue

Sweet Day, so cool, so calm, so bright,
The bridal of the earth and sky,
The dew shall weep thy fall tonight;
       For thou must die.

Sweet rose, whose hue, angry and brave,
Bids the rash gazer wipe his eye,
Thy root is ever in its grave,
       And thou must die.

Sweet spring, full of sweet days and roses,
A box where sweets compacted lie,
My music shows ye have your closes,
       And all must die.

Only a sweet and virtuous soul,
Like seasoned timber, never gives;
But though the whole world turn to coal,
       Then chiefly lives.

GEORGE HERBERT (1593–1633)

Comment

Here, in one of his greatest poems, Herbert notes the deathless character of the virtuous soul – a conclusion he draws from the Resurrection of Christ. In a contemplation of nature he sees a relentless cycle of life and death; the very dews are as tears for the fading and passing of nature's splendours. Even the lovely rose, which draws tears from the eyes of the 'rash gazer', has one foot in the grave; the loveliest of music rises and falls. But the soul which, like seasoned timber, has stood the test of time, differs from all else because it is immortal. I suspect that the poet wrote these lines at Eastertide when there could have been ringing in his ears the reassuring words of our Lord to Martha following the death of her brother. 'Your brother will rise again... I am the resurrection and the life; he who believes in me, though he die, yet shall he live, and whoever lives and believes in me, shall never die'. (St John ch.10, vv, 24–27). Martha was reasssured, as we can be when our loved ones cross life's horizon.

Prayer   *Lord of all life, by whom all souls live, we thank you for those whom your love has called from the life of trial and change to the life of rest. We trust them to your care, and we pray that by your grace we may be brought to enjoy with them the endless life of glory, through Jesus Christ our Lord.*

The supernaturalism of Nature

The centre-fire heaves underneath the earth
And the earth changes like a human face;
The molten ore bursts up among the rocks,
Winds into the soul's heart, outreaches bright
In hidden minds, spots barren river-beds,
Crumbles into fine sand where sunbeams bask –
God joys therein. The wroth sea's waves are edged
With foam, white as the bitter lip of hate,
When, in the solitary waste, strange groups
Of young volcanoes come up, cyclops-like
Staring together with their eyes on flame –
God tastes a pleasure in their uncouth pride.
Then all is still; earth is a wintry clod:
But spring wind, like a dancing psaltress passes
Over its breast to waken it, rare verdure
Buds tenderly upon rough banks, between
The withered tree-roots and the cracks of frost,
Like a smile striving with a wrinkled face.

Above, birds fly in merry flocks, the lark
Soars up and up, shivering for very joy;
Afar the ocean sleeps; white fishing gulls
Flit where the strand is purple with its tribe
Of nested limpets; savage creatures seek
Their loves in wood and plain – and God renews
His ancient rapture. Thus He dwells in all,
From life's minute beginnings, up at last
To Man – the consummation of this scheme
Of being, the completion of this sphere of life.

ROBERT BROWNING (1812–1889)

Comment

Wordsworth and Shelley are often described as the poets of Nature, and Browning as the poet of the human soul. But here, in a passage of surpassing beauty, Browning sees in Nature not only things beautiful and wonderful, but things which betray the mind and the hand of the living God. Nature is not only beautiful to the eye; it is challenging to the mind of man. It demonstrates both death and life. All can be still – 'earth is a wintry clod' – spring comes and all Nature is throbbing with life again, and 'God renews His ancient rapture'. One of the things we need to do from time to time is to be still, and to contemplate nature and to learn to press through what we see to the invisible God.

Prayer   *Heavenly Father, who hast filled the world with beauty: Open our eyes*
we beseech thee, to behold thy gracious hand in all thy works; that re-
joicing in thy whole creation, we may learn to serve thee with gladness;
that as we pass through things temporal we may never lose the vision
of things eternal; through Jesus Christ our Lord.

Sundays

Bright shadows of true rest! Some shoots of bliss;
        Heaven once a week;
The next world's gladness pre-possessed in this;
        A day to seek
Eternity in time; the steps by which
We climb above all ages; lamps that light
Man through his heap of dark days; and the rich
And full redemption of the whole week's flight.

The pulleys unto headlong man; Time's bower;
        The narrow way;
Transplanted Paradise; God's waking hour;
        The cool o' th' day!
The creature's jubilee; God's parley with dust;
Heaven here; man on those hills of myrrh and flowers;
Angels descending; the returns of trust;
A gleam of glory after six days' showers.

The Church's love feasts; Time's prerogative
        And interest
Deducted from the whole; the combs, and hive,
        And home of rest.
The milky way chalked out with suns; a clue
That guides through erring hours; and in full story
A taste of Heaven on earth; the pledge and cue
Of a full feast; and the outcourts of glory.

HENRY VAUGHAN (1622–1695)

Comment

Henry Vaughan was a country doctor and a loyal son of the Church. All his poems reflect the reality and strength of his faith. He has been called 'the poet of meditation', and since meditations are intensely personal experiences, their translation into poems frequently presents readers with difficulties in interpreting the poet's allegories and symbols. This poem, however, presents no such difficulty. Sunday was for Vaughan a day of great joy. The old pagan Sun Day was the first day of the week and from the moment of the Resurrection that day became for Christians 'the Day of the Lord' (Revelation ch.1 v.10). The poet sums up its meaning for him. It was 'a day of joy', 'a day to seek ', a day to express 'Eternity in time', a day to partake of 'the Church's love-feasts'. So regarded it could be 'Heaven once a week'. For Christians it must essentially be a day when they join in public worship. That does not mean 'no fun', 'no games', 'no recreation'. It means something positive, namely putting God first. The Lord's Own Service, on the Lord's own Day, in the Lord's own House', should be a 'must' for all Christians.

Prayer   *O God who makest us glad with the weekly remembrance of the glorious resurrection of Thy Son our Lord; vouchsafe us such a blessing through our worship on the first day of the week, that the days to follow it may be hallowed by thy abiding presence; through Jesus Christ our Lord.*

God's Grandeur

The world is charged with the grandeur of God.
    It will flame out, like shining from shook foil;
    It gathers to a greatness, like the ooze of oil
Crushed. Why do men then now not reck His rod?
Generations have trod, have trod, have trod;
    And all is seared with trade; bleared, smeared with toil;
And bears man's smudge and shares man's smell: the soil
Is bare now, nor can foot feel, being shod.

And for all this, nature is never spent;
    There lives the dearest freshness deep down things;
And though the last lights from the black West went
    Oh, morning, at the brown brink eastward, springs –
Because the Holy Ghost over the bent
    World broods with warm breast and with ah! bright wings.

GERARD MANLEY HOPKINS (1844–1889)

Comment

Gerard Manley Hopkins was by no means the first poet to see the glory of God the Creator mirrored in the world of nature. He opens his sonnet with a splendid line in which he sees the whole world of nature filled with manifestations of God – His beauty, His power and His Life. It has been said of Hopkins that he was 'a poet who had the poet's pen, the painter's brush, and the musician's ear', and this sonnet is but one of his works which sustains that judgement. He sees the beauty, but he sees too the things that man has done which mar the beauty. As a priest, he ministered in northern industrial towns and he expresses his sadness at the spoliation of nature by man, examples of which he saw all around him. There is pathos in his question, 'Why do men now take no notice of [i.e. not reck] the divine authority? He complains that man has been recklessly wanton in the way in which he has treated the world of nature so that the world is 'seared', 'bleared' and 'smeared'. But things are not hopeless. They never are in God's domain! Nature is never spent. The 'deep down things' will rise again, as does the sun every morning. Is not that 'ah! bright wings' an exclamation of the artist in him as the sun peeps above the horizon to shatter the darkness? What lessons are here for you and me? – warnings against wanton mutilation, against ruthless spoliation and the challenges of conservation!

Prayer   *Heavenly Father, you have filled the whole world with beauty. Open our eyes that we may see your hand in all your works. As we rejoice for all creation, help us to reverence all your gifts and so to respond to all that is useful and beautiful, that passing through things temporal we may not lose the vision of the eternal; through Jesus Christ our Lord.*

The Light of the Eternal Morning

The rising of the sun was noble in the cold and warmth of it, peeping down the spread of light he raised his shoulder heavily over the edge of grey mountain and wavering length of upland. Then the woods arose in folds, like drapery of awakened mountains, stately with depths of awe and memory of tempests. Autumn's mellow hand was on them as they own already, touched with gold and red and olive; and their joy towards the sun was less to a bridegroom than to a father.

Yet before the floating image of the woods could clear itself, suddenly the gladsome light leaped over the hill and valley, dispelling fear and the cloven hoof of darkness. Then life and joy sprang reassured from every crouching furrow. Every flower and bud and bird had a fluttering sense of them.

So, perhaps, shall break upon us the light of the eternal morning, when crag and chasm shall be no more, neither hill and valley, nor great unvintaged ocean; when glory shall not snare happiness, neither happiness envy glory, but all things shall arise and shine in the light of the Father's countenance.

RICHARD D. BLACKMORE (1825–1900)

Comment

Richard Blackmore was a barrister, but it was probably as a novelist of the nineteenth century that he was best known, not least for *Lorna Doone* a romance of Exmoor which was his first novel of distinction. He was a Christian, and his book on the Creation, from which the quotation is an extract, together with some verses which he wrote, reveal him as a true man of God. In this passage of his book he tries to do what many poets and saints have tried to do before – to express a conviction which he held of the joys of Heaven. Heaven is not a place but a state of being with God. Richard Blackmore is saying in effect what Easter says: that there is a future for good and none for evil, a future for all that is beautiful and good and true and none for the ugly, the bad and the false. The world in which we live is a vestibule of Eternity where, above all else, we must be able to speak the language of Heaven – which is Love, and in the spirit of Heaven – which is Joy. 'Joy, joy for ever! My task is done. The gates are passed and Heaven is won'. So said Sir Thomas More. We have a choice. We have to decide here and now where we stand.

Prayer   *O Lord, who has taught us that in thy Father's house there are many mansions: we thank thee for the heavenly home which thou hast gone to prepare for us. Make us ready, we pray thee, for that home, and in thy mercy bring us all at last to be partakers of its joys, that we may dwell with thee for evermore.*

What is Life?

And what is life? An hour-glass on the run,
A mist retreating from the morning sun,
 A busy, bustling, still repeated dream –
Its length? A moment's pause, a moment's thought
 And happiness? A bubble on the stream
That in the act of seizing shrinks to naught.

Vain hopes – what are they? Puffing gales of morn,
That of its charms divests the dewy lawn,
 And robs each flower of its gem, and dies –
A cobweb hiding disappointment's thorn
 Which stings more keenly through the thin disguise.

And thou, O trouble? Nothing can suppose,
And sure the Power of Wisdom only knows,
 What need requireth thee,
So free and lib'ral as thy bounty flows,
 Some necessary cause must surely be.

Then what is Life? When stripped of its disguise
 A thing to be desired it cannot be,
Since everything that meets our foolish eyes
 Gives proof sufficient of its vanity.
'Tis but a trial all must undergo
 To teach unthankful mortals how to prize
That happiness vain man's denied to know
 Until he's called to claim it in the skies.

JOHN CLARE (1793–1864)

Comment

John Clare wrote several hundred poems, many of them reflecting genius of a high order. But the tragic melancholy apparent in *What is Life?* breaks through many of his poems suggesting a sense of failure, of emotional instability and the illusion that the world was always conspiring against him. His livelier *Poems Descriptive of Rural Life and Scenery* were well received and won him reputation. But his fame was short-lived. Subsequent failures engendered a bitterness which seemed to imprison him. He became insane and spent the last seventeen years of his life in asylums. Even so he continued to write poems, many exquisitely beautiful, if moving in their sadness. And yet, as the last line of this poem betrays, and other mentions of 'my Creator God', and of 'God's sweet blessings', the light which comes from God broke through his darkness. Not many of us escape, from time to time, failures, frustrations, and a feeling that everything is going against us. Sometimes we feel, like the poet, that happiness will for ever elude us. But we can take heart that godly folk have sensed this darkness and found their way through to God who is Light. The man who wrote Psalm 139 was one such. Read what he says!

Prayer   *Read Psalm 139 – and in your own words commit yourself, as the Psalmist does, to the care of the inescapable God.*

The Spiritual Pasch

The very name of the (Easter) feast points to the way in which it is surpassed, if it is correctly explained. The word 'Pasch' means passage, because when the angel of death was striking down the first-born, he passed over the houses of the Hebrews. But with us the passage of the angel of death is a reality, for it passes over us once for all, when Christ raises us up to eternal life.

The year is the symbol of eternity for it continually turns round upon itself and never comes to rest. Christ, the father of the age to come, was offered as a sacrifice for us; he treats our former life as a thing of the past, and gives us the beginning of a new life by the bath of regeneration, according to the pattern of his own death and resurrection.

Everyone who has learned of the Pasch that was sacrificed on his behalf, should reckon the moment when Christ was sacrificed for him as the moment when his own life began. Now Christ is sacrificed for him when he recognises the grace and understands the life this sacrifice has won for him.

If he understands this, he should be eager to welcome the beginning of the new life, and never run back to the old, for it has reached its end. How can we who died to sin still live in it?

ANONYMOUS – AN ANCIENT HOMILY

Comment

The word 'Pasch' was in early days used both for the Jewish Passover and the Christian festival of Easter. It occurs in many of our Easter hymns e.g. the popular Easter hymn, 'At the Lamb's high feast we sing', used in the Eucharist has:

'Praise we Christ, Whose Blood was shed,
Paschal Victim, Paschal Bread;
With sincerity and love
Eat we Manna from above'

It is in effect another name for the Easter festival. The anonymous writer, who may well have lived in the first century A.D., has lifted Easter to the highest point in the Christian calendar and that because it is the feast which guarantees for man the triumph over sin and death which the Risen Christ has won for him. In his earthly ministry Christ's promise was that he would make all things new. Easter assures us that he does just that. He does not 'mend' a human life; he makes it a new life by what our author calls 'the bath of regeneration'. For us that means that however low we may sink in sin, Christ can still reach us if our hand is uplifted to meet his – and our prayer is that of the disciples: 'Lord, save us, we perish'.

Prayer

Create in me a clean heart, O God, and renew a right spirit within me. Give me the gladness of your help again, and support me with a willing spirit.

PSALM 51

My Fault, my own grievous Fault

You are under the power of no other enemy, and held in no other captivity, and want no other deliverance but from the power of your own earthly self. This is the one murderer of the divine life within you. It is your own Cain that murders your own Abel. Now everything that your earthly nature does is under the influence of self-will, self-love and self-seeking, whether it carries you to laudable or blameable practices. All is done in the nature and spirit of Cain and helps you to such goodness as when Cain slew his brother. For every action and notion of self has the spirit of Anti-Christ and murders the divine life within you.

Receive every day as a resurrection from death, as a new enjoyment of life. Meet every rising sun with such sentiments of God's goodness as if you had seen all things new created on your own account; and under the sense of so great a blessing let your joyful heart praise and magnify so glorious a Creator.

WILLIAM LAW (1686–1761)

Comment

William Law was a prolific writer of books which cover every aspect of the Christian life in its personal, moral and social content. So much indeed did he write that it is difficult to extract from his writings, short representative passages which can satisfy the whims of the anthologist. The quotations above come from two of his works – the first from *The Spirit of Love* and the second from his greatest and most memorable work *A Serious Call to the Devout and Holy Life*. The title above the first passage is not his but mine, as it seems to me that he is pressing upon his readers just there, that when a Christian lapses from the spirit of love to the spirit of hate, and that in any circumstance, there is none other whom he can blame for his fall. In the second passage, which follows an exhortation to the virtues demanded of a Christian in his daily life – temperance, humility, integrity, self-denial for example – he tells Christians that every day should be a resurrection day. Every day should be a day when, by the mercy of God, the sins of yesterday can be blotted out, and the divine life within us can begin again. St Paul cherished the same thought when he advised 'Do not let the sun go down on your anger' (Ephesians, ch.4 v.26). The first of the quotations above is a warning to us; the second is an assurance for us.

Prayer   *Lord, for thy tender mercies' sake, lay not our sins to our charge, but forgive all that is past: give us grace to amend our lives, to decline from sin and incline to virtue that we may walk with a perfect heart before thee, now and evermore.*

Easter Morn

Say, earth, why hast thou got thee new attire,
And stick'st thy habit full of daisies red?
Seems that thou dost to some high thought aspire,
And some new-found-out bridegroom mean'st to wed:
Tell me, ye trees, so fresh apparelled, –
So never let the spiteful canker waste you,
So never let the heavens with lightning blast you –
Why go you now, so trimly dressed, or whither haste you?

Answer me, Jordan, why thy crooked tide
So often wanders from his nearest way,
As though some other way thy stream would slide,
And fain salute the place where something lay,
And you, sweet birds that, shaded from the ray
Sit carolling and piping grief away,
The while the lambs do hear you, dance and play.
Tell me, sweet birds, what is it you so fain would say?

Ye primroses and purple violets,
Tell me why blaze ye from your leafy bed,
And woo men's hands to rend you from your sets,
As though you would somewhere be carried,
With fresh perfumes and velvets garnished?
But ah! I need not ask, 'tis surely so
You all would to your Saviour's triumph go,
There would ye all await, and humble homage do.

GILES FLETCHER (1588–1623)

Comment

Giles Fletcher, who was Rector of Alderton in Suffolk, was a member of a notable family in the literary world, but not as well-known as his brother, Phineas, who wrote the lovely hymn *Drop, drop slow tears*, or of his cousin John who was an outstanding playwright. Giles wrote *Christ's Victory and Triumph in Heaven and Earth over and after Death* shortly before his death. Like many another poet he was inspired by the coming of spring as he sees all nature bubbling and bursting with new life. He hears the trees, the birds, the lambs, the flowers joining in a song of triumph for Christ's resurrection. In the Orthodox Church Christians do not greet their friends on Easter morning with the 'Happy Easter' wish. They greet them with the declaration which embodies the recipe for true happiness in that it carries with it an assurance. One calls to another, 'Christ is Risen' and he is answered with the equally confident reply, 'He is risen indeed'.

Prayer *O God, who has made the earth so fair, and written thy glory in the heavens; help us inwardly to respond to all that is outwardly beautiful, and grant that as we pass through things temporal we may never lose the vision of the things eternal, through Jesus Christ our Lord.*

Conviction

I feel in myself the future life. I am like a forest once cut down; the new shoots are stronger and livelier than ever. The sunshine is on my head. The Earth gives me its generous sap, but Heaven lights me with the reflection of unknown worlds. You say that the soul is nothing but the resultant of the bodily powers. Why, then, is my soul more luminous when my bodily powers begin to fail? Winter is on my head, but eternal spring is in my heart. I breathe at this hour the fragrance of the lilies, the violets and the roses, as at twenty. The nearer I approach the end, the plainer I hear around me the immortal symphonies of the worlds which invite me. It is marvellous, yet simple. It is a fairy tale and it is history.

For half a century I have been writing my thoughts in prose and in verse; history, philosophy, drama, romance, tradition, satire, ode and song; I have tried all. But I feel I have not said the thousandth part of what is in me.

When I go down to the grave I can say like many others, 'I have finished my day's work'. But I cannot say, 'I have finished my life'. My day's work will begin again the next morning. The tomb is not a blind alley; it is a thoroughfare. It closes on the twilight; it opens on the dawn.

VICTOR HUGO (1802–1885)

Comment

Victor Hugo, poet, novelist, diplomat, playwright, revolutionary in the struggle against Napoleon – he was all these but he was something more. He was a man of God, a man of faith, a man of prayer. He lived most of his life in France, but also spent some of his years in the Channel Islands. In the above quotation he makes the strongest affirmation which mere words can make, that death is not the end. He affirms the Easter truth. Our Lord answered the plea of the penitent thief on the cross with the grand assurance: 'Today shalt thou be with me in paradise'. That was more than a promise of immortality. It was a promise of recognition and companionship. It was late in his day that the thief turned to Christ. But it was not too late. It never is! There is always hope – but how much better is it to turn to Christ, to love him and to serve him in the here and now rather than later.

Prayer   *Heavenly Father, in whose hands are the hearts of all thy children: Grant us the faith that commits all to thee, without question and without reserve; that trusting ourselves wholly to thy love and wisdom, we may meet all that life may bring, and death itself at last, with serenity and courage; through Jesus Christ our Lord.*

CANON FRANK COLQUHOUN

New Life

Well may I guess and feel
Why autumn should be sad;
But vernal airs should sorrows heal,
Spring should be gay and glad:
Yet as along this violet bank I rove,
The languid sweetness seems to choke my breath,
I sit me down beside the hazel grove,
And sigh, and half could wish my weariness were death.

Like a bright veering cloud
Gay blossoms twinkle there;
Warbles around a busy crowd
Of larks in purest air.

Shame on the heart that dreams of blessings gone,
Or wakes the spectral forms of woe and crime,
When nature sings of joy and hopes alone,
Reading her cheerful lesson in her own sweet time.

She joys that one is born
Into a world forgiven,
Her Father's household to adorn,
And dwell with her in Heaven.
So have I seen in spring's bewitching hour,
When the glad earth is offering all her best
Some gentle maid bend o'er a cherished flower,
And wish it worthier on a parent's heart to rest.

JOHN KEBLE (1792–1866)

Comment

'Spring should be gay and glad' says Keble. It should be gay in the real meaning of that lovely word which we should do well to use frequently to rescue it from its demotion to slang. 'Glad, merry and sweet is the blessed and lovely face that our Lord shows to our soul', wrote Mother Julian of Norwich. Keble sees that gladness, that merriment, that sweetness reflected in the sights, the scenes and the sounds of spring. But he expresses a cautionary note lest 'spring's bewitching hour' should evoke no answering response – lest it should become a moment of selfish enjoyment which turns the mind of man inward without prompting him to turn his mind upward to God and outward to his fellows. The flower which the 'gentle maid' plucked was the flower of love – of love, mark you!

Prayer   *O God of hope, fill us with all joy and peace in believing, and enable us to share with others the joy, the peace and the love which are your gifts to all believers; through Jesus Christ our Lord.*

Commemorating Anselm, Archbishop of Canterbury Teacher of the Faith, died 1109

God's Goodness

What God giveth to man in the world is either such as he can never lose, and none can ever take from him, or such that even though man lose it, yet by it he may obtain that, when this present life is ended, he may be ever with his Creator in a life of bliss. God giveth to man oftentimes in this life to live according to reason, and as He hath commanded, and as is right, to love his Creator; and in all things, without any contradiction, to obey His commandments; and this good no man, except he himself of his own will let it go, can take from him. This world's riches, whether he will or no, he must needs give up; but while he hath them, if he bestow them as his God hath commanded, he may so be able to attain everlasting life.

O immeasurable goodness of our Creator! O inestimable mercy! Himself in nothing ever needing man, yet of His goodness alone He created man; creating, He adorned him with reason, that he might be able to be partaker of His happiness and His Eternity, and so with Him possess for ever joy and gladness.

St Anselm (1033–1109)

Comment

Anselm's wealthy father prevented him from taking up the vocation to which he wished to dedicate his life, until he was 23 when he left home to join the monks of the Abbey of Bec. Three years later he became Prior. He excelled as a teacher, both by the written and spoken word. He became Archbishop of Canterbury in 1093. Determined as he was to put God before Caesar he found himself frequently at odds with the king who ultimately forced him to leave the country. Not until Rufus died could he return to England, and doing so he received a great welcome from the populace. Once again, however, he found himself having to challenge the king, Henry the First, who sought to usurp the rights of the Church, and once again he was expelled. He returned to his See in 1107. Among his greatest written works are treatises on *The Being of God* and on *The Atonement*. He has been accounted the greatest of the Church's theologians in the 800 years of the Church's history between St Augustine of Hippo and St Thomas Aquinas. Early in 1109 he was warned that his earthly life was coming to an end. He answered the warning, 'If God's will be so, I will gladly obey it; but if He be pleased rather that I should remain among you until I have solved a question which I am turning over in my mind concerning the origin of the soul, I should receive it thankfully'. Within days he died. His body rests in Canterbury Cathedral. As for Anselm so for us – whatever we do in life we also are called to humble and joyful acceptance of God's will.

Prayer   *Grant O Lord that we may cleave to thee without parting, worship thee without wearying, serve thee without failing; faithfully seek thee, happily find thee, and for ever possess thee, the One only God, blessed, world without end.*

St Anselm

Easter

Rise, heart, Thy Lord is risen; sing His praise
Without delays,
Who takes thee by the hand that thou likewise
With Him mayst rise;
That, as His death calcined thee to dust,
His life may make thee gold, and much more, just.

Awake, my lute, and struggle for thy part
With all thy art:
The cross taught all wood to resound His name
Who bore His same;
His stretched sinews taught all strings what key
Is best to celebrate this most high day.

Consort both heart and lute, and twist song
Pleasant and long;
Or, since all music is but three parts vied
And multiplied,
O, let thy blessed Spirit bear a part,
And make up our defects with His sweet art.

GEORGE HERBERT (1593–1633)

Comment

Another burst of Easter joy from George Herbert who is undoubtedly one of the finest poets in the whole realm of English literature, though maybe in his day somewhat overshadowed by John Donne. Herbert died at the age of 40 and many of his poems, including this one did not appear until after his death. It was not his only poem about Easter, but in this work, as in *Easter Wings* he has in mind both the crucifixion and the resurrection of Christ, the fall of Man, his redemption by Christ, and his rising to new life in the power of the Risen Christ. Metaphysical poet that he was, there are generally symbols to interpret as in this poem. 'Calcined thee to dust' and the line which follows it sees the fall of Adam, Man's redemption by the Cross – from 'dust' to 'gold', and more – the strength to be just. Verses two and three see Herbert calling for joyous music and song – music which vies with all other means of expressing joy. He adds that if giving of our best in this way may still fall short of the perfect offering, the Holy Spirit can be relied upon to make up our defects. It can be no accident that the world's finest music from *the Messiah* the B Minor Mass, on one level, the Crimond and Blaenwern on the other, has been inspired by our holy religion, or that singing has taken such a great part in Christian worship.

Prayer   *O Blessed Lord, who didst promise thy disciples that through thy Easter victory their sorrow should be turned to joy, and their joy no man should take from them; grant us so to know thee in the power of thy resurrection, that we may be partakers of that joy which is unspeakable and full of glory, for thy holy name's sake.*

CANON FRANK COLQUHOUN

Commemorating George, Patron Saint of England
Martyr, Fourth century

Soon, Lovely England

Grey walls, broad fields, fresh voices, rippling weir,
I know you well; ten faces, for each face
That passes smiling, haunt this hallowed place,
and nothing not thrice noted greets me here.

Soft watery winds, wide twilight skies and clear,
Refresh my spirit at its founts of grace,
And a strange sorrow masters me; to pace
These willowed paths, in this autumnal year.
Soon, lovely England, soon thy secular dreams,
Thy lisping comrades, shall be thine no more.
A world's loosed troubles flood thy gated streams
And drown, methinks, thy towers; and the tears start
As if an iron hand had clutched my heart,
And knowledge is a pang, like love of yore.

GEORGE SANTAYANA (1863–1952)

Comment

A beautiful lament by a Spanish poet written in Cambridge a few days before the outbreak of the 1914 war. That same poet had, four years earlier, written *Spinoza's Ethics* in which his own outlook on life is clear. 'To see things under the form of eternity is to see them in their historic and moral truth, not as they seemed as they passed, but as they remain when they are over'. 'Lovely England' has sufferd another holocaust since the poet wrote his sonnet, and no prayers are more urgent, here and throughout Christendom, than that peace and happiness, truth and justice, religion and piety may be established among us 'for all nations'. Very little is known about St George, his life and his martyrdom, though it is probable that he was martyred very early in the fourth century at Lydda in Palestine. The dragon legend did not appear until the twelfth century and, insofar as it conjures up the courage of a great man of God, it is not without its value. After all, there is no shortage of dragons prowling around the world today – greed, hatred, racism, drug abuse, promiscuity among them. They cannot be eliminated by wishful thinking or by Acts of Parliament. They call for Christians to battle with them in the power of the Spirit. Ephesians ch.6 vv.10–20 has something to say about this.

Prayer

O God, bless this kingdom that there may be peace and prosperity in its borders. In peace, so preserve it that it corrupts not; in trouble defend it that it suffers not; and so order it whether in plenty or in want, that it may faithfully serve thee and patiently seek thy kingdom, through Jesus Christ our Lord.

WILLIAM LAUD

Wayfaring

Surely Thou comest in the misty morning
*   With glint of glory under radiant skies;*
In silent mystery each rosy dawning
*   Unfolds Thy beauty to the watcher's eyes.*

I could not say in words of human spelling,
*   How Thou wilt walk the quiet road with me,*
My Fellow Pilgrim ever gently telling
*   Thy child of Bethlehem and Calvary.*

And when the moon shines forth in silver beauty,
*   As in the night when Wise Men came from far –*
Meekly to kneel and offer Thee their duty,
*   Led by the shining of Thy wondrous star;*

Yea, though the world seem swinging to disaster,
*   And life's day darkened by a sense of doom,*
Thou wilt be with me then, my Lord and Master,
*   I will not fear the valley's shadowed gloom.*

O Jesu, Jesu, Jesu, I would praise Thee
*   So lightening every step along the road;*
And when I fall, Thy loving hand will raise me,
*   And take me home to Thee, O Lord my God.*

FATHER ANDREW, S.D.C. (1869–1946)

Comment

The author was a priest of the Society of the Divine Compassion, a Religious Order within the Church of England, whose members made a rich contribution to the spiritual life and mission of the church earlier in this century. In this simple poem, Father Andrew is saying that there are days when God's presence with us on life's road is, as it were, accentuated by the natural beauty around us. Then comes a time when this is seemingly obliterated by the doom and gloom with which the world threatens. The first two lines of the fourth verse might have been written more recently as a natural response to the nuclear shadow which hangs over the world. Father Andrew's response to the doom which 'shadowed the valley's gloom' was the authentically Christian response, namely the confident acceptance that his Lord died that he might be forgiven, even when he fell to sin, he could rise again in the power of the Risen Christ. 'All sin', said St Augustine, 'is a kind of lying'. He might have added that it is also a kind of dying. But there is not sin which is beyond the pale of the forgiving Love of God. When you ponder the first two lines of the fourth verse, pray for peace, pray that the world may be spared from the grim fate of the nuclear horror.

Prayer for Peace   *Lead me from death to life, from falsehood to truth; lead me from despair to hope, from fear to trust; lead me from hate to love, from war to peace. Let peace fill our hearts, our world, our universe.*

St Mark the Evangelist

Oh, who shall dare in this frail scene
On holiest, happiest thought to lean,
> *On Friendship, Kindred, or on Love?*
Since not Apostles' hands can clasp
Each other in so firm a grasp,
> *But they shall change and variance prove.*

Yet deem not, on such parting sad
Shall dawn no welcome dear and glad:
> *Divided in their earthly race,*
Together at the glorious goal,
Each leading many a rescued soul,
> *The faithful champions shall embrace.*

Oh then the glory and the bliss,
When all that pained or seemed amiss
> *Shall melt with earth and sin away!*
When saints beneath their Saviour's eye,
Filled with each other's company,
> *Shall spend in love th'eternal day!*

JOHN KEBLE (1792–1866)

Comment

Keble spells out in verse one of the saddest quarrels and one of the most glorious reconciliations in the early Christian Church. John Mark, who may well have been the young man who fled naked when Jesus was arrested, accompanied Paul, and his uncle Barnabas on Paul's first missionary journey, but at Perga he suddenly left them and went home. Paul was dismayed by his departure and decided that he lacked endurance. When arrangements were being made for a second missionary journey, Barnabas was anxious that Mark should join them again. Paul made it clear, however, that he was unwilling to have anything further to do with a man who had 'played the quitter on them in Pamphylia'. A bitter argument followed, and so sharp was the disagreement that the two Apostles parted company and it seemed that the second missionary journey was 'off' (see Acts ch.15). However, the Holy Spirit took over to ensure that the end result would not be 'no missionary journey', but 'two missionary journeys' – one with Mark, partnering Barnabas, and the other with Silas partnering Paul! By the time Paul was writing his letters from prison, he and Mark had become reconciled and just before his death Paul sent a message to Timothy to 'Take Mark, and bring him with you' (see 2 Timothy ch.4 v.11). It was that same Mark who wrote the earliest of our four Gospels. There are lessons here which touch our quarrels and disagreements and which pose questions as to our readiness to seek reconciliation.

Prayer   *O Lord and Master, Jesus Christ, Word of the Everlasting Father, who hast borne our griefs and carried the burden of our infirmities; renew, by thy Holy Spirit in thy Church, the gifts of healing and send forth thy disciples again to preach the Gospel of thy kingdom, to cure the sick and relieve thy suffering children to the praise and glory of thy holy name.*

LITURGY OF ST MARK

Quickness

False life! a foil and no more, when
Wilt thou be gone?
Thou foul deception of all men
That would not have the true come on.

Thou art a Moon-like toil; a blind
Self-posing state;
A dark contest of waves and wind;
A mere tempestuous debate.

Life is a fixed, discerning light,
A knowing joy;
No chance, or fit; but ever bright,
And calm and full, yet doth not cloy.

'Tis such a blissful thing, that still
Doth vivify,
And shine and smile, and hath the skill
To please without Eternity.

Thou art a toilsome Mole, or less –
A moving mist,
But life is, what none can express,
A quickness, which my God hath kissed.

HENRY VAUGHAN (1621–1695)

Comment

Henry Vaughan was one of the so-named metaphysical poets – that is, poets who, according to the dictionary 'combined intense feeling with ingenious thought and elaborate imagery'. John Donne and George Herbert are similarly regarded. In this poem Vaughan is contrasting the false life with the real life, the latter being that which is God-inspired, God-directed. People are often content with a 'foil' – not the real thing. Man is 'moon-like', that is he is for ever changing. He is 'self-posing' – that is tying himself up in knots with problems he is not able to resolve. The reader is invited to contrast that sort of life, depicted in the first two verses of the poem, with the Life which is discerning, never fitful, never dull, never boring. Those who are dedicated to that life must nevertheless beware. Man is a 'toilsome mole' – that burrowing little mammal who runs around spoiling our lawns! He is 'a moving mist' which blurs the real life to which Vaughan is directing his readers. 'I am come that they might have life and life overflowing' (St. John ch.10 v.10).

Prayer

Teach me, good Lord, the art of Life, and so to reverence it day by day, that in work and in leisure, and in my relationship with all whom I shall meet, your Way may direct me, your Truth may hold me firm, and your Life may fill me with that Love which is Eternal.

Be Thyself

'Know thyself' was written over the portal of the antique world. Over the portal of the new world, 'Be thyself' shall be written. The message of Christ to Man was simple 'Be thyself'. That is the secret of Christ . . . and so he who would lead a Christian life is he who is perfectly and absolutely himself. He may be a great poet, or a great man of science, or a young student at a university, or one who watches sheep upon a moor; or a maker of dramas, like Shakespeare, or a thinker about God, like Spinoza; or a child who plays in a garden, or a fisherman who throws his net into the sea. It does not matter what he is, as long as he realises the perfection of the soul that is within him. All imitation in morals and in life is wrong. Father Damien was Christlike when he went out to live with the lepers because in such service he realised fully what was best in him. But he was not more Christlike than Wagner when he realised his soul in music; or than Shelley, when he realised his soul in song. There is no one type for man. And while to the claim of charity a man may yield and yet be free, to the claims of conformity no man may yield and remain free at all.

OSCAR WILDE (1854–1900)

Comment

Some may think it strange that Oscar Wilde should find place in a book of this nature. Distinguished playwright that he was, he outraged the conventions of his day by some of his writings and by much of his conduct. But in the essay from which the quotation is an extract, as well as in *De Profundis*, he reveals that behind the pose and facade which shocked people, there was a deep-seated belief waiting to break through. In *The Ballad of Reading Gaol*, written in the course of his two year sentence there, he asks 'How else but through a broken heart may Lord Christ enter in?' He came to realise that what he calls 'the perfection of the soul that is within' is what man is in the world to achieve. Only so can a man be the self which God means him to be. Christians know that the path to that end is discerned, sustained and achieved by communion with God. By that communion, and only by that communion, can man be himself! It is not that we have to set out to realise ourselves. We have to set out to serve by using such gifts as we have to the glory of God and the benefit of our fellows. So shall we realise ourselves.

Prayer *Guide us, teach us, and strengthen us, O Lord, that we may become such as you would have us be – pure, gentle, truthful, courteous, generous and loving – reaching ever towards that perfection which you have set before us as our true vocation.*

Night and Death

Mysterious night! when our first parent knew
      Thee from report divine, and heard thy name,
      Did he not tremble for this lovely frame,
This glorious canopy of light and blue?
Yet, 'neath a curtain of translucent dew,
      Bathed in the rays of the great setting flame,
      Hesperus with the hosts of heaven came,
And lo! Creation widened in man's view.
Who could have thought such darkness now concealed
      Within thy beams, O Sun! or who could find
Whilst flower and leaf, and insect stood revealed
      That to such countless orbs thou mad'st us blind!
Why do we then shun death with anxious strife?
If Light can thus deceive, wherefore not Life?

BLANCO WHITE (1775–1841)

Comment

The author of this great sonnet was a Roman Catholic priest who became an Anglican and subsequently a Unitarian. If that betrays a measure of uncertainty in his ecclesiastical and theological convictions, here are words which leave no one in doubt as to his belief about life after death. In *The Bijou*, which he wrote in 1828, he looks at the wonders of the natural world and ponders how 'our first parent' must have been bewildered by the process of divine creation – darkness and light, sun and moon and stars, birds of the air, trees and flowers and leaves. It is as though he could hear 'our first parent' as the process developed, exclaim 'Whatever next?' – and always the 'next' proved to be far more wonderful than he could have anticipated. The Light seemed always to prove his speculations to be far less wonderful than the Creator's consummations. In his last two lines he poses the same sort of question with which St Paul confronted King Agrippa when he was defending himself against the accusations being levelled against him. 'Why is it thought incredible by any of you that God raises the dead?'(Acts ch.26 vv.2–6). 'Be of good cheer about death', said Socrates, and Christians can say 'Amen' to that. But Christians can go beyond that comforting exhortation. They have the assurance which Easter confirms: 'As in Adam all die, even so in Christ shall all be made alive'.

Prayer   *Receive, O Lord, in tranquillity and peace, the souls of thy servants who have departed to be with thee. Grant them rest and place them in the habitations of life, the abodes of blessed spirits; give them the life that knoweth not age and the good things that pass not away; through Jesus Christ our Lord.*

ST IGNATIUS LOYOLA (1491–1556)

Commemorating Catherine of Sienna, Mystic, died 1380

Yet I say that God demands of us, that as He has loved us without any second thoughts, so He should be loved by us. We are bound to Him, and not He to us because before He was loved, He loved us... To show the love we have for Him, we ought to serve and love every rational creature and extend our charity to good and bad, that is as much to one who does us ill service, and criticises us, as to one who serves us, for His charity extends over just men and sinners.

We must receive that sweet Sacrament because it is the food of our souls, for without that food we cannot preserve the life of grace. A man should do what he can to remove such things as would hinder his approach and when he has done all he can, it is enough. It may seem to him that he has not perfect contrition, but he is not to stay away on that account, for his goodwill is sufficient and that is the real disposition required of him. I will not, therefore, have you act as those who neglect to fulfil the precept of the Church, because, as they say, they are not worthy, and so they pass years in sin and never receive the food of their souls... God alone is worthy of himself, and He can render us worthy by His own worthiness, which never diminishes.

ST CATHERINE OF SIENNA (1346–1380)

Comment

Catherine of Sienna was a great letter-writer and many hundreds of her letters have survived. Quotations from two of them appear here. She wrote to kings, priests, bishops, popes, scholars and others in humbler station who sought her advice. Very early in her life she had joined the Religious Order of St Dominic and after living as a recluse for three years, she moved out into the world to a ministry of healing in the course of which many miraculous cures were attributed to her. So much was she loved and admired that recipients of her letters received her counsel gladly. In a letter to Pope Gregory she persuaded him to leave the delights of Avignon to return to Rome where, as she told him, 'perils and malaria and discomforts await you'. For her part she demonstrated her love of God not only in her prayers and worship, but in the boundless charity she extended to all those whose needs came to her notice. Undoubtedly the Holy Sacrament was a source of strength to her and in the second letter extract above, she bids all who would know the love of God and mediate that same love to others, to be meticulous in their attendance at Holy Communion and in their reception of the Sacrament. What excuses for absenting ourselves do we make? Would St Catherine regard them as valid?

Prayer

O Eternal Trinity, with Thy light Thou dost illuminate me so that I might know all Thy truth. In the light of faith, I am strong, constant and persevering; in the light of faith, I hope. Suffer me not to faint by the way. Clothe me, O Eternal Truth that I may run my mortal course with true obedience and the light of holy faith.

ST CATHERINE

One Man's Life

Faith is a state of mind and the soul. The language of religion is not a set of formulae which register a basic spiritual experience. It must not be regarded in terms to be defined by philosophy, the reality which is accessible to our senses, and which we can analyse with the tools of logic. I was late in understanding what this meant. When I finally reached that point, the beliefs in which I was once brought up, and which in fact had given my life direction even while my intellect still challenged their validity, were recognised by me as my own right and by my free choice. . . I found love in the writings of those great mediaeval mystics, for whom self-surrender had been the means of self-realisation, and who in 'singleness of mind' and 'inwardness' had found strength to say 'Yes' to every demand which the needs of their neighbours made them face. Love, that much misused and misinterpreted word, meant for them simply an overflowing of the strength with which they felt themselves filled when living in true self-oblivion. And this love found natural expression in an unhesitating fulfilment of duty, and an unreserved acceptance of life whatever it brought them personally of toil, of suffering – or of happiness.

DAG HAMMARSKJÖLD (1905–1961)

Comment

Nowhere in *Markings*, which is in effect the story of Hammarskjöld's pilgrimage to God, is there anything which will tell those who handle the book in years to come that its author was a Civil Servant – a man of God who rose to become Secretary-General of the United Nations, and who saw the opportunities which his high office afforded him as a way in which he could fulfil a mission near to the heart of God. The quotation above is not, in fact, a part of *Markings* proper, but part of a radio talk which Dag made when he took up his office. In that memorable broadcast he left no one in doubt as to where he stood in his attitude to life. 'All men are equal as children of God', he said, and as he went from country to country he lived what he believed. In prose and poetry, some of it jotted down as airplanes whisked him around the world as adviser, as reconciler and as peacemaker, he makes it clear that his faith was the touchstone of his life. 'Love life and men as God loves them, then he can use you, and if he doesn't use you, what matter? In his hand, every moment has its meaning, its greatness, its glory, its peace'. Such a sentiment challenges all Christians to ask themselves: 'How does my faith reveal itself in my daily work?'

Prayer

Here is one of Dag Hammarskjöld's prayers:

Give me a pure heart that I may see Thee,
A humble heart – that I may hear Thee,
A heart of love – that I may serve Thee
A heart of faith – that I may abide in Thee.

St Philip and St James, Apostles

O little self, within whose smallness lies
All that man was, and is, and will become;
Atom unseen that comprehends the skies
And tells the tracks by which the planets roam;
That, without moving, knows the joys of wings,
The tiger's strength, the eagle's secrecy,
And in the hovel can consort with kings,
Or clothe a God with his own mystery,
O with what darkness do we cloak thy light
What dusty folly gather thee for food,
Thou who alone art knowledge and delight,
The heavenly bread, the beautiful, the good,
O living self, O God, O morning star,
Give us thy light, forgive us what we are.

JOHN MASEFIELD (1878-1967)

Comment

When we meet these two apostles in the Gospel story neither strikes us as an outstanding personality. Each might be described as 'a little self', hidden 'within whose smallness' our Lord saw great potential for ministry. Philip was decisive at the moment of his call and quickly enlisted Bartholomew to the service of his Christ. Subsequently he appears as the hesitant apostle, seeming to pass the responsibility for decision to another. In the feeding of the multitude he was baffled when our Lord turned to him in the emergency, and it was left to Andrew to spot the little lad whose ready co-operation saved the day. Again, when the Greek tourists in the Temple addressed their request to Philip (prompted perhaps by hearing his Greek name), he answered their 'Sir, we would see Jesus', by passing them over to Andrew. It was Philip too who, on the night before the Passion, said to Jesus, 'Lord, show us the Father', a request which earned for him the gentle rebuke of our Lord: 'Have I been so long time with you Philip and yet you do not know me?... I am in the Father, and the Father is in me'. Both James, of whom little is known, and the hesitant Philip might have said 'O little self... with what darkness do we clothe thy light'. Modest, hesitating saints they were, but used mightily for God's purpose! There are times when we feel ourselves to be so 'little' that we have nothing to offer in Christian ministry, but turning to God and praying. 'Give us thy light', we shall be shown the path to service and given the strength to follow it.

Prayer   *Lord God, strengthen us to meet all the experiences of life with undaunted courage, illuminate the darkness of our minds by the light of your visitation, and when we know the way, but hesitate to follow it, steel our wills to your service, through Jesus Christ our Lord.*

Commemorating Athanasius, Bishop of Alexandria, Teacher of the Faith

'And was made Man'

Now if they ask, why then did He not appear by means of other and nobler parts of creation, and use some nobler instrument, as the sun or moon, or stars, or fire, or air, instead of man merely? Let them know that the Lord came not to make a display, but to heal and teach those who were suffering. For the way for one aiming at display would be just to appear and to dazzle the beholders; but for one seeking to heal and teach, the way is, not simply to sojourn here, but to give himself to the aid of those in want, and to appear as they who need him can bear it; that he may not, by exceeding the requirements of the sufferers, trouble the very persons that need him, rendering God's appearance useless to them.... God takes to Himself an instrument, a part of the whole, the human body, and unites himself with that, in order that since men could not recognise Him in the whole, they should not fail to know Him in the part; and since they could not look up to His invisible power, might be able at any rate, from what resembled themselves, to reason to Him and to contemplate Him.

ST ATHANASIUS (296–373)

Comment

Athanasius has been called 'the Champion of Orthodoxy'. Ordained at the age of 21 he soon became known for his service to the Bishop of Alexandria, and for his writings, among them his great work on the Incarnation from which the quotation is an excerpt. But it was his defence of the Catholic Faith against the heresy of Arianism, which denied the Divinity of Christ, which set him high among the teachers of the Church. At the Council of Nicaea, he was present as the Bishop's secretary, and his speech against the heresy propagated by Arius resulted in the excommunication of the heretic. It was at that Council that the first Nicene Creed was promulgated. Three years later, in 328, Athanasius became Bishop of Alexandria. He ministered to his vast diocese with great devotion and when the Christian Faith was established in Ethiopia he appointed its first bishop. But his battles against the heretics never ceased, and frequently he found himself having to defend the Faith against the civil powers as well as the followers of Arius. In the course of his episcopate he was banished five times, covering seventeen years, and only for seven years before he died was the 'bishop who planted trees under which men of a later age might sit', able to apply himself to his own appointed work without hindrance. Men of the calibre of Athanasius – 'the Champion of Orthodoxy' may not rise up in every age – but in every age Christians must be alert to defend the truth against falsehood and the Faith against heresy.

Prayer *May the Spirit Who proceeds from Thee, O Lord, illuminate our minds and, as Thy Son hath promised, lead us into all truth; through Jesus Christ our Lord.*

Farewell to the World

The old order changeth, yielding place to new,
And God fulfils Himself in many ways,
Lest one good custom should corrupt the world.
Comfort thyself; what comfort is in me?
I have lived my life, and that which I have done
May He within Himself make pure! But thou,
If thou should'st never see my face again,
Pray for my soul! More things are wrought by prayer
Than this world dreams of. Wherefore let thy voice
Rise like a fountain for me night and day.
For what are men better than sheep or goats
That nourish a blind life within the brain,
If, knowing God, they lift not hands of prayer
Both for themselves and those who call them friend?
For so the whole round Earth is every way
Bound by gold chains about the feet of God.

ALFRED TENNYSON (1809–1892)

Comment

This extract, from Tennyson's *Morte d'Arthur* has within it perhaps the most well-known call to prayer in the whole realm of secular poetry. It sets out in three of its lines an essential truth about prayer, namely that it is supremely an activity which marks man off from the lower animals – an act lifting him into the conscious presence of his creator. There are innumerable references to prayer both in the Old and New Testaments, and all of them make it clear, in one way or another, that prayer is not an optional extra in the exercise of our religion, but an essential element in it. Jesus said, '*When you pray, say Our Father*', not '*If you pray . . .* '. Prayer is the activity in which we consciously and deliberately seek to align ourselves with God's purpose both for ourselves and His world. It calls not for eloquence but for earnestness, for silence as much as for speech, for contemplation and confession, for commitment and confidence, and for persistent and patient intercession. Prayer does not change God, but it changes the one who prays to God, since it opens his mind to the inflow of the Mind of God. There is nothing in our daily lives – the distressing, the trivial, the joyous, the disgraceful, the painful, the exhilarating – which we cannot lay before God in prayer. All such experiences touch us at the very centre of our being, our souls, and the pouring out of the soul to God through Christ in the strength of the Spirit is prayer. How do we think of prayer, and does our thinking lead us on to action?

Prayer   *Eternal Light, illuminate us; Eternal Power, strengthen us; Eternal*
Wisdom, instruct us; Eternal Mercy, have pity on us; and grant us
with all our hearts and minds to seek Thy face, and to love Thy name,
through Jesus Christ our Lord.

WILLIAM BRIGHT (1824–1901)

'When you pray...'

First must be put the fundamental principle that God is perfect love and wisdom; He has no need that we should tell Him of our wants and desires; He knows what is for our good better than we do ourselves, and it is always His will to give it... Consequently we must not in our prayer have any thought of suggesting to God what was not in His mind or purpose. The first requirement of prayer is that we trust to God for all blessings... The next requirement is that we should persevere in prayer in spite of disappointment. We are to go on praying... The purpose of God's delay may well be to detach our faith in Him from all trust in our own judgment. Scarcely anything deepens and purifies faith in God for His own sake as surely as perseverance in prayer, despite long disappointment.

The purification of confidence by perseverance leads us to the third and deepest requirement. The other two were enjoined upon all His hearers; this was urged upon His more intimate disciples... 'Whatsoever ye shall ask *in My name*; this will I do that the Father may be glorified in the Son. If ye shall ask anything in My name, I will do it (St John ch.14 vv.13/14). This means that the essential act of prayer is not the bending of God's will to ours... but the bending of our wills to His. The proper outline of a Christian's prayer is not, 'Please do for me what I want', but 'Please do in me, with me, and through me, what you want'.

WILLIAM TEMPLE (1881–1944)

Comment

William Temple's *Readings from St John's Gospel* is a classic commentary, profound in its depth of penetration and understanding, yet written in a manner which enables ordinary Christians, untrained in the language of theology, to appreciate the treasure of divine truth which is the Fourth Gospel. Naturally he draws special attention to our Lord's teaching on prayer which is set down in Chapters 14, 15 and 16 of that Gospel, and he goes further and expounds our Lord's pattern for prayer 'When you pray say: Our Father...' (St Luke ch.11 v.2).

Prayer   *My God and Father, help me to pray as my first work, mine unremitting work, my highest, finest and dearest work; as the work I do for thee, and by thee, and with thee, for thy other children and for the whole world. Infuse and influence it with Thy blessed Spirit that it be not unwilling, nor unworthy, nor in vain, that it be not occupied with my own concerns, nor dwell in the interests, dear to myself, but seek Thy purposes, Thy glory only, and all through Thy Son, my Saviour, Jesus Christ.*

ERIC MILNER WHITE

Asking aright

I asked for strength that I might achieve:
I was made weak that I might learn humbly to obey.
I asked for health that I might do greater things:
I was given infirmity that I might do better things.
I asked for riches that I might be happy:
I was given poverty that I might be wise.
I asked for power that I might have the praise of men;
I was given weakness that I might feel the need of God.
I asked for all things that I might enjoy life;
I was given life that I might enjoy all things.
I got nothing that I asked for –
But everything that I had hoped for.
Almost despite myself my unspoken prayers were answered;
I am, among all men, most richly blessed.

A SOLDIER'S PRAYER
ANONYMOUS

Comment

His 'askings' appear not to have been 'askings' at all – at least, not spoken. They
were, I imagine, the 'I wish I could . . . ', 'I wish that . . . 'type of unspoken desires which slip through the mind, and off the tongue, without a great deal of thought
from time to time. But this unknown soldier clearly possessed a deeper faith than
he realised, and that faith sustained hopes which, unrecognised and unspoken,
were in God's good time realised to his great joy. All of us will, from time to time,
falter in our 'askings', both for ourselves and for others, but God in His love will
not indict us for this. He will rejoice that we bring what we conceive to be our
deepest needs, and the deepest needs of others, before Him. To wish is one thing.
To pray is quite another. The unknown soldier's 'askings' were in fact 'wishings'.
But deep in his heart were unexpressed hopes which prompted him to recognise
his weakness, his infirmity and his poverty, not as punishments from God, but
testings of his faith. He passed all the tests, and thus became of 'all men most richly blessed'. It is as though God poses the question: 'Are you ready to accept what
I do with your 'wishings'?

Prayer   *Lord, we know not what we ought to ask of Thee; Thou only knowest*
what we need; Thou lovest us better than we know how to love our-
selves; Father, give to us Thy children, that which we ourselves know
not how to ask. We would have no other desire than to accomplish Thy
will. Teach us to pray. Pray Thyself in us; for Christ's sake.

FRANCOIS DE FENELON (1651–1715)

Prayers and their answers

Just a lovely little child – three years old,
And a mother with a heart – all of gold.
Often did that mother say,
'Jesus answers when we pray
For he's never far away.
Jesus always answers'.

Now that tiny little child had brown eyes,
And she wanted blue instead, like blue skies,
For her mother's eyes were blue,
Like forget-me-nots, she knew.
All her mother said was true.
Jesus always answers.

So she prayed for two blue eyes. Said 'Good-Night',
Went to sleep in deep content, and delight.
Woke up early, climbed a chair
By a mirror. Where, O where
Could the blue eyes be?
Jesus hadn't answered.

Hadn't answered her at all; nevermore
Could she pray; her eyes were brown as before.
Did a little soft wind blow?
Came a whisper, soft and low.
Jesus answered, He said 'No'.
Isn't 'No' an answer?

AMY CARMICHAEL (1867–1951)

Comment

Amy Carmichael was born in Northern Ireland and at the age of 20 felt called
to missionary work overseas. She spent a year in Japan and the rest of her life in
India caring for children at Dohnavur. In her day she was as well-known for her
caring work as is Mother Teresa today. Much of her writing is severely practical
but through it also there shines her spiritual motivation. She is indeed a mystic,
and both in her poems and prose writings – most now out of print, alas! – she
displays a spiritual perception and power which reveals how closely she walked
with God. This exquisitely beautiful prayer – rare among hers for its simplicity
– offers the answer to a question which puzzles not only little girls but adults too.
We may seek from God something for which we yearn and sense to be wholly good
for us, but His answer will be 'No' if, in His wisdom, our plea is ill-founded or
ill-advised.

Prayer   *We beseech Thee, O Lord, to look upon Thy servants, whom thou hast*
enabled to put their trust in Thee, and grant us both to ask such things
as shall please Thee, and also to obtain what we ask; through Jesus
Christ our Lord.

LEONINE SACRAMENTARY

An Earnest Prayer

Wilt thou not visit me?
The plant beside me feels thy gentle dew,
*   And every blade of grass I see*
From thy deep earth its quickening moisture drew.
Wilt thou not visit me?
Thy morning calls on me with cheerful tone,
*   And every hill and tree*
Lend but one voice − the voice of Thee alone.
Come, for I need thy love,
More than the flowers the dew, or grass the rain;
*   Come gently as thy holy dove;*
And let me in thy sight rejoice to live again.
I will not hide from them
When thy storms come, though fierce may be their wrath,
*   But bow with leafy stem,*
And, strengthened, follow on thy chosen path.
Yes, thou wilt visit me;
Nor plant, nor tree, thine eye delights so well,
*   As, when from sin set free,*
My spirit loves with thine in peace to dwell.

JONES VERY (1813–1880)

Comment

The prayer is one from the pen and from the heart of an American Unitarian minister, a friend of the more famous Ralph Waldo Emerson. His poems were few and appeared for the most part only in Christian magazines in the United States. In this poem this man of prayer is experiencing a period of dryness when, as it seemed to him, his God was more concerned with the grandeur of the natural world which, in its beauty, responded to its Creator's love. Some of this poet's time was spent as a patient in an asylum and it may be that this poem in which he pleads 'let me in thy sight rejoice to live again' was a plea for release from his mental condition. This was, in fact, effected by Emerson's intervention, who declared that, far from being insane, his friend was spiritually and mentally tired. Most Christians go through periods of spiritual dryness such as our poet was experiencing. But such periods call, not for a sorry surrender, but for patient perseverance. There is a word for it in *The Cloud of Unknowing*, that great classic of mysticism: 'Smite upon that thick cloud of unknowing with a sharp sword of longing love. Come what may, do not give up'.

Prayer   *Almighty God, in whom is no darkness at all: grant us Thy light per-*
petually, and when we cannot see the way before us, may we continue
to put our trust in Thee that so, being guided and guarded by Thy love,
we may be kept from falling, this day and all our days, through Jesus
Christ our Lord.

WILLIAM KNIGHT

Commemorating Julian of Norwich, Mystic, died 1417

All shall be well

On one occasion, the good Lord said, 'Everything is going to be all right'. On another, 'You will see for yourself that every sort of thing will be all right'. In these two sayings the soul discerns various meanings. The first, that he wants us to know that not only does he care for great and noble things, but equally for little and small, lowly and simple things as well. This is his meaning: '*Everything* will be all right'. We are to know that the least thing will not be forgotten.

Another is this: we see deeds done that are so evil, and injuries inflicted that are so great, that it seems to us quite impossible that any good can come of them. As we consider these, sorrowfully and mournfully, we cannot relax in the blessed contemplation of God as we ought. This is caused by the fact that our reason is now so blind, base, and ignorant that we are unable to know that supreme and marvellous wisdom, might and goodness which belong to the blessed Trinity. This is the meaning of His word, 'You will see for yourself that every sort of thing will be all right'. It is as if he were saying, 'Be careful now to believe and trust, and in the end you will see it all in its fullness and joy'. So from those same six words 'I shall make everything all right', I gain great comfort with regard to all the works that God has still to do.

MOTHER JULIAN OF NORWICH (1342–1417)

Comment

The mystic, Julian of Norwich, found no place in the calendar of the Book of Common Prayer, nor did she appear in Butler's *Lives of the Saints* but within living memory she has come to be recognised as one of the most remarkable women in the history of the Church in this land. Thomas Merton wrote of her in 1977 'She gets greater and greater in my eyes as I grow older... I think that Julian of Norwich is with Newman the greatest English Theologian'. Not too soon therefore has our Church found a place for her in the roll of its great saints. Julian became an anchoress – a woman who set herself aside to live a life which glorified God and afforded her opportunity to set down in writing an account of her 'shewings' or 'visions' to help others to know, to love and to trust the God to whom she was totally dedicated. She lived her life in a 'cell' hard by St Julian's Church in Norwich – a cell which is still there, and to which peole go from all over the world to pray where she prayed, to meditate where she meditated, and to renew their confidence in the love of God as she renewed hers. It was there that she wrote her *Revelations of Divine Love*, from which the above quotation is extracted. Words of hers, based on the above, have become an assurance which has gone around the Christian world: 'All shall be well, and all shall be well, and all manner of thing shall be well'.

Prayer *Most Holy Lord, the ground of our beseeching, who through your servant Julian revealed the wonder of your love; grant that as we are created in your nature and restored by your grace, our wills may be so made one with yours, that we may come to see you face to face and gaze on you for ever.*

The goodness and love of God

To know the goodness of God is the highest prayer of all, and it is a prayer that accommodates itself to our most lowly needs. It quickens our soul, and vitalises it, developing it in grace and virtue. Here is the grace most propriate to our need, and most ready to help. Here is the grace which our soul is seeking now, and which it will ever seek until that day when we know for a fact that he has wholly united us to himself. He does not despise the work of his hands, nor does he disdain to serve us, however lowly our natural need may be. He loves the soul he has made in his own likenesss. For just as the body is clothed in its garments, and the flesh in its skin, and the bones in their flesh, and the heart in its body, so too are we, soul and body, clothed from head to foot in the goodness of God. Yes, and even more closely than that, for all these things will decay and wear out, whereas the goodness of God is unchanging, and incomparably more suited to us. Our lover desires indeed that our soul should cleave to him with all its might, and ever hold on to his goodness...

The love of God Most High for our soul is so wonderful that it surpasses all knowledge. No created being can know the greatness, the sweetness, the tenderness of the love that your Maker has for us. By his grace and help therefore let us in spirit stand and gaze, eternally marvelling at the surpassing, single-minded, incalculable love that God, who is Goodness, has for us.

LADY JULIAN OF NORWICH (1342–1417)

Comment

Following her commemoration yesterday it seems fitting to use her words to lead us back to the theme of Prayer which we have been following this month. Julian described her *Revelations of Divine Love* as 'made to an uneducated person in A.D.1373', but it would seem that that means no more than that the Nuns of the Benedictine Priory, which gave her her schooling, did not teach her Latin! But that she was advanced in the life of prayer there can be no doubt and that she started to pray, as it were, at 'the right end' – that is in an awareness of the boundless love of God, and in a conviction that those who pray aright place themselves consciously and deliberately within the ambit of God's love. There are, of course, different types of prayer – adoration, thanksgiving, penitence, petition, intercession – but none has meaning unless it is addressed with conviction to God Who is Love.

Prayer   *Lord of Love, help us to love you and all others in you, and at the last to meet before you in your everlasting love; through Jesus Christ our Lord.*

Inside the Castle

Souls without prayer are like bodies, palsied and lame, having hands and feet they cannot use. Just so there are souls so infirm and accustomed to think of nothing but earthly matters, that there seems no cure for them. It appears impossible for them to retire into their own hearts; they are so accustomed to be with the reptiles and other creatures which live outside the castle, as to come at last to imitate their habits.

Let us think no more of those crippled souls. We will now think of these others who at last enter the precincts of the castle; they are still very worldly, yet have some desire to do right, and at times, though rarely, commend themselves to God's care. They think about their souls every now and then; although very busy, they pray a few times a month, with their minds generally filled with a thousand other matters, for where their treasure is, there is their heart also... At length they enter the first rooms in the basement of the castle, accompanied by numbers of reptiles which disturb their peace, and prevent them seeing the beauty of the buildings; still it is a great gain to have found their way in at all.

ST TERESA (1515–1582)

Comment

St Teresa wrote a book about prayer, a subject of which she is no mean teacher. She called her book *The Interior Castle*. She sees the soul as a great castle and just as prayer has many facets, so the castle, which is the soul, has many rooms. There are, she laments, so many who never enter the castle at all – those whose hearts and minds are wholly rivetted to the things of earth. There are others who step inside occasionally, and invariably with some hesitation – but even that gains something for themselves and maybe for their friends. But for the deepest and most valuable experience of all we must go into the innermost room of the castle, there to lay bare our souls to God our Maker undisturbed by the multitude of 'earthly matters' which rightly demand our attention at other times. It will be in the silence of that inner room that we see God face to face, that we experience His love for us, that we talk to Him as to our Father and take from Him a Father's love, a Father's guidance, a Father's forgiveness and a Father's encouragement to go on our way again rejoicing. Pose the question to yourself 'Have I penetrated the castle, and if so have I reached its innermost room?'

Prayer   *Govern all by Thy wisdom, O Lord, so that my soul will always be serving Thee as Thou dost will, and not as I may choose. Do not punish me, I beseech Thee, by granting that which I wish or ask, if it offend Thy love, which would always live in me. Let me die to myself, that I may serve Thee; let me live to Thee, who in Thyself art the true Life.*

ST TERESA

Let me lean Hard

Let me lean hard upon the Eternal Breast;
In all earth's devious ways, I sought for rest
And found it not. I will be strong, said I,
And lean upon myself. I will not cry
And importune all heaven with my complaint.
But now my strength fails, and I fall, I faint;
  Let me lean hard.
Let me lean hard upon the unfailing Arm;
I said I will walk on, I fear no harm,
The spark divine within my soul will show
The upward pathway where my feet should go;
But now the heights to which I most aspire
Are lost in clouds. I stumble and I tire,
  Let me lean hard.
Let me lean harder yet. That swerveless force
Which speeds the solar systems on their course
Can take unfelt, the burden of my woe,
Which bears me to the dust and hurts me so.
I thought my strength enough for any fate,
But help! I sink beneath my sorrow's weight.
  Let me lean hard.

ELLA WHEELER WILCOX (1855–1919)

Comment

It is as though the poet was indicting herself for putting her trust not in God but in her own native strength sufficient as, momentarily, it seemed to be. Trust in God in the affairs of our daily life with its problems to resolve, its difficulties to overcome and its daily tasks to discharge, does not supercede the application of our own prudent means to achieve the ends we desire. That way we should merely be tempting providence. To lean hard on God in prayer is not to impose upon him burdens which he expects us to bear alone. It is to put our trust where our love is and to know that, moving forward with an unfaltering trust in God's love for us is the sure way by which we shall be aware of the pull and the power of 'the unfailing Arm'. When the will is dedicated, the way is directed. 'There is but one way to browbeat this world', said Robert Browning, 'It is to go on trusting, namely, till faith move mountains.

Prayer *O Lord Jesus Christ, Who art the Way, the Truth, and the Life, we pray Thee to suffer us not to stray from Thee, who art the Way, nor to distrust Thee, who art the Truth, nor to rest in any other thing than Thee, who art the Life. Teach us by Thy Holy Spirit what to believe, what to do, and wherein to take our rest.*

ERASMUS (1466–1536)

Gratification

I longed for Wealth!
Aye! toiled for it with zeal that never grew cold,
Till everything I touched just turned to gold –
'Twould not buy health.

I longed for Fame!
Aye! sought to be renowned from pole to pole,
And, after striving years, I reached my goal –
But what's a Name!

I longed for Power!
Aye! strove to scale Ambition's lofty height –
And reached in time my pinnacle of Might –
Still life was sour!

I longed for Grace!
And as I turned my back on worldly things
I seemed to hear the beat of angel-wings
And see God's Face!

MARGARET PIERCE

Comment

Here is a poet who echoes an experience which may well have been her own, and in so doing she tells the sad tale of many more who go far beyond verse three of her poem, in frantic efforts to attain some goal which can afford them no lasting satisfaction. Wealth, Fame, Power, Ambition, Security – these are not intrinsically evil, unless they become the consuming passion of a man's life. The Tenth Commandment may not be heard very frequently in our churches today but the sin against which it warns us, namely covetousness, which is the ground of all vice, is the world's besetting sin. 'Take heed', said our Lord, 'and beware of covetousness, for a man's life does not consist in the abundance of his possessions' (St Luke ch.12 v.15). That is not an exhortation to be shiftless or thriftless in our daily lives. It is an exhortation to put first things first and to remember, as our poet reminds us, that Grace is first of all. The verses embrace a warning about the substance of our prayers and the conduct of our lives. There is no merit in tormenting ourselves with idle wishes for things which may well remain for ever beyond our reach; but to seek the Grace of God in our prayers is to open our minds and hearts for the inflow of His Spirit to enlighten and to inspire.

Prayer *O God, whose grace is sufficient for all our need: lift us, we pray thee, above our doubts and anxieties into the calm of thy presence; that guarded by thy peace we may serve thee without fear all the days of our life; through Jesus Christ our Lord.*

Purity of Motive

I asked the Lord that I might grow
        In faith and love and every grace;
Might more of his salvation know,
        And seek more earnestly his face.

I thought that in some favoured hour
        At once he'd answer my request;
And by his love's constraining power,
        Subdue my sins and give me rest.

Instead of this he made me feel
        The hidden evils of my heart,
And let the angry powers of hell
        Assault my soul in every part.

'Lord, why is this?', I trembling cried,
        'Wilt thou pursue thy worm to death?'
''Tis in this way,' the Lord replied,
        'I answer prayer for grace and faith'.

'These inward trials I employ,
        From self and pride to set thee free,
And break thy schemes of earthly joy,
        That thou may'st seek thy all in me'.

JOHN NEWTON (1725–1807)

Comment

The poet has apprently learnt two lessons which can help others who seek to pray. The first touches purity of motive; the second, that whilst the Christian's sincere prayer never goes unanswered, the answer, when it comes, may nevertheless be not what was anticipated. Here the prayer seemed to be wholly good – a prayer for 'faith and love and every grace', but it did not win from God the sense of release from sins which was anticipated. 'The hidden evils' of the heart rose up, as in anger as it were, to sustain their possession of the soul. God's answer to the prayer was in effect to say: 'There can be no rest such as you seek without repentance'. St Augustine expressed the truth succinctly when he said 'Before God can deliver us, we must undeceive ourselves'. That means that repentance is to alter our direction, looking at life from God's point of view rather than our own. Merely to experience grief for any sin of omission or commission to which we have fallen is but stage one of true repentance. We must move on from there to turn our sorrow into penitence and so clear the way for God's forgiveness and to experience renewal of 'faith and love and every grace'.

Prayer   *O God, our Judge and Saviour, set before us the vision of thy purity, and let us see sin in the light of thy holiness. Pierce our self-contentment with the shafts of thy burning love, and let that love consume in us all that hinders us from perfect service of thy cause; for as thy holiness is our judgment, so are thy wounds our salvation.*

WILLIAM TEMPLE (1881–1944)

St Matthias the Apostle

When earth's last picture is painted,
  And the tubes are twisted and dried,
When the oldest colours have faded,
  And the youngest critic has died,
We shall rest, and, faith, we shall need it,
  Lie down for an aeon or two,
Till the Master of All Good Workmen
  Shall put us to work anew.
And only the Master shall praise us
  And only the Master shall blame;
And no one shall work for money,
  And no one shall work for fame,
But each for the joy of the working,
  And each in his separate star,
Shall draw the Thing as he sees It
  For the God of the things as they are.

RUDYARD KIPLING (1865–1936)

Comment

Matthias might be called 'the unknown Apostle'. Appointed by lot to succeed the traitor Judas, he disappears at once from the story. Certainly he did not 'work for fame', or he might have earned more than one mention in Holy Scripture. Maybe he was one of the Seventy Disciples whom Jesus appointed, and who subsequently returned excitedly to report how well their mission had been received. Apocryphal tradition suggests that he preached the Gospel in Ethiopia, that he wrote a Gospel, that he suffered martyrdom in Jerusalem, spurning a suggestion of the prosecuting judge that he should renounce Christ with the affirmation 'God forbid that I should repent of the truth that I have truly found and become an apostate'. So there he is among the Twelve – unsung, all but unknown, working 'in his separate star', neither for money nor for fame, but winning undoubtedly 'the Master's praise'. There are a great many more who could be such – people whose gifts may be modest indeed. Blest as they are by the 'God of things as they are' they could 'draw the Thing as they see it', to God's glory and to his people's welfare. Fame is not a necessary hall-mark of Christian commitment, and 'the joy of the working, each in his separate star' is the richest reward a man could ever receive.

Prayer *O Lord Jesus Christ, in all the fullness of thy power so gentle, in thine exceeding greatness so humble: bestow thy mind and spirit upon us who have nothing whereof to boast; that clothed in true humility we may be exalted to true greatness. Grant this, O Lord, who livest and reignest with the Father and the Holy Spirit, one God for evermore.*

Worship

Worship is the most practical thing in all existence. It is a fundamental attitude of mind, and it consequently determines our approach to the whole of life. By it we recognise a standard to be accepted as absolute, as altogether good, and true, and beautiful, before which we must bow in respect and adoration. Those who have no such guide are left rudderless on an uncharted sea. Sooner or later they founder in their own abysmal ignorance, or they run aground in shallows and in miseries.

We might well be lost and terrified in the search for such an absolute to which we can attach our allegiance and find safety. For the Christian, however, it has been revealed and that, not as some austere and unattainable idea, but as a loving Creator, Redeemer and Friend, who is no mere figure in past history or remote influence beyond the furtherest star, but a Person who enters into most intimate union with us 'closer to us than breathing, nearer than hands or feet'. There is our hope and strength, the source of our hope and confidence in the grim but exhilarating battle of life.

To worship is –

to quicken the conscience by the holiness of God,
to feed the mind with the truth of God,
to purge the imagination by the beauty of God,
to open the heart to the love of God,
to devote the will to the purpose of God.

All this is gathered up in that emotion which most cleanses us from selfishness because it is the most selfless of all emotions – adoration.

WILLIAM TEMPLE (1881–1944)

Comment

So much and so eloquently did William Temple write and speak about the meaning and purpose of worship that I have extracted two paragraphs from two of his books. What he says applies equally to private and to public worship. Our private prayers must begin, continue and end with adoration. So too in public worship. Isaiah began his prayers with adoration: 'Holy, Holy, Holy, is the Lord of Hosts, the whole earth is full of His glory'. It is against the holiness of God that he became aware of this own sinfulness. That is, adoration moved him to penitence and to confession. The Church embraces within its acts of worship the elements of adoration, praise and thanksgiving and, as Temple reminds us, in the second of the quotations, it is as we do so that consciences are quickened, minds are fed, imaginations are purged, hearts are opened and wills are re-directed to the service of God. That is why attendance at public worship is for the Christian a matter not of convention but of conviction, not of convenience but of constraint.

Prayer   *Glory be to the Father and to the Son and to the Holy Spirit; As it was in the beginning is now and ever shall be, world without end. Amen.*

'If I could shut the gate'

If I could shut the gate against my thoughts
  And keep out sorrow from the room within,
If memory could cancel all the notes
  Of my misdeeds, and unthink my sin:
How free, how clear, how clean my soul should lie,
Discharged of such a loathsome company!

If there were other rooms without my heart
  That did not to my conscience join so near,
Where I might lodge the thoughts of sin apart
  That I might not their clam'rous crying hear;
What peace, what joy, what ease should I possess,
Freed from their horrors that my soul oppress!

But, O my Saviour, who my refuge art,
  Let thy dear mercies stand 'twixt them and me,
And be the wall to separate my heart
  So that I may at length repose me free;
That peace, and joy, and rest may be within,
And I remain divided from my sin.

ANONYMOUS (POSSIBLY 17TH CENTURY)

Comment

Pilgrims on the Christian Way must always beware of sentences which begin with 'If', for too often they are no more than excuses for delay or inactivity in the discharge of some discipline or duty. The priest and the Levite might well have passed the wounded traveller murmuring, 'Sorry for him. If only I were not going to the Temple... '. The Samaritan was undeterred by the 'ifs' and 'buts' which possibly ran through his mind as his eyes lighted upon the wounded Jew. So for ourselves. We cannot erase our misdeeds from our memories; we cannot 'unthink' our sins or push them out of sight in some secret room. Skeletons in the cupboard tend to remind us of their presence. But what we can do with our sins, as with our frustrations, our abject moral and spiritual failures, is to lay them before our Lord in penitence, to receive from him the forgiveness which heals. Having received his forgiveness we may well find that we have restitutions which must be made, that reconciliation must be sought or apology offered. Difficult though these may sometimes be, they are the necessary demands of true repentance and forgiveness. It is when I am wholly 'divided from my sin' by Christ Himself that He can erase 'all the notes of my misdeeds'.

Prayer   *O Lord, because we often sin and have to ask for pardon, help us to forgive as we would be forgiven; neither mentioning old offences committed against us, nor dwelling upon them in thought; blot out from our minds all those sins for which we have sought and received your forgiveness, and, so forgiven, enable us to go on our way rejoicing in the power of the Spirit, through Jesus Christ our Lord.*

Prayer of Intercession

If God is Almighty and all Loving, what possible difference can our prayers for other people make? Will He not act for the greatest good for those for whom we pray, irrespective of anything we may or may not do? These are great questions – questions that greatly bother some people, when vitality is low and faith is weakened.

Let me say first that in any reading of God's dealings with men it is clear that God will not do things regardless of us; He will not ride roughshod over anyone. For, wonderfully and humbly, He has chosen the role of partnership. We see the principle stated in these words Jesus spoke on the eve of the Passion: 'Henceforth I call you no longer servants, for the servant knoweth not what his master doeth; but I have called you friends' (St John ch.15 v.15). It is this principle that we see worked out in the realm of intercession...

That first, then second: Our Lord left us in no doubt at all that, not only were we to pray for people, but that this was something which He did Himself. He prayed for Simon Peter (St Luke ch.22 v.32)... He prayed for his disciples... As he came to His cross He prayed for those who had brought him there... And if He did what I have described, as indeed He did, the Christian will have no hesitation in doing likewise. Jesus said, 'Whatsoever ye shall ask in my Name, that will I do'.

KENNETH MATTHEWS
(FROM THE WATCHWORD)

Comment

We must note there the determining condition. When we pray in His Name for someone whom we know and love in need of comfort or guidance or healing, or for some purpose which we believe to be in line with the purpose of the Living God, it is not that we are trying to call God's attention to someone or something that He has overlooked. It is rather that, as a member of the family of which God is the Father, we talk to Him of our concern for another member or other members of the family, as our Lord bade us to do. The Christian rule of this kind of prayer can never be other than 'Thy will be done', and by intercession we affirm our belief in God's love and our concern for other members of His family. The answers to such prayer may well be that, in some way unbeknown to us, God may use our strong concerns put freely at His disposal, to achieve His purpose. Our prayer may indeed involve us in the achievement of God's purpose. Whilst petition and intercession are not the most important types of prayer – the most important is adoration, – 'Hallowed be Thy Name' – they must find a place in a Christian's prayer life just because he, as a member of the family of God, cannot but be concerned for the welfare of other members of the family. God achieves His purposes for His people through his people, and to petition or to intercede may result in a challenge from God to us to spring into action. We must not cease to pray, but we must never forget the cardinal rule which is ever, 'Thy will be done'.

Prayer   *Almighty God, our heavenly Father, who lovest all and forgettest none, we bring to Thee our supplications for all Thy children everywhere... May Thy blessing be upon them, for the sake of Jesus Christ our Lord.*

JOHN HUNTER (D.1849)

Obedience

I said, 'Let me walk in the fields'.
He said, 'No, walk in the town'.
I said, 'There are no flowers there'.
He said, 'No flowers but a crown'.

I said, 'But the sky is black,
    There is nothing but noise and din',
But he wept as he sent me back, –
    'There is more', he said, 'there is sin'.

I said, 'But the air is thick,
And fogs are veiling the sun'.
He answered, 'Yet souls are sick,
And souls in the dark undone. . . '

I said, 'I shall miss the light,
    And friends will miss me, they say'.
He answered me, 'Choose to-night –
    If I am to miss you or they'.

I cast one look at the field,
Then set my face to the town;
He said 'My child, do you yield?
Will you leave the flowers for the crown?'

Then into his hand went mine,
And into my heart came he;
And I walk in a light divine
The path I had feared to see.

GEORGE MACDONALD (1824–1905)

Comment

The poet expresses his own desires but recognises in his conclusion that God's purpose for him, though contrary to what he sought, enables him to walk in 'a light divine'. It was a politician, not a priest – Gladstone no less – who declared that 'there is one proposition in which the whole matter, as it is relevant to human duty, may be summed up; that all our works, alike inward and outward, great or small, ought to be done in obedience to God'. God's first law to man was a law of obedience. In 'keeping of God's commandments there is great reward'. Undoubtedly obedience to the law of God is the distinguishing mark of our religion and, as our poet says, in another of his writings, 'I find the doing of the will of God leaves me no time for the disputing of His plans'. There are times in our own spiritual pilgrimage when we are tempted to turn a blind eye to what we know to be in tune with God's commandments and to pursue our own will and way. Humble acceptance of God's dispensations may not always be the easy path to follow, but it will be the surest and the one which leads to peace of mind.

Prayer *Make us of quick and tender conscience, O Lord; that understanding we may obey every word of Thine, and discerning, may follow every suggestion of Thine indwelling Spirit. Speak, Lord, for Thy servant heareth. Through Jesus Christ our Lord.*

CHRISTINA ROSSETTI (1830–1894)

Commemorating Dunstan, Archbishop of Canterbury, died 988

. . . Give thy thoughts no tongue,
Nor any unproportioned thought his act.
Be thou familiar, but by no means vulgar.
The friends thou hast, and their adoption tried,
Grapple them to thy soul with hoops of steel,
But do not dull thy palm with entertainment
Of each new-hatched unfledged comrade. Beware
Of entrance to a quarrel, but, being in,
Bear't that the opposed may beware of thee.
Give every man thine ear but few thy voice:
Take each man's censure, but reserve thy judgment. . . .
This above all: to thine own self be true,
And it must follow, as night the day,
Thou canst not then be false to any man.

WILLIAM SHAKESPEARE (1564–1616)

Comment

Both as a statesman and as a churchman Dunstan undoubtedly stands among the greatest in English history. He was successively Abbot of Glastonbury, Bishop of London and Archbishop of Canterbury. Holding such offices he could not escape from time to time the 'entrance to a quarrel' whether with Church or State. The teenage King Edwy, whose moral laxity Dunstan rebuked, drove him into exile, but his successor Edgar recalled him as his chief adviser. Such was his influence and power under successive kings that Dunstan became the virtual ruler of England, and London became one of the world's chief trading centres. Within the Church itself the Archbishop was fiercely opposed for his strict enforcement of discipline in the lives of the clergy. Censured by many and often, Dunstan remained true to himself and to his vocation, and it followed 'as night the day' that he came to be regarded with great admiration throughout the land. He spent his last days in Canterbury praying, making music and writing, and Church and State alike came to realise that a holy man had been amongst them through the years, serving them faithfully as a true man of God. His holiness had been too hard for some to bear but all came to realise that he had spoken for God, even before kings, and England and her Church were the stronger and the holier for his work and witness. Certainly he had demonstrated by his words, by his counsels and by his actions that being true to his commitment to Christ had resulted in his not being 'false to any man' even though his integrity frequently brought him suffering. His life and his witness can direct us to this prayer:

Prayer   *God our Father, as we praise you for the life and witness and work of your servant Dunstan, who remained true to his calling in the face of fierce opposition, grant that we too, who are within the Church which he served, may likewise be true to ourselves and used by you to bear witness to the Way, the Truth and the Life of our Lord and Saviour Jesus Christ.*

Sursum Corda

I place before my inward eyes myself with all that I am – my body, soul, and all my powers – and I gather round me all the creatures which God ever created in heaven, on earth, and in all the elements, each one several-ly with its name, whether birds of the air, beasts of the forest, fishes of the waters, leaves and grass of the earth, or the innumerable sand of the sea, and to these I add all the little specks of dust which glance in the sunbeams, with all the little drops of water which ever fell or are falling from dew, snow, or rain, and I wish that each of these had a sweetly sounding stringed in-strument, fashioned from my heart's inmost blood, striking on which they might each send up to our dear and gentle God a new and lofty strain of praise for ever and ever. And then the loving arms of my soul stretch out and extend themselves towards the innumerable multitude of all creatures, and my intention is, just as a free and blithesome leader of a choir stirs up the singers of his company, even so to turn them all to good account by inciting them to sing joyously, and to offer up their hearts to God – 'Sur-sum corda'.

HENRY SUSO (1295–1366)

Comment

The author quoted above was a German mystic whose writings were admired by, among others, Thomas à Kempis. He spent his boyhood in a Dominican convent, and at the age of 18 he made himself a 'Servant of the Eternal Wisdom'. Through-out his life he was sought after as a wise spiritual director. Like many mystics, before him and since, he strove in effect to express the inexpressible beauty and splendour of God. He saw the lifting up of the human heart to the Being and Maj-esty of God as a necessary prelude to progress in the spiritual life. The quotation is drawn from a book of his Meditations. Like many mystics who followed him, and many poets throughout Christian history, he saw the Beauty, the Splendour, the Majesty of God revealed in the natural world, and he pictured all Creation gathered around him so that he, and all God's creatures, could lift up their hearts 'in strains of praise for ever and ever'. This lifting of our hearts in adoration to the Living God is the beginning of all prayer and praise. A man's heart is the sanc-tuary of his soul. To lift it up to God is to open it for God's indwelling. That must be the beginning of prayer. In the cloister garden of Gloucester Cathedral there is a sundial bearing wise advice. It reads:

> Give God thy heart, thy service and thy gold,
> The day wears on and the time is waxing old.

Prayer *Blessing and honour, and thanksgiving and praise, more than we can utter, more than we can conceive, be unto Thee, O holy and glorious Trinity, Father, Son and Holy Spirit, by all angels, all men, all crea-tures for evermore.*

BISHOP LANCELOT ANDREWES (1553–1626)

God knows

So heart be still:
What need our little life
Our human life to know,
    If God hath comprehension?
In all the dizzy strife
Of things both high and low,
    God hideth His intention.

    God knows. His will
Is best. The stretch of years
Which wind ahead, so dim
    To our imperfect vision,
Are clear to God. Our fears
Are premature: In him
    All time hath full provision.

    Then rest; until
God moves to lift the veil
From our impatient eyes,
    When as the sweeter features
Of Life's stern face we hail,
Fair beyond all surmise
God's thought around His creatures
    Our mind shall fill.

M. LOUISE HASKINS (1875–1957)

Comment

Louise Haskins was the poet who became known all over the Commonwealth when King George the Sixth quoted her in a Christmas broadcast: 'Go out into the darkness and put your hand into the hand of God'. There is an aspect of prayer in which we do just that. We find ourselves in the darkness of suffering, of doubt, of bewilderment. We may not be able even to fashion words with which to speak to God. We merely stretch out our hand to grasp his, knowing as our poet says, that 'God hath comprehension in all the dizzy strife' in which we may, at any moment, be immersed. If our eyes are directed towards God and our minds are set on him, if our hearts are opened to the inflow of his love, then he knows our state though words may fail us. Mother Frances Dominica, of the Society of All Saints, warns us in her perceptive study of prayer in its several aspects to 'Beware of using too many words when you pray. Use words only if they mean something and are a useful means of reaching closer to God. Remember that prayer is a two-way thing, you to God but also God to you. If you bombard him with a non-stop flow of words you will never hear what he is saying to you'. Clearly Louise Haskins knew the value of what might be called the prayer of silent trusting. Facing 'Life's stern face', and putting her hand into the hand of God, she was able to rise from her knees and say: 'I went forth and finding the hand of God, trod gladly into the night. And he led me towards the hills and the breaking of the day in the lone East'.

Prayer   *Lord, I know that the reality of prayer is not measured by eloquence but by earnestness. I ask only that you take my hand and lead me through the darkness as through the light.*

Prayer in Christ's Name

To pray 'in the name of Jesus' may perhaps be explained most simply in this way. A magistrate orders something, 'in the name of the King'. What does that mean? In the first place it means: I myself am nothing. I have no power, nothing to say for myself – but it is in the name of the King. Thus, to pray in the name of Christ means: I dare not approach God without a mediator; if my prayer is to be heard, then it will be in the name of Jesus; what gives it strength is that name. Next, when a magistrate gives a command in the name of the King, it naturally follows that what it commands will be the King's will; he cannot command his own will in the name of the King.

The same thing is true of praying in the name of Jesus, to pray in such a way that it is in conformity with the will of Jesus. I cannot pray in the name of Jesus to have my own will; the name of Jesus is not a signature of no importance, but the decisive factor... To pray in the name of Jesus means to pray in such a manner that I dare name Jesus in it, that is to say think of Him, think of His holy will together with whatever I am praying for.

Finally, when a magistrate gives an order in the name of the King, it means that the King assumes that responsibility. So too with prayer in the name of Jesus, Jesus assumes the responsibility and all the consequences. He steps forward for us, steps into the place of the person praying.

SÖREN KIERKEGAARD (1813–1855)

Comment

In his short life this Danish philosopher won high regard for his philosophical writings, but it was not until the last five years of his life that he contributed so richly to Christian thinking and Christian practice. He was one who fought his way through, from atheism to Christianity and, having once found Christ, he produced many books which revealed a total acceptance of Christian theology, not least in its devotional demands. Only in recent years, however, has the depth of his spiritual thinking been appreciated for the benediction it affords to the searcher after God. Recalling the forms of prayer – 'through Jesus Christ our Lord', 'we ask in the Name of Jesus Christ', he expounds in simple terms the profound meaning of prayer in Christ's Name. His writings about the Christian Faith were by no means merely academic. He knew what it was to suffer physically, and indeed mentally at the hands of a Danish *'Private Eye'* which taunted him for his deformed body and peculiarities of dress. Here is one of his prayers:

Prayer   *Father in Heaven, when the thought of Thee wakes in our hearts, let it not awaken like a frightened bird that flies about in dismay, but like a child waking from its sleep with a heavenly smile. We ask this in the name of Jesus.*

What is Prayer?

Prayer is the soul's sincere desire,
Uttered or unexpressed,
The motion of a hidden fire
That trembles in the breast.

Prayer is the burden of a sigh,
The falling of a tear,
The upward glancing of an eye
When none but God is near.

Prayer is the simplest form of speech
That infant lips can try;
Prayer is the sublimest strains that reach
God's Majesty on high.

Prayer is the Christian's vital breath,
The Christian's native air,
His watchword at the gate of death;
He enters heaven with prayer.

JAMES MONTGOMERY (1771–1854)

Comment

There is no single all-embracing definition of the exercise which we call prayer, though James Montgomery, who wrote a number of our hymns including *Angels from the realms of glory*, at least establishes one truth about it. That truth is that it is not something which touches only certain aspects of the Christian's life. He speaks of it as 'vital breath', vital to the life of the soul as is breath to the life of the body. He reminds us that it can be 'uttered or unexpressed' – that is, it is not invariably expressed in words but in an attitude to all life, which on occasion can be the mere 'upward glancing of an eye to God'. It can indeed be the prayer of silence. The saints through the ages have all tried to do what the poet is doing. To Clement of Alexandria prayer is 'conversation with God', to St Francis de Sales prayer is being 'absorbed with God'. Theologians, philosophers and poets have in their turn declared themselves to be men and women of prayer by expressing what prayer has meant to them. But maybe it is not the word of any one of these which challenges the cynic or the sceptic, nor the word of holy men like George Herbert, Jeremy Taylor, Martin Luther, Brother Lawrence and hundreds more. Maybe it is the word of folk whom people regard as 'men of the world' whose witness is the more telling. J. Edgar Hoover could declare with confidence that 'the force of prayer is greater than any possible combination of man's controlled powers, because prayer is man's greatest means of tapping the infinite resources of God.'

Prayer *Lord, may we know not what we ought to ask of Thee; Thou only knowest what we need; Thou lovest us better than we know how to love ourselves. Father, give to us, Thy children, that which we ourselves know not how to ask. Teach us to pray. Pray Thyself in us; for Christ's sake.*

FRANCÒIS FENELON (1651–1715)

Commemorating John and Charles Wesley, Priests, Poets, Teachers of the Faith

The holiest of men still need
Christ as their prophet as the
Light of the world. For he does
not give them light but from
moment to moment; the instant He
withdraws, all is darkness. They
still need Christ as their King
for God does not give them a
stock of holiness. But unless
they receive a supply every moment,
nothing but unholiness
would remain. They still need
Christ as their Priest, to make
atonement for their holy things.

    Even perfect holiness is
acceptable to God only through
Jesus Christ.

JOHN WESLEY (1703–1791)

O Thou Who camest from above
The fire celestial to impart,
Kindle a flame of sacred love
On the mean altar of my heart.

There let it for Thy glory burn
With inextinguishable blaze,
And trembling to its source return
In humble prayer and fervent praise.

Jesus, confirm my heart's desire,
To work, and speak, and think for Thee,
Still let me guard the holy fire,
And still stir up the gift in me.

Still let me prove Thy perfect will,
My acts of faith and love repeat,
Till death thy endless mercies seal,
And make the sacrifice complete.

CHARLES WESLEY (1707–1788)

Comment

It is impossible to compass in a few words what the Wesley brothers did for England, and indeed for the Christian world, in the course of the eighteenth century. John was the elder, and following his conversion he declared it to be his object 'to promote, as far as I am able, vital practical religion, and by the grace of God, to beget, preserve and increase the life of God in the souls of men.' This he did, with such zeal and enthusiasm, travelling around the country on horseback for seven or eight thousand miles a year, that even those who were critical of his methods could not but listen to him with respect though occasionally, as he discloses, he was pelted with garbage. He founded the Methodist Movement, hoping at its outset that it would remain within the bosom of the Church of England. His brother Charles followed his example in the itinerant ministry but His richest contribution was undoubtedly his gift to the Christian world of nearly six thousand hymns of which hundreds are known and sung throughout Christendom. Both these priests of the Church were men of great piety and courage, and each possessed a magnetic personality which drew people to them and enabled them to win the multitudes for God and His Church.

Prayer   Here is John Wesley's Rule which can easily be fashioned into a prayer:

Do all the good you can
By all the means you can,
In all the ways you can,
In all the places you can,
At all the times you can,
To all the people you can,
As long as ever you can.

Commemorating The Venerable Bede
Priest, Monk of Jarrow, died 735

The Death of Bede

So until Ascensiontide he worked with his pupils to conclude his translation of St John's Gospel into the English tongue: but the Tuesday before
Ascensiontide his sickness increased upon him. Nevertheless, he taught and
bade his scholars work, saying cheerfully, 'Write with speed now, for I cannot tell how long I may last'.

The day broke (that is, Wednesday), and about the third hour the scribe
said, 'There is yet a chapter wanting: it is hard for thee to continue vexing
thyself'. 'This is easily done', said Bede. 'Take thy pen again and write
quickly'. And joyfully he dictated until the evening at the ninth hour.

'Dear Master', said the boy, 'there is yet one sentence to be written.'
He answered, 'Write it quickly'. Soon after, the boy said, 'It is finished now'.

Bede answered, 'Thou hast well said, It is finished'. Raise my head in
thy arms, and turn my face towards the holy spot where I was wont to pray,
for I desire to sit facing it and call upon my Father'.

So they held him up on the pavement, and he chanted, 'Glory be to the
Father, and to the Son, and to the Holy Spirit'. Then, as he named the
Holy Spirit, his spirit took leave, and departed to the Heavenly Kingdom.

FROM A LETTER WRITTEN BY ONE CUTHBERT –
A PUPIL OF BEDE

Comment

Church and State owe a tremendous debt of gratitude to Bede who has been called
the 'Father of English History'. Born in 673, near Jarrow, he entered a monastery
at the tender age of 7 and remained there for the rest of his life, being ordained
priest at the age of 20. He appears never to have gone outside Northumbria, though
he gathered to himself sufficient scholarship, and sufficient information touching
the life of Church and State, to enable him to write no less than forty substantial
books, his Ecclesiastical History of the English Nation being the most well known.
His scholarship and saintly character were known and admired throughout the
Church, and his application to the demands of his priestly vocation shines through
all his writings, not least those in which he set out 'to annotate briefly the Holy
Scriptures'. His wise advice to the Bishop of York of his day, one Egberct, is such
that it should be heeded by all bishops, as well as those responsible for their appointment. He wrote to the bishop about the high importance of 'episcopal visitation, confirmation and frequent Communion' – that is, of those pastoral
responsibilities of the bishop alongside which, I suspect, administration must pale
into insignificance.

Prayer   *We beseech Thee, Lord Jesus, that to whom Thou dost vouchsafe sweet
draughts of the words of thy knowledge, Thou wilt also, of thy goodness, grant that we may, in due time, come to Thee, the fountain of
all wisdom, and ever stand before Thy face; for Thy sake.*

BEDE

Commemorating Augustine
First Archbishop of Canterbury, 605

Who could fully tell the joy that has sprung up in the hearts of all the faithful because the race of the Angles, through the grace of Almighty God and the labours of your brotherhood, has had the light of holy faith poured out on it and the darkness of error driven away?

Now in purity of mind they trample down those idols which previously they served in insane fear. They worship Almighty God with pure hearts, and by the rules that they have learnt from the holy preaching, they are restrained from falling into evil deeds. With their souls they serve the divine commandments and in their minds they are raised up by them. They bow down to the ground continually in prayer, that their minds may not lie prostrate. Whose work is this if not the work of him who says: 'My Father is working even now, and I am working'?

It is by His power and not by the wisdom of men that the world is converted, and to prove this he has chosen unlearned men to be his preachers and has sent them into the world. This too is what he is doing at the present time, for he has deigned to do mighty works among the Angles through weak men.

POPE GREGORY THE GREAT (A.D.604)

Comment

This day cannot pass without re-telling the familiar story which resulted in the appointment of Augustine as first Archbishop of Canterbury. There were three fair-complexioned boys for sale in Rome's market, and Gregory was told that they were Angles or Angli. 'They are well named for they have angelic faces and it becomes such to be companions with the angels in heaven', Gregory commented. When he learnt that they were pagans from 'Deira', he continued with his puns! 'De ira', he exclaimed. 'They shall be saved from God's ire'. On being told that the king of Deira was called 'Aella', he resolved that 'Alleluia' must be sung in Aella's land'. He set off at once with some of his monks but was recalled to Rome by Pope Pelagius. Later, during his own Pontificate, he sent Augustine and forty missionaries to England and it was they who worked for England's reconversion to the Christian Faith. 'Re-conversion' is the appropriate word for the ancient British Church had already been at work in the land and Augustine found the Church of Saint Martin in Canterbury. King Ethelbert was himself baptised and, despite tensions between Augustine and the bishops of the ancient British Church, the cause of Christ and His Church triumphed.

Prayer

O God, who has graciously preserved our nation through the years and hast led us in wondrous ways: Grant that we may be worthy of our high calling. Purge from among us the sins that dishonour Thee. Give us true religion; crown our faith with righteousness; and make of us a holy people, to Thy praise and honour, through Jesus Christ our Lord.

Thanking God

In the Christian community thankfulness is just what it is anywhere else in the Christian life. Only he who gives thanks for little things receives the big things. We prevent God from giving us the great spiritual gifts He has in store for us, because we do not give thanks for daily gifts. We think we dare not be satisfied with the small measure of spiritual knowledge, experience and love, that has been given to us, and that we must constantly be looking forward eagerly for the highest good. Then we deplore the fact that we lack the deep certainty, the strong faith, and the rich experience that God has given to others, and we consider this lament to be pious.

We pray for the big things and forget to give thanks for the ordinary, small – yet really not small – gifts. How can God entrust great things to one who will not receive from Him the little things? If we do not give thanks daily for the Christian fellowship in which we have been placed, even where there is no great experience, no discoverable riches, but much weakness, small faith, and difficulty; if, on the contrary, we only keep complaining to God that everything is so paltry and petty, so far from what we expected, then we hinder God from letting our fellowship grow according to the measure and riches which are there for us all in Jesus Christ.

DIETRICH BONHOEFFER (1906–1945)

Comment

One of the first lessons a little child is taught is to say 'Thank-you'. This might suggest that thankfulness should be ingrained in us all from childhood, and that gratitude should be a natural response for gifts human and divine. It will not have escaped our notice that the theme of thanksgiving recurs frequently in the Psalms. 'It is a good thing to give thanks unto the Lord' (Psalm 92); 'Enter into his gates with thanksgiving and into his courts with praise' (Psalm 100). Our Lord's poignant question following the healing of the ten lepers 'Where are the nine?' is itself indicative of surprise that so elementary a response should be lacking. Thanksgiving should find a place in our private prayers as in our public worship.

Prayer   *Thank you, Lord, for all your goodness to us; for the world which you have made and for the strength to serve you in it; for daily revelations of yourself, in nature, in art and in the lives of your faithful people; for the Bible which declares your Word, and for all other writings which reveal your truth, for the tasks to which you are calling us, and for the courage we need to fulfil them. But above all we thank you for your Son our Saviour Jesus Christ, through whom we see you, our Father. May his Spirit live in us ever, making us strong to serve you with joy and gladness all the days of our life; through Jesus Christ our Lord.*

The Coronet

When for the thorns with which I long, too long,
    With many a piercing wound,
    My Saviour's Head have crowned,
I seek with garlands to redress that wrong;
    Through every garden; every mead,
I gather flowers (my fruits are only flowers).
    Dismantling all the fragrant towers
That once adorned my shepherdess's head;
And now, when I have summed up all my store,
    Thinking (so I myself deceive)
    So rich a chaplet thence to weave
As never yet the King of Glory wore,
    Alas! I find the Serpent old,
    That, twining in his speckled breast
    About the flowers disguised, does fold,
    With wreaths of fame and interest.
Ah, foolish man, that would'st debase with them
And Mortal glory, Heaven's diadem!
But Thou who only could'st the Serpent tame,
Either his slippery knots at once untie,
And disentangle all his winding snare;
Or shatter too with him my curious frame,
And let these wither – so that he may die –
Though set with skill, and chosen out with care;
That they, while Thou on both their spoils dost tread,
May crown Thy feet, that could not crown Thy head.

ANDREW MARVELL (1621–1678)

Comment

There is a form of prayer, known variously as meditation or contemplation, which does not necessarily express itself in words but consists of devotional reflection upon God's being or upon some passage of scripture. Andrew Marvell, who was one of the so-named metaphysical poets, is engaged in that sort of prayer in this poem. He contemplates Christ's crown of thorns and yearns to replace it with another crown, one of flowers consisting of his personal service to God. But he reflects that often when he has tried to do just that the devil steps in to shatter his noblest ideals. He is in effect calling upon God to 'wither' the devil in man just as the flowers wither and die. What was true for the poet is true for us. Within us is a 'lower nature' and a 'higher'. The soul within us aspires to offer 'flowers'; the self within us concerns itself with 'fame and interest'. The soul seeks God; the self 'spoils' the seeking. The poem closes with an unspoken prayer.

Prayer   *O Christ, who by the thorns which were pressed upon your head hast drawn the thorns from the sorrows of this world, and offered us a crown of joy and peace, help us to suffer with cheerfulness in your service, press on with undaunted courage in the Way you have shown us, in the Truth you have declared, and in sharing the Life which you offer to all who follow you.*

Meditation

There is a way into the greenwood which is not much used in these days of feverish rush. Its name in the Scriptures is 'Meditation'. (My meditation of Him shall be sweet'. Psalm 104, v 34). We should plough a deeper furrow if we knew more of that way. We should be quieter then, and there is nothing creative in noise. 'Friend, when dost thou *think*', asked the old Quaker after listening to a modern timetable; we cannot think by machinery. We cannot consider the lilies without giving time to the lilies. Often our flash of haste means little. To read a book in an hour (if the book has taken half a life-time to write) means nothing at all. To pray in a hurry of spirit means nothing. To live in a hurry means to do much but to effect little. We build more quickly in wood, hay and stubble than in gold, silver, precious stones; but the one abides, the other does not.

If he who feels the world is too much with him will make for himself a little space, and let his mind settle like a bee in a flower on some great word of his God, and brood over it, pondering it till it has time to work in him, he will find himself in the greenwood.

A MY C ARMICHAEL (1867–1951)

Comment

Earlier in the month there was quoted a poem by Amy Carmichael and some notes about her and her work appear on the page. The home for children which she started became in time the Dohnavur Fellowship which is now self-supporting – a great Family of 700 men, women and children, with its own schools, hospitals, church, workshops, weaving-sheds and clinics – all inspired by Amy Carmichael with, as she puts it, 'our Unseen Leader moving on before us'. Following an accident in 1932 this great missionary became housebound, but despite her infirmity the work continued. She remained Head of the Family though no longer able to contribute physically to its life and work. But she continued to direct its activities and to sustain it spiritually with her writings and prayers. The quotation above is from *Gold by Moonlight*, one of about forty books of spiritual guidance which she wrote in the course of her life. It is good to be advised by a lady who was herself so busy about the Lord's work, that it is both wise and necessary for a Christian to withdraw from activities from time to time to 'settle like a bee in a flower' on some great word of God, 'to brood over it'. The quotation is an extension of our thought yesterday about meditative and contemplative prayer. An old Italian proverb suggests that 'solitude is intolerable', but like so many proverbs, that is no more than a half truth. In an age when there is so much noise, and so little silence, so much activity and so little stillness, so much anxiety and so little serenity, we need to withdraw from the bustling world from time to time to settle ourselves in solitude which someone has called 'the audience chamber of God'.

Prayer   *Teach me, good Lord, to look beyond this world, and to set every day into the frame of the heavenly vision. By prayer and sacred study, open for me a door into heaven that I may hear and heed only your voice, and so return to my tasks in the world with a new understanding, a new hope and a new courage.*

A Poet's Prayer

Lord, not for light in darkness do we pray,
Not that the veil be lifted from our eyes,
Not that the slow ascension of our day
    Be otherwise.

Not for a clearer vision of the things
Whereof the fashioning shall make us great,
But for remission of the peril and stings
    Of time and fate.

Not for a fuller knowledge of the end
Whereto we travel, bruised yet unafraid,
Nor that the little healing that we lend
    Shall be repaid.

Not these, O Lord. We would not break
    the bars
Thy wisdom sets about us; we shall climb
Unfettered to secrets of the stars
    In thy good time.

We do not crave the high perception swift
When to refrain were well, and when
    fulfil,
Nor yet the understanding strong to sift
    The good from ill.

Not these, O Lord, for these thou hast revealed.
We know the golden season when to reap
The heavy-fruited treasure of the field,
    The hour to sleep.

Not these. We know the hemlock from the rose,
The pure from stained, the noble from the base,
The tranquil holy light of truth that glows
    On Pity's face.

We know the paths wherein our feet should
    press,
Across our hearts are written thy decrees.
Yet now, O Lord, be merciful to bless
    With more than these.

Grant us the will to fashion as we feel,
Grant us the strength to labour as we know,
Grant us the purpose, ribbed and edged
    with steel,
    To strike the blow.

Knowledge we ask not – knowledge thou
    hast lent;
But Lord, the will – there lies our bitter need.
Give us to build above the deep intent
    The deed, the deed.

JOHN DRINKWATER (1882–1937)

Comment

There is neither space nor need to explain the poet's words. They embody the thoughts of one who was himself a man of prayer and they sum up admirably the thoughts on prayer which we have been following through the month.

Prayer   *Read the verses again, and this time not as a poem but as a prayer of your own, sealed with your own 'Amen'.*

Commemorating the visit of the Blessed Virgin Mary to Elizabeth

Ave Maria; blessed Maid!
Lily of Eden's fragrant shade,
Who can express the love
That nurtured thee so pure and sweet,
Making thy heart a shelter meet
For Jesu's holy Dove?

Ave Maria! Mother blest,
To whom caressing and caressed,
Clings the Eternal Child;
Favoured beyond Archangels' dreams,
When first on thee with tenderest gleam
The new-born Saviour smiled.

Ave Maria; thou whose name
All but adoring love may claim,
Yet may we reach thy shrine;
For He, thy Son and Saviour, vows
To crown all lowly lofty brows
With love and joy like thine.

Bless'd is the womb that bare Him,
bless'd
The bosom where his lips were press'd
But rather bless'd are they
Who hear His word and keep it well,
The living homes where Christ shall dwell,
And never pass away.

JOHN KEBLE (1792–1866)

Comment

As the Mother of Jesus, Mary is pre-eminent among the saints. Although she figures prominently in the birth stories and, of course, at the foot of the Cross, hers is very much a background role in our Lord's ministry. Yet she moves through it with that supreme dignity which itself certifies the uniqueness of her divine assignment. It was on her visit to Elizabeth that she broke her silence with a song which Christendom has been singing ever since – 'My soul doth magnify the Lord', the *Magnificat* – a sweet song indeed but a stern one which has been described as 'the most revolutionary document in the world'. It is Mary's song which, first in the Gospel story, condemns pride and exalts humility. It is Mary's song which proclaims what the rich must do in respect of the poor and the well fed in respect of the hungry. Professor Barclay writes truly 'There is loveliness in the Magnificat but in that loveliness there is dynamite. Christianity begets a revolution in each man and a revolution in the world'. But for this revolution the dynamite is not of nitroglycerin mixed with an absorbent, but of the human will motivated by the gifts of the Spirit. Something of this revolution is present in every authentic Christian life. Thus every Christian must face the question 'Is it present in my life?'

Prayer   *O God, who when the fullness of time was come didst send forth thy Son, born to Mary, to redeem mankind. Vouchsafe evermore to dwell in our hearts. Inspire us with thy purity, strengthen us with thy might, guide us into all truth; that we may conquer every adverse power and be wholly devoted to Thy service and confirmed to Thy will, through Jesus Christ our Lord.*

Commemorating Justin, Martyr at Rome, c.165

The Godhead

Father of Heaven, and Him, by whom
It, and us for it, and all else for us
   Thou mad'st, and govern'st ever, come
And re-create me, now grown ruinous;
    My heart is by dejection, clay,
     And by self-murder, red.
From this red earth, O Father, purge away
All vicious tinctures, that new fashioned,
I may rise up from death, before I'm dead.

   O Son of God, who seeing two things,
Sin and death, crept in, which were never made,
   By bearing one, tryed'st with what stings
The other could Thine heritage invade;
    O be Thou nail'd unto my heart,
     And crucified again.
Part not from it, though it from Thee
   would part,
But let it be, by applying so Thy pain,
Drown'd in Thy blood, and in Thy
   passion slain.

   O Holy Ghost, whose temple I
Am, but of mud walls, and condensed dust,
   And being sacrilegiously
Half wasted with youth's fires, of pride
   and lust,
    Must with new storms be weather-beat;
    Double in my heart Thy flame,
Which let devout sad tears intent; and let
(Though this glass lanthorn, flesh, do
   suffer main)
Fire, Sacrifice, Priest, Altar be the same.

          JOHN DONNE (1572–1631)

Comment

Justin, who was brought up in a pagan home, embraced the Christian Faith at the age of 30, and from then until his martyrdom in 165 A.D. his writings, of which there are many, were concerned to defend the Christian Faith against the charge that it conflicted with Reason. He was one of the great Christian Apologists who sought to inform educated people about the Christian Faith and to defend the Church's right to exist despite the opposition of the State. It could be said that in his First, as in his Second *Apology*, he expounded the teaching which Donne sets down in the first three verses quoted above from his *Litany*. Justin believed in the transcendence, that is the 'otherness', of the Living God, which did not deny his Fatherhood; he believed in the Incarnation, God becoming 'one of us' to achieve in Christ what Donne expounds in his second verse, and in the outpouring of the Holy Spirit to work through those in whom he dwelt. He dwells in us through Baptism into the Body of Christ, the Church. Thus he attached great importance to the two Gospel Sacraments, Holy Baptism and the Eucharist.

Prayer   *Jesus, Light of the world, shine upon our minds; Spirit of Truth, make clear your Truth to us; Father of Heaven, sanctify us through your Truth, and give us courage to hold fast to it.*

The Hound of Heaven

I fled Him down the nights and down the days:
I fled Him down the arches of the years;
I fled Him down the labyrinthine ways
Of my own mind; and in the mist of tears
I hid from Him, and under running laughter.
Up vistaed hopes I sped;
and shot, precipitated
Adown Titanic glooms of chasmed fears
From those strong Feet that followed, followed, after.
But with unhurrying chase,
And unperturbed pace,
Deliberate speed, majestic instancy,
They beat – and a Voice beat
More instant than the Feet –
'All things betray thee, who betrayest Me'.

FRANCIS THOMPSON (1859–1907)

Comment

Pentecost – Whit Sunday – frequently falls in June and many Sundays following it are known as Sundays after Pentecost. Pentecost is the Feast of the Holy Spirit and the Birthday of the Church. We could do well in the course of this month to dwell upon what St Paul calls in his letter to the Galatians (Ch.5) 'the fruit of the Spirit'. Before he lists the fruits, however, he lists the temptations of our lower nature against which we have to fight. His catalogue of the evil things, including such sordid sins as sexual immorality, hatred, jealousy, fits of rage, selfish ambition, envy, drunkenness, reads like a few pages of a daily paper. (Sexual immorality was not merely condoned in his day; it was regarded as normal human activity). The committed Christian does not fall into any of these willingly, but the struggle against temptations to them is no less severe on that account. Like Francis Thompson, Christians tend sometimes to turn their backs on Christ and his values. The struggle to live up to the demands of the Spirit – love, joy, patience, kindness, goodness, faithfulness, gentleness, self-control – is fierce and frightening. The Psalmist found it so too. But he found, as Francis Thompson finds, that God is inescapable. ('If I climb up into heaven thou art there, and if I go down to hell thou art there also'). For Christians, conscience has to be informed, awake and alert, lest they find themselves engulfed in the 'gloom of chasmed fears'.

Prayer *Spirit of God, keep alive in me the beacon light of conscience, and by the power of your Spirit enable me to follow where conscience leads, through Jesus Christ our Lord.*

The Voice of Conscience

Father of all in every age
*   In every clime adored,*
By saint, by savage and by sage,
*   Jehovah, Jove or Lord!*

Thou Great First Cause, least understood,
*   Who all my sense confined*
To know but this, that Thou art good,
*   And that myself am blind.*

You gave me in this dark estate,
*   To see the good from ill,*
And, binding nature fast in fate,
*   Left free the human will.*

What conscience dictates to be done,
*   Or warns me not to do,*
This, teach me more than hell to shun,
*   That more than Heaven pursue.*

If I am right, Thy grace impart
*   Still in the right to stay;*
If I am wrong, O, teach my heart
*   To find that better way.*

ALEXANDER POPE (1688-1744)

Comment

The poet gives early recognition in the fourth verse quoted – there are 13 in all! – of the place of conscience in the Christian pilgrimage. Conscience was described by Cardinal Newman as the 'true vicar of Christ in the soul, a prophet in its information, a monarch in its peremptoriness, a priest in its blessings or anathemas, according as we operate it or disobey it'. So long as conscience is informed, awake and alert, it will do for us what the poet knows it is doing for him. In particular it will warn us against the temptations of the flesh set out in the grim list which St Paul mentions in his letter to the Galatians (ch.5). Furthermore, should we fall, it will give us no peace of mind until we have sought God's forgiveness, and, it may be, our neighbour's. Different translations of the New Testament give different names to the evils to which the flesh is prone, but that does not change the substance of the evils nor does it 'date' them. In the sphere of temptation and evil not much has changed since St Paul's day. Satan may give new names and new substance to original sin but, dressed in whatever garments, the temptations of the flesh are the same for us as for those first Christians whom St Paul was warning.

Prayer *Help me, Lord, to wait for you, to wish for you and to watch for you. Give me a conscience which will ever be informed, awake and alert, that the sanctuary of my soul may not be defiled and the witness of my life may ever be to your glory.*

Examining Conscience

To begin your examination properly, place yourself in the presence of God and invoke the Holy Spirit that he may enlighten you and enable you to see yourself clearly as you really are, praying humbly with St Augustine, 'Teach me to know thee, O Lord, and to know myself', or saying with St Francis of Assisi 'Who art Thou, O Lord, and who am I?' Protest that you wish to note your progress, not for your own satisfaction but to rejoice in it for God's sake; not for your own glory, but for his, that you may thank him. Protest also if you seem to have made little spiritual progress, or even fallen back, that you will not give way to discouragement and become faint-hearted and lukewarm, but on the contrary that you will stir yourself to greater efforts, that you will humble yourself and strive, with God's grace, to remedy your defects. Having done this, consider carefully and peaceful-ly, how you have behaved up to the present towards God, your neighbour and yourself. . .

A lute player, having tested the strings of his lute, tightens or loosens them when he finds them out of tune; so, having tested the passions of your soul, its love and its hate, its desires, its fears and its hopes, you should likewise tune them if necessary, by means of God's grace, that you may play the melody you desire which is the praise of God's glory.

ST FRANCIS DE SALES (1567–1622)

Comment

The quotation is from a book entitled *Introduction to the Devout Life* written and pub-lished by St Francis de Sales more than 300 years ago at the time when Francis was Bishop of Geneva. The translation, by Dom Michael Day, is in everyday 'down to earth' language designed, firstly, not for scholars or experts in the spiritual life, but for all humble Christian followers after the Way, the Truth and the Life of Christ. The author is making the point here that all who are committed to Christ and His Church must examine themselves carefully and regularly in the course of their prayers, not merely to seek release from their sin through repentance, but also to mend what is wrong in their inclinations, and to make a new start in the pursuit of those fruits of the Spirit which we must develop to the glory of God and for our own peace of mind. Such an examination of conscience, such a testing of 'the passions of your soul', points the Christian once more to 'the fruit of the Spir-it' to which he re-dedicates himself.

Prayer　　*O all-good God, thou dost not forsake unless forsaken; thou never takest away thy gifts until we take away our hearts. As thou hast not deprived us of the operation of thy love, so help us not to deprive thee of our love and service.*

ST FRANCIS DE SALES

Commemorating Boniface, Bishop, Missionary, Martyr, 754

The Christian Militant

A man prepared against all ills to come,
That dares to dead the fire of martyrdom:
That sleeps at home; and sailing there at ease,
Fears not the fierce sedition of the Seas;
That's counter-proof against the Farm's mishaps,
Undreadful too of courtly thunderclaps:
That wears one face (like heaven) and never shows
A change, when Fortune either comes, or goes;
That keeps his own strong guard, in the despite
Of what can hurt by day, or harm by night:
That takes and re-delivers every stroke
Of Chance (as made up all of rock or oak)
That sighs at others' deaths; smiles at his own
Most dire and honest crucifixion.
Who for true glory suffers thus; we grant
Him to be our Christian militant.

ROBERT HERRICK (1591–1674)

Comment

The author, a parish priest, could well have had St Boniface in mind as he wrote that poetic definition of a Christian Militant. Boniface, a Devonian, was born in 680 and after his Exeter education he resolved to pursue a dream of his youth to be a missionary. His first attempt was thwarted but, with the encouragement of the Pope, he faced 'the fierce sedition of the seas' to cross to Germany where his ministry was richly blessed though he experienced many a change with Fortune coming and going. In 732 he became Bishop of the German people. During his episcopate of thirty years he faced an unceasing struggle preserving order in the Church and evangelising the heathen. He summoned help from England and helpers came 'like a swarm of bees out of a hive' says his biographer. A moment came when the Christian Militant sighing, 'at others' deaths', found himself forced to indict the Bishop of Mainz who had murdered his father's murderer. In time he himself became Bishop of Mainz and so remained until his martyrdom. On the eve of Pentecost he was attacked by an armed crowd endeavouring to resist his work. 'Let us not return evil for evil', said Boniface to those who tried to persuade him to resist with force. 'Strengthen yourselves in the Lord, and he will redeem your souls. Fear not them which can destroy the body, but put your trust in God, who will give you an eternal reward, and admit you to His heavenly Kingdom'. Whether he smiled at 'his own most dire and honest crucifixion', we do not know, but we do know that a copy of the Holy Gospels was in his hand as the death blow came to him.

Prayer *Father in Heaven, you have promised that those who endure to the end shall be saved, steel our wills with such courage, that come what may in opposition to your purpose and to our salvation, we may not falter, through Christ our Lord.*

The Joy of Love

He who acts out of the pure love of God, not only does he not perform his actions to be seen by men, but does not do them even that God may know of them. Such an one, if he thought it possible that his good works might escape the eye of God would still perform them with the same joy, and in the same pureness of love.

Whoever loves another does so according to his own attributes and properties. Therefore since the Lord is within you and is all powerful, he gives you power, and loves you with the same.

Since he is wise he loves you with wisdom.
Since he is good he loves you with goodness.
Since he is holy he loves you with holiness.
Since he is just he loves you with justice.
Since he is merciful he loves you with mercy.
Since he is compassionate he loves you with compassion.
Since he is gentle he loves you with gentleness.

St John of the Cross (1542–1591)

Comment

Love had to be the first 'fruit of the Spirit' in St Paul's list (Galatians ch.5). But it was not the love which some of his day would have in their minds. It was the love of that 'new commandment' of which Jesus spoke. 'A new commandment give I unto you that you love one another'. 'New!', some would exclaim. 'Love is not new. It is as old as the hills', to which Paul would have retorted, 'No, no, passion may be as old as the hills, but not the love of the Jesus sort'. To Jesus, love was a selfless, boundless, compassionate, forgiving and sacrificial quality which touches our individual relationships and our social responsibilities as citizens of God's world. The schoolboy howler that 'The New Testament ends with Revolutions' was by no means totally wrong! The 'bovver boys' of Thessalonica damned the early Christians as 'these that have turned the world upside down'. That is just what Christian love does when it finds itself confronted by selfishness, hatred, racism, inhumanity, corruption and the like. The cynic must be reminded that he may look no further than our own country to know that it was Christian love that gave us our first schools and colleges, first hospitals, first homes for the aged. These were social results of obedience to our Lord's new commandment – that you love one another. These were some of the first fruits of the Spirit's indwelling in the hearts of Christians and in the Church of Christ. Christ's commandment was new because it went far beyond the summary of the Law. He called his disciples to love one another *'as I have loved you'*.

Prayer   *O God of Love, we pray Thee to give us love; love in our thinking, love in our speaking, love in our doing, and love in the hidden places of our souls, that so at length we may be worthy to dwell with Thee, Who art Eternal Love.*

William Temple (1881–1944)

Pentecost

So free, so bright, so beautiful and fair
the Holy Dove descends the earthly air:
in startling joyance come
from its immortal home,
it bears the Glory that all men share.
Through ancient space and newest time, it brings
transcendent reason to a world of things:
it shows each mind and heart
how to assume its part
in dances born of God's imaginings.
On wings of subtlest flame, the Holy Dove
flies through the human world and offers love:
it teaches Heart and Mind
how to transcend their kind
and praise the God who lets all being move.
So free, so bright, so beautiful and fair
the Holy Dove flies through the mortal air:
always there descending,
always there ascending,
it brings the Glory that all men may share.

JOHN BENNETT (BORN 1920)

Comment

The poet, a Professor of English, in a Wisconsin college, uses the symbol of the Holy Spirit – the Dove, who silently and gently; 'flies through the human world and offers love'. Extending the symbolism we could say that the dovecotes to which the Spirit comes are the hearts and minds of God's people, but it is only as those hearts and minds of all God's people are open and prepared that the Spirit can enter with His gifts of love, and it is only as the Love which comes from God is shared, that God's imaginings are realised and his glory is revealed.

Prayer   *O God of Love, we pray Thee to give us love: love in our thinking, love in our speaking, love in our doing, and love in the hidden places of our souls;*
Love of our neighbours, near and far;
Love of our friends, old and new;
Love of those with whom we find it hard to bear; and
Love of those who find it hard to bear with us;
Love of those with whom we work, and of those with whom we play;
Love in joy, love in sorrow, love in life and love in death that so at length we may be worthy to dwell with Thee, Who are Eternal Love.

WILLIAM TEMPLE 1881–1944)

'And the second is this . . . '

George Herbert's chiefest recreation was music... his love of music was such that he went usually twice every week to the Cathedral Church in Salisbury and, before his return thence, he would usually sing and play his part at an appointed private music meeting... In one of his walks to Salisbury he saw a poor man with a poorer horse that was fallen under his load; they were both in distress and needed present help; which Mr Herbert perceiving, put off his canonical coat, and helped the poor man to unload, and after to load his horse. The poor man blessed him for it; he blessed the poor man; and was so like the Good Samaritan that he gave him money to refresh both himself and his horse; and told him that if he loved himself he should be merciful to his beast. Thus he left the poor man; and at his coming to the musical friends at Salisbury, they began to wonder that Mr George Herbert, which used to be so trim and clean, came into that company so soiled and discomposed; but he told them the occasion. And when one of the company told him that he had disparaged himself by so dirty an employment, his answer was, that the thought of what he had done would prove music to him at midnight; and that omission of it would have upbraided and made discord in his conscience whensoever he should pass by that place. 'For if I be bound to pray for all that be in distress, I am sure that I am bound, so far as it is in my power, to practise what I pray for'.

IZAAK WALTON (1593–1683)

Comment

That 'good Samaritan story', recorded by Izaak Walton in his *Life of George Herbert* who was parish priest of Bemerton during the last three years of his life, is set down in our thoughts about Love – the first fruit of the Spirit – because in one sense the incident is trivial. It was not some mighty act of Christian service which would find place in the ecclesiastical media of the day, or some massive contribution to charitable funds of which the world would be told. The fact is that so much which can be counted as 'love of neighbour' consists of acts of seemingly trivial service to our neighbours whether these live in our own road, worship in our own church, starve in Ethiopia, or suffer indignity because they differ from us in colour. Ours is the duty to offer a ministry of love in these and every circumstance of need – whether known by the world or only by ourselves. This embodies too a ministry of listening to the outpourings of grief of a neighbour weighed down by sorrow, distress or anxiety. Our neighbour may be on our doorstep or far away. It is not distance which brings him into that category. It is need.

Prayer *Heavenly Father, I ask you to keep my eyes open to the needs of neighbours near and far; alert my conscience, direct my action, strengthen my will to offer them the service of my love, through Jesus Christ our Lord.*

Commemorating Columba, Abbot of Iona, Missionary, 597

Columcille

On some island, I long to be,
a rocky promontory, looking on
the coiling surface of the sea.

To see the waves, crest on crest,
of the great shining ocean, composing
a hymn to the Creator without rest.

To see without sadness the strand
lined with bright shells, and birds
lamenting overhead a lonely sound.

To hear the whisper of small waves.
against the rocks, that endless sea-
sound, like keening over graves.

To watch the sea-birds sailing,
in flocks, and most marvellous
of monsters, the turning whale.

To see the shift from ebb-tide
to flood and tell my secret name:
'He who set his back on Ireland'.

ST COLUMBA (521–597)
VERSION: JOHN MONTAGUE

Comment

Columba was born in Ireland and clearly loved his homeland, though he spent most of his years outside it. He founded many monasteries in his native land, at Kells, at Durrow, at Raphoe, at Drumhome and at Derry, declaring that the last-named was 'sweeter and dearer' to him than all the others. However, he was not to be there long for when he quarrelled with the king, relations between them became so strained that he and a number of his brothers left the country. He landed in Iona on the west coast of Scotland and from there, having built a small church and some cells for their home, after two years he engaged himself in missionary journeys during which he converted the Picts to the Faith and became known in a considerable area around the firths of Clyde and Forth. He was much sought after as a friend, as a teacher, as a pastor and as a confessor. His biographer, one Adamnan, recalls that in addition to taking upon himself his full share of the manual labours of the monastery, he spent much time in prayer and in making copies of the Holy Gospels. He records Columba as being 'polished in speech, sanctified in work, great in counsel, unwearied in prayer and fasts and vigils... loving to all... and gladdened in his inmost heart with the joy of the Holy Spirit'. Such a thought must surely prompt us to make an affirmation of trust in God as St Columba did and in his words:

Prayer

Alone with none but Thee, my God, I journey on my way, I have no fear when Thou are near O King of night and day. More safe am I within Thy hand than if a host did round me stand.

ATRRIBUTED TO ST COLUMBA

Unkindness

Lord, make me coy and tender to offend:
In friendships first, I think, if that agree
      Which I intend
      Unto my friend's intent and end;
I would not use a friend as I use Thee.

When that my friend pretendeth to a place,
I quit my interest, and leave it free;
      But when Thy grace
      Sues for my heart, I thee displease;
Nor would I use a friend as I use Thee.

If any touch my friend or his good name,
It is my honour and my love to free
      His blasted fame
      From the least spot or thought of
      blame;
I could not use a friend as I use Thee.

Yet can a friend what Thou hast done
      fulfil?
O, write in brass, 'My God upon a tree
      His blood did spill
      Only to purchase my good-will';
Yet use I not my foes as I use Thee.

My friend may spit upon my curious floor,
Would he have gold? I lend it instantly;
      But let the poor,
      And Thee within them, starve at
      door;
I cannot use a friend as I use Thee.

GEORGE HERBERT (1593–1633)

Comment

The good priest who helped the labourer and his load - see the story on June the Eighth – indicts himself for his inconsistencies, and most of all for the recollections that he has, that his service of his Lord often falls short in fidelity to his service to his friends. Kindness is Love in action. Our little acts of kindness may on occasion be motivated by something less than pure love. They may be tainted by self-interest. But deliberate unkindness, expressed whether in a word or action, deals a mortal blow to love of neighbour, and creates a situation which calls for apology and reconciliation. Furthermore, the ministry of kindness has converting power, whereas unkindness, meted out by a Christian to a cynical man of the world, is likely to win the retort comparable with the enigmatic utterance recorded in St Luke's Gospel: 'If they do this when the wood is green, what will happen when it is dry?' (St Luke ch.23 v. 31). In other words he will say, 'If that's how a Christian behaves, what can you expect from people who are not?'

Prayer   *Lord, I expect to pass through this world but once; any good thing that I can do, or any kindness that I can show to any fellow creature, let me do it now; help me to requite injury with kindness and so to fulfil your law of love.*

St Barnabas the Apostle

All qualities are not only good, but infinitely perfect, as they are in God; and it is absolutely impossible that they should have any evil or defect in them, as they are in the one God, who is the great and universal All. But the same qualities, thus infinitely good and perfect in God, may become imperfect in the human creature; because, in the creature, they may be divided and separated from one another by the creature itself. God could not possibly create a creature to be an infinite All, like himself, but only creatures that are finite and limited. Yet neither could He bring any creature into existence, save by imparting to it His own qualities and the freedom of His own nature, and so giving it the capacity of dividing and separating these qualities from one another. . .

There is no evil, no guilt, no deformity in any creature but in its dividing and separating itself from something which God had given to be in union with it. This, and this alone, is the whole nature of all good and evil in the creature, both in spiritual and material things. . . The qualities of fire and strength that constitute an evil wrath in the soul, are in themselves very good qualities and necessary to every good life; but they become an evil wrath when separated from some other qualities with which they should be united. That which in a devil is an evil selfishness, a wrathful fire, a stinging motion, is in a holy angel the everlasting kindling of a divine life, the strong birth of heavenly love, a real cause of an ever-springing, ever triumphant joyfulness, an ever-increasing sensibility of bliss.

WILLIAM LAW (1686–1761)

Comment

This extract from the writings of William Law, though difficult, repays quiet reflection. It is most appropriate as we praise God for the life and witness of St Barnabas. St Luke describes him as a good man 'full of the Holy Ghost and of Faith', and all we know about him confirms Luke's judgement. Barnabas was the man who, having given himself to Christ, sold his lands so that the little Christian community could live as such, sharing their possessions. He was the man without whose commendation of Paul's conversion and integrity, the Christian church might never have heard the name of Paul, for all others suspected Paul's intentions. He was the man who quarrelled – yes quarrelled! – with Paul, when Paul refused to allow John Mark to join them for the second Missionary journey (see Acts ch.15). Barnabas stood by young Mark and saw in him potential for powerful witness in the service of his Lord if only he were given a second chance. Subsequently Barnabas took Mark with him on a mission to his homeland, Cyprus. Subsequently too the rift was mended and Paul himself came to value Mark's ministry. Barnabas had all the human qualities, sufficient 'fire and strength', for example, to hold his own in the battle with Paul regarding Mark's defection. But most of all he was 'a good man', and that goodness was demonstrated 'both in spiritual and material things'. How did it triumph within him? It triumphed because he was 'full of the Holy Ghost'.

Prayer   *Fill us with your Spirit, Lord, that our faith may grow in strength and your goodness shine in our lives.*

From Love to Joy

Ah! heavenly joy! But who hath ever heard,
Who hath seen joy, or who shall ever find
Joy's language? There is neither speech nor word;
Naught but itself to teach it to mankind.
 Scarce in our twenty thousand painful days
We may touch something: but there lives beyond
The best of art, or nature's kindest phrase –
The hope whereof our spirit is fair and fond.
The cause of beauty given to man's desires
Writ in the expectancy of starry skies,
The faith which gloweth in our fleeting fires,
The aim of all good that here we prize;
 Which but to love, pursue and pray for well
Maketh earth heaven, and to forget it hell.
Eternal Father, who didst all create,
In whom we live, and to whose bosom move
Till its loud praises sound at heaven's high gate
Perfect thy kingdom in our passing state,
That here on earth Thou may'st as well approve
Our service, as Thou ownest theirs above,
Whose joy we echo and in pain await.

ROBERT BRIDGES (1844–1930)

Comment

Robert Bridges gives us the right lead into our meditations on the second of the fruits of the Spirit. With his 'Ah! heavenly joy' and his 'whose joy we echo', he indicates the source of the joy which is of the Spirit and the precious responsibility which is ours to 'echo' that joy in the world. We can and should desire joy for ourselves but we cannot create it. It can never be a consequence of superficial things such as wealth or even health. These may ensure happiness but they cannot guarantee joy. Joy is heavenly in the sense that it comes unsought as we are 'in the Spirit', speaking the language of heaven, which is love, and ordering our lives with the laws of heaven as our Lord proclaimed them. Such joy can be so anchored in our hearts that it abides even when circumstances conspire against us. The psalmist was not the first to experience the truth that though sorrow may endure for a night, joy comes again in the morning (Psalm 30 v.5). The joy which is the fruit of the Spirit may sometimes be sullied by sorrow or by suffering, but these have no power to destroy it though they may conceal its light. The joy which is of the fruit of the Spirit is imperilled only by sin.

Prayer *Heavenly Father, give me the joy of your Spirit in my heart that what-*
ever life brings in its course the joy of heaven may abide in me to comfort
and to sustain.

Joy

'God beholds thee individually, whoever thou art. He calls thee by thy name. He sees thee and understands thee. He knows what is in thee, all thy own peculiar feelings and thoughts, thy dispositions and likings, thy strength and thy weakness. He views thee in thy day of rejoicing and thy day of sorrow. He sympathises in thy hopes and in thy temptations. He interests himself in all thy anxieties and remembrances, in all the risings and falls of thy spirit. . . Thou does not love thyself better than He loves thee. Thou canst not shrink from pain more than He dislikes thy bearing it: and if he puts it on thee, it is as thou art wise, for a greater good afterwards. . .

Doubt, gloom, impatience, have been expelled; joy has taken their place, the hope of heaven and the harmony of a pure heart, the triumph of self-mastery, sober thoughts, and a contented mind. How can charity towards all men fail to follow, being the mere affectionateness of innocence and peace. Thus the spirit of God creates in us the simplicity and warmth of heart which children have, nay, rather the perfectness of His heavenly hosts, high and low being joined together in His mysterious work; for what are implicit trust, ardent love, abiding purity, but the mind both of little children and of the adoring Seraphim! . . .

Whatever troubles come upon you, body, or estate, from within or from without, from chance or from intent, from friends or foes – whatever your trouble be, though you be lonely, O children of a heavenly Father, be not afraid!

CARDINAL NEWMAN (1801–1890)

Comment

'Doubt, gloom, impatience! . . . whatever troubles come upon you . . . joy has taken their place'. One might have thought that the Cardinal would not have set joy by the side of such a list of human troubles, but he was right. The word which he could not couple with his list is the word happiness. The troubles could eliminate happiness, but they could not eliminate joy. Joy is distinctly a Christian experience. Its springs are deep down. Happiness is an experience which is ours when everything is going right for us. Joy, on the other hand, is a divine gift. Happiness comes from 'doing'. 'If ye know these things, happy are ye if ye *do* them' (St John ch.13 v.17). Joy comes from 'being' – that is being in Christ. 'These things I speak in the world, that they might have my joy fulfilled in themselves (St John ch.17 v.13). Someone has said that joy is the echo of God's life within us. 'All seek it', said St John Chrysostom, 'but it is not found on earth'.

Prayer   *God of hope, fill thy children with all joy and peace in believing, that we and they may abound in hope in the power of the Holy Ghost; through Jesus Christ our Lord.*

(ST PAUL , ROMANS CH.15 V.13)

Commemorating Basil the Great
Bishop of Caesarea and Teacher of the Faith, d.379

The Holy Spirit's action

The Spirit is present like the sun to each individual who is capable of receiving him, and emits an influence which is sufficient to help them all, but is not divided; they profit by sharing in him according to their natures, not according to his power. Through him hearts are raised high, the weak are led by the hand and those who are advanced gain perfection. He it is who shines on those whose hearts are purified and stainless and makes them truly spiritual through the common union they have with him.

Even as bright and shining bodies, once touched by a ray of light falling on them, become ever more glorious and themselves cast another light, so too souls that carry the Spirit, and are enlightened by the Spirit, become spiritual themselves, and send forth grace upon others. This grace enables them to foresee the future, to understand mysteries, to grasp hidden things, and to dance with the angels. So is their joy unending, so is their perseverance to God unfailing, so do they acquire likeness to God, and so – most sublime of all – do they themselves become divine.

ST BASIL THE GREAT (c.330–379)

Comment

Though born of Christian parents Basil was not himself baptised until he was a young man of 29. It was then that he turned his back on the extravagances of his youth, and began to seek ways in which he could serve God. He travelled about for some time to observe how other men fulfilled their ordained ministry. He found many living in isolation from one another and conceived the plan of gathering them together in community, believing that their witness might thereby be more powerful in the world. He was, in fact, the first priest to found a monastery – at least in the East – in which monks could live together under strict rules and spend their time in manual work, in mission, in prayer and in study. Basil became Bishop of Caesarea in 370 and from that time until his death, his was a life in which his service of God and the church was pursued against both state opposition and abuses and heresies within the Church itself. Basil was a man of great learning who was noted for his eloquence, his statesmanlike ordering of the Church's life and worship, and his sensitivity to the needs of the poor for whom he built hospitals and provided relief. Nor was he lacking a sense of humour for when an angry imperial officer threatened to 'tear out' his liver, he replied: 'I should be very much obliged if you would do so, as it gives me a great deal of trouble where it is.'

Prayer   *O Lord our God, show us the course wherein we should go. Let thy Spirit curb our wayward senses, and guide and enable us unto that which is our true good, to keep thy laws and in all our works evermore to rejoice in thy glorious and gladdening Presence, for thine is the glory for ever and ever.*

ST BASIL THE GREAT

Dominion

I went beneath the sunny sky
When all things bowed to June's desire –
The pansy with its steadfast eye,
The blue shells on the lupin spire.

The swelling fruit along the boughs,
The grass grown heady in the rain,
Dark roses fitted for the brows
Of queens, great kings have sung in vain.

My little cats with tiger bars,
Bright claws all hidden in content;
Swift birds that flashed like darkling stars
Across the cloudy continent.

And all these things seemed very glad,
The sun, the flowers, the birds on wing,
The jolly beasts, the furry clad
Fat bees, the fruit, and everything.

But gladder than them all was I
Who, being man, might gather up
The joy of all beneath the sky,
And add their treasure to my cup.

And travel every shining way,
And laugh with God in God's delight,
Create a world for every day,
And store a dream for every night.

JOHN DRINKWATER (1882–1937)

Comment

You may have noticed that our commemoration of St Basil the Great yesterday did not interrupt our meditations on the Holy Spirit and the fruit of the Spirit – joy. The quotation yesterday was from Basil's treatise *Of the Holy Spirit*, and you will have sensed his own joy in his phrases describing the effects of the Holy Spirit's indwelling in the heart of man. 'To dance with the angels... so is their joy unending' and the words of a man who had himself experienced the Spirit's indwelling and the subsequent exhilaration of heavenly joy. The poet John Drinkwater experiences the same joy at the wonders, the liveliness and the beauty in the whole of God's creation. 'The joy of all beneath the sky' lifted his own spirit so that he was truly in communion with the Holy Spirit impelling him to 'laugh with God in God's delight'. There they are, the fourth-century bishop and the twentieth-century poet: one talks of dancing with the angels and the other of laughing with God. Each was for a moment possessed by the Spirit and it was the Spirit's joy which bubbled over in those expressive phrases.

Prayer   *O God, may I live to have one day of unsullied joy!*

LUDWIG VON BEETHOVEN (1770–1827)

'A thing of beauty'

A thing of beauty is a joy for ever:
Its loveliness increases; it will never
Pass into nothingness; but still will keep
A bower quiet for us, and a sleep
Full of sweet dreams, and health, and quiet breathing.
Therefore, on every morrow, are we wreathing
A flowery band to bind us to the earth
Spite of despondence, of the inhuman dearth
Of noble natures, of the gloomy days,
Of all the unhealthy and o'er-darkened ways
Made for our searching: yes, in spite of all,
Some shape of beauty moves away the pall
From our dark spirits. Such the sun, the moon,
Trees old and young, sprouting shady boon
For simple sheep; and such are daffodils
With the green world they live in; and clear rills
That for themselves a cooling covert make
'Gainst the hot season; the mid-forest brake
Rich with a sprinkling of fair musk-rose blooms.

JOHN KEATS (1795–1821)

Comment

The familiar lines are from *Endymion*, one of John Keats' early poems which was received by the literary world with something less than enthusiasm when it first appeared, but which came to be accounted among his best. Its length alone denies it a place in popular anthologies. The young poet writes with exuberance about the world about him and sees in all its beauty, qualities which are not only pleasing to the eye but which evoke a response from the very soul of man. True beauty, whether in the natural world or in the character of man, in art or music or literature, is of God. The joy which it affords us is the joy of the spirit, a joy which will 'never pass into nothingness' so long as we see the hand of God in all that is beautiful, good and true. St Francis of Assisi's *Canticle – Great Lord of King and Earth and Sky and Sea* similarly reflects his shining joy as he looks out upon God's world. It was said of Francis that in him 'the joy of God erupted like a volcano'. Whenever the hand of God is seen at work in the world of nature and in the world of human nature, there joy is kindled in the heart of man. If we feel little joy we should do well to make time, in our over-active lives, to reflect quietly on nature in these two forms, and to pray for eyes to see.

Prayer

Lord, give me joy in my heart, the joy which comes from seeing you in all that is beautiful and good and true; and, prompted by your Spirit, help me day by day to bring joy to the hearts of others in ministries of kindness.

Peace

My soul there is a country
  Far beyond the stars,
Where stands a wingèd sentry
  All skilful in the wars:
There above noise, and danger,
  Sweet Peace sits crowned with smiles,
And One born in a manger
  Commands the beauteous files.
He is thy gracious Friend
  And – O my soul awake! –
Did in pure love descend
  To die here for thy sake.
If thou canst get but thither,
  There grows the flower of Peace,
The Rose that cannot wither,
  Thy fortress, and thy ease.
Leave then thy foolish ranges,
  For none can thee secure
But One, who never changes,
  Thy God, thy life, thy cure.

HENRY VAUGHAN (1622–1695)

Comment

This is perhaps the best known of the poems of Henry Vaughan, brought together in his two volumes of religious poetry in *Sparks from the Flint*. It gives us a good opening for our thoughts about the third of the fruits of the Spirit – Peace. Vaughan lived in the troublous years of the seventeenth century and, as a Royalist, saw some of his dearest friends killed, and his brother, who was a priest, deprived of his benefice. He wrote, 'Certain Divine Raies break out of the soul in adversity like sparks of fire on the afflicted flint'. In this poem, written in just such a time of adversity, he declares his stance for life. He is talking, of course, of that Peace within the soul, which can sustain us even in the midst of the bitterest trials. It is what The Book of Common Prayer calls 'the peace which the world cannot give'. Only the wilful sin which remains unconfessed, or the eyes 'open to the world but closed to God', can deprive us of that peace of the soul. After the torment of his early life St Augustine could write in his *Confessions*, 'Thou hast touched me and I have been translated into thy peace'.

Prayer *Give us, O Lord, that peace which the world cannot give. Take from our souls all strife, all bitterness, all despair, and help us ever to remember that the peace which is our final good can be found only in you.*

Blessed are the Peacemakers

The Christian virtues come to fruition in the man who preserves the simplicity of Christian peace. No one can be called a child of God without first deserving the name of peacemaker. It is peace which frees a man from slavery, and ennobles him. In God's eyes his condition as well as his character is changed, for peace makes a son of a servant, and a free man of a slave. Peace in the community is God's will; it is the sweetness of Christ and the perfection of sanctity. Peace is the rule of justice, the mistress of learning, the guardian of morals; its restraining influence is everywhere to be commended. It is the goal of our prayers, an easy and effective way of making atonement, the complete fulfilment of all our longings. Peace is the mother of love, the bond of friendship, the clearest proof of that innocence which craves satisfaction of God, which seeks fulfilment and has its longing satisfied. Peace must be preserved by precepts which have binding force, for the Lord Jesus Christ has said 'My peace I give unto you'.

God has commanded us to preserve his gift; . . . We must love peace and cherish harmony, for they are the very conditions which produce charity and sustain it. . . The community should be closely knit in peace. . . We should guard peace before all the virtues, for God is always present in peace. Love peace and all is peaceful. God's Church was established in the simplicity of peace. If you embrace that perfect discipline in Christ, you may well rejoice.

ST PETER CHRYSOLOGUS (C.450 A.D.)

Comment

The quotation is from a sermon preached by the fifth-century Bishop of Ravenna, called 'Chrysologus', which means 'golden-worded', for his ability to grip the attention of his hearers as he expounded the Scriptures in words and illustrations which became memorable. Many of his sermons are extant and all of them are short! Based on our Lord's words 'Peace I leave with you, my peace I give unto you', this Doctor of the Church makes it clear that peace does not reside in outward things but dwells within the soul of man. It is a fruit of the indwelling of the Holy Spirit. It is not something which withers through an onslaught of sorrow or suffering or pain, but it is something which we lose, if and when we cherish envy, anger, pride, avarice and selfish ambition. George Herbert said, 'Where there is peace, God is'. He could have added as truly, 'Where God is, there is peace'.

Prayer   *Blessed Lord,*
Drop thy still dews of quietness
Till all our strivings cease;
Take from our souls the strain and stress,
And let our ordered lives confess
The beauty of thy Peace.

J.G. WHITTIER (1807–1892)

My Peace I leave with you

Thy Peace! Thou pale, despisèd Christ!
  What Peace is there in Thee,
Nailed to the Cross that crowns the world
    In agony?

What Peace was Thine? Misunderstood,
  Rejected by Thine own,
Pacing Thy grim Gethsemane,
    Outcast and lone.

What Peace hast Thou to give the world?
  There is enough of pain;
Always upon my window beats
    The sound of rain.

For millions come to Golgotha
  To suffer and to die,
Forsaken in their hour of need,
    And asking, Why?

Man's Via Crucis never ends,
  Earth's Calvaries increase,
The world is full of spears and nails,
    But where is Peace?

'Take up thy cross and follow Me,
  I am the Way, my son,
Via Crucis, Via Pacis,
    Meet and are one'.

GEOFFREY STUDDERT-KENNEDY (1883–1929)

Comment

Here is the eminent padre of the European War coming to grips with the problem which haunted his soldier friends as it haunts many a Christian pilgrim. Not all of them would understand his conclusion: '*Via Crucis, Via Pacis,* meet and are one'. The Way of the Cross does not, from a superficial glance, appear to lead to Peace, but such is the truth. On the first Good Friday evening the friends of Jesus would have made their way home disillusioned and dispirited. Christ's Cross was as hideous as any they had seen before. But that same Cross is now central to the world's history – B.C. – A.D. The Christ who was rejected and scorned and apparently defeated, triumphed over death and all that he had taught and promised and claimed was vindicated. The way of the cross is spelt out for us in selflessness, in acts and words and needs of love, in apologies, in reconciliations. All these are painful, burdensome, humbling – but they make for Peace.

Prayer   *Let your Spirit, O Lord, so fill my heart that I may be a peacemaker, and so strengthen my soul that I may bear manfully whatever crosses I must, to pass to others the peace which you have given me.*

Peace and War

Waste

Waste of Muscle, waste of Brain,
Waste of Patience, waste of Pain,
Waste of Manhood, waste of Health,
Waste of Beauty, waste of wealth,
Waste of Blood, and waste of Tears,
Waste of Youth's most precious years,
Waste of ways the Saints have trod,
Waste of Glory, waste of God, –
      War!

GEOFFREY STUDDERT-KENNEDY (1883–1929)
WRITTEN IN PERIOD 1914-18

Nightmare

Darkest night of man's imagination,
When nuclear horrors hold him in their grip:
Bleak desolation foul desecration
Of man, of beast, of plant – God's
      workmanship.
Death stalks the lifeless land, and everywhere
Are bodies strewn – listless, inert, deceased.
Man breaks the sombre silence with a prayer
That from this nightmare he may be released.
But still men pile their weapons of destruction,
Still hurl they turgid threats from sea to sea,
Ignoring still the palpable deduction,
That none can win a war if none there be.
   From faleshood, fear and folly and from
      hate,
   Preserve your people, Lord, from this
      grim fate.

CYRIL BULLEY
WRITTEN IN 1983

Comment

Our thoughts about Peace could not be concluded without facing its impious denial. This century has been marred by two tragic wars and it seems that its closing years are to be shadowed by the threat – pray God not the reality – of a nuclear holocaust. War is the very negation of that fruit of the Spirit which is Peace. War is evil. Of that there can be no doubt. In the course of the Church's history a view has been sustained that it would be morally defensible if its purpose were to banish a greater evil. On the other hand many great Christian leaders have concluded that there is nothing which can justify a war, and the more so since a modern conflict could not discriminate between armies and civilians and could indeed result in the blasphemous destruction of God's world and millions of his children. But the tide to destruction is never irresistible. Strife between nations, strife within industries, strife of whatever kind can be resolved in the power of God. Cranmer's prayer points the way: 'that peace and happiness, truth and justice, religion and piety' may be established among us for all generations. 'Peace and happiness' are not self-poised. They derive from 'truth and justice'. They in their turn are not self-poised. They derive from religion, and religion is sustained only by piety, and that includes your piety and mine.

Prayer   *Father in Heaven, we pray that your Being may be known and acknowledged throughout the world, that your laws, revealed to us through the ministry of your Son, our Lord, may be reverenced throughout the world, so that living together in love, your children may inherit that peace which is the gift of your Spirit.*

'More than conquerors'

I was interned in March 1943. The Japanese Military Police raided the prison, searched our luggage and arrested some sixty of us. It is not my purpose to relate the torture they inflicted upon us, but rather to tell you of some of the spiritual experiences of that ordeal, which was to be a challenge to my courage, my faith and my love.

The beatings and long hours of ignoble pain were a severe test. In the middle of the torture they asked me if I still believed in God. When, by God's help, I said 'I do', they asked me why God did not save me. By the help of His Spirit I said, 'God does save me. He does not save me by freeing me from pain or punishment, but He saves me by giving me the spirit to bear it'. When they asked me why I did not curse them I told them that it was because I was a follower of Jesus Christ who taught me that we were all brethren. When I muttered 'Forgive them', I wondered how far I was being merely dramatic, and if I really meant it, because I looked at their faces as they stood round, taking it in turns to flog me, and their faces were hard and cruel. But, by the grace of God, I saw those men not as they were, but as they had been. Once they were little children . . . happy in their parents' love, and it is hard to hate little children. So I saw them, not as they were, but as they were capable of becoming, redeemed by the power of Christ, and I knew that I should say 'forgive'.

LEONARD WILSON (1897–1970)

Comment

'The fruit of the Spirit is . . . long-suffering'. The quotation is a small part of a broadcast which Bishop Leonard Wilson, who was Bishop of Singapore at the time the Japanese occupied the island, made to the nation on a Sunday morning in 1946. The whole world knew something of what he had gone through but his broadcast, which was concerned less with the sufferings and more with the grace which had sustained him throughout, disclosed for the first time the quality of the long-suffering with which the Spirit had endowed him for that ordeal. The Greek word which the Authorised Version of the Bible translates 'long-suffering' has been translated 'patience' in all the subsequent translations. Maybe the combination of the two words best tells us what this particular fruit of the Spirit really is. It is the power by which we can endure patiently: suffering, pain, insult, injury, unkindness, chronic illness, physical disabilities and the like, without answering them with bitterness. There are times, of course, when some of these can be overcome, and should be. There are other times when, as the world puts it, we have 'to grin and bear it'. Christians can do that in the power of the Spirit. But we must remember that at no time must any such sufferings be responded to with bitterness. That way closes the door to the Spirit's influence and offers no healing and no comfort.

Prayer

O God, give me strength to change the things I can change, to accept with patience the things I cannot change, and the wisdom to know the difference.

REINHOLD NIEBUHR

Alban, First Martyr of Britain d.304

The Good Great Man

How seldom, friend, a good great man inherits
  Honour or wealth, with all his worth and pains!
It sounds like stories from the land of spirits
If any man obtain that which he merits
  Or any merit that which he obtains.

The Reply

For shame, dear friend! Renounce this canting strain!
What wouldst thou have a good great man obtain?
Wealth, title, dignity, a golden chain,
Or throne of corpses which his sword hath slain?
Greatness and goodness are not means, but ends,
Hath he not always treasures, always friends, –
The good great man? Three treasures, – love, and light,
  And calm thoughts, equable as infants' breath;
And three firm friends, more sure than day and night, –
  Himself, his Maker, and the Angel Death.

SAMUEL TAYLOR COLERIDGE (1772–1834)

Comment

Not a great deal is known about St Alban, the first English martyr, and what we do know comes from Bede who wrote his history some 400 years after the martyrdom. That he was 'born in fertile Britain's land' is a fact established by his biographer. Of his early years nothing is known, save that he was a pagan. Bede tells us that he sheltered a Christian priest who was fleeing from persecution. So impressed was he with the priest's serenity and faith that Alban himself became a Christian and was baptised by the priest. When the persecutors tracked down the fugitive's hiding-place Alban impersonated the priest and dressed himself in the priest's clothing. He declared his adherence to the Christian faith to the judge and refused the opportunity he was given to retract his profession. Scourging did not shake his constancy and the judge ordered his immediate execution. A church was built by the Christian community on the site of his martyrdom and that was later superceded by St Alban's Abbey. The priest shared his treasures – 'love and light, and calm thoughts' with his pagan host with such effect that he too turned to the Source of those treasures and in doing so found 'himself, his Maker' and, with consummate courage, 'the angel of death'. The citizens of the city of St Albans can look back with pride on the 'good and great man' who in effect struck out its pagan name – Verulamium – and christened it with his baptismal name. May it be given to us to change the world in which we live.

Prayer   *Praise to you, O God, for your servant Alban's witness and courage. Give to the people of our land, in which he died a martyr's death, the courage to stand firm in the faith of their fathers.*

Patience

They who tread the path of labour where My feet have trod;
They who work without complaining do the holy will of God;
Nevermore thou needest seek Me; I am with thee everywhere;
Raise the stone, and thou shalt find Me; cleave the wood and I am there.

Where the many toil together, there am I among My own;
Where the tired workman sleepeth, there am I with him alone.
I the Peace, which passeth knowledge, dwell amid the daily strife;
I the Bread of Heaven, am broken in the sacrament of life.

Every task, however simple, sets the soul that does it free;
Every deed of love and mercy done to man, is done to Me.
Nevermore thou needest seek Me; I am with thee everywhere;
Raise the stone, and thou shalt find Me; cleave the wood and I am there.

HENRY VAN DYKE (1852–1933)

Comment

Patience is a virtue to which the Christian's attention is frequently drawn in Holy Scripture. 'Let patience have her perfect work, that ye may be perfect and entire, wanting nothing' exhorts the author of the General Epistle of St James (ch.1 vv.3, 4). 'Let us run with patience the race that is set before us, looking unto Jesus', writes the author of the letter to the Hebrews (ch.12 v.1). It is interesting that in the various translations of the Bible the word 'patience' is replaced by, for example, constancy, endurance, perseverance, and even 'gallant determination'. These are, indeed, more accurate descriptions of the Greek word in the New Testament. The patience which is the fruit of the Spirit is not something passive – a mere ability to bear whatever comes in work, in responsibility, in suffering and much else. It is something active, enabling the worker, enabling the sufferer, to welcome the trials which the task brings and the strain which the suffering inflicts and to triumph over them. The Christian is exhorted not merely to 'take what comes' passively, but actively to turn what comes into something great and glorious. Such was the 'patience' of the martyrs who died not in tears but in triumph. They saw that spiritual power is greater than material. Our 'testings' may be less than theirs only in extent, though this is not invariably so, but the spiritual resources available to us are not one whit less than those available to them.

Prayer   *O Lord God, when thou givest to thy servants to endeavour any great matter, grant us also to know that it is not the beginning, but the continuing of the same, until it be thoroughly finished, which yieldeth the true glory; through him that for the finishing of thy work laid down his life, our Redeemer, Jesus Christ.*

SIR FRANCIS DRAKE (1540–1596)

The birth of St John the Baptist

The last and greatest Herald of heaven's King,
Girt with rough skins, hies to the deserts wild,
Among that savage brood the woods forth bring,
Which he than man more harmless found and mild.
His food was locusts, and what there both spring,
With honey that from virgin hives distilled;
Parched body, hollow eyes, some uncouth thing
Made him appear, long since from earth exiled.
There burst he forth: 'All ye whose hopes rely
On God, with me amidst these deserts mourn,
Repent, repent, and from old errors turn!'
  Who listened to his voice, obeyed his cry?
Only the echoes, which he made relent,
Rung from their flinty caves, 'Repent! Repent!'

WILLIAM DRUMMOND (1585–1649)

Comment

'John the Baptist leapt into the arena fully armed'. So says a Scottish New Testament scholar. The word 'leapt' is apt indeed for anyone coming new to the New Testament could not but be surprised to be confronted with this gaunt and somewhat forbidding figure so early in the story. It is good first to remember that he is 'anchored' in history. He is no shadowy figure of holy Scripture for we find him mentioned in the writings of the Jewish historian Flavius Josephus. He was born about six months before Jesus and in his early years he clearly lived an austere life. About the year AD 26 he emerged as a powerful preacher, declaring that the kingdom of heaven was at hand and that he was the forerunner of the Messiah. He was the prophet in whom the voice of ancient prophecy came alive. He denounced evil and rounded fiercely upon those who perpetrated it whether they were leaders, one might say, in 'church' or 'state'. But his message was not merely negative. He could, and did, call the Pharisees and Sadducees a 'generation of vipers' but having said his worst about the evils of his day, he pointed the people to what might be if they followed the new way. He was the great protester of the first century. He led no marches and carried no banners. His message was never 'Rebel!'. Nor was it 'Reform!', though reformation was sorely needed in 'church' and 'state', in personal, social and national life. He was a preacher with one recurring text: 'Repent'. He said in effect 'Turn away from sin. Turn to God', and so saying he pointed to Christ. 'Repentance', said Milton, 'is the golden key that opens the palace of Eternity'. We must ask ourselves whether we have found the golden key of repentance. If not maybe another 're..' word is called for – namely reflection.

Prayer *Lord, for thy tender mercies' sake, lay not our sins to our charge, but forgive us all that is past; and give us grace to amend our lives, to decline from sin and incline to virtue that we may walk with a perfect heart before thee, now and evermore.*

Twelve years of 'long-suffering'

After I had lain in prison about seven weeks, the quarter sessions were to be held in Bedford. There a bill of indictment was preferred against me... and the chief justice gave his sentence...

'You must be had back again in prison and there lie for three months following; and at three months' end, if you do not submit to go to church to hear divine service, and leave your preaching, you must be banished from the realm: and if, after such a day as shall be appointed you to be gone, you shall be found in the realm, or to be found to come over again without special licence from the king, you must stretch by the neck for it, I tell you plainly'.

Thus I departed from them; and I can truly say, I bless the Lord Jesus Christ for it, that my heart was sweetly refreshed in the time of my examination, and also afterwards at my returning to the prison, so that I found Christ's words more than bare trifles, where he saith: 'I will give you a mouth and wisdom which all your adversaries will not be able to gainsay or resist'.

JOHN BUNYAN (1628–1688)

Comment

Bunyan was in Bedford Gaol for twelve years. He was long-suffering, he was patient, but he was active in the service of the Lord for whom he was suffering. From that long imprisonment came many devotional books including, of course, one of the literary classics of all time – *The Pilgrim's Progress*. He could have spent his years feeling sorry for himself but accepting the situation passively. He could have spent his time writing vicious words against 'the authorities', that is, responding with bitterness. He chose none of these and the world is the richer for his choice. In many ways he was a John Baptist of his age. He might well have been indiscreet in his utterances and unwise in some of his actions. Even though that were so, he accepted his punishment with patience and grasped it eagerly as a way by which with his pen, if not with his voice, he could continue to proclaim his faith in Christ and to point the way for other pilgrims to follow. He was 'down' but still able to raise others 'up'. His song of contentment can be ours:

> He that is down needs fear no fall,
>   He that is low, no pride;
> He that is humble, ever shall
>   Have God to be his guide.

The Pilgrim's Progress has gone all over the world in its many languages – and so too has one of his and our most popular hymns: 'Who would true valour see'.

Prayer *Teach us, O Father, in whatsoever state we are, therewith to be content, that we may know both how to be abased and how to abound; that in prosperity we may bless thee who givest us richly all things to enjoy, and in adversity may not suffer our faith in thy love to fail, through Jesus Christ our Lord.*

Divina Commedia

Oft hàve I seen at some cathedral door
*   A labourer, pausing in the dust and heat,*
*   Lay down his burden, and with reverent feet*
Enter and cross himself, and on the floor
Kneel to repeat his paternoster o'er;
*   Far off the noises of the world retreat;*
*   The loud vociferations of the street*
Become an indistinguishable roar.

So, as I enter here from day to day,
*   And leave my burden at this minster gate,*
Kneeling in prayer, and not ashamed to pray,
*   The tumult of the time disconsolate*
To inarticulate murmurs dies away,
*   While the eternal ages watch and wait.*

H.W. LONGFELLOW (1807–1882)

Comment

Longfellow's frequent experience summed up in his first verse is one of which I saw a copy in Killarney Cathedral some years ago. A postman dumped his sack of mail in the aisle, knelt down, crossed himself, and prayed. I confess I was left wondering whether he should have been doing that when the State was paying him to deliver letters! But if his timing was wrong, his motive was right. There are times when our daily work seems to 'get us down', perhaps because it is repetitious or boring, or because suddenly it presents us with difficult decisions, or because we are anxious about its outcome. Our Lord's warning to us on those occasions is, 'Be not anxious'. Significantly enough that warning appears in St Matthew's Gospel almost immediately after The Lord's Prayer. 'Therefore I say unto you take no thought for your life... ' (St Matthew, ch.6 v.25). Again a Greek word has not been accurately translated and modern translations of the New Testament make the warning more explicit when they say e.g. 'Be not anxious... ', or 'Do not worry... '. We answer 'But I am anxious – I do worry'. Longfellow's labourer, my postman, Longfellow himself, all had the answer. Worry achieves nothing that is good. Indeed there are evidences that worry and anxiety can result in mental or physical exhaustion. Knowing his Bible, Jesus doubtless had in mind as he uttered his warning, the confidence which the prophet Isaiah expressed to those about him who were anxious: 'Thou wilt keep him in perfect peace, whose mind is stayed on Thee' (Isaiah, ch.26 v.3). Here is a prayer from the Orthodox Church which we can make our own.

Prayer   *Grant calmness and control of thought to those who are facing uncertainty and anxiety: Let their heart stand fast believing in the Lord. Be thou all things to all men, knowing each one and his petition, each house and its need, for the sake of Jesus Christ.*

RUSSIAN LITURGY

Good and great God, can I not think of thee,
  But it must, straight, my melancholy be?
Is it interpreted in me disease,
  That laden with my sins, I seek for ease?
O be thou witness, that the reins dost know
  And hearts of all, if I be sad for show.
And judge me after, if I dare pretend
  To aught but grace, or aim at other end.
As thou art all, so be thou all to me,
  First, midst, and last, converted one, and three;
My faith, my hope, my love: and in this state,
  My judge, my witness, and my advocate.
Where have I been this while exiled from thee?
  And whither rapped, now thou but stoop'st to me?
Dwell, dwell here still: O, being everywhere,
  How can I doubt to find thee ever, here?
I know my state, both full of shame, and scorn,
  Conceived in sin, and unto labour born,
Standing with fear, and must with horror fall,
  And destined unto judgement after all.
I feel my griefs too, and there scarce is ground
  Upon my flesh t'inflict another wound.
Yet dare I not complain, or wish for death
  With holy Paul, lest it be thought the breath
Of discontent; or that these prayers be
  For weariness or life, not love of thee.

BEN JONSON (1573–1637)

Comment

The poet suddenly realises that he has brought suffering upon himself through the burden of his sins. Maybe he had thought that, for example, the injury he had done to another, would soon pass from his memory, but it haunted him still. So for many a Christian, who knows 'his state, both full of shame and scorn', who knows of things he has done, things he has said, duties he has left undone, injuries he has inflicted, who can say with the poet 'I feel my griefs'. In other words he is suffering for his sins, he is worrying, he is anxious. He could hide his sins but he could never be free from anxiety. So it is for us. St Teresa realised this when she wrote 'My soul is like a mirror in which the glory of God is reflected, but sin, however insignificant, covers the mirror with smoke'. But the simple recognition of sin within our lives is the beginning of salvation from its ill effects. Recognition followed by repentance is not only the path to forgiveness. It brings serenity to the sanctuary of the soul.

Prayer   *Lord, sanctify us wholly, that our whole spirit, soul and body may become thy temple. Do thou dwell in us and be thou our God, and we will be thy servants, through Jesus Christ.*

BISHOP KEN (1637–1711)

Irenaeus, Bishop of Lyons, Martyr, c.200

Four things

Four things a man must learn to do
If he would make his record true;
To think without confusion clearly;
To love his fellow men sincerely;
To act from honest motives purely;
To trust in God and Heaven securely.

HENRY VAN DYKE (1852–1933)

Comment

The life of Irenaeus exemplifies the truth of Henry Van Dyke's brief summary of the elements in the life of any man if 'his record is to be true'. Irenaeus was born about the year 125 AD. He was brought up to love the Scriptures, to study them in their original languages, to read widely in the realms of philosophy and literature. It is not fanciful to assume that he learnt about the Christian Faith from men who had known the Apostles personally. Certainly he embraced the Faith and was ordained to the priesthood at an early age, and served in the city of Lyons. The bishop at that time was one Pothinus who suffered martyrdom in the course of a virulent period of persecution. His fellow clergy had sent Ireneaus to Rome to seek the Pope's help and on his return he became Bishop of Lyons and remained so for twenty years. By that time the persecution had ceased and the peril besetting the Church was then within the Church rather than without. The heresy of Gnosticism was not wholly anti-Christian but it embraced pagan features which, at best, confused Christians and at worst denied elements of the Christian Faith. Irenaeus was a man who could 'think without confusion clearly' and as a result he was able to confound the heresy of Gnosticism without engendering bitterness among his fellow Christians. They in their turn recognised that their bishop was acting 'from honest motives purely' and thus no 'rival church' was set up. Irenaeus is regarded as the first great exponent of Christian theology. His defence of the Christian Faith against the heresy of Gnosticism in particular is contained in his greatest work, still extant, entitled *Against the Heresies*. One sentence of that great work must suffice to declare that he trusted 'in God and heaven securely'. He wrote: 'God's splendour is the source of life, and those who see him share his life; because he was beyond the reach of man's mind, incomprehensible and invisible, he made himself visible, intelligible and knowable so that those who see and accept him may possess life'.

Prayer *Give perfection to beginners; give intelligence to the little ones; give aid to those who are running their course; give sorrow to the negligent, fervour of spirit to the lukewarm and to the perfect a true humility, for the sake of Jesus Christ our Lord.*

St Peter the apostle

To St Peter

St Peter once: 'Lord, doest Thou wash my feet?' –
Much more I say: Lord, dost Thou stand and knock
At my closed heart more rugged than a rock,
Bolted and barred, for Thy soft touch unmeet.
Nor garnished nor in any wise made sweet?
Owls roost within and dancing satyrs mock,
Lord, I have heard the crowing of the cock
And have not wept; as, Lord, thou knowest it,
Yet still I hear Thee knocking, still I hear:
'Open to Me, look on Me eye to eye,
That I may wring thy heart and make it whole;
And teach thee love because I hold thee dear
And sup with thee in gladness soul with soul,
And sup with thee in glory by and by'.

CHRISTINA ROSSETTI (1830–1894)

Comment

The Prince of the Apostles is lovable, so human in his weaknesses, so impetuous
in his enthusiasms, so appealing in his humility, so unpredictable in his reactions,
so passionate in his love for his Master, so deeply concerned for those who embraced the Faith. He knew how to work hard for a living, for the Sea of Galilee
was no fisherman's 'picnic'. Maybe it was then that he learnt how 'to curse and
to swear' when his net broke. But that was in his 'Simon days'. It was in his 'Peter
the Rock' days that he made his great confession of faith – 'Thou art the Christ',
yet subsequently he lapsed and denied Christ – 'I know not the man'. The Peter
in him impelled him to follow his Master into the courtyard of the high priest but
the Simon in him prompted him to mingle with the crowd, to be incognito. When
the end came, in the Neronian persecutions, it is said that the Christians of Rome
tried to persuade their bishop to go into hiding until the tyranny was overpast.
Legend tells us that he refused, and refused again, but at length he broke, and
in the dead of night slipped through the city gate and along the Appian Way to
go into hiding. He was suddenly confronted with a vision of Christ. 'Domine, quo
vadis?' He turned back and suffered martyrdom – on a cross. It is interesting to
reflect that we might never have known of Peter's weakness but for Peter himself.
St Mark, the author of the earliest of our four Gospels, relied for his information
on St Peter. Peter indeed regarded Mark as his spiritual son (see 1 Peter, ch.5
v.13). One can almost hear Mark saying to his friend, 'Oughtn't we perhaps to
leave that bit out as it reflects so badly on you?', and Peter answering, 'No son,
put it all in. Your readers must know that even when I fell so low, the Lord raised
me up'. Maybe we fall much lower and more often than did St Peter, but we know
from him that we can rise again.

Prayer *Lord, give me the strong faith in you which your servant Peter professed;*
lift me up when I stumble as you lifted him. Inspire me with your love
as you inspired him. All this I ask for your glory.

An Ode

The spacious firmament on high,
With all the blue ethereal sky,
And spangled heavens, a shining frame,
Their green Original proclaim.
The unwearied sun from day to day,
Does his Creator's power display,
And publishes to every land
The works of an almighty hand.

Soon as the evening shades prevail,
The moon takes up the wondrous tale,
And nightly to the list'ning earth
Repeats the story of her birth;
Whilst all the stars that round her burn,
And all the planets in their turn,
Confirm the tidings as they roll,
And spread the truth from pole and pole.

What though in solemn silence all
Move round the dark terrestrial ball;
What though nor real voice nor sound
Amid their radiant orbs be found;
In reason's ear they all rejoice,
And utter forth a glorious voice,
For ever singing as they shine:
'The hand that made us is divine'.

JOSEPH ADDISON (1672–1719)

Comment

We should not let midsummer pass without deviating somewhat from our theme to ponder the wonders of the universe. It is perhaps in high summer that we are most moved by the beauty around us, to see the glory of the living God bursting through its wonders. Poets all through history, and saints too, have added their songs of praise to the Psalms of David. All have reached the same conclusion that 'the heavens declare the glory of God and the firmament shows his handiwork'. Francis of Assisi wrote ecstatically about the world of nature. Augustine of Hippo in his search for God begins by equating the beauties of nature with God. He asked the sea, the winds, the sky, the stars, the sun, the moon 'and all that can be admitted by the door of the senses', and all in turn replied, 'We are not your God'. To this he replied: 'Since you are not my God, tell me about him. Tell me something of my God'. Clearly and loudly they answered, 'God is he who made us'. Augustine adds, in his *Confessions*, 'I asked these questions simply by gazing at these things, and their beauty was all the answer they gave.'

Prayer   *Heavenly Father, who hast filled the world with beauty: Open our eyes to behold thy gracious hand in all thy works; that rejoicing in thy whole creation, we may learn to serve thee with gladness; for the sake of him by whom all things were made, thy Son, Jesus Christ our Lord.*

AMERICAN PRAYER BOOK

A beauteous evening

It is a beauteous evening, calm and free;
The holy time is quiet as a Nun
Breathless with adoration; the broad sun
Is sinking down in his tranquillity;
The gentleness of heaven broods o'er the Sea;
Listen! the mighty Being is awake,
And doth with his eternal motion make
A sound like thunder – everlastingly.
Dear Child! dear Girl! thou walkest with me here,
If thou appear untouched by solemn thought,
Thy nature is not therefore less divine:
Thou liest in Abraham's bosom all the year;
And worshipp'st at the temple's inner shrine,
God being with thee when we know it not.

WILLIAM WORDSWORTH (1770–1850)

Comment

In St Paul's list of the fruits of the Spirit we come now to one which is difficult to define but easy to recognise. Wordsworth sets us on the right path in this beautiful sonnet in which he speaks of 'the gentleness of heaven'. By those words alone he cites the origin of gentleness as a gift of the Spirit. In the New Testament the Greek word translated as 'gentleness' has more than one meaning. Writing to the Corinthians, St Paul draws out its meaning in a contrast. He asks, 'Shall I come to you with a rod, or with love in a spirit of gentleness?' (1 Cor. ch.4 v.21). By that he means surely that he does not intend being – in modern parlance – heavy-handed with them over their weaknesses. Other uses of the same Greek word suggest that it is the quality of submission to the will of God, humble enough to be easily teachable, considerate in our dealings with our fellow men and particularly so when we may have the advantage over them in knowledge, experience or worldly goods. The well-known children's hymn *Jesu, meek and gentle*, has sometimes been criticised for presenting an unbalanced picture of Christ, but it does nevertheless present an aspect of Christ's personality which Christians should reflect in their lives, in their relationship with fellow Christians and indeed with all Creation. John Galsworthy has some fine words about gentleness which press home the lesson –

To all the humble beasts there be,
To all the birds on land or sea,
Great Spirit! sweet protection give,
That free and happy they may live.
And to our hearts the rapture bring
Of love for every living thing;
Make of us all one kin, and bless
Our ways with Christ's own gentleness.

Prayer *Lord of the loving heart, may mine be loving too; Lord of the gentle hands, may mine be gentle too; Lord of the willing feet, may mine be willing too. So may I grow more like Thee in all I speak and do.*

George Herbert's Gentleness

On Mr Herbert's coming to Bemerton there came to him a poor old woman, with an intent to acquaint him with her necessitous conditions, as also with some troubles of her mind; but after she had spoken some few words to him, she was surprised with a fear, and that begat a shortness of breath, so that her spirits and speech failed her; which he perceiving, did so compassionate her, and was so humble, that he took her by the hand, and said 'Speak, good mother, be not afraid to speak to me; for I am a man that will hear you with patience; and will relieve your necessities too, if I am able, and this I will do willingly, and therefore Mother, be not afraid to acquaint me with what you desire'. After which comfortable speech, he again took her by the hand, made her sit down by him, and understanding that she was of his parish, he told her he would be acquainted with her, and take her into his care. And having with patience heard and understood her wants (and it is some relief for a poor body to be but heard with patience), he like a Christian clergyman, comforted her by his gentle behaviour; but because that cost him nothing, he relieved her with money too, and so sent her home with a cheerful heart, praising God and praying for him. Thus worthy, and thus lowly, was Mr George Herbert in his own eyes; and thus lovely in the eyes of others.

IZAAK WALTON (1593–1633)

Comment

The story is contained in Izaak Walton's *Life of George Herbert*, the godly parish priest of Bemerton who spent no more than the last three years of his short life in ministry in that parish. The biographer gives many such instances of meekness and gentleness which marked Herbert's service to his parishioners. They knew that they had among them a gifted scholar and an aristocrat, but they knew too that among them was a humble man of God – lowly, meek, gentle, kindly, a man in whose life and ministry, the love of Christ, the compassion of Christ and the care of Christ marked his relationships with all his flock, the 'high and mighty' and the 'meek and lowly'. George Herbert had time for the poor old woman, time to listen to her sorry tale, time to counsel her, time to help her. But it should not be deduced from Walton's story that time for others must be a duty only of a 'Christian clergyman'. The story has something to say to each one of us. It is undoubtedly incumbent upon every Christian to have time for people, time to listen, time to understand, time to counsel, and time to sympathise, which last means 'to suffer with'.

Prayer *Take from us, O God, all pride and vanity, all boasting and forwardness, and give us the true courage which shows itself by gentleness; the true wisdom that shows itself by simplicity; and the true power that shows itself by modesty; through Jesus Christ our Lord.*

CHARLES KINGSLEY (1819–1875)

St Thomas the Apostle

A Doubting Heart

Where are the swallows fled?
　　Frozen and dead
Perchance upon some bleak and stormy shore,
　　O doubting heart!
　　Far over purple seas
　　They wait, in sunny ease,
　　The balmy southern breeze,
To bring them to their northern homes once
　　more.

Why must the flowers die?
　　Prisoned they lie
In the cold tomb, heedless of tears or rain.
　　O doubting heart!
　　They only sleep below
　　The soft white ermine snow
　　While winter winds shall blow,
To breathe and smile upon you soon again.

The sun has hid his rays
　　These many days.
Will dreary hours never leave the earth?
　　O doubting heart!
　　The stormy clouds on high
　　Veil the same sunny sky
　　That soon (for spring is nigh)
Shall wake the summer into golden mirth.

Fair hope is dead, and light
　　Is quenched in night.
What sound can break the silence of despair?
　　O doubting heart!
　　The sky is overcast,
　　Yet stars shall rise at last,
　　Brighter for darkness past,
And angels' silver voices stir the air.

ADELAIDE PROCTOR (1825–1864)

Comment

Poor old Thomas! The Church will last for ever, and for ever he will be known as 'Doubting Thomas'. He was, in fact, just that for a time, but his was the kind of doubt that did not close the door upon faith. It was true that, momentarily, there was nothing to 'break the silence of despair'. But in a sky which was overcast he discerned at length the rising of the stars. The doubts which Thomas had, never closed the door to faith. He faced them. He thought through them – and won. Let it never be forgotten that the apostle who alone among them all expressed his doubts about the Risen Christ, was the first apostle to affirm Christ's Divinity – 'My Lord and My God'.

Prayer　　Lord Jesus Christ, you have taken away the sin of the world and are alive for evermore. Grant us the faith that doubts not your word and trusts where it cannot see'; that as we take hold upon your promises, we may rest in your love, now and always.

The Little Black Boy

My mother bore me in the southern wild,
And I am black, but Oh! my soul is white;
White as an angel is the English child,
But I am black, as if bereaved of light.

My mother taught me underneath a tree,
And sitting down before the heat of day,
She took me on her lap, and kissed me,
And, pointing to the east, began to say: –

'Look on the rising sun – there God does live,
And gives his light, and give his heat away;
And flowers, and trees and beasts and men
  receive
Comfort in morning, joy in the noonday.

And we are put on earth a little space,
That we may learn to bear the beams of love;
And these black bodies and this sunburnt face
Is but a cloud, and like a shady grove.

For when our souls have learned the heat to
  bear,
The cloud will vanish; we shall hear his
  voice,
Saying: 'Come out from the grove, my love
  and care,
And round my golden tent like lambs rejoice'.

Thus did my mother say, and kissed me;
And thus I say to little English boy.
'When I from black and he from white
  cloud free,
And round the tent of God like lambs we joy,

I'll shade him from the heat, till he can bear
To lean in joy upon our Father's knee;
And then I'll stand and stroke his silver hair,
And be like him, and he will then love me'.

WILLIAM BLAKE (1757–1827)

Comment

Written two hundred years ago here is a poem which seems to foretell the intolerance and friction which strikes now at the heart of the national life in so many countries of the world. The last verse of this touching poem must not be dismissed as mere sentiment. It points to the only way in which there can be a coming together of peoples – black and white, brown and yellow. Intolerance will always build walls of separation. Gentleness, with all its ingredients of compassion, understanding, humility and meekness, will alone pierce those walls. These are qualities which are essentially spiritual – qualities which cannot be fashioned by legislation. Laws can, alas! inhibit their effective power – as in South Africa. Only the gifts of the Spirit, embraced by God's people irrespective of their colour, can shatter the racist walls of division and these only if Christians are prepared to stand up to be counted in the councils of the nation.

Prayer

O God, let us be united, let us speak in harmony; let our minds apprehend alike; common be our prayer, our resolution, our deliberations. Alike our feelings, unified our hearts. Common be our intentions. Perfect be our unity.

A HINDU PRAYER

Gentleness in Judgment

The world has often seen examples of the presumptuous religious individual who is perfectly secure in his own God-relationship, flippantly assured of his own salvation, but self-importantly engaged in doubting the salvation of others, and in offering to help them. However, I believe that it would be a fitting expression for a genuinely religious attitude if the individual were to say: 'I do not doubt the salvation of any human being; the only one I have fears about is myself. Even when I see a man sink very low, I should never presume to doubt his salvation; but if it were myself, I should doubtless have to suffer this terrible thought. A genuine religious person is always mild in his judgment of others, and only in his relationship to himself is he cold and strict as a master inquisitor. His attitude towards others is like that of a benevolent patriarch to the younger generation: in relation to himself he is old and incorruptible.

SOREN KIERKEGAARD (1813–1855)

Comment

The thoughts are those of a Danish philosopher whose religious works have caught the attention of the Christian world only in recent years. Here he contributes to our meditations on 'gentleness' by exhorting us not to judge others harshly even if we see them sink very low. To be considerate towards our fellow men, even when we see them err, is indeed to be both gentle and humble. St Paul bids the Corinthians: 'By the meekness and gentleness of Christ, I appeal to you – I, Paul, who am 'timid' when face to face with you, but bold when away!' (2 Corinthians ch.10, v.1). Writing from prison, and very much aware of the tensions his converts were facing and the disappointments they suffered as some had slipped away, or were behaving in a way which could not but destroy the unity of the Church he pleads: 'Be completely humble and gentle; be patient, bearing with one another in love' (Ephesians ch.4 v.2). Paul is convinced that if Christians can 'bear with one another in love' nothing that another person does will ever make us 'write him off'. We may dislike a person because of his behaviour but we have no right to hate, to harbour bitterness or to seek revenge. We may protest that gentleness of response is unnatural. It is indeed unnatural. It is *supernatural* – the response of God within us. It is a gift of the Spirit.

Prayer *Incline us, O God, to think humbly of ourselves, to be severe only in the examination of our own conduct, to consider our fellow creatures with kindness, and to judge all they say and do with the charity which we would desire from them ourselves.*

JANE AUSTEN (1775–1817)

Commemorating Thomas More, Martyr, 1535

Saint Thomas More

I'll lay my heart's affection at your feet,
Thomas – you loved so many and so much;
Your children – whom you could not bear to beat,
Instructing them with patience and goodwill;
Your wife (who kept her own opinion still),
Her monkey (with unpleasant habits),
Your own tame fox, the children's rabbits,
The weasel in his hutch.

Erasmus, often peevish and too clever,
(Sometimes in doubtful taste),
Norfolk and Wolsey, soon to be disgraced,
The waterman who rowed you down the river,
Henry, your cruel, fond, conceited king
You loved, it seemed in spite of everything.
But venerated his first lawful queen,
Unhappy Katharine,
And pitied Anne. The essential human stuff,
Deeply perceived and felt – that was enough.

In just this way – however odd it strikes us –
Our maker, God, not only loves but likes *us.*

SISTER CYRILLA, C.S.M.V.

Comment

Never can a holy man's life have been so amply covered in so small a space! Here was a man – a family man, a man who loved his wife, his children, his Church, his country, his God, but a man who would not 'render unto Caesar the things that were God's'. Refusing to recognise the royal supremacy over the Church which Henry the Eighth claimed, he was imprisoned in the Tower of London where he spent fifteen months writing devotional books. In a letter written from the Tower to his daughter he said that God's grace had made him 'content to lose goods, land and life as well' rather than to act against his conscience. He was not fearless – nor was he faithless. Thus he could write to Margaret his daughter: 'Do not let your mind be troubled over anything that shall happen to me in this world. Nothing can come but what God wills, and I am very sure that whatever that can be, however bad it may seem, it shall indeed be the best'.

Prayer   *O God, our refuge and strength, have mercy on your Church in the midst of oppression. Deliver your people by your mighty aid from tyranny; keep them faithful in the hour of trial, and restore to them the blessings of freedom and peace; through Jesus Christ our Lord.*

Goodness

Good critics who have stamped out poet's hopes,
Good statesmen who pulled ruin on the state,
Good patriots who for a theory risked a cause,
Good kings who disembowelled for a tax,
Good popes who brought all good to jeopardy,
Good Christians who sat still in easy chairs
And damned the general world for standing up –
Now may the good God pardon all good men!

Earth's crammed with heaven,
And every common bush afire with God;
But only he who sees takes off his shoes,
The rest sit round and pluck blackberries,
And daub their natural faces unaware
More and more from the first similitude.

ELIZABETH BARRETT BROWNING (1806–1861)
FROM *Aurora Leigh*

Comment

Goodness is a lovely word covering so much that is beautiful in character. The Greek word so translated is elsewhere translated kindness, gentleness, even sweetness. The quotations, the first from Book 4 of Elizabeth Barrett Browning's long poem *Aurora Leigh* and the second from Book 7, detached as they are from the full poem, seem to present a contrast. The one an outburst against the misuse of the word *Good* – an error which persists! – the other which turns the reader's eyes towards *The Good*. Barnabas the Apostle is described as 'a good man' and that appellation is immediately defined: 'a good man, full of the Holy Ghost and of faith'. The poetess is making it crystal clear that the critics, statemen, patriots, kings, popes and Christians whom the world has labelled 'good' are not necessarily entitled to be so named. The world must find a different adjective for them. That does not mean of course, that none who reach high office in the world are ever 'good'. It means that goodness is of the very essence of God – God's character – and thus goodness does not consist in the outward things we do which may or may not be praiseworthy and laudable. Goodness is 'God-ness'. It is love in action. Barnabas was a good man – his heart was a sanctuary for God. 'Of all virtues and dignities of the mind' said St Bernard of Clairvaux, 'goodness is the greatest, being the character of the Deity, and without it man is a busy, mischievous, wretched thing'. It is our duty to look beyond Barnabas to our Lord himself who 'went about doing good'.

Prayer   *Lord, as I pass through this world but once, enable me to 'go about doing good'. Help me to requite injury with kindness, selfishness with compassion and indifference with caring love, and to do these things always to your glory and the growth of your kingdom.*

Reversibility

Angel so gay, know you the misery,
The shame, the weeping, the remorse, the grief,
The vague fears of those nights beyond belief
Which crumple up the heart's security?
Angel so gay, know you the misery?

Angel so good, know you aversion,
The fists clenched in the dark, the bitter tears,
When Vengeance calls its hellish volunteers,
And comes to captain our decision?
Angel so good, know you aversion?

Angel so healthy, know you maladies,
Which, down the vast halls of dim hospitals,
Like exiles drag their way rheumatical,
Seeking rare sun, mouthing inaudibly?
Angel so healthy, know you maladies?

Angel so lovely, know you greying hair,
The fear of age, this desolation
Of reading horror of devotion
To eyes which long fulfilled our ardent prayer?
Angel so lovely, know you greying hair?

Angel so happy, joyful, radiant,
The dying David would have asked to live
By the enchantment that your body gives;
But I for prayers alone am supplicant,
Angel so happy, joyful, radiant!

CHARLES-PIERRE BAUDELAIRE (1821–1867)
TRANSLATED JOANNA RICHARDSON

Comment

These verses by the French poet Baudelaire present a salutary reminder that to go about doing good is not an easy option. The field in which 'angels of mercy' can work is wide; the areas where help is needed are frequently distressing; the proffered service may be rejected, perhaps more so among the aged who may well feel that acceptance is tantamount to the surrender of independence. The angel is bidden to approach 'greying hair' with an understanding sensitivity. But the angel must not be deterred; he must press on 'happy, joyful, radiant'. So for us. We do not become good because of what we do. It is rather that indwelt by God's good Spirit, goodness is within us and the scope for its exercise is as wide as the family of God throughout his world – our nearest and dearest, our neighbours and friends, the sick and wounded, strangers steeped in grief and misery and desolation in the Third World – not forgetting those averse to us – all are within the ambit of God's love, and all therefore should be within the ambit of our goodness.

Prayer   *Blessed be the God and Father of our Lord Jesus Christ, the Father of mercies and God of all comfort who comforts us in all our affliction so that we may be able to comfort those who are in any affliction, with the comfort with which we ourselves are comforted by God. (St Paul 2 Cor.1, vv.3, 4).*

A Good Friend

To have a good friend is one of the highest delights of life; to be a good friend is one of the noblest and most difficult undertakings. Friendship depends not upon fancy, imagination or sentiment, but upon character. There is no man so poor that he is not rich if he have a good friend; there is no man so rich that he is not poor without a friend. But friendship is a word made to cover many kindly impermanent relationships. Real friendship is abiding. Like charity, it suffereth long and is kind. Like love, it vaunteth not itself, but pursues the even tenor of its way, unaffrighted by ill-report, loyal in adversity, the solvent of infelicity, the shining jewel of happy days. Friendship has not the iridescent joys of love, though it is closer than is often known to the highest, truest love. Its heights are ever serene, its valleys know few clouds. To aspire to friendship one must cultivate a capacity for faithful affection, a beautiful disinterestedness, a clear discernment. Friendship is a gift, but it is also an acquirement. It is like the rope with which climbers in the high mountains bind themselves for safety, and only a coward cuts the rope when a comrade is in danger. From Cicero to Emerson, and long before Cicero, and forever after Emerson, the praises of friendship have been set forth. Even fragments of friendship are precious and to be treasured. But to have a whole real friend is worthy of high endeavour, for faith, truth, courage and loyalty bring one close to the Kingdom of Heaven.

'ATMOS'

Comment

Our anonymous author sets between his first sentence and his last a recipe for friendship which every Christian can endorse. All the way through, the accent is on the word 'good'. He infers that it is as possible to have a bad friend as it is to *be* a bad friend, and leaves his readers to assume that that would debase the word 'friend'. It would indeed drag friendship through the gutter. Friendship must have about it the hallmark of goodness, and lacking that it cannot be genuine. How urgent a duty it is for adult Christians to press home upon young Christians that they should test their friendships by that scale, that they should pose to themselves the question: 'Is he (or she) pressing friendship upon me for genuine companionship, or is there some ulterior motive – drug pushing, for example, or illicit sex?'. This gift of the Spirit called goodness touches the whole gamut of life, both in its personal and social contacts. The mature Christian knows how to *be* a good friend and knowing that will find himself attracting good friends. Young people – and that includes young Christians – must be encouraged to make good friends, but they must be warned too that they may meet those with ill intent who could trap them into a bad friendship.

Prayer   *Jesus, Fountain of love, look upon my friends and all who seek my friendship. Help them to love you with all their hearts, that they may think and do only such things as are well-pleasing to you.*

AFTER ST ANSELM (1033–1109)

The Higher Good

Father, I will not ask for wealth or fame,
Though once they would have joyed my carnal sense:
I shudder not to bear a hated name,
Wanting all wealth, myself my sole defence.
But give me, Lord, eyes to behold the truth;
A seeing sense that knows the eternal right;
A heart with pity filled, and gentlest ruth;
A manly faith that makes all darkness light;
Give me the power to labour for mankind;
Make me the mouth of such that cannot speak;
Eyes let me be to groping men and blind;
A conscience to the base; and to the weak
Let me be hands and feet; and to the foolish, mind;
And lead still further on, such as thy kingdom seek.

THEODORE PARKER (1810–1860)

Comment

A poet sets out his priorities! Wealth and fame would have satisfied him once, but when his eyes had been opened to the truth, his heart was filled with pity and with the 'gentlest ruth' – i.e. compassion. He acknowledges that there could have been goodness of a kind in his 'carnal sense' but having found the higher good which the Spirit planted within him he prays for the gifts which would enable him to spread God's goodness around the world in which he moved. He believed that under God he would be able to do that, even for 'groping men and blind'. All of us meet such in our pilgrimage, and all of us meet 'the base'. We must never forget that deep down in the souls of 'groping men and blind' and in 'the base' there is the spark of goodness which God himself set there. Our goodness to such people may in turn fan that spark of goodness within them. The Moslem poet Nizami tells a story of a dead dog in the gutter of the market place of an Eastern town. The rotting body evoked from passers-by comments of disgust. 'Loathsome!' said one. 'What a stench!' said another. 'How revolting!' said a third. As the circle of people increased a gentler voice was heard: 'Have none of you noticed its pearly white teeth?'. The little group dispersed, and as the man with the gentler voice left, another whispered: 'Surely that must be Jesus, for who else would say a good word about a dead dog?' Goodness begets goodness.

Prayer   *O Lord Jesus, acknowledge what is thine in us and help us to acknowledge what is thine in others. Take away from us all that is not thine, and give us the humility to encourage all that is thine in others.*

AFTER ST BERNARDINO (A.D.1380)

Commemorating Benedict, Abbot of Monte Cassino, c.550

In the first place when you begin something good you must beg of the Lord with unflagging prayer to bring it to completion, so that he, who has already been so gracious as to count us among his sons, will never be saddened by our evil deeds... Let us stand up on our feet then, for Scripture rouses us saying: 'It is full time now for you to awake from sleep'. And having opened our eyes to the light of God, let us listen attentively to what the divine voice cries out to us: 'To-day if you would hear his voice, harden not your hearts'; and again, 'He who has ears to hear let him hear what the spirit says to the churches'...

Just as there is an evil bitter zeal which cuts us off from God and leads to hell, so there is a good zeal which shields us from vice and leads to God and eternal life... Girding our loins then with faith and the observance of good deeds; let us so follow his paths under the guidance of the gospel that we may be worthy to see him who has called us into his kingdom. If we desire to live in the dwelling-place of his kingdom there is no means of reaching it except by the way of good deeds.

ST BENEDICT (C.480–550)

Comment

The name of Benedict among the saints of God is known throughout the Christian Church all over the world. He was not a priest, not a bishop, but a layman whose religious life began at the age of fourteen or fifteen when, dismayed and disgusted by life as he saw it in Rome, he decided to become a hermit and lived for a time in a cave some 50 miles from the city. His fame as a man of God, as a healer, as a counsellor spread and soon he had around him many disciples, living in caves on the mountains and looking to him as their leader. At the age of 50 he withdrew to Monte Cassino and there he founded the Benedictine Order of monks. As monasticism grew in the West a great many Benedictine Monasteries were founded and for these Benedict drew up a Rule, an extract from which appears above. Subsequently other religious orders were founded – the Dominicans and the Franciscans. All the Orders have one thing in common. All who came, clergy and laymen, were men eager to dedicate their lives to God. He attached the utmost importance to the Rule of Life he drew up for the Order. He bound himself to it irrevocably and admitted to the Order only those who could promise strict obedience to its every detail. If there is one thing which Christians generally can learn from Benedict it is just that they themselves need to have their Rule of Life – some time each day for prayer, some time each Sunday for public worship, some times each week for quiet meditation.

Prayer   *O gracious and holy Father, give us wisdom to perceive thee, diligence to seek thee, patience to wait for thee, eyes to behold thee, a heart to meditate upon thee, and a life to proclaim thee; through the power of the Spirit of Jesus Christ our Lord.*

The Incomprehensible

Far in the Heavens my God retires,
My God, the mark of my desires,
And hides his lovely face;
When he descends within my view,
he charms my reason to pursue,
But leaves it tired and fainting
In the unequal chase.

Or if I reach unusual height
Till near his presence brought,
There floods of glory check my flight,
Cramp the bold pinions of my wit,
And all untune my thought;
Plunged in a sea of light I roll,
Where wisdom, justice, mercy shines;
Infinite rays in crossing lines
Beat thick confusion on my sight,
And overwhelm my soul.

Great God! behold my reason lies
Adoring; yet my love would rise
On pinions not her own:
Faith shall direct her humble flight
Through all the trackless seas of light,
To Thee, th'Eternal fair, the infinite unknown.

ISAAC WATTS (1674–1748)

Comment

In St Paul's list of the fruits of the Spirit, we come now to 'faith'. In translations of the New Testament subsequent to the Authorised Version the Greek word is more accurately translated 'fidelity' or 'faithfulness'. Fidelity to the things of God, faithfulness to the ways of God, as they are marked out for us in the life and ministry of Jesus Christ, are of course meaningless unless we begin with a faith in God Himself. This is the problem with which Isaac Watts is concerning himself in the mystical verses. It may surprise some lovers of the poet's beautiful hymns – they include 'When I survey', 'Jesus shall reign' – that he should regard God as 'incomprehensible'. In his early life Watts fought his way through problems to a sturdy and serene faith in 'the infinite Unknown'. The truth is, of course, that we cannot *comprehend* God. He is, as it were, too big for our little minds. But we can *apprehend* God. We can grasp him mentally and spiritually because 'he descends within our view' in the person of Jesus Christ. Looking at Christ, reading the words of Christ, seeing the acts of Christ, penetrating the thoughts of Christ – all these enlighten and fortify Reason, all these afford an answer to the question which has teased the minds of men from the beginning, 'What is God like?'.

Prayer   *Faithful Lord, grant to us we pray all such things as will strengthen our faith. Fill us with your love, keep us steadfast in love, and preserve us faithful all the days of our life.*

The Faith of an Explorer

It was his steadfast and unalterable conviction that for a man who has wrapped his will in God's will, put his life consciously in the stream of his divine life, freed his soul from all personal ambitions, taken his life on trust – that for such a man there is an over-ruling providence which guards and guides him in every incident of his life, from the greatest to the least. He held that all annoyances, frustrations, disappointments, mishaps, discomfort, hardships, sorrows, pains, and even final disaster itself, are simply God's ways of teaching us lessons that we could never else learn. That circumstances do not matter, are nothing; that there is no situation in human life, however apparently adverse, nor any human relationship, however apparently uncongenial, that cannot be made, if God be in the heart, into a thing of perfect joy; that in order to attain this ultimate perfection, one must accept every experience and learn to love. The worth of life is not to be measured by its achievements or success, but solely by the motive of one's heart and the effort of one's will.

GEORGE SEAVER (1890–1976)

Comment

The words are those of George Seaver in his book *The Faith of Edward Wilson*, the doctor who accompanied Scott on his last expedition to the Antarctic. Wilson reached the South Pole along with four companions in January 1912. Undoubtedly he was a man of indomitable courage and that proved to be an asset even more valuable than his medical skill and his zoological knowledge. But courage can itself be fragile. Wilson's was strong as it was based on a profound faith in God and in the conviction that all things work together for good to those who love God. Maybe we shall never in our lives face that sort of testing of the faith that is in us. Even so in all the enterprises for good to which we put our hands and hearts we have to trust God even if we cannot at that moment trace him. Trust in God does not supersede prudence – in other words it is not enough to say a prayer and do nothing. That is to tempt Providence. The faith, the trust which will sustain us through the shadows of life as through the sunshine is the trust of the psalmist – 'In God have I put my trust, I will not be afraid what man can do unto me' (Psalm 56 v.11). Such trust, sustained by prayer and worship, offers no guarantee of immunity from the sufferings, the trials, the anxieties and the problems which are the common lot of mankind. But it can and does lift us above them so that by God's grace we are in control. Charles Spurgeon, the nineteenth-century evangelist, took up this theme in one of his addresses. 'When you have no helpers', he said, 'see all your helpers in God. When you have many helpers, see God in all your helpers. When you have nothing but God, see all in God. Under all conditions stay your heart only on God'.

Prayer　　*Lord Jesus Christ, who alone art wisdom, and knowest what is best for us, mercifully grant that it may happen to us only as it is pleasing to you and as seems good in your sight, for thy name's sake.*

KING HENRY THE SIXTH 1421

All things are full of God

All things are full of God. Thus quote
 Wise Thales in the days
When subtle Greece to thought awoke
 And soared in lofty ways.
And now what wisdom have we more?
 No sage-divining rod
Hath taught than this a deeper lover,
 AND THINGS ARE FULL OF GOD.

The light that gloweth in the sky
 And shimmers in the sea,
That quivers in the painted fly
 And gems the pictured lea,
The million hues of Heaven above
 And Earth below are one,
And every lightful eye doth love
 The primal light, the Sun.

E'en so, all vital virtue flows
 From life's first fountain, God;
And he who feels, and he who knows,
 Doth feel and know from God.
As fishes swim in briny sea,
 As fowl do float in air,
From thy embrace we cannot flee;
 We breathe, and thou art there.

Go, take thy glass, astronomer,
 And all the girth survey
Of sphere harmonious linked to sphere
 In endless bright array.
All that far-reaching Science there
 Can measure with her rod,
All power, all laws, are but the fair
 Embodied thought of God.

JOHN STUART BLACKIE (1809–1895)

Comment

The author of these confident verses was a Professor of Greek in Edinburgh University, and was throughout his life associated closely with various social, educational and political movements. He brought to his work the insights of a virile faith in God and among his many learned writings is a volume of *Lay Sermons*. The Thales who first made the declaration that 'All things are full of God' was one of the Seven Wise Men of Greece, regarded in his day (BC 640) as the first Greek philosopher. His wisdom led him to faith in God. Blackie sustains the theme suggesting that all the researches into the universe – the laws of nature, the discoveries of astronomy and other sciences – can still be seen as 'but the embodied thoughts of God'. It was in the closing years of the sixteenth century that the German astronomer Kepler said excitedly: 'Has not God waited six thousand years for someone to contemplate his work with understanding?'

Prayer   *'The heavens declare the glory of God: and the firmament proclaims his handiwork. One day tells it to another and night to night communicates knowledge'. Praise be to God!*

Sing to the Lord!

What else can I do, a lame old man, but sing hymns to God? If I were a nightingale, I would do the nightingale's part; if I were a swan, I would do as a swan. But now I am a rational creature, and I ought to praise God: this is my work; I do it, nor will I desert my post, so long as I am able to keep it. And I exhort you to join me in this same song.

EPICTETUS, GREEK STOIC, IST CENTURY

My intention is, just as a free and blithesome leader of a choir stirs up the singers of his company, even so to turn them all to good account by inciting them to sing joyously, and to offer up their hearts to God.

HENRY SUSO, MYSTIC (1295–1366)

Dance my heart, dance to-day with joy. The strains of love fill the days and nights with music and the world is listening to its melodies. Mad with joy, life and death dance to the rhythms of this music. The hills and the sea and the earth dance. The world of man dances in laughter and tears. Behold, my heart danceth in the delight of a hundred arts; and the Creator is well pleased.

KABIR, INDIAN MYSTIC, 15TH CENTURY

Till you can sing and rejoice and delight in God, as misers do in gold and kings in sceptres, you never enjoy the world.

TRAHERNE, ENGLISH MYSTIC, 17TH CENTURY

Comment

So through the centuries, and the world over, holy men have borne their witness to the power of music and singing both as a means of expressing the praise of God and of sensing his indwelling in their hearts. Our faith in God, our fidelity to the things of God, our faithfulness to Christ's Way, Christ's Truth and Christ's Life – all these tend to fluctuate in reality between the 'high' and the 'low'. It was ever so, and nothing is more reassuring to Christian pilgrims than the mystics whose lives are so wrapped up in God that they are able both to enter into the experience of waverers and to point them to ways by which faith can be strengthened and vision can be renewed. It is interesting and significant that they note the importance of singing to this end. Few people take part in, or listen to a rendering of the chorus in Handel's *Messiah* without being deeply moved by the way in which it expresses what we might think of as the inexpressible; in which too it lifts the spirit and binds the company together in a fellowship born of the Spirit. In recent years the church's hymnody has been enriched by many of the chorus-type hymns – despised alas by many purist musicians. Let it be said that the faith of many has been strengthened by these uplifting modern hymns. One who despises, for example, a chorus such as *Sing Hosanna to the King of Kings* deprives many a flagging spirit of rich renewal.

Prayer *Lord, increase my faith. Teach me, inspire me, assist me to adore. Let my adoration be pure, deep and whole, thankful and joyous. Give me your grace that the adoration of my heart and my lips may express itself in my daily life, to your glory ever.*

The Possessor of the Earth

I could sit there quietly and, looking on the waters, see fishes leaping at flies of several shapes and colours. Looking on the hills, I could behold them spotted with woods and groves. Looking down the meadows, I could see here a boy gathering lilies and lady-smocks, and there a girl cropping columbines and cowslips, all to make garlands suitable to this present month of May.

As I thus sate, joying in mine own happy condition, I did thankfully remember what my Saviour said, that the meek possess the earth.

IZAAK WALTON (1593–1683)

Comment

Izaak Walton had in mind the Beatitude: 'Blessed are the meek for they shall inherit the earth' (St Matthew ch.5 v.5). But 'meek' is not now regarded as a complimentary adjective! To describe someone as 'a meek little man' is almost to suggest that he is spineless, incapable of saying 'boo' to a goose. Fortunately the Greek word which the Bible translates as 'meek' has a very different meaning, and in translations subsequent to the earliest – subsequent, that is, to the Authorised Version – and the Revised Standard Version – the real meaning is made clear by using words more in line with what the evangelist had in mind. Thus the New English Bible translates the verse as: 'Blessed are those of a gentle spirit, for they shall have the earth for their possession'. Another modern translation, that of J.B. Phillips, expresses the sentiment in modern English with, 'Happy are the kind-hearted for they shall have kindness shown to them'. Classical Greek suggests that the Beatitude could be expressed: 'Blessed is the man who is self-controlled'. All of which suggests that the 'meekness' is something very gentle, very kind-hearted but all the time very strong and compelling in its attractiveness. Meekness is a gift of the Spirit which, far from evoking contempt from another person, evokes from him warm admiration. The meek will indeed 'inherit the earth' – i.e. he will win the heart of every one by his kindness, his humility, his integrity, his self-control. Professor William Barclay, a twentieth-century New Testament scholar to whom the Church owes a great debt for his exposition of the New Testment, suggests that a translation of that particular Beatitude which might embrace all these nuances of the Greek word, could be:

> O the bliss of the man who is always angry at the right time and never angry at the wrong time, who has every instinct, and impulse and passion under control. Because he himself is controlled, who has the humility to realise his own ignorance and his own weakness, for such a man is a king among men.

Prayer   Here is a one line prayer that this gift of the Spirit of meekness which embodies so many virtues, may be ours:

> The things, good Lord, that we pray for, give us the grace to labour for.

ST THOMAS MORE (1478–1535)

A Song to David

Tell them I AM, Jehovah said
To Moses; while earth heard in dread,
And smitten to the heart,
At one above, beneath, around,
All nature, without voice or sound,
Replied, O Lord, THOU ART.

Thou art – to give and to confirm,
For each his talent and his term;
All flesh thy bounties share:
Thou shalt not call thy brother fool;
The porches of the Christian school
Are meekness, peace and prayer.

Open, and naked of offence,
Man's made of mercy, soul and sense;
God's armed the snail and wilk;
Be good to him that pulls thy plough;
Due food and care, due rest, allow
For her that yields thee milk.

Rise up before the hoary head,
And God's benign commandment dread,
Which says thou shalt not die;
'Not as I will, but as thou wilt',
Prays He whose conscience knew no guilt;
With whose blest pattern vie.

CHRISTOPHER SMART (1772–1771)

Comment

Every stanza of Christopher Smart's beautiful *Song to David* has within it some pearl of religious truth and these are no exception. He sees each endowed with God-given talents and he is at pains to direct how these should be used. We may not, for example, call our brother 'fool' because of the words over the door of the school in which the Christian is taught: 'meekness, peace and prayer'. Replace 'meekness' with any of the wider translations mentioned in yesterday's *Comment* and the poet's injunction holds still. But he goes further. He says in effect that that same gentleness, humility, self-control, and kindness which are due from us to our fellows are due too to the animals which serve us. They are God's creatures and Man, though he stands at the pinnacle of God's creation and is 'made of mercy, soul and sense' has no right, human or divine, to ill-treat them or to be other than good to them. The lilies of the field, the sheep, the sparrow, all have their rights too. The right attitude of Man to his fellow Man and to all God's creation will be discerned as we look at Christ with whose 'blest pattern' we must vie.

Prayer   *God our Father, Lord of all creation, help us to extend the kindness due from us to our fellows to all dumb creatures who serve us by their labours or their companionship.*

Mary's Meekness

Behold, how completely Mary traces all to God, lays claim to no works, no honour, no fame. She conducts herself as before, when as yet she had naught of all this. She demands no higher honours than before. She is not puffed up, does not vaunt herself, nor proclaim with a loud voice that she has become the Mother of God. She seeks not any glory, but goes about her wonted household duties, milking the cows, cooking the meals, washing pots and kettles, sweeping out the rooms, and performing the work of maidservant or house-mother in lowly and despised tasks, as though she cared naught for such exceeding great gifts and graces. She was esteemed among other women and her neighbours no more highly than before, nor desired to be, but remained a poor townswoman, one of the great multitude...

When men accord us praise and honour, we ought to profit by Mary's example... We ought neither to reject this praise and honour as though they were wrong, nor to despise them as though they were naught... We should ascribe them to God in heaven to whom they belong.

MARTIN LUTHER 1483–1546)

Comment

We recall Mary's song – the *Magnificat*, which Luther surely had in mind when he wrote those words. Mary's soul magnified the Lord because 'He that is mighty hath magnified me, and holy is his name'. This is meekness, this is self-control, this is humility. She was not saying that she was a worthless creature in the sight of God, nor that she could not understand why she had been chosen by God for so high a calling. She realised that God had 'magnified' her, God had endowed her with a responsibility which was unique. It was not hers to question God's decision. It was hers to accept it – meekly, humbly, thankfully. The fact that 'all generations' would call her blessed – induced in her not pride but humility. William Temple, the former Archbishop of Canterbury, wrote in his *Christ in His Church*: 'Humility means that you feel yourself, as a distinct person, out of count, and give your whole mind and thought, to God himself in worship and to the fulfilment of his will in Christian love'. Mary realised that in the purpose God assigned to her she was 'a distinct person'. She could answer in no other way than to 'magnify the Lord'. The same must be true of the gifts with which God endows us – the gift of parenthood, the talents with which we are severally endowed, the opportunities of service which are put in our way, gifts of leadership, gifts of understanding, and of empathy. It is ours to recognise that by them God has magnified us and looks to us to use what he has ordained to his glory and his people's welfare.

Prayer   *Lord of the Church, you have given to your servants a diversity of gifts that they may share them with their brethren. Grant us the humble heart to receive and the generous heart to share, that your purpose may be perfected in us to the welfare of your people and the glory of your name.*

God's Dwellings

Lord, thou hast told us that there be
Two dwellings which belong to thee,
  And those two – that's the wonder,
  Are far asunder.
The one the highest heaven is,
The mansions of eternal bliss,
  The other is the contrite
  And humble sprite.

Not like the princes of the earth,
Who think it much below their birth
  To come within the door
  Of people poor;
No such is thy humility
That though thy dwelling be on high,
  Thou dost thyself debase
  To the lowest place.

Where'er thou seest a sinful soul
Deploring his offences foul,
  To him thou wilt descend
  And be his friend.
Thou wilt come in, and with him sup,
And from his low state raise him up,
  Till thou hast made him eat
  Blest angels' meat.

Thus thou wilt him with honour crown
Who in himself is first cast down,
  And humbled for his sins,
  That thy love wins.
O God! since thou delight'st to rest
In the humble contrite breast,
  First make me so to be,
  Then dwell with me.

THOMAS WASHBOURNE (1606–1687)

Comment

Thomas Washbourne is probably best known for his poem entitled *The Circulation* which he wrote soon after William Harvey published his thesis on the circulation of the blood. In that poem he accepted the physician's thesis – 'Our famous Harvey hath made good the circulation of the blood' – and he makes it clear that the discovery in no way affected belief in the spiritual nature of man – 'Go then, my dust, to dust, but thou my soul return unto thy rest above the pole'. In *God's Two Dwellings* he confirms this conviction and sees God himself coming 'to the lowest place' in the Incarnation of Our Lord who in turn lifts man to dwell with him. Man's meekness and humility win for him God's love.

Prayer   Give us, Lord Jesus, the grace of meekness and patience; help us to bear with the faults of others gently and humbly and to strive ever to root out our own faults.

A Temperate Man

Now as touching his qualities wherewithal he was specially endued, like as some of them were rare and notable, so ought they not to be put in oblivion. Wherefore among other things it is to be noted that he was a man of such temperate nature, or rather so mortified, that no manner of prosperity or adversity could alter or change his accustomed conditions; for, being the storms never so terrible or odious, nor the prosperous estate of the time never so pleasant, joyous, or acceptable, to the face of the world his countenance, diet or sleep never altered or changed, so that they which were most nearest and conversant about him never or seldom perceived by no sign or token of countenance how the affairs of the prince of the realm went. Notwithstanding, privately with his secret and special friends he would shed forth many bitter tears lamenting the miseries and calamities of the world.

Again he so behaved himself to the whole world, that in no manner or condition he would seem to have any enemy, although in very deed he had both many great and secret enemies, whom he always bore with such countenance and benevolence that they could never take good opportunity to practise their malice against him but to their great displeasure and hindrance in the end.

RALPH MORICE (16TH CENTURY)

Comment

So who is this temperate man of whom Ralph Morice writes? He is none other than Archbishop Cranmer, who was Archbishop of Canterbury from 1533 to 1556 when he was executed because he refused to 'render unto Caesar the things that were God's'. Throughout his episcopate the man closest to him who could measure his response to the many trials he had to bear and to the decisions he had to take was his personal secretary, Ralph Morice. His testimony of the Archbishop's bearing through his troubled life can be relied upon as the witness of the one closest to him. St Paul's last 'fruit of the Spirit' appears – at least in the Authorised Version as 'temperance' – a word, like meekness, which has been reduced in our day to bear reference only to the consumption of alcohol! Ralph Morice uses the word temperate as it was understood in his day as in Paul's – that is, self-control, self-restraint. It is not surprising that translations of the Bible subsequent to the Authorised Version all use one or other of those two words. A man who loses his temper loses control of himself as certainly as a man who consumes alcohol excessively. So indeed does a man who is prodigal in the use of his time. Each is intemperate, lacking in a fruit of the Spirit which governed so splendidly Cranmer's reaction to the trials which beset him.

Prayer *May God the Father watch over us; May Christ take care of us; May the Holy Spirit enlighten us and control us that we may be temperate in all things.*

Man

Man putteth the world to scale
  And weigheth out the stars;
Th'eternal hath lost her veil,
  The infinite her bars;
His balance he hath hung in heaven
  And set the sun there.

He measures the lords of light
  And fiery orbs that spin;
No riddle of darkest night
  He dares not look within;
Athwart the roaring wrack of stars
  He plumbs the chasm of heaven.

The wings of the wind are his;
  To him the world is given;
His servant the lightning is,
  And slave the ocean even;
He scans the mountains yet unclimbed
  And sounds the solid sea.

With fingers of thought he holds
  What is or e'er can be;
And, touching it not, unfolds
  The sealed mystery.
The pigmy hands, eyes, head God gave
  A giant's are become.

But tho' to this height sublime
  By labour he hath clomb,
One summit he hath to climb
  One deep the more to plumb –
To rede himself and rule himself,
  And so to reach the sun.

SIR RONALD ROSS (1837–1932)

Comment

Sir Ronald Ross was an eminent physician and bacteriologist who has among his other claims to fame, a measure of the credit for discovering that malaria is spread by mosquitoes. He was a scientist of no mean stature but he cherished no notion that Man could be regarded as the lord of creation. 'Giant' he may well have become and indeed has become in many fields of medicine and technology, but as the matter which he controls is God-given, man must take care 'to rede and rule himself', that is to counsel and control himself so that he may order things only in ways which are pleasing to God. Does this say something to us about nuclear energy and a great many other human advances?

Prayer   *Father, teach us your will and how to follow it. Teach us the best way of doing the best things, lest we spoil the end by unworthy means.*

St Mary Magdalen

Magdalen at Michael's gate
  Tirlèd at the pin;
On Joseph's thorn sang the blackbird;
  'Let her in! Let her in!'

'Hast thou seen the wounds?' said Michael,
  'Know'st thou thy sin?'
'It is evening, evening', sang the blackbird.
  'Let her in! Let her in!'

'Yes, I have seen the wounds,
  And I know my sin'.
'She knows it well, well, well', sang the blackbird.
  'Let her in! Let her in!'

'Thou bringest no offerings'. said Michael,
  'Naught save sin'.
And the blackbird sang, 'She is sorry, sorry, sorry,
  Let her in! Let her in!

When he had sung himself to sleep,
  And night did begin,
One came and opened Michael's gate,
  And Magdalen went in.

HENRY KINGSLEY 1830–1876)

Comment

Mary of Magdala – 'out of whom went seven devils'. We do not know precisely what that means. It could be that she had been a woman of the streets, a woman whose past did not bear close examination. In his moving poem Henry Kingsley pictures Mary Magdalen lifting the latch 'at Michael's gate' but gaining no immediate entrance. 'The blackbird' intercedes on her behalf. 'She knows she has sinned. She knows she has wounded her Master. She is sorry'. So here she stands in the calendar of saints. Small wonder that, since there are no less than fourteen references to her in the Gospel, only two of them hint at her past, and all reveal her as one who had committed herself wholly to the love and service of her Lord. For Mary of Magdala the path to saintship was not a path of innocence but of penitence. So too for us. We may fail our Lord in all sorts of ways – trivial and grave. None of us is innocent, nor was any one of those whom the church labels 'saints'. They stood 'at Michael's gate' as penitents. Thus did they enter into the joy of their Lord.

Prayer *Make me a clean heart, O God, and renew a right spirit within me.*
           Cast me not away from thy presence, and take not thy Holy Spirit from me.

PSALM 51, VV.10–11

Temperance

If now we consider how we ourselves stand in respect of this virtue of temperance, we discover that it must bring its sobering realisms into our social, personal and spiritual life... I often think that when St Paul wrote his classic list of fruits of the Spirit, he gave us unconsciously a wonderful account of his own growth in this spiritual realism. We should hardly think of the virtue of temperance as specially characteristic of St Paul, and even to the end of his days he probably found it difficult; yet in this he discovers the final proof of the Creative Spirit in his soul. He begins upon a note of convinced fervour. The fruit – the harvest – of the spirit is love, joy, peace'. No three words could better express the rich beatitude which in his holiest moments has flooded his soul. He pauses. We seem to see him thinking... How does that Spirit act on my troubled spirit in those less expansive moments? Surely in long-suffering, gentleness and kindness which I know must control all my actions in the world of men... At the very end we reach those unexpected characters which are the earnest of his total transformation in the Spirit: fidelity, meekness, moderation... These are the real fruits of his subjection to God. Paul, whose first idea had been to breathe fire and slaughter upon the Christians, and whose second idea had been to be 'all out' for Christ... learns that the final gift of the Spirit is not intensity of life, but Temperance.

EVELYN UNDERHILL (1875–1941)

Comment

The quotation is from Evelyn Underhill's *The House of the Soul'*. She is not saying, of course, that we should not be 'all out' for Christ. She is saying that even in this godly intention, which is part of the mission of the Church to which every member of the Church is committed, we should not be impatient and intemperate in the way we approach our brethren who are indifferent to, or who deny, the claims of Christ. Time was when Paul himself would breathe out 'fire and slaughter' on – as he thought – Christ's behalf. He came to know better – by the power of the Spirit. The harvest of the Spirit may be expressed in nine words – love, joy, peace, long-suffering, gentleness, goodness, faith, meekness, temperance – but we are not permitted, following examination procedure – merely to attempt any six! Even in the matter of evangelism we must not try to bully people into the Kingdom.

Prayer   *Lord, help me to bear my witness for you always and everywhere by word and by deed but help me too to do this humbly and gently in the power of the Spirit.*

The Fruit . . . and the Failures?

If I could shut the gate against my thoughts,
  And keep out sorrow from this room within,
Or memory could cancel all the notes
  Of my misdeeds, and I unthink my sin:
How free, how clear, how clean my soul should lie,
Discharged of such a loathsome company.

Or were there other rooms within my heart
  That did not to my conscience join so near,
Where I might lodge the thoughts of sin apart,
  That I might not their clamorous crying hear;
What peace, what joy, what ease should I possess,
  Freed from their horrors that my soul oppress.

But, O my Saviour, who my refuge art,
  Let thy dear mercies stand 'twixt them and me,
And be the wall to separate my heart
  So that I may at length repose me free;
That peace and joy and rest may be within,
  And I remain divided from my sin.

JOHN DANIEL (c.1620)

Comment

Here is a cry from the heart of a Christian acutely conscious of his failures. The fruit of the Spirit is indeed a harvest of 'love, joy, peace, long-suffering, gentleness, fidelity, meekness and self-control', and he could recall failures on all those counts, failures of commission and omission. He is saying 'If only I could wipe the slate clean and silence the prickings of conscience!' Then he realises that whilst he cannot do that, Christ can, and does for all who throw themselves onto his mercy. Our poet wins through. He accepts conscience as the divine voice in the human soul, responds to it and finds that peace and joy fill his heart. It is ever so. We open our hearts to the Spirit. Sometimes the harvest is rich and we are uplifted. Sometimes it is meagre and we are prompted to steel our wills to renewed effort. Sometimes the harvest fails. . .

> *Yet still there whispers the small voice within,*
> *Heard through Gain's silence, or o'er Glory's din;*
> *Whatever creed be taught or land be trod,*
> *Man's conscience is the oracle of God.*

So said Lord Byron. The faltering Christian listens for the oracle and heeds it.

Prayer

Heavenly Father, by the quickening power of your Holy Spirit keep my conscience awake and alert, strengthen my will to follow where it leads, lift my spirit that it may be one with your Spirit in seeking all that is good and true.

St James the Apostle

O great Apostle! rightly now
  Thou readest all thy Saviour meant,
What time his grave yet gentle brow
  In sweet reproof on thee was spent.
'Seek ye to sit enthroned by me?
  Alas! ye know not what ye ask.
The first in shame and agony,
  The lowest in the meanest task –
This can ye be? and can ye drink
  The cup that I in tears must steep,
Nor from the whelming waters shrink
  That o'er me roll so dark and deep'

'We can – thine are we, dearest Lord,
  In glory and in agony,
To do and suffer all thy word;
  Only be Thou for ever nigh' –
'Then be it so – my cup receive,
  And of my woes baptismal taste;
But for the crown, that Angels weave
  For those next me in glory placed,
I give it not by partial love;
  But in my Father's book are writ
What names on earth shall lowliest prove,
  That they in heaven may highest sit'.

JOHN KEBLE (1792–1866)

Comment

James and John, the sons of Zebedee and Salome, were among our Lord's first Apostles. In his verses, drawn from *The Christian Year*, John Keble has in mind the incident in the Gospel in which Salome appeared to be seeking preferential treatment for her sons! Jesus surnamed them Boanerges, and although this means 'sons of thunder' it was probably a commendation of their burning zeal for Christ and his cause rather than a criticism of the impetuosity which they may have inherited from their mother. Jesus clearly observed and admired that zeal and it is significant that the two brothers, along with Peter, were the chosen witnesses of his Transfiguration and his closest companions through the agony of Gethsemane. James became the first Christian martyr – slain by Herod Agrippa the First who decided that persecuting the Christians was the surest way of winning the approval of the Jews. Clearly James was a man whose commitment to Christ was marked by an ardent zeal to win others to The Way. Zeal is a fine quality to cherish but it has its dangers. St Paul acknowledged that the Jews were zealous for God (Romans ch.10 v.2), but their zeal was misdirected in that it was based on a rigid obedience to the trivia of law. The zeal of James for Christ and his Church was a zeal for loyalty, for love, for mercy, and for goodness. In that we can, and should emulate him.

Prayer *Lord, you have taught us through your servant Paul that 'it is fine to be zealous provided the purpose is good'. Keep your purpose of love ever before us and so fill us with your Spirit that we may hold fast to it day by day.*

Commemorating Anne, Mother of the Blessed Virgin Mary

A Mother brings her child to God

Deep in the warm vale the village is sleeping,
 Sleeping the firs on the bleak rock above;
Nought wakes, save grateful hearts, silently creeping
 Up to their Lord in the might of their love.

What Thou hast given to me, Lord, here I bring thee,
 Odour and light and the magic of gold;
Feet which must follow thee, lips which must sing thee,
 Limbs which must ache for thee, ere they grow old.

What thou hast given to me, Lord, here I tender
 Life of mine own life, the fruit of my love;
Take him, yet leave him me, till I shall render
 Count of the precious charge, kneeling above.

CHARLES KINGSLEY (1819–1875)

Comment

The Four Gospels in our Bible are not the only Gospels ever written. There are many others known as 'Apocryphal' (i.e. Hidden). Some of these are authentic and orthodox but were deemed to be less suitable for the Canon of Scripture than the Four. It is to the Apochryphal Gospels that we could turn for details of the life of St Anne. But we need not do so, for the Mother is seen in her Child, and we need not doubt that as Mary the Mother of Jesus brought him up with such affection, such tenderness and such wisdom, she for her part was recalling her own infancy and childhood when her Mother Anne was bringing her up in the fear of God. Anne brought her child Mary to God as did the mother in Kingsley's poem, and Mary for her part brought Jesus to God. No mother ever invented a better recipe for raising a child – as our American friends describe the process – than did Mary who doubtless learnt it at her mother's knee. 'Jesus increased in wisdom and stature, and in favour with God and man', embodies Mary's recipe which no mother could better. This was a four-square growth – mentally, physically, spiritually and socially. Anne was a mother in Israel indeed and we discern both her character and her wisdom in her daughter Mary. It is right and proper for a mother to bring her child to God in Holy Baptism, for example. But this is but a beginning, for spiritual, mental and social growth demand as much careful thought as does physical growth. The Spanish proverb which declares that 'an ounce of mother is worth a ton of priest' is not far from the truth if it is suggesting that when a mother brings her child to God in Holy Baptism she cannot say to the priest: 'There you are. His spiritual growth is now your responsibility'.

Prayer *Father, let your blessing rest upon our homes. As we remember Anne who bore in her womb the Mother of our Lord, so we pray for all mothers that, bringing their children to God, they may with firm resolve lead them on to holy living.*

The Price of Discipleship

Christ took upon himself this human form of ours. He became Man even as we are men. In his humanity and his lowliness we recognise our own form. He has become like a man so that men should be like him. And in the Incarnation the whole human race recovers the dignity of God and the image of God. Henceforth any attack on the least of men is an attack on Christ, who took the form of man, and in his own Person restored the image of God in all that bears a human form. Through fellowship and communion with the incarnate Lord, we recover our true humanity, and at the same time we are delivered from that individualism which is the consequence of sin, and retrieve our solidarity with the whole human race. By being partakers of Christ incarnate we are partakers in the whole humanity which he bore. We know now that we have been taken up and born in the humanity of Jesus, and therefore that new nature we now enjoy means that we too must bear the sins and sorrows of others. The incarnate Lord makes his followers the brothers of all mankind. The philanthropy of God, revealed in the Incarnation, is the ground of Christian love towards all on earth that bears the name of man. The form of Christ incarnate makes the Church into the Body of Christ. All the sorrows of mankind fell upon that form, and only through that form can they be borne.

DIETRICH BONHOEFFER (1906–1943)

Comment

If ever a man was able to count *The Cost of Discipleship*, which is the title of the book from which the quotation is culled, that man was Dietrich Bonhoeffer. He was a German pastor sent into exile for his opposition to the Nazi regime. On the outbreak of the Second World War he returned to his native country to work for the Church and to bear his witness to the evils of Nazism, warning the German people constantly about the dangers of the road along which they were being driven. He was arrested in 1943 and imprisoned in Buchenwald. It was in prison there that he wrote a number of letters affirming his faith. Shortly before he was hanged by Hitler's personal orders, he wrote in one of his letters what I would call a layman's exposition of the quotation from his book. 'You must never doubt that I am travelling my appointed road with gratitude and cheerfulness. My past life is replete with God's goodness, and my sins are covered by the forgiving love of Christ crucified. I am thankful for all those who have crossed my path, and all I wish is never to cause them sorrow, and that they, like me, will always be thankful for the forgiveness and mercy of God'. Here is one of Bonhoeffer's prayers which can be meaningful for us even though our tribulations are never likely to match his.

Prayer   *Heavenly Father, I praise and thank thee for all thy goodness and faithfulness throughout my life. Thou hast granted me many blessings. Now let me accept tribulation from thy hand. Thou wilt not lay on me more than I can bear. Thou makest all things to work together for good for thy children.*

The Retreat

Happy those early days, when I
Shined in my Angel-infancy!
Before I understood this place
Appointed for my second race.
Or taught my soul to fancy aught
But a white, celestial thought;
When yet I had not walked above
A mile or two from my first Love,
And looking back, at that short space
Could see a glimpse of his bright face;
When on some gilded cloud or flower
My gazing soul would dwell an hour,
And in those weaker glories spy
Some shadows of eternity;
Before I taught my tongue to wound
My conscience with a sinful sound,
Or had the black art to dispense
A several sin to every sense;
But felt through all this fleshly dress
Bright shoots of everlastingness.

O how I long to travel back,
And tread again that ancient track!
That I might once more reach that plain
Where first I left my glorious train;
From when the enlightened spirit sees
That shady City of Palm-trees.
But ah! my soul with too much stay
Is drunk, and staggers in the way!
Some men a forward motion love,
But I by backward steps would move,
And, when this dust falls to the urn,
In that state I came, return.

HENRY VAUGHAN (1622–1695)

Comment

A poignant poem this in which the mystical poet Henry Vaughan looks back upon the innocency of childhood, before 'the world' took possession of his soul and laid its spoiling hand on his life. It is a poem of universal application. In childhood we knew nothing of those sins of the flesh which precede St Paul's list of the harvest of the Spirit, and even the fruits of the Spirit seemed to possess us without any conscious effort on our part. In adult life 'the enlightened spirit' may cast a glance at 'that shady city of Palm-trees' – i.e. the ideal of innocence, but it must be but a glance. Our task is to press on, looking unto Jesus, our Way and Truth and Life, and seeing ever in him those fruits of the Spirit which must be our agenda for life.

Prayer   Spirit of purity and grace, our weakness, pitying, see:
O make our hearts thy dwelling place and worthier thee.

HARRIET AUBER (1763–1862)

Commemorating William Wilberforce, Social Reformer, 1833

Christianity assumes her true character, no less than she performs her natural and proper office, when she takes under her protection those poor degraded beings on whom philosophy looks down with disdain or perhaps with contemptuous condescension. On the very first promulgation of Christianity it was declared by its great Author, as 'glad tidings to the poor'; and, ever faithful to her character, Christianity still delights to instruct the ignorant, to succour the needy, to comfort the sorrowful, to visit the forsaken.

Animated, Sir, by this unfeigned spirit of friendship for the natives of India, their religious and moral interests are undoubtedly our first concern; but the course we are recommending tends no less to promote their temporal well-being than their eternal welfare; for such is their real condition that we are prompted to endeavour to communicate to them the benefits of Christian instruction, scarcely less by religious principle than by the feelings of common humanity. Not, Sir, that I would pretend to conceal from the House, that the hope which, above all others, chiefly gladdens my heart, is that of being instrumental in bringing them into the paths by which they may be led to everlasting felicity. But still, were all considerations of a future state out of the question, I hesitate not to affirm, that a regard for their temporal well-being would alone furnish abundant motives for our endeavouring to diffuse among them the blessings of Christian light and moral instruction.

WILLIAM WILBERFORCE (1759–1833)

Comment

The quotation is part of a speech which Wilberforce made in Parliament. Wilberforce was undoubtedly a great man of God and a visionary. He was an Evangelical, a member of the Clapham Sect, and he and his fellow Christians found the best expression for their piety in the field of humanitarian activity. They were desperately concerned about the poor, about conditions in the places where they were employed, about the education of the young and about the slave trade, and they found support on both sides of the political fence, though within the Church itself alas! there were high and dry conservative clergy who were opposed to, or indifferent to, the anti-slavery cause. Gradually, however, people began to think for themselves, and Christians were no longer content to toe the party line. The breakthrough came in 1807, though another quarter of a century elapsed before the cause finally triumphed. The historian Trevelyan describes Wilberforce as 'the classic example of the use of the cross-bench politician in our two-party public life. . . an agitator who always retained his powerful gift of social charm'. That, with his deep Christian conviction, assured the success of the causes to which he gave his life. God be praised for his life and work!

Prayer   *Heavenly Father, lover of mankind, who raised up your servant William Wilberforce to bring liberty to the captives and to free the oppressed. Grant that, by the teaching of your Church and the zeal of your people, all chains of oppression on earth may be broken, and your love reign supreme, through Jesus Christ our Lord.*

Christ and Ourselves

I wish a greater knowledge, than t'attain
The knowledge of myself: A greater gain
Than to augment myself; a greater treasure
Than to enjoy myself; a greater pleasure
Than to content myself; how slight, and vain
Is all self-knowledge, pleasure, treasure, gain;
Unless my better knowledge could retrieve
My Christ; unless my better gain could thrive
In Christ; unless my better wealth grow rich
In Christ; unless my better pleasure pitch
On Christ; or else my knowledge will proclaim
To my own heart how ignorant I am;
Or else my gain, so ill improved, will shame
My trade, and show how much declined I am;
Or else my treasure will but blur my name
With Bankrupt, and divulge how poor I am;
Or else my pleasures, that so much inflame
My thoughts, will blab how full of sores I am;
Lord, keep me from myself; 'Tis best for me
Never to own my Self, if not in thee.

FRANCIS QUARLES (1592–1644)

Comment

Francis Quarles became a student of Christ's College, Cambridge at the age of 14 and came into prominence as cupbearer to the Princess Palatine when he was 18. That was a strange prelude to a literary life which revealed him as an ardent student of the Bible. He became private secretary to the Archbishop of Armagh in 1625 and from then until his death in 1644 his output of works on the Christian religion and Christian morals was considerable. He was deeply religious, concerned not only to teach others but to increase his own faith. His poem *Christ and Our Selves* betrays something of the struggle which went on within him in his quest for the good life in Christ. So acute was his sense of personal failure that he saw himself as waging a continual battle with self. Doubtless he would have endorsed Tennyson's 'self-reverence, self-knowledge, self-control' as leading 'to sovereign power', but all these qualities, noble as they are, could conclude with spiritual bankruptcy unless they led him to Christ ever and again. A heart which is full of self leaves no room for the entry of the Spirit and offers no hope for a rich harvest of the Spirit.

Prayer   *Almighty God, give me desire, overmastering and perpetual, to consecrate myself to thee, my life to thy kingdom, my love to all whom you love.*

AFTER ERIC MILNER-WHITE

Immanence

I come in the little things,
Saith the Lord:
Not borne on morning wings
Of majesty, but I have set My Feet
Amidst the delicate and bladed wheat
That springs triumphant in the furrowed sod.
There do I dwell in weakness and in power;
Not broken or divided saith our God!
In your straight garden plot I come to flower;
About your porch my Vine
Meek, fruitful doth entwine;
Waits at the threshold, Love's appointed hour.

I come in the little things,
Saith the Lord;
Yea! on the glancing wings
Of eager birds, the softly pattering feet
Of furred and gentle beasts, I come to meet
Your hard and wayward heart. In brown
     bright eyes
That peep from out the brake, I stand confest,
On every nest
Where feathery Patience is content to brood
And leave her pleasure for the high emprize
Of motherhood –
There doth my Godhead rest.

I come in the little things,
Saith the Lord;
My starry wings
I do forsake,
Love's highway of humility to take;
Meekly I fit my stature to your need,
In beggar's part
About your gates I shall not cease to plead –
As man, to speak with man –
Till by such art
I shall achieve My Immemorial Plan
Pass the low lintel of the human heart.

EVELYN UNDERHILL (1875–1941)

Comment

A wonderful poem indeed about the Christ whose company the Christian seeks even as he is engaged in 'the little things'. Christ fits his stature to our need. Our needs change from day to day and year to year. None is too trivial, too little, for him to meet. For those with hearts which yearn, and eyes which see, we meet him on 'love's highway of humility'.

Prayer   *What better prayer than to read the poem again and fashion your own personal prayer about 'the little things' uppermost in your mind just now.*

❧

Laugh!

Laugh and be merry, remember, better the world with a song,
Better the world with a blow in the teeth of a wrong.
Laugh for the time is brief, a thread the length of a span.
Laugh and be proud to belong to the old proud pageant of man.
Laugh and be merry; remember, in olden time,
God made heaven and earth for joy he took in a rhyme,
Made them and filled them full with the strong red wind of his mirth,
The splendid joy of the stars: the joy of the earth.
So we must laugh and drink from the deep blue cup of the sky,
Join the jubilant song of the great stars sweeping by,
Laugh, and battle, and work, and drink of the wine outpoured,
In the dear green earth, the sign of the joy of the Lord.
Laugh and be merry together, like brothers akin,
Guesting awhile in the rooms of a beautiful inn,
Glad till the dancing stops, and the lilt of the music ends.
Laugh till the game is played; and, you be merry, my friends.

JOHN MASEFIELD (1878–1967)

Comment

August – the holiday month! Perhaps this is the month for a lighter touch in the quotations meeting the beauties of the natural world and 'all creatures great and small'. The true Christian life is not one which excludes fun and laughter, humour and merriment. 'I am come', said our Lord, 'that they might have life and have it more abundantly', and the 'abundantly' means 'overflowing', life in all its fullness. The Christian life is not a dull dispirited experience. It is a life bubbling over with joy and one which certainly does not exclude laughter and fun – and humour, so long as it is 'clean' and never unkind. To say this is not to forget that life has its shadows as well as its sunlight. It is to remember as Thomas Carlyle put it, that everyone's life is 'a little gleam of Time between two Eternities'. John Masefield, who was Poet Laureate from 1930–1967, knew something of both aspects of life – the sorrowful and the joyful, the serious and the frivolous. In this poem he exhorts us to 'laugh and be merry together' and this can be an expression of Christian fellowship. But there must be two warnings for Christians. The first, that we may never laugh at another's misfortune. The second, to remember that whilst it is true that our Lord's first public engagement was to be present at a party, where undoubtedly the wine flowed freely, and there was much laughter and merriment, we may be certain that the wine was not drunk to excess and that everyone had a good time – good that is in its noblest meaning.

Prayer   *Teach me, O Lord, the art of life; help me to see friendship as a holy tie and fellowship one with another as sacred. Help me to enjoy life to the full and to bring that same enjoyment to others, enhanced by merriment and unsullied by sin – and this to our common good and to your glory.*

Dewdrops

The dewdrops on every blade of grass are so much like silver drops that I am obliged to stoop down as I walk to see if they are pearls, and those sprinkled on the ivy-woven beds of primroses underneath the hazels, white-thorns, and maples are so like gold beads that I stooped down to feel if they were hard, but they melted from my finger. And where the dew lies on the primrose, the violet and whitethorn leaves, they are emerald and beryl, yet nothing more than the dews of the morning on the budding leaves; nay, the road grasses are covered with gold and silver beads, and the further we go the brighter they seem to shine, like solid gold and silver. It is noth-ing more than the sun's light and shade upon them in the dewy morning; every thorn-point and every bramble-spear has its trembling ornament: till the wind gets a little brisker, and then all is shaken off, and all the shining jewellery passes away into a common spring morning full of budding leaves, primroses, violets, vernal speedwell, bluebell and orchids, and common-place objects.

JOHN CLARE (1793–1864)

Comment

A wonderful appreciation of a common enough sight which usually goes unnotic-ed. John Clare, who was adjudged insane for the last 27 years of his life, neverthe-less wrote many hundreds of poems about birds and animals, flowers and trees. In these and in prose passages of exquisite beauty he saw a hand mightier than Man's and sensed a Presence real though unseen. The world wrote him off as 'mad' but he clearly shared a wisdom which the world could not penetrate. Even as a patient in an asylum in Northampton he found a solace in his solitude and as he wandered alone in the grounds of the hospital he wrote of this:

> There is a charm in solitude that cheers
> A feeling that the world knows nothing of;
> A green delight the wounded mind endears
> After the hustling world is broken off,
> Whose whole delight was crime – at good to scoff,
> Green solitude, his prison, pleasure yields.
> The bitch fox heeds him not, the birds seem to laugh.
> He lives the Crusoe of his lonely field
> Whose dark green oaks his noontide leisure shield.

This is the insane teaching a much needed lesson to the sane, for do we not our-selves face the danger of cluttering up our lives with so much ceaseless activity that we can find no space for a moment's solitude during which we can probe the purpose of life more deeply and find communion with the author of life more clearly?

Prayer *Give me, O Lord, the grace of detachment from the things of the world and in the silence help me to set my life into the frame of the heavenly vision that I may see you in all things lovely and reflect your love in my life day by day.*

Leisure

What is this life, if, full of care,
We have no time to stand and stare?

No time to stand beneath the boughs
And stare as long as sheep or cows.

No time to see, when woods we pass,
Where squirrels hide their nuts in
  grass.

No time to see in broad daylight
Streams full of stars, like skies at
  night.

No time to turn at Beauty's glance,
And watch her feet, how they can
  dance.

No time to wait till her mouth can
Enrich that smile her eyes began.

A poor life this if, full of care,
We have no time to stand and stare.

WILLIAM H. DAVIES (1871–1940)

Comment

Here is another poet who opted out of society. He lived the life of a tramp – a life in which he found time to stand and stare, and more time to set down his thoughts, often profound and often amusing. Here is an example of his standing and staring. He calls the poem *A Great Time*.

Sweet Chance, that led my steps abroad,
    Beyond the town, where wild flowers grow –
A rainbow and a cuckoo, Lord,
    How rich and great the times are now!
        Know, all ye sheep
        And cows that keep
On staring, that I stand so long
    In grass that's wet from heavy rain –
A rainbow and a cuckoo's song
    May never come together again:
        May never come
        This side the tomb.

The poet's standing and staring afforded him an experience he had not hitherto enjoyed, but its outcome was something precious which would be with him for ever – even on the other side of the tomb. He was not the first poet who by standing and staring had found enrichment of mind and spirit. A Christian may meditate on the works of God on his knees or in his arm-chair at home, in his garden, or on walks in the country. He may not express himself as, for example, did Wordsworth or indeed as this poet, but if he 'stands and stares', he may find the serenity and the inspiration which they found.

Prayer Leaving the things which are too high for us, in quietness and confidence may we find our strength renewed. Through your words and your works reveal to us your light and, knowing the Way, help us to walk steadfastly in it. This we ask through Jesus Christ our Lord.

Commemorating Dominic, Priest, Friar, 1170–1221

So noble in character, so ardently on fire with divine love was Dominic that there can be no doubt that he was a chosen vessel of grace. Except when he was moved to pity and compassion he always displayed great firmness of mind. A joyous heart is reflected in the countenance, and Dominic revealed his tranquillity of soul by the joyful kindliness of his look. Everywhere in word and deed, he showed himself to be a herald of the gospel. By day no one was more affable or more friendly with his brethren and companions, no one more fervent than he in vigils and prayer at night. His conversation was always either with God or about God; rarely did he speak on other matters, and this practice he commended to his disciples.

He often exhorted his friars, both in his writings and by his words, to study constantly the sacred scriptures, in the old and new testaments. He always carried with him a copy of the gospel according to St Matthew and the epistles of St Paul; these he had studied to such an extent that he almost knew them by heart.

Gregory IX said of him: 'I knew him as a wholehearted follower of the apostolic way of life, and there is no doubt that he shares in heaven the glory of the apostles themselves'.

·HISTORY OF THE ORDER OF PREACHERS

Comment

St Dominic shares with St Francis of Assisi the insight of realising that his day needed a new slant to the monastic life. Hitherto monks were expected to renounce the world and to separate themselves from the world, believing that thereby they could serve God the better. Dominic established the Order of Friars who did indeed renounce the world, but they believed that they should at the same time mingle with the world and give themselves humbly to mission especially among the unlettered, the poor and the under-privileged. The Dominican Friars were established as an Order in 1215 and, led by St Dominic, they went about preaching the gospel and ministering to the poor. Dominic became known and loved not only for taking the light of the gospel into dark places in Spain and in Italy, but also for his limitless compassion to the sick and the needy. Approaching a village with some of his friars on one occasion he asked them to stand still at its entrance and he exclaimed: 'Look at those roofs, what sorrows and tears, what sins and difficulties they cover. Oh! that we might relieve some of them as we pass by'. That is precisely what they did.

Prayer *Pour out your Spirit, O Lord, on all who preach the gospel. Inflame them with the fire of your love and give grace to all who hear your Word to take it to themselves and to pass on its message of love both by their words and by their deeds, through Jesus Christ our Lord.*

Commemorating Oswald, King of Northumbria, d.642

The Fatherland

Where is the true man's fatherland?
*   Is it where he by chance is born?*
*   Doth not the yearning spirit scorn*
In such scant borders to be spanned?
Oh, yes! his fatherland must be
As the blue heaven wide and free.

Is it alone where freedom is,
*   Where God is God and man is man?*
*   Doth he not claim a broader span*
For the soul's love of home than this?
Oh, yes! his fatherland must be
As the blue heaven wide and free!

Where'er a human heart doth wear
*   Joy's myrtle-wreath or sorrow's gyves*
*   Where'er a human spirit strives*
After a life more true and fair,
There is the true man's birthplace grand,
His is a world-wide fatherland!

Where'er a single slave doth pine,
*   Where'er one man may help another, –*
*   Thank God for such a birthright,*
*   brother, –*
That spot of earth is thine and mine!
There is the true man's birthplace grand,
His is a world-wide fatherland!

J. RUSSELL LOWELL (1818–1891)

Comment

Russell Lowell, the American poet and hymn writer who was once Ambassador in London, expresses sentiments in *The Fatherland* which Oswald expressed in his life as a king. Once he had established his kingdom he resolved to make the people aware of that greater Kingdom of which Jesus is Lord. He sent a message to Iona asking that a bishop might be sent to preach the gospel and to strengthen the church throughout his land. The bishop who came was Aidan, but as his English was weak Oswald frequently accompanied him as interpreter. The Church in his fatherland was mightily strengthened by his own proclamation of the gospel and by his personal behaviour. Motivated by the laws of Christ's kingdom Oswald was determined to ensure that his kingdom should be 'as the blue heaven wide and free'. Life should be 'more true and fair. . . where one man may help another'. A story from Bede illustrates Oswald's concern. Sitting with the bishop on Easter Day, a servant told the king that a great number of beggars had gathered outside asking for help. Oswald ordered that the silver dish be filled with food to be distributed among the beggars, and the dish itself should be broken into pieces and given to them. Read Lowell's poem again. Are we as conscious of the 'world-wide fatherland' as our holy religion calls us to be? 'Where one man may help another'? What of poverty, starvation, inhumanity, racism, apartheid?

Prayer   *Pour upon us, O Lord, the spirit of brotherly kindness that wherever in your world our brothers and sisters are in need we may not be slow to help one another.*

The Transfiguration of Our Lord

Transfiguration

Think not to roam at will the distant hill
And drink the heady wine of morning air,
To linger long beside some sparkling rill
Amidst the marshy, flower-strewn
  meadows there.
These things in surfeit tend to be but loss
For we are nailed to life as to the cross.

Long may our sojourn be upon this plain,
And dim the way our feeble footsteps tread,
While all our strivings seem to be but vain
And heart is weary, inspiration dead.
Yet in the furnace gold is purged of dross
And Christ has triumphed for us on the
  Cross,

So lift your heart to Christ upon the mount,
Drink deep to fill its emptiness again.
He fills us all, turns all to good account,
For he descends the footpath to the plain
To heal the leper, making whole the loss,
Before he nails us with him to the Cross.

SISTER SHEILA MARGARET C.S.M.V.

Comment

The incident in our Lord's ministry which Sister Sheila Margaret interprets so beautifully in her poem is one of great significance. It is recorded in the Gospels of Matthew, Mark and Luke and all are at one in presenting it as a moment of great significance, a moment when the somewhat bewildered disciples, distressed by the insistence of Jesus that he would be made to suffer and be crucified, were suddenly uplifted by the vision of their Christ in his glory. The face of Jesus 'shone like the sun', and a voice was heard, 'This is my son, my chosen, listen to him' (St Luke ch.9 v.35). Here was a vision splendid; here for a moment they could see the crown beyond the cross; here they could catch the truth that if indeed their Christ must be humiliated there must be another end to the story and that of victory and triumph. All this flashed upon them momentarily as they saw their Christ in his glory. Peter's reaction was to stay where they were – physically, mentally, spiritually. 'Master, it is good for us to be here and let us make three tabernacles, one for thee, one for Moses and one for Elias' (St Mark ch.9). Peter's reaction is one which, maybe, we experience from time to time – following some rich religious experience, some great act of worship, some invigorating holiday where we have communed with the wonders of God's world. But our Lord led Peter and his friends from the mountain to the plain, from the glory to the trials. So for us. It is good to seek moments of 'transfiguration' – in a retreat, in Sunday worship, in our prayers – but from the mountain of glory we have to descend to the plain – of work, of pain maybe, of difficulties, of problems, of suffering. That we can do with confidence that the glory will shine through for us as it did for the apostles.

Prayer   *God whom it belongs ever to adore, teach me, inspire me, assist me to adore – and, seeing you in all your glory, help me to reflect that glory in my life.*

The Donkey

When fishes flew and forests walked
  And figs grew upon thorn,
Some moment when the moon was blood
  Then surely I was born.

With monstrous head and sickening cry
  And ears like errant wings,
The devil's walking parody
  On all four-footed things.

The tattered outlaw of the earth,
  Of ancient crooked will;
Starve, scourge, deride me; I am dumb.
  I keep my secret still.

Fools! For I also had my hour
  One far fierce hour and sweet;
There was a shout about my ears,
  And palms before my feet.

G.K. CHESTERTON (1874–1936)

Comment

Chesterton lights upon the most despised of the animal world – the one which bears the name than which few can be more insulting when applied by one human to another. The poor donkey recognises himself as an ugly beast, obstinate and wilful. But he nurses a secret which prompts him to look with some pity upon those who deride him and ill-treat him. He remembers the time – and will never forget – when he was privileged to carry the Christ on his back, what time people waved palms and shouted 'hosanna'. Chesterton was too sensitive a man and too deeply committed to Christ as the Lord of all life merely to write what some might regard as no more than a funny story about a donkey. The poem says more than can be seen by the eye. The Christian in his pilgrimage will have his shadowed days – days of anxiety, days of frustration, days when nothing 'goes right', days of loneliness, days of despair. Christians must remember when passing through such a period of depression that they have a 'secret still' and the power of that secret – Christ crucified and Christ risen – will carry them through the dark days enabling them to rise again. Cowper concludes one of his poems entitled *The Nightingale and the Glow-Worm* thus:

  Hence jarring sectaries may learn
  Their real interest to discern;
  That brother should not war with brother,
  And worry and devour each other.

Prayer   *Lord, who alone art God, the gracious and merciful; who commandest them that love thy name to cast away all fear and care, and to lay their burden upon thee; Receive us under thy protection and give us that everlasting rest which thou hast promised to them that obey thy word, through Jesus Christ our Lord.*

FROM AN ANCIENT PRIMER

The Imaginary Invalid

I remember going to the British Museum one day to read up the treatment for some slight ailment of which I had a touch – hay fever, I fancy it was. I got down the book, and read all I came to read; and then, in an unthinking moment, I idly turned the leaves, and began indolently to study the diseases generally. I forget which was the first distemper I plunged into – some fearful devastating scourge I know – and before I had glanced half down the list of 'premonitory symptoms', it was borne in upon me that I had got it.

I sat for a while, frozen with horror; and then, in the listlessness of despair, I again turned over the pages. I came to typhoid fever, read the symptoms – and discovered that I had typhoid fever, must have had it for months without knowing it – wondered what else I had got; turned up St Vitus's Dance and found, as I expected, that I had that too. I began to get interested in my case, and determined to sift it to the bottom and so started alphabetically. I read up ague, and learned that I was sickening for it. Bright's disease, I was relieved to find, I had only in a modified form and, so far as that was concerned, I might live for years. Cholera I had with several complications; and diphtheria too. I plodded conscientiously through the twenty-six letters, and the only malady I could conclude I had not got was housemaid's knee.

JEROME K. JEROME (1859–1927)

Comment

The insertion of this passage in the August selection is not primarily to raise a smile though it should certainly do just that. It is to lead into a few thoughts about anxiety. Reading from the Authorised Version of the Bible we hear Jesus saying 'Take no thought' – for your life, your raiment, your food, your words, and we deduce from that, that those to whom he was speaking were weighed down with worries of one kind and another. 'Take no thought', however, does not mean 'Do not think about'. It is not a word against prudence. Translations of the New Testament subsequent to the Authorised Version make our Lord's meaning clear. He is saying: 'Do not be anxious... do not worry'. But remember that he is talking to people worrying about their own welfare. We *must* concern ourselves about the welfare of others. We *must* be prudent about our own welfare. But worry is a want of trust in God our Heavenly Father, and it is that against which our Lord is warning his friends.

Prayer

Lord, you have taught us not to be anxious but to put our whole trust in you. Silence our murmurings, allay our fears and dispel our doubts, that we may rise above our anxieties and put our whole confidence in you.

The Cricket

Little inmate full of mirth,
Chirping on my kitchen hearth,
Whereso'er be thine abode
Always harbinger of good.
Pay me for thy warm retreat
With a song more soft and sweet;
In return thou shalt receive,
Such a strain as I can give.

Thus thy praise shall be expressed,
Inoffensive, welcome guest!
While the rat is on the scout,
And the mouse with curious snout,
With what vermin else infest
Every dish, and spoil the best;
Frisking thus before the fire,
Thou hast all thy heart's desire.

Though in voice and shape they be
Formed as if akin to thee,
Thou surpassest, happier far,
Happiest grasshoppers that are;
Theirs is but a summer's song
Thine endures the winter long.
Unimpaired and shrill, and clear
Melody throughout the year.

Neither night nor dawn of day
Puts a period to thy play;
Sing then – and extend thy span
Far beyond the date of man;
Wretched man, whose years are spent
In repining discontent,
Lives not, aged though he be,
Half a span, compared with thee.

WILLIAM COWPER (1731–1800)

Comment

Cowper, a barrister by profession and a devout Christian by conviction, became a lay assistant to John Newton, the curate of Olney. Together they compiled the *Olney Hymns* – a collection which embraces a great number of the most popular hymns used throughout Christendom. *The Cricket*, based on a Latin collection, reveals the sensitivity with which Cowper approached all created things – birds, trees, flowers, insects, not forgetting his tame hare given him by a parishioner when he was recovering from a mental breakdown. 'I kept him', he wrote, 'for his humour's sake'. He sees in the little cricket qualities which man could emulate. The cricket plays and sings not only in the summer but in the long winter too. The lay assistant poet-hymn-writer is indeed preaching a sermon – about 'the good', about contentment and about singing the praises of the Creator.

Prayer   *Father, preserve me from 'repining discontent' and help me to fill my days with praise and bear my witness to the world in the sweet melody of love.*

Commemorating Laurence, Deacon, Martyr, 258

Look Home

Retired thoughts enjoy their own delights,
As beauty doth, in self-beholding eye;
Man's mind a mirror is, of heavenly sights,
A brief, wherein all marvels summed lied;
Of fairest forms and sweetest shapes the
*   store,*
Most graceful all, yet thought may grace
them more.

The mind a creature is, yet can create,
To nature's patterns adding higher skill
Of finest works, wit better could the
*   state*
If force of wit had equal power of will;
Device of man in working hath no end;
What thought can think, another
*   thought can mend.*

Man's soul of endless beauties image is,
Drawn by the work of endless skill and
*   might;*
This skilful might gave many sparks of
*   bliss,*
And to discern this bliss a native light
To frame God's image as his work
*   required,*
His might, his skill, his word, and will
*   conspired.*

All that he had, his image should present;
All that it should present, he could afford;
To that he could afford his will was bent,
His will was followed with performing
*   word.*
Let this suffice, by this conceive the rest:
He should, he could, he would, he did his
*   best.*

ROBERT SOUTHWELL (1561–1595)

Comment

The poet Robert Southwell was a Jesuit who wrote most of his poetry in prison. Since he himself was a martyr, it seems appropriate that his poem should appear as the martyr Laurence is being commemorated. Laurence was a deacon in Rome during the persecutions under the Emperor Valerian. He saw his bishop led to his execution and shouted defiantly to the soldiers: 'Should the bishop go to the sacrifice without his attendant deacon?' He was arrested immediately and as he left he heard his bishop's answer: 'My son, in three days thou shalt follow'. Ordered to surrender all the treasures of the Church within twenty-four hours, Laurence gathered together the city's beggars, the lame and the halt. 'These', he said to the Prefect, 'are the Church's treasures'. He was condemned and executed. He might have taken the view that he could evade the challenge since he was but a deacon. But when the test came he knew that '*he should*', he had faith that '*he could*', he concluded that '*he would*'. Thus he was martyred. 'He *did* his best'.

Prayer   *O Lord, who hast promised a blessing for all who suffer for righteousness' sake: Grant to all our brethren persecuted for the truth, that they may rejoice in being counted worthy to suffer dishonour for thy name. Strengthen their faith and renew their love, that in their patience they may possess their souls and win their persecutors to penitence and new brotherhood in Thee, for the sake of him who suffered shame and reproach and remained invincible in his love, even thy redeeming Son, Christ our Lord.*

BISHOP GEORGE APPLETON

Commemorating Clare of Assisi, Virgin, 1253

When as Saint Francis was at Assisi, oftentimes he visited Saint Clare and gave her holy admonishments. And she having exceeding great desire to once break bread with him, oft-times besought him thereto, but he was never willing to grant her this consolation; wherefore his companions, beholding the desire of Saint Clare, said to Saint Francis: 'Father, it doth appear to us that this severity accordeth not with heavenly charity: since thou givest not ear unto Sister Clare, a virgin so saintly, so beloved of God, in so slight a matter as breaking bread with thee, and above all, bearing in mind that she through thy preaching abandoned the riches and pomps of the world. And, of a truth, had she asked of thee a greater boon then this, thou oughtest so to do unto thy spiritual plant'.

Then replied Saint Francis: 'Doth it seem good to you that I should grant her prayer?' Replied his companions: 'Yea, Father, fitting is it that thou grant her this boon and consolation'. Then spake Saint Francis: 'Since it seems good to you, it seems so likewise unto me. But that she might be the more consoled, I will that this breaking of bread take place in Saint Mary of the Angels; for she has been for so long shut up in St Damian that it will rejoice her to see again the house of Saint Mary, where her hair was shorn away and she became the bride of Jesus Christ; there let us eat together in the name of God' . . . .

St Francis then made ready the table on the bare ground as he was wont to do. And the hour of breaking bread come, they sat down together, Saint Francis and Saint Clare, and all the other companions took each his place at the table with all humility.

FROM THE LITTLE FLOWERS OF SAINT FRANCIS

Comment

St Clare is a newcomer to the Church of England's calendar of commemorations. She was born in 1193 and at the age of 18 she was deeply moved by a course of Lenten sermons by Francis in the church of San Giorgio. Fired by his words she decided to give her life to Christ within a religious Order and, directed by Francis, she entered a Benedictine convent. Eventually Francis found her and the Sisters of the Order a house on the outskirts of Assisi and it was there that the Poor Clares were established and from there that Clare and her Sisters did their work of teaching and ministry to the poor. She was Abbess of the Order until her death in 1253 after a long drawn-out illness. She was deeply moved herself by the poverty, the humility and the charity of Christ, and these she emulated for love of God and his children. There are within the Church a great many Religious Communities for women, the Poor Clares among them. Their dedication and their ministry deserve remembrance in our prayers.

Prayer   *O Lord, who for our sakes became poor, we ask you to strengthen all our religious communities, that those who have taken up the Cross to follow you in poverty, humility and charity, may by their consecration and the power of their prayers, be the means of drawing many into the fellowship of your Church, through Jesus Christ our Lord.*

Poetical Sketches

The first by a shepherd

> Welcome, stranger, to this place,
> Where joy doth sit on every bough,
> Paleness flies from every face;
> We reap not what we do not sow.
> Innocence doth like a rose
> Bloom on every maiden's cheek;
> Honour twines around her brows,
> The jewel health adorns her neck.

The second by a young shepherd

> When the trees do laugh with our merry wit,
> And the green hills laugh with the noise of it,
> When the meadows laugh with lively green
> And the grasshopper laughs in the merry scene.
> When the greenwood laughs with the voice of joy,
> And the dimpling stream runs laughing by,
> When Edessa, and Lyca, and Emilie,
> With their round mouths sing ha, ha, he,
> When the painted birds laugh in the shade,
> Where our table with cherries and nuts is spread;
> Come live and be merry and join with me,
> To sing the sweet chorus of ha, ha, he.

The third by an old shepherd

> When silver snow decks Sylvia's clothes,
> And jewel hangs at shepherd's nose,
> We can abide life's pelting storm
> That makes limbs quake, if hearts be warm.
> While Virtue is our walking staff
> And Truth's a lantern to our path,
> We can abide life's pelting storm
> That makes limbs quake, if hearts be warm.
> Blow, boisterous wind, stern winter's frown,
> Innocence is a winter's gown:
> So glad, we'll bide life's pelting storm
> That makes limbs quake, if hearts be warm.

WILLIAM BLAKE (1757–1827)

Comment

William Blake is best known for his *Jerusalem*, sung so often and with such fervour. Here he exalts joy, innocence, laughter, singing, merriment, and through the lips of the old shepherd he gives the clue to the life which will not be broken however boisterous the winds of adversity may beat against it. And the clue? It is Virtue, which is the 'Walking staff', and Truth which is the lantern which lights the way.

Prayer   *Light of the World, shine upon our minds and hearts. Spirit of Truth, guide us into all truth. Father in Heaven, be our strength and stay that with hearts warmed by your love we may go on our way rejoicing.*

Commemorating Jeremy Taylor, Bishop of Down and Connor, Pastor, Teacher, 1667

Prayer – a Parable and a Definition

So have I seen a lark rising from its bed of grass, and soaring upwards, singing as he rises, and hopes to get to heaven and climb above the clouds; but the poor bird was beaten back with the loud sighings of an eastern wind, and his motion made irregular and inconstant, descending more at every breath of the tempest than it could recover by the libration and frequent weighing of his wings; till the little creature was forced to sit down and pant, and stay till the storm was over; and then it made a prosperous flight, and did rise and sing, as if it had learned music and motion from an angel, as he passed sometimes through the air, about his ministries here below; so is the prayer of a good man.

Prayer is the peace of our spirit, the stillness of our thoughts, the evenness of our recollection, the seat of meditation, the rest of our cares and the calm of our tempests. Prayer is the issue of a quiet mind, of untroubled thoughts. It is the daughter of charity and the sister of meekness.

JEREMY TAYLOR (1613–1667)

Comment

Jeremy Taylor, sometime chaplain to Charles the First, Rector of Uppingham, chaplain to the Royalist Army and Bishop of Down and Connor, could not be excluded from any list of Anglican divines. His contribution to the spiritual life of his day is memorable and indeed immeasurable in his many writings. Two of these have exercised a profound effect on Anglican spirituality, namely *The Rule and Exercise of Holy Living* and *The Rule and Exercise of Holy Dying*. Taylor's devotional writings, from which the above quotations were extracted, have been described as 'combining transparent lucidity with rhetorical vigour and powerful imagery', qualities which have captured the attention even of those who lay no claim to scholarship.

Prayer   *O Thou who dwellest in every humble heart, and dost consecrate it for thy sanctuary: hallow our hearts within us, that they may be houses of prayer, the dwelling places of thy spirit wherein thou dost reveal thy holy mysteries; through Jesus Christ our Lord.*

JEREMY TAYLOR

Childhood

There was a time when I was very small,
  When my whole frame was but an ell in height;
Sweetly as I recall it, tears do fall,
  And therefore I recall it with delight.
Then seemed to me this world far less in size,
  Likewise it seemed to me less wicked far;
Like points in heaven I saw the stars arise,
  And longed for wings that I might catch a star.

Wondering, I saw God's sun, through western eyes
  Sink in the ocean's golden lap at night,
And yet upon the morrow early rise,
  And paint the eastern heaven with crimson light.
With childish reverence my young lips did say
  The prayer my pious mother taught to me:
'O gentle God! O let me strive alway
  Still to be wise and good and follow thee!'

So prayed I for my father and my mother
  And for my sister, and for all the town;
The king I knew not, and the beggar-brother,
  Who, bent with age, went sighing up and down.
They perished, the blithe days of boyhood perished,
  And all the gladness, all the peace I knew!
Now have I but their memory, fondly cherished –
  God! may I never, never lose that too!

JENS NAGGESEN (1764–1816)
TRANS. H.W. LONGFELLOW

Comment

Nostalgic thoughts of a Scandinavian poet which will not be entirely foreign even to folk who are long past childhood and adolescence. The simple poem must bring to our minds our Lord's attitude to children. The women who took their children to him for a blessing clearly discerned in him a person who would understand their desire and be sensitive to their request. Jesus resisted his disciples' intention to drive them away. But there is a lesson even more important than that. Not only did he show his love and care for the children, but he saw their presence as affording an opportunity to teach the adults a lesson: 'I tell you, whoever does not accept the kingdom of God like a child will never enter it; (St Mark ch.10 v.16). 'Like a child' – what can that mean? Children fail in all sorts of ways, similar to the failures of adults. But children are by nature humble and obedient; they do not bear grudges; they are trustful. He who would enter the kingdom of God must not come with a proud heart or a defiant spirit which nurses grievances and fails to forgive. Furthermore he must trust God as a child trusts his parents. Our Lord did indeed say: 'Except you become as little children . . . , ' but that was not an exhortation to be childish, but to be childlike.

Prayer *O Lord, whose way is perfect, help us to trust in your goodness, that following you with a childlike trust we may possess quiet and contented minds casting all our care on you.*

The Pessimist

Nothing to do but work,
*   Nothing to eat but food,*
Nothing to wear but clothes,
*   To keep one from going nude.*
Nothing to breathe but air,
*   Quick as a flash 'tis gone;*
Nowhere to fall but off,
*   Nowhere to stand but on.*

Nothing to comb but hair,
*   Nowhere to sleep but in bed,*
Nothing to weep but tears,
*   Nothing to bury but dead.*
*   Nothing to sing but songs,*
*   Ah! well, alas! alack!*
Nowhere to go but out,
*   Nowhere to come but back.*

Nothing to see but sights,
*   Nothing to quench but thirst,*
Nothing to have but what we've got,
*   Thus through life we are cursed.*
Nothing to strike but a gait;
*   Everything moves that goes.*
Nothing at all but common sense
*   Can ever withstand these woes.*

BENJAMIN FRANKLIN KING (1857–1894)

Comment

With his tongue deep in his cheek Benjamin King composes what might be called the working creed of the pessimist. Life is basically futile and there is nothing man can do about it – nothing, in his view at least, save what comes by common sense. The poet was not a philosopher but a humorist; but his little joke can prompt a serious consideration. Philosophically, pessimism is the doctrine that there is an imbalance in life which operates inevitably against goodness and happiness. Optimism, on the other hand, is the disposition which anticipates the most favourable outcome to events. Philosophically, optimism holds that goodness pervades reality. The Christian expresses that by his belief in the ultimate triumph of good over evil. Evil does indeed stalk defiantly across the stage of the world. But our Lord offers a reassuring promise: 'Be of good cheer, I have overcome the world' (St John ch.16 v.33). Another Benjamin – Jowett, nineteenth-century Master of Balliol and a priest – spoke of 'apostolic optimism' – that is, recognition of the world's sinful condition whilst remembering that, as God is the Lord of history, in the end 'all shall be well and all manner of thing shall be well'.

Prayer   *O Thou who art the Source from which we come, the End to which we travel, and the Centre on which we rest, help us to put our trust in thee for ever. Enable us to surrender our wills to thine, and to sacrifice each desire which is contrary to thy law; for the sake of Jesus Christ our Lord.*

WILLIAM KNIGHT (19TH CENTURY)

Bewildered Alice

'Cheshire puss', Alice began, rather timidly as she did not at all know whether it would like the name... 'Would you tell me please which way I ought to go from here?'

'That depends a good deal on where you want to go', said the Cat.

'I don't much care where... ', said Alice.

'Then it doesn't matter which way you go', said the Cat.

'... as long as I get somewhere', Alice added as an explanation.

LEWIS CARROLL (1832–1898)

Comment

Poor little Alice! there were times when she must have felt that she was 'Alice in Blunderland' – so frequently did she say the wrong thing or pose a seemingly silly question. There are many familiar quotes from Lewis Carroll's 'Alice' books, but none more familiar than Alice's question and the Cat's answer. The philosopher John Kemeny uses the question and answer as the caption for one of the chapters in his *Philosophy of Science*. But if the Alice books have philosophic and scientific overtones, so too, and even more markedly, do they have theological overtones. Their author was, after all, a priest – Charles Lutwidge Dodgson – and he puts into Alice's mouth questions which prompt answers which are in effect 'sermonettes'. One commentator has said that 'the Cat's answer expresses very precisely the cleavage between Science and Ethics'. Carroll himself might have expressed it differently. He might well have said something along the lines of Einstein's words that 'Science without religion is blind'. It doesn't know where to go! But 'Religion without Science is lame'. It knows which way to go but needs science and technology to enable it to get there! Poor Alice hadn't made up her mind where she wanted to be, and until she had resolved that problem, neither the Cat nor any other being could help her! The Christian knows where he wants to go. He has been told as much by the Christ to whom he is committed. That knowledge has a personal and a social reference. He also knows the way to get there, for that same Christ has said 'I am the Way'. Beyond that he needs but one more assurance – that in following the Way he may be sustained by the grace of God to continue in the Way to his life's end. He has that assurance in Christ's promise 'Lo, I am with you always'.

Prayer   *O Lord Jesus Christ who didst say to thy servant Thomas the Apostle, I am the Way and the Truth and the Life. Mercifully grant that we looking to thee by faith, may find in thee the Way that leads to the Father, the Truth that makes us free, and the life that is Life indeed, now and always.*

CANON FRANK COLQUHOUN

To the Cuckoo

Hail, *beauteous singer of the grove!*
　　Thou messenger of Spring!
Now heaven repairs thy rural seat,
　　And woods thy welcome ring.

Delightful visitant! with thee
　　I hail the time of flowers,
And hear the sound of music sweet
　　From birds among the bowers.

The school-boy, wandering through the wood
　　To pull the primrose gay,
Starts, the new voice of spring to hear,
　　And imitates thy lay.

What time the pea puts on the bloom,
　　Thou fli'st thy vocal vale,
An annual guest in other lands,
　　Another Spring to hail.

Sweet bird! thy bower is ever green,
　　Thy sky is ever clear;
Thou hast no sorrow in thy song,
　　No winter in thy year!

O could I fly, I'd fly with thee!
　　We'd make with joyful wing,
Our annual visit o'er the globe,
　　Companions of the spring.

JOHN LOGAN (1748–1788)

Comment

The soft flute-like call of the cuckoo in April is music to the ear, for whatever the weather-men say, the cuckoo's arrival from Africa is the authentic announcement that spring has come. Mrs Cuckoo, a somewhat promiscuous lady, deposits her eggs in any convenient nest, be it the homestead of a robin, a wagtail or a pipit, and the foster parents accept the situation without a murmur. The enigmatic male bird is heard but not seen. He arrives, fulfils his mission and departs. John Logan is one of many poets who have told the cuckoo's story in verse. In his penultimate verse the poet confesses that he is envious of the cuckoo's apparently easy life – no sorrow and no winter, all joy and eternal spring. We may never have expressed it quite like that as we face our sorrows or pass through our winters of dis-content. Socrates said that the way to make a discontented man happy was not to add to his possessions but to diminish his desires. Paul had a surer answer which he gave to the Philippians: 'I have learned in whatever state I am therewith to be content' (Philippians ch.4 vv.10–13).

Prayer 　*Heavenly Father, give us contented and trustful hearts, that, casting all our cares on you, and bearing all our trials cheerfully, we may for ever be united to you in your love in this world and the next, through Jesus Christ our Lord.*

The Mind called out of Darkness

I owe to literature something more than my earthly welfare. Adrift early in the life upon the great waters, if I did not come to shipwreck, it was that I was rescued, like the ancient Mariner, by guardian spirits, 'each one a lovely light', who stood as beacons to my course.

Infirm health and a natural love of reading, threw me into the company of poets, philosophers, and sages, to me good angels and ministers of grace.

From these silent instructors I learned something of the divine, and more of the human, religion. They were my interpreters in the House Beautiful of God, my guides among the Delectable Mountains of Nature. They reformed my prejudices, chastened my passions, tempered my heart, purified my tastes, elevated my mind, and directed my aspirations. I was lost in a chaos of undigested problems, false theories, crude fancies, obscure impulses, and bewildering doubts, when these bright intelligences called my mental world out of darkness, like a new Creation.

THOMAS HOOD (1799–1845)

Comment

Here is a fine expression of gratitude from the heart and pen of a man who at the tender age of 16 was already contributing humorous and serious articles to established magazines. As a punster, unrivalled in his day, he contributed to *Punch* and himself edited similar periodicals. In his short life of 45 years he juggled with words in so masterly a fashion, moving rapidly from the pathetic to the humorous and back, that fun, fact and fiction are all happily blended in his poems. Whilst there is none which would find its way into an anthology of religious poems, there are many which would reveal that the poet's heart was in the right place. Himself in constant suffering he reveals his sympathy with other sufferers. He went through periods of misfortune and ill-health and preserved throughout his sense of humour. His poem 'I remember, I remember' sees him looking back on a childhood which was clearly happy – and if indeed it ends rather pathetically 'But now, 'tis little joy to know I'm farther off from heaven than when I was a boy' – that in itself reveals that he was a man of God. We must emulate him in his gratitude to all who helped him become what he was and achieve what he did. The 'intelligences' who in his early days called him 'out of darkness' and set him into 'a new Creation' were never forgotten.

Prayer *O God our Father, we thank you that you have set your truth in the hearts and minds of many who in their turn have shared the treasures with others. We pray for all who write what many read or speak where many hear, that they may so serve you that your name may be hallowed and your kingdom come, through Jesus Christ our Lord.*

Robin Redbreast

Sweet robin, I have heard them say
That thou wert there upon the day
The Christ was crowned in cruel scorn
And bore away one bleeding thorn, –
That so the blush upon thy breast,
In shameful sorrow was impressed,
And thence thy genial sympathy
With our redeemed humanity.

Sweet robin, would that I might be
Bathed in my Saviour's blood like thee;
Bear in my breast, whate'er the loss,
The bleeding blazon of the cross;
Live ever, with thy loving mind,
In fellowship with human kind;
And take my pattern still from thee,
In gentleness and constancy.

GEORGE WASHINGTON DOANE (1799–1850)

Comment

In the course of literary history the robin redbreast has attracted the praise of many poets and the legend to which this poet refers is one which, we might like to think, the friendly little bird must proudly accept as authentic. Of all the wild birds the robin is the one which seeks and enjoys the company of man. So intimate does he become that he positively invites man to woo him, and that not merely when he anticipates the gift of a worm. The little fellow has a personality of his own, a jubilant song of his own, a colour of his own and an emotional quality of his own. To our poet he had too a message of his own, a message of which we might well be reminded when next the robin redbreast meets us in the garden. In the second verse of his poem our poet expresses the wish that he might be marked with 'the bleeding blazon of the Cross'. In fact every Christian is so marked at his baptism. It is not merely a sign of his membership of the Body of Christ. It is a sign of Christ's victory of love over hatred, of good over evil. Under such a sign we live, and live not to ourselves, but 'in fellowship with human kind'. Taking his pattern from the intimacy with himself of the robin, the poet decides that he will fashion his life 'in gentleness and constancy' towards his brother man. Yes! let us go with our poet and see the redbreast as affording a reminder to us of what Christ has done for us. 'He died that we might be forgiven, He died to make us good', and as a reminder too of that 'gentleness and constancy' which we owe to our brother man.

Prayer   *Grant O God, that we who have been signed with the sign of the Cross in our baptism, may never be ashamed to confess the faith of Christ crucified, but may manfully fight under his banner against sin, the world and the devil, and continue Christ's faithful soldiers and servants unto our lives' end.*

THE BOOK OF COMMON PRAYER

Commemorating Bernard, Abbot of Clairvaux, 1153

Seeking God First

It is our nature's law that makes a man set higher values on the things he has not got than upon those he has, so that he loathes his actual possessions for longing for the things that are not his. And this same law, when all things else in earth and heaven have failed, drives him at last to God, the Lord of all, whom hitherto alone he has not had.

It is, however, a practical impossibility to make such a trial of all other things before we turn to God. Life is too short, our strength too limited, the number of competitors for this world's goods too great; so long a journey, such unfruitful toil, would wear us out. We want to satisfy all our desires, and find we cannot get possession of all desirable things. Much wiser would we be to make the choice not by experiment but by intelligence, this we could do easily and not without result. Indeed God gives us reason for this very purpose, that it may guide the senses in their choice and see to it that they will therefore be not satisfied except by that which reason has approved. . . There will therefore be no ascent to God for, for you, the gift of reason will have been bestowed on you in vain, if, like the beasts, you let yourself be guided by your senses, while reason just looks on. They run indeed whose steps are not controlled by reason; but they run not along the track. How can they win, seeing they want the prize only when they have tried all else and failed? Theirs is an endless road, a hopeless maze, who seek for good before they seek for God.

ST BERNARD OF CLAIRVAUX (1091–1153)

Comment

Bernard, son of a Burgundian nobleman, was born in 1091. By his own insistent desire he abandoned the academic life when he was 21 to become a monk. Four brothers followed him into the Benedictine monastery at Citeaux, but his stay there was brief as the English Abbot invited him to be the founder of a daughter house at Clairvaux. From there he conducted missions throughout Europe and became known, loved and respected throughout the Christian world. It was written of him that 'when the princes of the world bowed down to him, when bishops awaited his bidding, when the Pope sought his advice and made him a general legate of the world, he was never puffed up. . . when everyone thought him the greatest, he was in his own opinion the least'. Humility was the mark of his life and greatness never obliterated it. He was, he said, the minister, not the author of mighty works.

Prayer *Lord Jesus Christ, who by precept and example has taught us that the greatest of all is the servant of all, and that the humble shall be exalted; Make us content to take the lowest place; and if it shall please thee to call us higher, do thou preserve within us a simple and lowly spirit; to thy great glory.*

The Lowliest Task

Let the lowliest task be mine,
Grateful, so the task be thine.

If there be some weaker one,
Give me strength to help him on;
If a blinder soul there be,
Let me guide him nearer thee.
Make my mortal dreams come true,
With the work I fain would do;
Clothe with life the weak intent,
Let me be the thing I meant;
Let me find in thy employ,
Peace that dearer is than joy;
Out of self to love be led
And to heaven acclimated,
Until all things sweet and good
Seem my natural habitude.

Thus did Andrew Rykman pray;
Are we wiser, better grown,
That we may not, in our day,
Make his prayer our own?

J.G. WHITTIER (1807–1892)

Comment

Two of the Christian world's best-loved hymns – 'Immortal love for ever full', and 'Dear Lord and Father of mankind' – were written by this nineteenth-century Quaker poet, John Greenleaf Whittier. The simple poem above has an interesting story around it, a story which carries further the virtue of humility of yesterday's reading. The Andrew Rykman mentioned in the last verse was a Dutchman whose tombstone bore a prayer which attracted Whittier's attention. Gripped by the prayer's exaltation of humility Whittier thought it well worthwhile to afford it a wider reading – and praying – public. Hence the poem which is itself a prayer. Only yesterday we were thinking of the humility of St Bernard of Clairvaux. It was he who wrote: 'It is no great thing to be humble when you are brought low; but to be humble when you are praised is a great and rare attainment'. To be prepared to do the lowliest acts of service to our fellow men without seeking a reward is to put one's foot on the path to that true humility which is the genuine proof of Christian virtue. The same John Greenleaf Whittier, who warmed to Andrew Rykman's willingness to take on the lowliest tasks for those weaker than himself, practised what he preached and in another of his poems entitled *What of the Day?'* he said:

> *If but the least and frailest, let me be*
> *Ever more numbered with the truly free*
> *Who find thy service perfect liberty!*

The humblest example ever was by One who washed his disciples' feet – He who said: 'I am among you as he that serveth'.

Prayer   *What can be better than the prayer at the head of this page?*

Diary of a Church Mouse

Here among long discarded cassocks,
Damp stools, and half split open hassocks,
Here where the vicar never looks
I nibble through old service books.
Lean and alone I spend my days
Behind this Church of England baize. . .
Christmas and Easter may be feasts
For congregations and for priests,
And so may Whitsun. All the same
They do not fill my meagre frame.
For me the only feast at all,
Is autumn's Harvest Festival,
When I can satisfy my want
With ears of corn around the font.
I climb the eagle's brazen head
To burrow through a loaf of bread.
I scramble up the pulpit stair
And gnaw the marrows hanging there. . .
Within the human world I know
Such goings on could not be so,
For human beings only do
What their religion tells them to.
They read their Bible every day
And always, night and morning, pray,
And just like me the good church mouse
Worship each week in God's good house.
But all the same it's strange to me
How very full the church can be
With people I don't see at all
Except at Harvest Festival.

JOHN BETJEMAN (1906–1984)

Comment

This is a somewhat abbreviated version of Sir John Betjeman's amusing poem – and it could
be said that its sting is in its tail! Let it first be said, however, that here is a man – Poet
Laureate in fact – who was a devout Christian and a most regular worshipper who could
laugh and make other people laugh. His first amusing poem – *Whatever will rhyme with summer* – was written whilst he was at his Preparatory School and throughout his life he brought
joy to the hearts of the high and the low, the simple and the 'lettered'. One of his serious
poems will appear later in this book – during the Christmas period. Let this one stand,
however, to remind us all to imitate the church mouse in one of its vagaries, that is, to 'Worship each week in God's Own House'.

Prayer   *O God, who makest us glad with the weekly remembrance of the glorious resur-*
rection of thy Son our Lord; vouchsafe us such a blessing through our worship
on the first day of the week, that the days to follow it may be hallowed by thy
abiding presence; through Jesus Christ our Lord.

Southend

I do not like Southend-on-Sea:
It sometimes haunts my memory
With visions drab and slatternly.
An equatorial atmosphere,
Scented with shrimps and beastly beer
Affects me most depressingly
When someone says, 'Southend-on-Sea'.

And yet, and yet, there have I seen
A mother thronèd like a queen –
So blessed Mary might have been
Once by the Lake of Galilee;
The Babe held so caressingly,
The little Baptist playing near,
Like that brown youngster over there.

And I have seen lights on the sea,
A light in kind eyes thanking me
For just some common courtesy:
The sea and sand can shine like gold,
The place the peace of Heaven can hold –
There is another part of me
That just adores Southend-on-Sea.

FATHER ANDREW, S.D.C. (1869–1946)

Comment

Henry Hardy became known as Father Andrew when he and two other priests founded the Society of Divine Compassion – a religious Order ministering to the poor more especially in Plaistow. He wrote prose, poetry and plays and exercised through these and parish missions a greatly appreciated ministry in different parts of the country. His verses could be simple – as the above – or profound, even mystical, but whether laying bare his own soul or seeking to teach a simple lesson, they never fail to arrest attention. In this simple poem he says to every Christian: 'Do not be hasty in your judgments', and 'Look for the best in everything and everyone'. There were things in Southend-on-Sea which clearly 'put him off', yet he remembers that some of his happiest days were spent there – days made happy by fellow human beings, with whom he was at pains to establish contact by a 'common courtesy'. 'If a man be gracious and courteous to strangers', said Francis Bacon, 'it shows that he is a citizen of the world'. But it is Hilaire Belloc who seals the truth most aptly by telling us what it is in courtesy that can transform human relationships:

> *Of Courtesy – it is much less*
> *Than courage of heart or holiness*
> *Yet in my walks it seems to me*
> *That the Grace of God is in courtesy.*

No wonder the reverend Father's common courtesy transformed his memory of Southend on Sea!

Prayer   *Fill us, O Lord, with the Spirit of graciousness, of courtesy and of brotherly kindness, so that under your benediction we may ourselves be glad and bring joy to the hearts of those whom we meet day by day.*

St Bartholomew the Apostle

God give us men! A time like this demands
Strong minds, great hearts, true faith and ready hands!
Men whom the lust of office does not kill,
Men whom the spoils of office cannot buy,
Men who possess opinions and a will,
Men who love honour, men who cannot lie.

JOSIAH G. HOLLAND (1819–1881)

Comment

Fine words indeed, and although they were written for 'a time like this' – mid-nineteenth century - they are apposite for the troubled closing years of this twentieth century. But why in particular should they be chosen for the Feast Day of St Bartholomew? Thereby hangs an interesting tale:

Bartholomew was one of our Lord's Twelve Apostles mentioned in the synoptic gospels – Matthew, Mark and Luke. Eusebius, who is known as the father of ecclesiastical history, and who became Bishop of Caesarea early in the 4th century, records that in the closing years of the second century a Christian philosopher named Pantaenus went to preach the gospel in India and there, to his surprise, found Christians who told him that Bartholomew had preached Christ there, and had left behind him a Hebrew copy of St Matthew's Gospel. He also leant that Bartholomew had been martyred – flayed alive in Armenia. The name Bartholomew means 'Son of Tolmai'. We might call it his family name. The name does not occur in the Fourth Gospel but scholars are now agreed that the Nathanael whom Philip introduced to Jesus is, in fact, the Bartholomew of the synoptic Gospels. The story is in the first chapter of St John's Gospel and the deduction scholars have made is tenable in that the name Nathanael does not occur in the synoptics, nor does the name Bartholomew occur in the fourth Gospel. Furthermore, in the list of the apostles mentioned in Matthew and Mark, the names of Philip, who introduced Nathanael to Jesus, and Bartholomew are side by side; that at least suggests that they were particularly close to each other. At that point we come to our Lord's estimate of Nathanael: 'Behold an Israelite indeed, in whom is no guile'. What a wonderful testimonial that was – and from the One who sees not as man sees but as God sees. Read the poet's words above again and see how they match Bartholomew. Guile is deception, dishonesty, duplicity, slyness, sharp practice, or in slang terms 'hanky panky'. The Christian recipe for good personal and social relations and for public service is to be, as was Bartholomew, 'without guile'.

Prayer   *Uphold us, O Lord of life, with your free Spirit. Save us from guile, from praising what is good whilst practising what is bad, from speaking the truth whilst living a lie, from thinking high thoughts while following low standards. Give us strong minds, great hearts and a true faith, that we may live and serve, to your glory.*

The Moth

The great moth winged with many eyes
frets from its breast its silver dust.
Caught in the net my lamp has cast,
he beats and circles till he dies.

His life was set on some true path
until his kind inhabited night
betrayed him to a craze of light,
light meaningless and cold like death –

or so I said, who watched him perch
upon his sterile radiant heaven
a love unjoined, a gift ungiven –
strange failure in the eternal search:

and so turned back my pen to prayer
that might be language for a moth;
'O overcome me, Power and Truth;
transmute my ignorance, burn it bare;
so that against your flame, not I
but all that is not You may die'.

JUDITH WRIGHT (CONTEMPORARY)

Comment

The lines are by one of Australia's most well-known poets. She writes of an incident the like of which we have all witnessed as a moth is drawn irresistibly to a light. Light is a dominant theme in all the Gospels and more especially in St John's, where we read of our Lord's description of himself as the Light of the World, and where we are given his guarantee for ourselves (St John ch.8 v.22). The Christian who is in earnest is drawn irresistibly to our Lord as the Light of the world. He too is bidden to be a light in the world in which he lives – the world of home, of work, of leisure, of social responsibility. He seeks, like the moth, to be drawn ever nearer to the Light, so near as to be in complete union with Christ. Thus does he enjoy not only the light of Life but also the assurance that all that is inconsistent in his own life with the Light of Life will wither and die. Like the poet's moth he can say: '. . . against your flame, not I but all that is not You may die'. Browning puts it in another way:

> *You groped your way across my room,*
> *In the dear dark dead of night;*
> *At each fresh step a stumble was;*
> *But, once your lamp alight,*
> *Easy and plain you walked again;*
> *So soon all wrong grew right.*

Prayer *O God, with whom is the well of life, and in whose light we see light, increase in us, we beseech thee, the brightness of divine knowledge, whereby we may be able to reach thy plenteous fountain; import to our thirsting souls the draught of life, and restore to our darkened minds the light from heaven; through Jesus Christ our Lord.*

(MOZARABIC LITURGY)

Footprints in the Sand

One night a man had a dream. He dreamed he was walking along the beach with the Lord Jesus. Across the sky flashed scenes from his life. For each scene he noticed that there were two sets of footprints in the sand, one set belonging to him and one set belonging to the Lord.

When the last scene of his life flashed before him, he looked back at the footprints in the sand. He noticed that many times along the path of his life, there was only one set of footprints. He also noticed that this happened at the very lowest and saddest times of his life.

This really bothered him and he questioned his Lord about it: 'Lord, you said that once I decided to follow you, you would walk with me all the way. But I have noticed that during the most troublesome times of my life there is only one set of footprints. I cannot understand why, when I needed you most, you would leave me'.

The Lord replied: 'My precious, precious child, I love you, and I would never leave you. During your times of trial and of suffering, when you saw only one set of footprints in the sand, it was then that I carried you'.

ANONYMOUS

Comment

'And be assured, I am with you always, to the end of time'. Those are the closing words of St Matthew's Gospel as Jesus sent out the eleven disciples, commissioning them to carry the gospel around the world. It was a staggering commission and but for the assurance which followed it the eleven might well have wilted beneath it. That they did not, is proof itself of the assurance of the abiding presence of their Lord with them. Christ's promise to those first disciples is Christ's promise to us. Life for all of us has its moments of sorrow and joy, of disappointments and fulfilment, of sickness and health, of success and failure. If we forget to thank him when all is going well, maybe we shall forget to realise his presence when the way is hard. In his *Auguries of Innocence* William Blake (he, of *Jerusalem!*) has a relevant word:

> *Joy and woe are woven fine,*
> *A clothing for the soul divine;*
> *Under every grief and pine,*
> *Runs a joy with silken twine.*
> *It is right it should be so;*
> *Man was made for joy and woe;*
> *And when this we rightly know,*
> *Through the world we safely go.*

Our anonymous dreamer would surely be ready to join in the negro spiritual: 'Nobody knows the troubles I've seen, nobody knows but Jesus'. He knows, but he waits to be invited to share them.

Prayer *May God the Father bless us: May Christ take care of us: May the Holy Spirit lighten us all the days of our life. The Lord be our Defender and Keeper now and for ever.*

BISHOP AEDELWALD

How we Learn

Great truths are dearly bought. The common truth
  Such as men give and take from day to day,
Comes in the common walks of easy life,
  Blown by the careless wind across our way.

Bought in the market, at the current price,
  Bred of the smile, the jest, perchance the bowl,
It tells no tale of daring or of worth
  Nor pierces e'en the surface of a soul.

Great truths are greatly won. Not found by chance
  Nor wafted on the breath of summer dream,
But grasped in the great struggle of the soul,
  Hard buffeting with adverse wind and stream.

Not in general mart, 'mid corn and wine,
  Not in the merchandise of gold and gems,
Not in the world's gay halls of midnight mirth,
  Nor 'mid the glaze of regal diadems.

But in the day of conflict, fear and grief,
  When the strong hand of God, put forth in might,
Plows up the subsoil of the stagnant heart,
  And brings the imprisoned truth-seed to the light.

Wrung from the troubled spirit in hard hours
  Of weakness, solitude, perchance of pain,
Truth springs, like harvest, from the well-plowed field,
  And the soul feels it has not wept in vain.

HORATIUS BONAR (1808–1889)

Comment

Horatius Bonar was a Scottish Presbyterian minister who wrote a number of poems and hymns, among the latter several which are sung throughout Christendom. 'Fill thou my life, O Lord my God', and 'I heard the voice of Jesus say . . . ' are among the most popular. In this poem he is concerned with great truths and common truths, and he makes the point that the latter are easy to come by, whereas the former will forever elude us unless and until dormant minds are awakened, stagnant hearts are ploughed and languid spirits are aroused. We should remind ourselves that the distinction which the poet is drawing does not imply that only divine truth is sacred. All truth is precious and it becomes a Christian to be meticulous about the truths of 'the common walks of easy life', of 'the market . . . the merchandise . . . and the world's gay halls of midnight mirth'. But it will be 'the great truths' which, once embraced, will fortify the Christian in his efforts to hold to 'the common truths'. The 'great truths' have to do with the Being of God, of his Revelation of himself in Christ and of Christ's government of God's world. The greatest Truth is illimitable and incontrovertible for the greatest Truth is God in Christ.

Prayer *Light of the world, shine upon our minds and hearts. Spirit of truth, guide us into all truth. Holy Father, sanctify us through thy truth, and make us wise unto salvation, through Jesus Christ our Lord.*

THE REV. L. TUTTIETT (1825)

Commemorating Augustine, Bishop of Hippo
Teacher of the Faith, 430

O eternal truth and true love and beloved eternity! You are my God, and I sigh to you by day and by night... So I set about finding a way to gain the strength that was necessary for enjoying you. And I could not find it until I embraced the mediator between God and man, the man Christ Jesus, who is over all things, God blessed forever, who was calling unto me and saying: I am the way, the truth and the life; and who brought into union with our nature that food which I lacked the strength to take: for the Word was made flesh that your wisdom, by which you created all things, might give suck to our souls' infancy.

Late have I loved you, O Beauty so ancient and so new; late have I loved you! For behold you were within me, and I outside; and I sought you outside, and in my ugliness fell upon those lovely things that you have made. You were with me and I was not with you. I was kept from you by those things, yet had they not been in you, they would not have been at all. You called and cried to me and broke open my deafness; and you sent forth your beams and shone upon me and chased away my blindness: you breathed fragrance upon me, and I drew in my breath and do now pant for you: I tasted you and now hunger and thirst for you; you touched me and I have burned for your peace.

St Augustine (354–430)

Comment

Augustine, who on any reckoning must be regarded as among the greatest of the Church's saints, was for many years among the greatest of the world's sinners. He was brought up as a Christian by his mother Monica, but in his adolescence he abandoned the Faith to become a wild teenager, morally corrupt and intellectually indisciplined. He left home to read Rhetoric at university, and sank ever deeper into the mire of sin. A single book by Cicero made him realise that there must be something more in life than he had found. He began to seek the Truth – the great Truth which we were thinking of in yesterday's reading. He turned to the Bible and rejected it, being repelled by the Old Testament. His search continued. He left for Milan and there came under the influence of the Bishop, Ambrose. At length his mind was made up. He believed in God; he believed in God in Christ. It was still a long time before he could bring himself to abandon his profligate way of life. At length, and at the age of 33, he was baptised. Four years later he was ordained and within four further years he became Bishop of Hippo. One of his greatest books is his *Confessions*, where he sets out his life 'warts and all' and tells the story of his conversion part of which is the quotation above.

Prayer   *Almighty God, who by the light of your word converted Augustine to the catholic faith, and made him a pre-eminent teacher and pastor of your people; grant that we who put our trust in your abundant grace, may ever hold fast to the truths of the gospel and grow in the likeness of him whom the gospels proclaim, even your son Jesus Christ our Lord.*

One Man's Prayer

Give me a good digestion, Lord,
And also something to digest.
Give me a healthy body, Lord,
With sense to keep it as its best.
Give me a healthy mind, good Lord,
To keep the good and pure in sight,
Which seeing sin in not appalled,
But finds a way to set it right.

Give me a mind that is not bored,
That does not whimper, whine or sigh,
Don't let me worry overmuch
About that fussy thing called I.
Give me a sense of humour, Lord,
Give me the grace to see a joke,
To get some happiness from life,
And pass it on to other folk.

Anonymous

Comment

I hope that no one will dismiss the anonymous poet's prayer as impious! It is after all rightly directed to the Living God and if it savours too much of the 'Give me... give me', it does conclude by seeking to get some happiness in life 'to pass it on to other folk'. It is indeed a 'tall order' to place before God but its consistent requests are all laudable – a healthy body, a clean mind, a desire to put right things that are wrong, a lively spirit and an intention to avoid being self-centred. But the part of the prayer which deserves special mention is: 'Give me a sense of humour Lord'. Good clean humour is one of the spices of life which we should encourage and enjoy. In a very learned book called *The Imprisoned Splendour* by Dr Raynor Johnson of the University of Melbourne I read: 'The functioning of the Higher Mind shows the two qualities of artistry and humour and it does not require an intensive search to find both of these in the pageant of evolution... Lest a sense of humour should be thought unfitting in the serious business of the Mind's development, I commend to biologically-minded students the neck of the giraffe, the girth of the hippopotamus, the nose of the elephant, and the tail of the pig for a consideration of their survival value'. Lest it be thought that author lacked a faith in God let me add that in the portion of his book entitled 'The Significance of the Whole' he declares his faith by sharing Browning's confidence expressed in *Rabbi Ben Ezra*':

> *Grow old along with me!*
> *The best is yet to be,*
> *The last of life, for which the first was made:*
> *Our times are in His hand*
> *Who saith, 'A whole I planned,*
> *Youth shows but half; trust God: see all, nor be afraid!'*

Even so I hope that the Creator preserves his giraffes from having too many sore throats!

Prayer   *see* above.

Pied Beauty

Glory be to God for dappled things –
For skies of couple-colour as a brindled cow;
For rose-moles all in stipple upon trout that swim:
Fresh fire-coal chestnut-falls; finches' wings;
Landscape plotted and pierced – fold, fallow and ploughed;
And all trades, their gear and tackle trim.

All things counter, original, spare, strange;
Whatever is fickle, freckled (who knows how?)
With swift, slow; sweet, sour; adazzle, dim;
He fathers-forth whose beauty is past change:
$\qquad\qquad$ *Praise Him.*

GERARD MANLEY HOPKINS (1844–1889)

Comment

The priest-poet Gerard Manley Hopkins was another who could see reflection of God in the natural world – of flowers and trees and birds and stars. Long before the world had ever heard of him, for nothing of his was published until after his death, his friendship with the poet Robert Bridges gave him the opportunity to share his exciting thoughts with one whose work he admired. 'What fun it would be if you were a classic!' he said to Bridges, little thinking that one day he himself would be just that. Hopkins pressed on with his priestly duties in the squalor of industrial towns and his perceptive power for beauty in the small as in the large was never broken. He could sing *A Song to the Decaying Year* with its 'grey heaven' and its 'blue grey flocks of trees'. He wrote ecstatically about the colours of the rainbow, about the spring flowers, and the cuckoo with its 'magic cuckoocall'. He could delight in 'the dappled things', the 'brindled cow', the stippled trout, and in his different poems and moods could rejoice over the fickle and freckled. He went *Hurraying in Harvest*, and says:

> *I walk, I lift up, I lift up heart, eyes.*
> $\quad$ *Down all that glory in the heavens to glean our Saviour.*
> $\quad$ *And eyes, heart, what looks, what lips yet gave you a*
> *Rapturous love's greeting of realer, of rounder replies?*

Hopkins is, of course, counted among the mystical poets and it is to be expected that some of his lines may well be understood fully only by him. But one thing is clear throughout, and that is that he looked upon the world as God's world and saw, even in the tiny things a beauty and a love which would outshine 'Solomon in all his glory', and for them all he praised God.

Prayer

$\qquad$ *Bless the Lord all created things: sing his praise and exalt*
$\qquad\qquad$ *him for ever.*
$\qquad$ *Bless the Lord all men of upright spirit:*
$\qquad\qquad$ *Bless the Lord you that are holy and humble in heart.*
$\qquad$ *Bless the Father, the Son and the Holy Spirit:*
$\qquad\qquad$ *Sing his praise and exalt him for ever.*

Commemorating Aidan, Bishop of Lindisfarne
and
John Bunyan, Author

Oswin, King of Northumbria... bestowed a very good horse upon Bishop Aidan, although, good man, he used commonly to perform his journeys on foot. Yet, notwithstanding, for the easier passage of rivers and other such like occasion, he had accepted the king's gift, and one day as he made use of it by riding, a poor man, encountering him, begged for alms. The good bishop, being full of pity, a special observer of the poor, and a father of the afflicted, instantly dismounting, wills that his horse, with all the royal harness, should be given to the poor man. The king had speedy notice thereof; whereupon, going into dinner with Aidan, he said: 'What is this that thou hast done, my Lord Bishop, in giving to the poor man the royal horse which thou shouldst have kept for thine own use? Were there not meaner horses, or other kinds of things good enough to be given to the poor man so that thou didst not part with that horse which I gave thee for thine own personal service?' The bishop, cutting him short, made answer, 'What is this that thou sayest, O king? Is that son of a mare which I have given away, of more esteem with thee than that son of God to whom I have given it?'

Now was my heart filled full of comfort and hope and now I could believe that my sins should be forgiven me. I was now so taken with the love and mercy of God that I thought I could have spoken of his love and mercy to me even to the very crows that sat upon the lands before me, had they been capable to have understood me; wherefore I said in my soul with much gladness, 'Surely I will not forget this forty years hence'. But alas! within less than forty days I began to question all still'.

Comment

Two incidents in the lives of two holy men, very different from each other in background, in experience, in outlook, in education – but alike in their Christian commitment. The Aidan story comes from the *Story Books* of Little Gidding; the Bunyan story from his own *Grace Abounding*. Aidan was the saintly Bishop of Lindisfarne who worked with Oswald the King of Northumbria in converting the people in his realm. John Bunyan was, as all the world knows, the tinker who became an evangelist and ultimately found himself in prison under repressive measures imposed by the Royalists after the Restoration of the Monarchy in 1660. It was in prison that he wrote his *Pilgrim's Progress*. There was a sequel to each of the stories. Aidan's courageous answer to the king – brought the king to his knees in penitence. He promised that from that day forward he would 'never set any limits' to what he would 'bestow and give amongst the sons of God'. As for John Bunyan, the day did come 'within less than forty days' that he questioned the reality of God's forgiveness but later the true message of the Cross came to him dramatically: 'He hath made peace through the blood of his cross' and he was able to say: 'God and my soul were friends in this blood'.

Prayer   *God our Father, we know that it is by your grace that the flame of love is kindled in the hearts of all who turn to you; we praise you for the witness of all who in our own land have, by their words and deeds, kindled that same love in the hearts of others. As we rejoice in their triumphs we pray that we may profit by their examples, through Jesus Christ our Lord.*

Gradatim

Heaven is not reached at a single bound;
    But we build the ladder by which we rise
    From the lowly earth to the vaulted skies.
And we mount to its summit round by round.

I count this thing to be grandly true;
    That a noble deed is a step towards God,
    Lifting the soul from the common clod
To a purer air and a broader view.

We rise by the things that are under our feet;
    By what we have mastered of good and gain;
    By the pride deposed and the passion slain,
And the vanquished ills that we hourly meet.

We hope, we aspire, we resolve, we trust,
    When the morning calls us to life and light,
    But our hearts grow weary, and e'er the night,
Our lives are trailing the sordid dust.

We hope, we aspire, we resolve, we pray
    And we think that we mount the air on wings
    Beyond the recall of sensual things,
While our feet still cling to the heavy clay.

Wings for the angels, but feet for men!
    We may borrow the wings to find the way –
    We may hope, and resolve, and aspire, and pray;
But our feet must rise or we fall again.

Heaven is not reached in a single bound;
    But we build the ladder by which we rise
    From the lowly earth to the vaulted skies,
And we mount to its summit round by round.

JOSIAH G. HOLLAND (1819-1881)

Comment

Our reflections in June and July were based on 'the fruit of the Spirit'. Day by day through those months we followed St Paul's list of the spiritual gifts which make up the harvest of the Spirit – love, joy, peace, long-suffering, gentleness, goodness, fidelity, and self-control. The point was made that it was important to see them in their totality as the Spirit's harvest. Yet, as this poet reminds us, we do not reach heaven 'at a single bound'. The nine elements of the harvest are, as it were, steps in the ladder to heaven, each lifting our souls 'from the common clod to a purer air and a broader view'. In one way we shall pursue the same aim during this month, yet the 'steps' will have different names. They are known as the 'three theological virtues' and the four 'cardinal virtues', and they have for long been regarded as the basis for what is called moral theology which is concerned with human behaviour, personal and social. To ponder these seven virtues will be a far more pleasant and valuable exercise than their technical names 'theological' and 'cardinal' might suggest.

Prayer

Help us, Heavenly Father, to use all the faculties with which you have endowed us for our own neighbours' happiness and to your great glory, through Jesus Christ our Lord.

The Cross and Virtue

Was it necessary for the Son of God to suffer for us? It was very necessary, and on two counts: First as a remedy for our sins, and secondly as a model for us in our behaviour... If anyone wants to live a perfect life, he has only to despise the things that Christ despised on the cross, and to desire what Christ desired. The cross provides an example of every virtue.

If you are looking for an example of charity, 'Greater love has no man than this, that a man lay down his life for his friends'...

If you are looking for patience, you will find it in its highest form on the cross... Christ suffered greatly and with patience on the cross. When he suffered he did not threaten. 'Like a lamb that is led to the slaughter he opened not his mouth'.

If you are looking for an example of humility, look at the cross. There, God willed to be judged by Pontius Pilate and to die.

If you are looking for an example of obedience, follow him who was obedient to the Father, even unto death.

If you are looking for a model of contempt for earthly things, follow him who is the 'King of Kings and Lord of Lords', 'in whom are hid all the treasures of wisdom and knowledge'.

ST THOMAS AQUINAS (1225–1274)

Comment

The words of St Thomas Aquinas, quoted above, offer but a glimpse of that great saint's mind about the sort of behaviour which is expected of a Christian. It is appropriate that we begin with St Thomas for it was he, in a great work known as the *Summa Theologica*, who first faced the fact that, in the matter of what might be called social behaviour, there would sometimes be a tension between authority and freedom. Clearly there must be a limit to the freedom of the individual; a Christian cannot be accorded an unfettered freedom to deny freedom to others. Yet the true freedom of the individual must be safeguarded or he will not be able to give of his best in the service of God and his neighbour. Long before the days of Jesus Christ's ministry there had been great teachers – for example Plato who was born in 429 BC – who put before their citizens certain aims and ideals – that is, virtues – which were necessary if the citizens were to enjoy a tolerable existence. These were: Prudence, Temperance, Justice and Fortitude. It was St Ambrose (fourth century) who gave these the name 'cardinal virtues' by which he meant that they are the virtues on which all the others depend. (The Latin word *cardo*, means 'a hinge'). When our Lord told his disciples that he was giving them a 'new commandment', that did not mean that he was scrapping the old commandment and all the old virtues. It meant that he was fulfilling them – filling them all with a new dimension, a new meaning. Thus the Christian Church took to itself these pre-Christian virtues, called the 'cardinal' to demonstrate that the specifically Christian virtues – faith, hope and love, far from denying the old, 'baptised' and fulfilled the old.

Prayer   *Lord God, help me ever to remember that virtue is the health and beauty of the soul. So, 'Come down O Love Divine, seek Thou this soul of mine and visit it with thine own ardour glowing'.*

AFTER R.F. LITTLEDALE

Commemorating Gregory the Great, Bishop of Rome, Teacher of the Faith

Faith comes to the Angles

Glory to God in the highest, and peace to his people on earth, for a grain of wheat fell into the earth and died, that he might reign not only in heaven. Through his death we live, by his weakness we are strengthened, by his death we are freed from suffering, through his love we seek in Britain brothers whom we do not know, and by his gift we find those whom in our ignorance we were seeking.

For who could fully tell the joy which has sprung up in the hearts of all the faithful because the race of the Angles, through the grace of Almighty God and the labours of your brotherhood, has had the light of holy faith poured out on it and the darkness of error driven away? Now in purity of mind they trample down those idols which previously they served in insane fear. They worship Almighty God with pure hearts, and by the rules that they have learnt from the holy preaching, they are restrained from falling into evil deeds. With their souls they serve the divine commandments, and in their minds they are raised up by them. They bow down to the ground continually in prayer, that their minds may not lie prostrate on the earth. Whose work is this, if not the work of him who says: 'My Father is working now, and I am working?'

It is by his power and not by the wisdom of men that the world is converted, and to prove this he has chosen unlearned men to be his preachers, and has sent them into the world. This too is what he is doing at the present time, for he has deigned to do mighty works among the Angles through weak men. But in this heavenly gift, dearest brothers, there is something to cause great joy and great fear.

St Gregory the Great (540–604)

Comment

It was through the initiative of Gregory the Great that Augustine became the Apostle to the English and the first Archbishop of Canterbury. It would not, however, be true to say that Augustine introduced the Christian faith to our land for, in fact, he found in Canterbury itself a Christian Church in which our forefathers worshipped long before his mission came. Augustine's mission was a new beginning and a splendid one, even though he failed to unite this newly founded English Church with the British Church presided over by the British Bishops. Even so the Anglican Calendar of Saints of the Church could not have omitted the name of Gregory the Great whose enthusiasm and vision brought to the ailing British Church new life and new zeal. Commemorating him as we do we should not miss the opportunity to pray for re-union of our Church with the Holy Roman Church of which Gregory was Pope.

Prayer *O God who biddest us to dwell with one mind in thine house, of thy mercy put away from us all that causes us to differ, that through thy bountiful goodness we may keep the unity of the Spirit in the bond of peace, through Jesus Christ our Lord.*

E.B. Pusey (1800–1882)

An Ode
In Imitation of Alcaeus

What constitutes a State?
Not high-raised battlement or laboured mound,
Thick wall or moated gate;
Not cities proud with spires and turrets crowned;
Not bays and broad-armed ports,
Where, laughing at the storm, rich navies ride;
Not starred and spangled ports,
Where low-browed baseness wafts perfume to pride.
No! – men, high-minded men,
With powers as far above dull brutes endued
In forest, brake, or den,
As beasts excel cold rocks and brambles rude, –
Men who their duties know,
But know their rights, and, knowing, dare maintain;
Prevent the long aimed blow,
And crush the tyrant while they rend the chain: –
These constitute a State;
And sovereign Law, that State's collected will,
O'er thrones and globes elate
Sits empress, crowning good, repressing ill.
Smit by her sacred frown,
The fiend, Dissension, like a vapour sinks;
And e'en the all-dazzling Crown
Hides his faint rays, and at her bidding sinks.
Since all must life resign,
Those sweet rewards which decorate the brave
'Tis folly to decline,
And steal inglorious to the silent grave.

WILLIAM JONES (1746–1794)
NOTE: IT IS SAID THAT DR SAMUEL JOHNSON ADDED THE LAST FOUR LINES

Comment

Alcaeus was one of the greatest Grecian lyric poets. Only fragments of his poetry have survived but these reveal that he praised what we now call the cardinal virtues as the essential foundation stones of a civilised State. He wrote at the close of the seventh and beginning of the sixth centuries before Christ. The poem finds place here to emphasise the truth that these four virtues – prudence, temperance, fortitude and justice – are not essentially Christian. William Jones, imitating the Greek poet, exalts them as the ingredients of good citizenship but, or course, makes no claim that they are in essence, Christian. It is important to remember this in a day when so many confuse good citizenship with Christian commitment, and in a day too when the secular state attaches the name Christian to what are no more than civic duties. These virtues are a state's demand upon everyone who would claim citizenship of it. For a Christian they mean all that – and more, as we shall see as we probe more deeply into them.

Prayer   *Eternal God, by whose providence our land has been blest with leaders who have set temperance, justice, prudence and fortitude as the foundation stones of our national life; Grant that we may not forget the one foundation stone who is Christ our Lord, lest having gained so much that is wholesome and good, we may yet lose our own soul; we ask this of your mercy.*

An Emperor's Meditations

Say to thyself at daybreak: I shall come across the busy-body, the thankless, the overbearing, the treacherous, the envious, the unneighbourly. All this has befallen them because they know not good from evil. But I, in that I have comprehended the nature of the Good that is beautiful, and the nature of Evil that it is ugly, and the nature of the wrong doer himself that it is akin to me, not as partaker of the same blood and seed but of intelligence and a morsel of the Divine, can neither be injured by any of them – for no-one can involve me in what is debasing – nor can I be angry with my kinsman and hate him. For we have come into being for co-operation, as have the feet, the hands, the eyelids, the rows of upper and lower teeth. Therefore to thwart one another is against Nature; and we do thwart one another by showing resentment and aversion.

Does a man do thee wrong? Go in and mark what notion of good and evil was his that did the wrong. Once perceive that and thou wilt feel compassion, not surprise or anger. For thou hast still thyself either the same notion of good and evil as he or another not unlike. Thou needest must forgive him then. But if thy notions of good and evil are no longer such, all the more easily shalt thou be gracious to him that sees awry . . . If a man makes a slip enlighten him with loving-kindness and show him wherein he hath seen amiss.

MARCUS AURELIUS (121–180)

Comment

The *Meditations* of this Roman Emperor are the meditations of a man who embraced the cardinal virtues as the signposts for his life. That he took those signposts seriously is evidenced throughout, for he frequently addresses the warnings in his meditations to himself. He mentions 'sins of omission and commission'. He says that 'a man must be arched and buttressed from within, else the temple wavers to the dust'. But he offers no guarantee against this spiritual disaster, nor does he tell what a man is to do with his sins. In other words he writes as a godly man who strove himself to stick to the cardinal virtues and urged others to do so, but he was not a Christian. Pious Stoic though he was and strict adherent to temperance, prudence, fortitude and justice, he lines up not with Jesus but with Nero. Pilate did indeed order that the inscription on the cross of Christ should be written 'in Hebrew, Latin and Greek'. The three civilisations had reached a climacteric. God in Christ was to make all things new. The cardinal virtues were to be baptised, to make their contribution to Christ's new world.

Prayer   *Give us, O Lord, a steadfast heart, which no unworthy thought can drag downwards; an unconquered heart which no tribulation can wear out; an upright heart which no unworthy purpose can tempt aside. Bestow upon us understanding to know thee, diligence to seek thee, wisdom to find thee and a faithfulness which may finally embrace thee; through Jesus Christ our Lord.*

ST THOMAS AQUINAS

Abiding Virtues

Thou who hast made these hearts to answer thine –
Infused thy virtues, faith, hope, charity,
Mirror'd thine image here that all may see,
If such be earthly what must be divine;
Thou who hast taught, by riddle, type, and sign,
The weakness of our immaturity
The measure of Thy strength one day to be,
By precept upon precept, line on line; –

Lord, take these signs and longings, hopes and fears,
The throb of love, the pulse of penitence,
The praise of all thy love has done – shall do –
And teach us – as Thy fuller light appears
And brightness at the gates of earthly sense, –
Who love Thy grace, to love Thy glory too.

ROBERT HUGH BENSON (1871–1914)

Comment

This author, son of an Archbishop of Canterbury, who spent the last thirteen years of his life as a Roman Catholic priest, leads us into our thoughts about 'faith, hope and charity'. The virtues of prudence, temperance, fortitude and justice, could be seen as the 'earthy' pre-Christian virtues about which Monsignor Benson poses the question: 'If such be earthy, what must be divine?' Obviously he must conclude that 'faith, hope and charity' stand high above all others. St Paul in his letter to the Corinthians sets all other virtues momentarily aside declaring: 'And now abideth faith, hope and charity. . . ' (1 Cor. ch.13). In our thoughts about the virtues we too can set the so-named cardinal virtues momentarily aside to see them later in the light of 'faith, hope and charity'. That is precisely what Paul did. Casting his eye towards the Christless world, and realising that it embraced men of vast intellectual knowledge, men of civic rectitude, men of wisdom, men of courage, he knew what was lacking in them and fearlessly expressed it. F.W.H. Myers in a poem about St Paul sums up the Apostle's feelings and motives:

Then with a thrill the intolerable craving
Shivers throughout me like a trumpet call –
O to save these – to perish for their saving –
Die for their lives, be offered for them all.

Those to whom he was addressing his preaching possessed so much in moral stature but lacked so much in spiritual insight and spiritual strength. Only Christ could give them that. Only Christ could baptise what they had with faith, with hope and with love.

Prayer   *O my God, I believe in thee and all that thy Church doth teach because thou hast said it and thy word is true: O my God, I hope in thee for grace and for glory, because of thy promises, thy mercy and thy power; O my God, I love thee because thou art good and gracious, and for thy sake I love my neighbour as myself.*

Faith

Now God forbid that Faith be blind assent
    Grasping what others know, else Faith were nought
But learning as of some far continent
    Which others sought,
And carried thence, better the tale to teach,
Pebbles and shells, poor fragments of the beach.
Now God forbid that Faith be built on dates,
    Cursive or uncial letters, scribe or gloss,
What one conjectures, prove or demonstrates,
    This were the loss
Of all to which God bids that man aspire,
This were the death of life, quenching of fire.
Nay, but with Faith I see. Not even Hope,
    Her glorious sister, stands so high as she.
For this but stands expectant on the slope
    That leads where He
Her source and consummation sets His seat,
Where Faith dwells always to caress His Feet.
May she, if proof and tortured argument
    Content thee – teach thee that the Lord is there,
Or risen again; I pray thee be content,
    But leave me here,
With eye unsealed by any proof of thine,
With eye unsealed to know the Lord is mine.

ROBERT HUGH BENSON (1871–1914)

Comment

Faith does not require that the Christian must have full intellectual understanding of every article of the Creed. To say 'I believe' is not necessarily to say 'I know'. Furthermore, as our author implies, there is no sure path to faith by way of 'dates, cursive or uncial letters, scribe or gloss'. It is a Christian maxim that we must believe in order to understand. As the writer of the Epistle to the Hebrews puts it: 'Without faith it is impossible to please God, for he that cometh to God must believe that God is, and that he is the rewarder of them that seek him'. It was a great scholar, long versed in the human sciences, who exclaimed after his life's studies: 'Now I know enough to know that I know nothing'. A sincere and virile faith is not something which only a theologian can enjoy. The man who said to our Lord: 'Lord, I believe, help thou mine unbelief', was not making a contradictory statement. He had made the leap of faith, but tucked away in his mind were, maybe, little nagging doubts – 'Help thou mine unbelief'. He was saying what any and every committed Christian might say with equal sincerity. Once we assert our faith in God in Christ and in the Church, which guards *the Faith*, our struggles are not over but they become struggles not of the intellect but of the will. We can answer the unbeliever and declare that 'the Lord is mine'.

Prayer   *Lord, strengthen our faith that it be not dead and ineffectual, but lively, showing itself in good works and conforming ever more closely to the image of Christ in whom we believe. We ask this through that same Christ Jesus our Lord.*

AFTER DEAN ADDISON (1605)

The Blessed Virgin Mary

The Greatness of Humility

Behold, how completely Mary traces all to God, lays claim to no works, no honour, no fame. She conducts herself as before, when as yet she had naught of all this; she demands no higher honours than before. She is not puffed up, does not vaunt herself, nor proclaim with a loud voice that she is become the Mother of God. She seeks not any glory, but goes about her wonted household duties, milking the cows, cooking the meals, washing pots and kettles, sweeping out the rooms, and performing the work of maid-servant or householder in lowly and despised tasks, as though she care naught for such exceeding great gifts and graces. She was esteemed among other women and her neighbours no more highly than before, nor desired to be, but remained a poor townswoman, one of the great multitude...

When men accord us praise and honour, we ought to profit by the example of the Mother of God... We ought neither to reject this praise and honour as though they were wrong, nor to despise them as though they were naught. We ought to ascribe them to Him in heaven to whom they belong.

MARTIN LUTHER (1483–1546)

Comment

There are three major festivals of the Blessed Virgin in the Alternative Services Book – namely The Presentation of Christ in the Temple (2 February), the Annunciation (25 March), and the Nativity of the Blessed Virgin (8 Sept.). The Book of Common Prayer's additional commemoration, the Visitation is now on 31 May. Standing as she does pre-eminent among the saints as the Mother of Christ our Redeemer, the Christian Church has throughout its history accorded her 'all but adoring love', by which phrase John Keble rightly reserves acts of adoration for God in Christ, but sets the Blessed Virgin above all the other saints of God. Very early in Christian history – from about the year 200 AD – the Church accorded her the title 'God-bearer', or 'Mother of God' – a title which the founder of the German Reformation – Martin Luther – was apparently happy to use. Although in the 5th century some efforts were made to withdraw the title, two Councils of the Church in 431 and 451 upheld it, and it has been used ever since. Luther's passage, from his *Magnificat*, is particularly fine since he lifts her high in our estimation and exhorts us to emulate her in her humility. Today being her birthday we can in all humility offer her our birthday greeting in the ancient salutation:

> Hail Mary! full of grace, the Lord is with thee,
> blessed art thou among women, and blessed is the
> fruit of thy womb, Jesus –

and we can pray that as she so readily became a willing instrument in the hand of God for his work, we too must see ourselves as those upon whom he relies for the working out of his purpose in his world.

Prayer

O Almighty God, who didst endue with singular grace the Blessed Virgin Mary, the Mother of ur Lord; Vouchsafe we beseech thee, to hallow our bodies in purity, and our souls in humility and love; through the same our Lord and Saviour Jesus Christ.

Personal Faith

I see his blood upon the rose
And in the stars the glory of his eyes,
His body gleams amid eternal snows,
His tears fall from the skies.

I see his face in every flower;
The thunder and the singing of the birds
Are but his voice – and carven by his power
Rocks are his written words.

All pathways by his feet are worn,
His strong heart stirs the ever-beating sea
His crown of thorns is twined with every thorn,
His cross is every tree.

I saw the Sun at midnight, rising red
Deep-hued yet glowing, heavy with the stain
Of blood-compassion, and I saw It gain
Swiftly in size and growing till It spread
Over the stars; the heavens bowed their head
As from Its heart so dripped crimson rain.
Then a great tremor shook It, as of pain –
The night fell, moaning, as It hung there dead.

O Sun, O Christ, O bleeding Heart of flame!
Thou giv'st Thine agony as our life's worth,
And mak'st it infinite, lest we have dearth
Of rights wherewith to call upon thy Name;
Thou pawnest Heaven as a pledge for Earth,
And for our glory sufferest all shame.

JOSEPH MARY PLUNKET (1887–1916)

Comment

Both the poems are by the nineteenth century poet who wrote many mystical verses. In fact they embody a profession of his personal faith. Whether it is the 'blood upon the rose', or 'the Sun at midnight, rising red', both were pointers to the Living God the Creator and to the redeeming work of Christ. Faith is a higher faculty than reason. Indeed to contrast it with reason is an error for its true contrast is with the senses. Our poet sees 'blood on the rose' and sees a 'cross in every tree' and in his second poem he sees 'Sun at midnight, rising red'. He sees all these with his physical eyes but with his inward eye he sees Christ himself. That is personal faith – to go as far as our eye can see – or, if you like, as reason can take us, and then to make the leap of faith. We may not be able to do this as readily as the mystic can but for all of us there is a point where the intellect fails. The leap of faith takes us beyond that point which confronts us with God. John Donne summed it up by saying that 'Reason is our soul's left hand, Faith is our soul's right hand. By these we reach divinity'.

Prayer

Increase our faith, O Lord our God, in Thee and in Thy Christ; increase our love, O our Redeemer, to Thee and to Thy righteous people; increase a sure hope in us of our salvation; increase strength in us to overcome sin and to stand firm against temptation; for Thy Names's sake.

(SIXTEENTH CENTURY)

The Church – its Faith and Life

When Christ's visible presence was withdrawn from men's sight, what was left as the fruit of his ministry? Not a formulated creed, nor a body of writings in which a new philosophy of life was expounded, but a group of men and women who found themselves knit together in a fellowship closer than any that they had known and who became the nucleus of the whole Christian Church. As the fellowship expanded, it drew within its bounds people of every type, every nation and every class.

The name of this fellowship which ought ideally to be so close as to constitute a single personality, is the Church. St Paul speaks of the Church as the Body of Christ, and what he means first and foremost by that is, of course, that Jesus of Nazareth used the body of flesh and blood in order to live before men the life which interprets to them the very being of God. So the Church exists on earth to do the self-same thing. It is the means whereby Christ becomes active and carries out his purpose in the world; that is what it is for, and that is what makes it the Church, the life of his Spirit within it, rising out of its faith in him. And that remains true of it even when people who are members of the Church from time to time become very feeble in their faith, so that the activity of his Spirit by means of them is very much hampered and limited.

WILLIAM TEMPLE (1881–1944)

Comment

There is what might be seen as a progression in faith. To believe in God is initial faith. To accept Christ as the Incarnate Son of God is to establish a personal fellowship with God. To immerse ourselves in Christ, reading his mind, discerning his purpose, and sealing our commitment to him is to appropriate faith. To assimilate Christ so that we become what C.S. Lewis described as 'little Christs' is active faith – and that is something which must engage body, mind and spirit, and that not in isolation but within the fellowship of the Church. There must be an 'end product' of faith not merely in our personal behaviour and relationships but also in our active membership of the Church.

> *If faith produce no works, I see*
> *That faith is not a living tree.*
> *Thus faith and works together grow;*
> *No separate life they e'er can know;*
> *They're soul and body, hand and heart;*
> *What God hath joined, let no man part.*

In the Eucharist we say: 'We are the Body of Christ'. Each of us is, by our faith, a limb of the Body. The thought can prompt pertinent self-questioning. An active limb contributing to the Church's witness and work in the world? A weak limb? A paralysed limb – impeding or frustrating Christ's purpose?

Prayer *Lord God, we pray for your Church throughout the world. May its faith be strong, its witness firm and its worship sincere. May we and all who are bound together in the fellowship of faith advance its honour to your glory and to the well-being of your people, through Jesus Christ our Lord.*

Before the Dawn

Thou, for whom words have exhausted their sweetness –
Thou, the All-end of human desire –
Thou, in whose Presence the ages are hourless,
      Gather me higher!

Hushed in the chambers where Reason lies sleeping,
Ere the Day claim us, to which we are told, –
Wrapped in the veil of Thy slumbering beauty,
      Fold me, oh fold!

Fill me afresh with the wonder awakening–
Draw me again with Thy splendour and might–
Open my lids but a moment, and grant me
      Sight of Thy sight!

Out of the furthest high Throne of Thy Dwelling,
A motionless Flame on the Bosom of Thought,
Deign to uncover Thyself, O Eternal
      Seeker and Sought!

Pure in the Body that offers Thee homage,
Blest in the thought that embraces Thee far,
Next to Thy secret and innermost breathing
      Thy worshippers are!

ALICE MARY BUCKTON (   )

Comment

Here is a splendid affirmation of faith in the Living God combined with what amounts to a prayer for its sustenance and strengthening. Our faith has to take many batterings. When it is at its strongest we can be assured of vision and venture and victory. When it is at its weakest we sink into what John Bunyan called the 'Slough of Despond'. Our poet prays that her faith may be increased – 'Gather me higher', that she may be filled 'afresh with the wonder awakening', that she may be granted a new sight of God who is both 'Seeker and Sought'. There is a reminder in that line that as we are seeking God, God himself is seeking us. The shepherd searches for the lost sheep; the housewife goes to great trouble to find the missing coin; the property-owner scans the sky-line day by day for a sight of his lost son. Shepherd, housewife and farmer rejoice when the 'sought' is 'found'. In her last verse the poet discloses, and this too from her own experience, that her faith is most richly renewed. The highest activity of the Church which is the Body of Christ is its worship of the Living God. It is when we are caught up in worship, altogether with one accord in one place, that we become most conscious of the presence of the Spirit within us, then that our faith is strengthened, then that we are emboldened to bear witness to it in the world.

Prayer

      Strong Son of God, immortal Love,
         Whom we, that have not seen thy face,
         By faith, and faith alone, embrace,
      Believing what we cannot prove.
            Amen

ALFRED, LORD TENNYSON (1809–1892)

The Church's Faith

The Christian faith is not primarily about being virtuous: it is one of its greatest handicaps that it has been saddled with that reputation. It is actually about being human, and that inevitably involves being a sinner. The speciality of the Christian faith is helping us to cope with sin, through the mechanism of Redemption, Repentance and Grace. Grappling with this, the Church – which is itself sinful – cannot help getting its hands dirty. It must regard physical violence as a blasphemy against creation, but it must still send out chaplains to the armed forces. It may be appalled by government policy on divorce and abortion, but it must still minister to the Minister, as it must to prostitutes and prisoners and men who sell pornography...

The Church should permeate and infiltrate the world, not make a private collection of those it favours. What matters is not whether socialism is more Christian than capitalism, but that both should be influenced by Christianity, and that there should be Christians on both sides. In rather the same way, I am less interested in something called 'Christian broadcasting' than I am in finding Christians broadcasting – and preferably they should not all be in one department labelled Religious Programmes, but in everything from News to Popular Music. For in the end, the best way of showing forth the Church in the world is to show that the Church is not its buildings and not its clergy, not even its services on Sunday, but its people out and about in their everyday lives, being Christians – which is being truly human according to God's will.

GERALD PRIESTLAND
FROM 'WHO NEEDS THE CHURCH?'

Comment

Gerald Priestland, erstwhile Religious Affairs Correspondent for the BBC up-dates and, maybe, extends what William Temple, the former Archbishop of Canterbury wrote in his book *Christian Faith and Life*, an extract from which was our quotation on September 10th. Some might see Priestland's opening line as in conflict with his closing lines. Indeed the Church's 'people out and about in their everyday lives' in their relationships with other people, in society, and in their contributions to debates concerning the social, national and international problems of our day, must in very truth be virtuous. Peter exhorted the Christians: 'Add to your faith, virtue', and then proceeded to indicate what that meant for them as to their influence in the world (read 2 Peter ch.1 vv.1–10).

Prayer   *Father, may the world not mould us today, but may we be so strong as to help to mould the world; through Jesus Christ our Lord.*

THE REV. J.H. JOWETT (1864)

Commemorating Cyprian, Bishop of Carthage, Martyr, 258

A letter from one priest to another

I have learnt of the splendid proofs you have given of your faith and courage and I have received with such elation the news of your noble confession of faith that I reckon I share in your merits and praise that was given you. For since we have one Church, one shared purpose and one harmonious charity, how can one priest not rejoice at the praises earned by a fellow priest as if at his own? What sort of brotherhood does not rejoice in a brother's joy?

I cannot express the exultation and the joy that I felt when I heard of your brave declaration and its happy outcome. In confessing your faith you showed the way to your brethren... You have persuaded the people to declare themselves Christians by first making profession of your own faith on behalf of all. I do not know which to praise you for first: your eager and firm faith or the love with which your brothers in Christ follow you. Your exemplary courage as a bishop has been publicly proved, and your brothers in Christ have shown their unity by imitating you. So long as you are unanimous in thought and word, it is as if the whole Roman Church made a profession of faith...

I have been instructed by the warning voice of God's providence and admonished by the salutary counsels of divine pity that the day when I shall be put to the test is approaching... Let us remember each other with one heart and mind. Let us pray for each other always and lighten our burdens and anxieties by our mutual love.

St Cyprian (d.258)

Comment

Here is an instance of a bishop writing to a brother bishop Cornelius, and praising him for his 'noble confession of faith'. Cornelius died in exile, probably as a martyr. Cyprian became Bishop of Carthage in the year 248. For many years the African Church had enjoyed a peaceful existence, but in those same years it had become lax and it was thus not equipped to deal with the inevitable persecution which began under the Emperor Decius. Vast numbers of Christians apostatized, some fled the country, and many were martyred. Pressed by the faithful, Cyprian withdrew for a time but returned to his See in the year 251. The persecution was followed by a plague which killed thousands and in this Cyprian directed humanitarian work for the relief of Christians and pagans alike. A further persecution followed and as a result Cyprian was banished, but in 258 he was recalled to face a further examination by the Consul. Once more he refused to renounce his faith and following the sentence: 'Our pleasure is that Thascius Cyprianus be executed with the sword', he replied: 'Thanks be to God' and the Christians hard by shouted: 'Let us also die with him'. We shall not be exiled for our faith. We shall not be martyred. But tests of the strength of our faith will come. God grant that we shall triumph when they do, so that we can say 'Thanks be to God'.

Prayer *Arm us, O Lord, with your grace, and assist us with your Holy Spirit, that in all the temptations and tests which come to us, our faith may not break.*

Commemorating Holy Cross Day

The Second Crucifixion

Loud mockers in the roaring street
    Say Christ is crucified again:
Twice pierced His gospel-bearing feet,
    Twice broken His great heart in vain.
        I hear, and to myself I smile,
        For Christ talks with me all the while.
No angel now to roll the stone
    From off his unawaking sleep,
In vain shall Mary watch alone,
    In vain the soldiers vigil keep.
        Yet while they deem my Lord is dead
        My eyes are on His shining head.
Ah! never more shall Mary hear
    That voice exceeding sweet and low
Within the garden calling clear:
    Her Lord is gone, and she must go.
        Yet all the while my Lord I meet
        In every London lane and street.
Poor Lazarus shall wait in vain,
    And Bartimeus still go blind;
The healing hem shall ne'er again
    Be touched by suffering humankind
        Yet all the while I see them rest,
        The poor and outcast, in His breast.
No more unto the stubborn heart
    With gentle knocking shall He plead
No more the mystic pity start,
    For Christ, twice dead, is dead indeed.
        So in the street I hear men say,
        Yet Christ is with me all the day.

RICHARD LE GALLIENNE (1866–1947)

Comment

Holy Cross Day, also known as the feast of the Exaltation of the Cross, is first mentioned in Christian literature early in the seventh century. In 629 the reigning emperor recovered the supposed true Cross of Christ from the Persians, and on this day it was exposed each year for venerations by Christians. In our day such veneration often takes place as a devotion on Good Friday. Christians venerate the Cross as the symbol of our redemption. For us it is 'the wondrous Cross on which the Prince of glory died'. They can boast no victories of their own 'save in the Cross of Christ'. Surely a cross should hang somewhere in every Christian home as a silent witness to all the family and to all who visit them, that Christ is Lord in that home and in the hearts of those who live beneath its roof. Our poet answers the mockers. He sees his Lord, talks with him, meets him in the street and finds him at his side throughout the day. He discerns too how what happened on the Cross has changed the history of the world. With what care Christians must walk lest they crucify Christ afresh!

Prayer

Grant, O God, that we who have been signed with the sign of the Cross, in our baptism, may never be ashamed to confess the faith of Christ crucified, but may manfully fight under his banner against sin, the world, and the devil, and continue Christ's faithful soldiers and servants unto our lives' end.

B.C.P.

Hope

For human nature, Hope remains alone
Of all the deities; the rest are flown.
Faith is departed. Truth and honour dead,
And all the graces too, my friends, are fled.
The scanty specimens of living worth,
Dwindled to nothing, and extinct on earth.
Yet whilst I live and view the light of heaven,
Since Hope remains and never has been driven
From the distracted world – the single scope
Of my devotion is to worship Hope.
When hecatombs are slain, and altars burn,
When all the deities adored in turn,
Let Hope be present, and with Hope, my friend,
Let every sacrifice commence and end.
Yes, indolence, injustice, every crime,
Rapine and Wrong, may prosper for a time;
Yet shall they travel on to swift decay,
Who tread the crooked path and hollow way.

THEOGNIS OF MEGARA (6TH CENTURY BC)
TRANS. JOHN H. FRERE

Comment

Theognis was a poet and party-politician who flourished in the 6th century BC.
He exercised a great influence following the overthrow of a tyrannical oligarchy.
He is credited with having written about 1400 lines of poetry about the virtues
and vices of man and his total work earned the title *Manual of Man*. He is quoted
here to reveal that even the pagans had a sense of Hope which resided in 'the deities' – that is hope was not for them something self-generated. In their acts of
worship – 'hecatombs' are acts of worship involving animal sacrifices – they believed that the virtue of hope resided in and could be experienced by the worshipper.
Possessing it, man would find that 'indolence, injustice, every crime' would 'travel on to swift decay'. In cherishing such beliefs the pagans were well ahead of those
in our day who link the virtue of hope with the baseless emotional optimism at-
taching to our worldly affairs. Though 'I hope I win the pools', or 'I hope England
wins the Test', are harmless enough as transitory expressions, they have nothing
to do with Christian Hope which Paul describes as an 'anchor of the soul both
sure and steadfast'. But Christians are not left to deal with vague 'deities'. Their
hope is in the hope of salvation. They believe that union with God is the final end
of man. The Christian indeed seeks happiness but he seeks it because it redounds
to the glory of God. Reading his lines on hope we might hear our Lord saying
to this pagan poet: 'Thou art not far from the Kingdom of God'.

Prayer   *God of Hope, fill us with all joy and peace in believing, so that by the*
power of your Holy Spirit we may abound in hope.

Hope

O God the soul of hope of the world,
The only refuge for unhappy men,
Abiding in the faithfulness of Heaven,
Give me a strong succour in this testing place.
O King, protect thy man from utter ruin,
Lest the weak flesh surrender to the tyrant,
Facing innumerable blows alone.
Remember I am dust, and wind, and shadow,
And life as fleeting as the flower of the grass,
But may the eternal mercy which hath shone from time of old
Rescue thy servant from the jaws of the lie,
Thou who didst come from on high in the cloak of the flesh,
Strike down the dragon with the two-edged sword
Whereby our mortal flesh can war with the winds
And break down strongholds, with our Captain, God, Amen

THE VENERABLE BEDE (673–735)
TRANS. HELEN WADDELL

Comment

Here the Venerable Bede expresses in Christian language what the pagan Theognis asserted in his. But he enlarges the theme too. He sees hope as man's refuge and protector 'from utter ruin', and Christ as the one who can kill the dragon of despair, which is hope's denial. Of course he sustains what may be regarded as the futurity of hope – 'The hope which is laid up for you in Heaven' (Col.ch.1 v.5), and 'Looking for that blessed hope and the glorious appearing of the great God and our Saviour Jesus Christ' (Titus ch.2 v.13) – but he concerns himself with the here and now, and the sin of despair into which man can fall so easily to his own hurt and health. We have every right, and indeed duty, to hope for the best for our world today, provided that we bend heart and mind and soul to work for the best. Paul Tillich in his *The Shaking of the Foundations* has an encouraging word to say on that score: 'If you can find hope in the ground of history, you are united with the great prophets who were able to look into the depth of their times, who tried to escape it, because they could not stand the horror of their visions, and yet who had the strength to look to an even deeper level, and there to discover hope'. Someone has put that more poignantly by saying that for Christians to describe a human situation, or a person, as hopeless is 'to slam the door in God's face'. In a world which is dark with suffering, with strife, with poverty and with grief, Christians must be, said Matthew Arnold, 'beacons of hope'. How do we stand in the light of that exhortation?

Prayer   *O Lord God, in whom we live and move and have our being, open our eyes that we may behold thy fatherly presence ever about us. Draw our hearts to thee with the power of thy love. Teach us to be anxious for nothing, and when we have done what thou hast given us to do, help us, O God our Saviour, to leave the issue to thy wisdom. Take from us all doubt and mistrust. Lift our thoughts up to thee, and make us to know that all things are possible to us through thy Son our Redeemer.*

BISHOP WESTCOTT (1825–1901)

'The Fell of Dark'

I wake and feel the fell of dark, not day.
What hours, O what black hours we have spent
This night! what sights you, heart, saw; ways you went;
And more must, in yet longer light's delay.
With witness I speak this. But where I say
Hours I mean years, mean life. And my lament
Is cries countless, cries like dead letters sent
To dearest him that lives alas! away.
I am gall. I am heartburn. God's most deep decree
Bitter would have me taste; my taste was me;
Bones built in me, flesh filled blood brimmed the curse.
Selfyeast of spirit a dull dough sours. I see
The lost are like this, and their scourge to be,
As I am mine, their sweating selves, but worse.

GERARD MANLEY HOPKINS (1844–1889)

Comment

All God's people, be they holy men like Herbert, Donne, Cowper, Clare, Augustine and others less well known, suffered their days of despair. Doubtless, so do we – days when we 'wake and feel the fell of dark', days when the light of hope has banished, days of sickness, of suffering, of sorrow, of disappointment and defeat. Moses knew that God's people would face trials of all kinds and before he died he gave them this assurance: 'The eternal God is your refuge and underneath are the everlasting arms'. A contemporary parish priest has written a prayer based on those words – a prayer which shall fill the rest of this page so that it can be turned to with ease when we 'feel the fell of dark', whatever the dark may be.

Prayer   The Everlasting Arms

Underneath us are the everlasting arms, the arms of him
who is male and female, Father and Mother, the arms of
God who to me is 'You'.
If I fall into sin –
I fall into the everlasting arms of the Father
of the Prodigal Son –
of the waiting Father, waiting to forgive and love.
If I fall into sickness, disaster or trouble –
I fall into the everlasting arms of the Father
of our Lord Jesus Christ who suffered for us,
and suffers with us
and fills our suffering
with his loving presence
and will bring us through suffering to glory
If I fall into death –
I fall into the everlasting arms of the Father
of our risen, ascended and glorified Lord
who brings us through death to resurrection
and eternal life.

THE REV. PETER STOKES (CONTEMPORARY)

The Eternal Hope

'Jesus offers paradise hereafter. Lenin offers paradise now'. That is the stuff that makes revolutions but it is, for Christians, a quite false antithesis. So far from anaesthetizing the social conscience, the eternal hope is what sharpens and stimulates it – the sanction and the incentive of all attempts to serve and ameliorate this world below. It is because man is heir of so high a destiny that the Christian must labour to make this world a place worthy to be a home for the children of God, to take their part as citizens of the earthly city in caring for education and social welfare, in abolishing war, poverty and disease, living here as colonists of the heavenly city.

As the eternal hope has grown dim it has been supplanted in Western civilisation by the secular belief in Progress... May it not be that the apathy and the restlessness so prevalent and so dangerous in our own time are results of the loss of that eternal hope which invests life here with its value and significance?

Now the Christian hope is essentially religious. It is not a matter of scientific experiment – which in any case could not yield the evidence – , nor of pathological introspection. It is the corollary of faith in God as he is shown to us in Jesus Christ, the God to whom persons are dear, who is 'not the God of the dead but of the living'. If it be true that God has created us moral and spiritual personalities capable of communion with himself, that implies a non-temporal relationship – in Christian language an eternal life in which we may be here and now partakers. It does not seem possible to believe that this eternal relationship is ruptured or destroyed when a Christian's heart stops beating.

BISHOP RUSSELL BARRY (1890–1976)

Comment

In the course of his ministry Russell Barry wrote no less that 26 books, many of them substantial volumes. Soon after the World War started in 1939 he sustained the faith of many with his book entitled *Faith in Dark Ages*. When the light of hope was flickering in the minds and souls of many Christians, here was a Christian leader who helped to keep that light burning. The quotation above is from *Questioning Faith* and here too he grappled with problems which disturb many Christians, and again set many minds at rest and challenged many to look afresh at the Christian Faith to find in it a hope which the world could not offer. In this passage he deals with what we may see as 'the two hopes' – the one which 'sharpens and stimulates the social conscience' and prompts Christians, despite their fears for the immediate future, not to give way to despair, and the hope of the eternal – the 'hope which is laid up for you in heaven' (Col. ch.1 v.5). The second of these is dubbed by the unbeliever as 'pie in the sky', wishful thinking, but as another writer said some years ago: 'It is for Christians to elucidate rather than to deny that cynical phase'. Try it with an unbelieving friend! Begin if you like by saying: 'Yes, indeed, but it is "some pie", for eternal life is nothing less than sharing the life of the Living God'. 'Eternal' means not only 'timeless'. It is a qualitative term meaning also 'perfection'.

Prayer   *Help me to remember, Lord, that good actions are the invisible hinges of the doors of heaven, and as the word which you have written on the brow of every man is Hope, inspire and strengthen me to press on in all things which serve your purpose for your world.*

AFTER VICTOR HUGO

Spes Unica Nostra

Where should a man find hope, if not in man?
And yet what man of us who doth not know
How 'twixt his thought of good – and what he can –
An unbridged stream of difference doth flow?
One voice insistent speaks within the breast,
Far other is the life we manifest.

Yet 'tis the inward Voice we trust the most;
And could we see a life, interpret it,
And make it flesh here upon earth, our boast
Should be to crown that life and follow it.

Now, since One Life beyond imagining
Hath all fulfilled, life, lifted to a faith,
Becomes a sacramental following
Of that One Love triumphant most in death.
So hail we Him with banner red unfurled
Of sacrifice – the Hope of all the world.

FATHER ANDREW, S.D.C. (1869–1946)

Comment

Father Andrew's poem – *Our only Hope* – strikes the right note with which to sum up our thoughts on the virtue of hope. There is a wordly hope which is legitimate and worthy – the hope for example of a better world order which excludes war as a means of settling differences, the hope that hunger and poverty can be eliminated from the world's scene. But to follow this up in a Christian manner there has to be 'in the life we manifest' something which can transform our hope into effective desire, and can then transform effective desire into Christian action. Father Andrew appears to have just this in mind in the first two verses of his poem. He goes on to make it clear that this hope, like the hope of Eternal life, can be realised only in Christ. It becomes indeed 'a sacramental following'. This is where the Church comes in, for whether we are concerned to fashion a better world here and now, or to be ourselves concerned with the hope of eternal life, Christ is 'the hope of all the world'. As to the first – the fashioning of a better world – the Church which is the Body of Christ (and that means you and me and all who call themselves Christians) cannot stand by impotent and dumb before the world's blasphemies of hunger and racism, strife and wars. We must stand up, not merely 'to be counted', but to put our witness, our wills and our weight behind efforts to eliminate these evils. As to the second – the hope of eternal life – read again the last paragraph of Bishop Russell Barry's words which formed part of yesterday's quotation.

Prayer　　*God is our hope and strength; a very present help in trouble. Therefore will we not fear. . . the Lord of hosts is with us.*

PSALM 46

Commemorating Saints and Martyrs of Australia and the Pacific New Guinea

Bird shaped island, with secretive bird voices,
Land of apocalypse, where the earth dances,
The mountains speak, the doors of the spirit open,
And men are shaken by obscure trances.

The forest-odours, insects, clouds and fountains
And like the figures of my inmost dream,
Vibrant with untellable recognition;
A wordless revelation is their theme.

The stranger is engulfed in those high valleys,
Where mists of morning linger like the breath
Of Wisdom moving on our specular darkness:
Regions of prayer, of solitude, and of death!

Life holds its shape in the molds of dance and music,
The hands of craftsmen trace its patternings;
But stains of blood, and evil spirits, lurk
Like cockroaches in the interstices of things.

We in that land begin our rule in courage,
The seal of peace gives warrant to intrusion;
But then our grin of emptiness breaks the skin,
Formless dishonour spreads its proud confusion.

Whence that deep longing for an exorcizer,
For Christ descending as a thaumaturge
Into his saints, as formerly in the desert,
Warring with demons on the outer verge.

Only by this can life become authentic,
Configured henceforth in eternal mode:
Splendour, simplicity, joy – such as were seen
In one who now rests by his mountain road.

JAMES McAULEY (1917–1976)

Comment

What a thrilling story can be told about all those who are embraced in today's commemoration – a story too long and with too many heroes of the faith to mention all by name. Even so the names of Bishop Broughton, who became the first Bishop of Australia – imagine Australia as a single diocese! – and Bishop Patteson of Melanesia must not be forgotten. On this day in 1871 John Patteson was killed with five stab wounds, each representing five islanders who had been kidnapped by evil-minded white traders. But the martyrs of New Guinea are too many to be numbered or named individually. They were the men and women, from this country and from Australia, who saw it as their duty to remain at their posts in 1942. They were slaughtered by the Japanese. 'We could never hold up our faces again', Bishop Philip Strong had said, 'if for our own safety we all forsook Him and fled when the shadows of the Passion began to gather round Him and His Church in Papua'. James McCauley, one of Australia's leading poets, writes of a country he came to love and in the last verse of his poem has in mind Bishop Alan de Boismenu, the Roman Catholic Bishop who was contemporary with Bishop Philip Strong.

Prayer   *We praise you, O God: we acknowledge you to be the Lord. The noble army of martyrs praise you. . . Day by day we magnify you, and we worship your Name, ever world without end.*

St Matthew the Apostle

Only this morn, in Custom's hut,
I sat upon the shore,
When suddenly a shadow fell,
A Form stood at my door.
Two eyes of flame looked into mine,
They read my very soul,
They saw my restless discontent,
The ache to be made whole –
The loathing of my better self
For my ill-gotten gain –
The cool contempt of fellow men
That stung my heart with pain.
And then – a Voice came to my ears,
(O that such thing could be!)
A voice vibrant with love and TRUST,
Cried 'Matthew, follow Me'.

SISTER ROSALIND MARY, C.S.M.V. (1895–1972)

Comment

Sister Rosalind Mary, of the Wantage Community, spent most of her professed life working in parishes in different parts of this country – visiting the sick in homes and hospitals.
She was, too, experienced as a teacher of adults as of the young. Maybe it was this that
prompted her to write about St Matthew who of all the evangelists was concerned chiefly
with Christ's teaching.

Matthew was a civil servant in the employ of the Roman Empire and his particular job
was to collect taxes for this foreign power. He was bitterly hated by his fellow Jews and
seen by them as an agent of the enemy. Clearly an educated man, he must have taken oral
reports about Jesus and his teaching as worthy of serious consideration, and it may be that
he was spiritually and mentally ready to hear 'the voice vibrant with love and trust' on that
momentous day in his life when he abandoned his profession and decided to cast his lot
in with Jesus. Fortunately he took his education – and his pen! – with him, and to him
we owe the first handbook of the teaching of Jesus. Clearly he used Mark's Gospel when
he was writing about the events of the life of Christ, but for the teaching of Jesus, and especially for the Sermon on the Mount, we are indebted to St Matthew. He was a Jew determined to convince and convert the Jews. Further, he was a Churchman. Alone of the writers
of the Synoptic Gospels (the first three) he uses the word Church, and he it is who sets out
the Divine command succinctly: 'Go ye therefore and teach all nations'. He has been called
the 'systematizer' of Christ's teaching, an ability he brought with him from his civil service
days. A great New Testament scholar writes of him: 'Matthew's picture of Jesus is the picture of the man born to be King. Jesus walks through Matthew's pages as if in the purple
and gold of royalty'. His proclamation today would indeed be: 'Jesus is Lord. His is the
Kingdom and the Power and the Glory'.

Prayer   *Praise be to you O God for the life and witness of your servant Matthew. Give*
your people strength to follow the teaching of our Lord and Saviour Jesus Christ
which by your servant's zeal is set forth in the Gospel bearing his name.

'The greatest of these is Charity'

God is love, or rather Charity; generous, outgoing, self-giving Love. When all the qualities which human thought attributes to reality are set aside, this remains. Charity is the colour of the Divine personality, the spectrum of Holiness. We believe that the tendency to give, to share, to cherish, is the mainspring of the universe, the ultimate cause of all that is, and reveals the nature of God; and that therefore when we are most generous we are most living and most real... When we look out towards this Love which moves the stars and stirs in the child's heart, and claims our total allegiance, and remember that this alone is Reality – and we are only real so long as we conform to its demands – we see our human situation from a fresh angle; and perceive that it is both more humble and dependent, and more splendid than we had dreamed. We are surrounded and penetrated by great spiritual forces, of which we hardly know anything. Yet the outward events of our life cannot be understood, except in that unseen and intensely living world, the Infinite Charity which penetrates and supports us, the God whom we resist and yet whom we trust; who is ever at work, transforming the self-centred desire of the natural creature into the wide-spreading outpouring love of the citizen of Heaven.

EVELYN UNDERHILL (1875–1941)

Comment

We introduce our thoughts on the third so-named 'theological virtue' under the name made familiar by the Authorised Version of the Bible in the concluding verse of St Paul's wonderful analysis of the content of Christian love: 'And now abideth faith, hope, charity, these three; but the greatest of these is charity' (1 Cor. ch. 13). Subsequent translations of the New Testament have translated the Greek word *agape* as *love* and this is not only more accurate but more meaningful since in our age the lovely word *charity* has been diminished in the popular mind as meaning no more than tossing a coin into a tin in return for a button-hole flag, or responding to an appeal following some natural disaster. Such responses are, of course, humanitarian and are to be applauded. But *agape* – Christian love – is vastly more demanding than this, as Evelyn Underhill makes clear in this extract from her book *The School of Charity*. Christian love is in fact God at work within us. God is Charity, is Love – and when God possesses our hearts we need no nudging from without to prompt us to respond in any and every human situation. When there is a special need for a special outpouring of God's love through us, as for example in some world tragedy, it is right that we should be informed. But the Christian must be a continuous channel of charity. As a citizen of heaven he must accept the solemn responsibility for the wide-spreading outpouring of God's love.

Prayer   *Pour upon us, O Lord, the spirit of brotherly kindness, so that sprinkled with the dew of your benediction we make glad the lives of our neighbours, and be made glad by your peace in our hearts, through Jesus Christ our Lord.*

I in Thee and Thou in me

I am but clay in thy hands, but thou art the all-loving artist;
  Passive I lie in thy sight, yet in my selfhood I strive
So to embody the life and love thou ever impartest
  That in my spheres of the finite I may be truly alive.

Knowing thou needest this form, as I thy divine inspiration,
  Knowing thou shapest the clay with a vision and purpose divine,
So would I answer each touch of thy hand in its loving creation,
  That in my conscious life thy power and beauty may shine.

Reflecting the noble intent thou hast in forming thy creatures;
  Waking from sense into the life of the soul, and the image of thee;
Working with thee in thy work to model humanity's features
  Into the likeness of God, myself from myself I would free.

One with all human existence, no one above or below me;
  Lit by thy wisdom and love, as roses are steeped in the morn;
Growing from clay to statue, from statue to flesh, till thou know me
  Wrought into manhood celestial, and in thine image reborn.

So in thy love will I trust, bringing me sooner or later
  Past the dark screen that divides these shows of the finite from thee.
Thine, thine only, this warm dear life, O loving Creator,
  Thine the invisible future, born of the present must be.

CHRISTOPHER PEARSE CRANCH (1813–1892)

Comment

A fine poem in which the poet expounds the truth of God's need of our love of him in order
that his love may through us be imparted to others. 'By divine charity we love God above
all else for his own sake and our neighbours for God's sake', said Thomas Aquinas. Jeremy
Taylor in his *Eight Signs of Purity of Intention in Holy Living* sets out the ways by which our
love of God expresses itself, ways which have been regarded as 'classical' in the literature
of Christian ethics. These are – and I take the liberty of up-dating some of the good man's
words and phrases – that Man:

1. values religious ends before temporal
2. is not solicitous of the opinion and censures of others
3. behaves as well in private as in public i.e. in the world as
   in church
4. is not troubled about the effect of his actions of loving God
5. is not envious of his neighbour's perfections of character
6. despises sensual pleasures and worldly reputation
7. uses the means God has given him with thankfulness
8. rejoices in the failure of a temporal end which defeats a spiritual
   end.

That is indeed a touchstone against which to measure the genuineness of our love of God.
It has to be pure, not counterfeit, for only thus can God shape us 'with a vision and purpose
divine', only thus will Christians be able to say 'Into the likeness of God, myself from myself I would free'.

Prayer   *My God, I love thee, not because I hope for heaven thereby, nor yet because
who love thee not are lost eternally. Not from the hope of gaining aught, nor
seeking a reward, but as Thyself has loved me, O ever loving Lord.*

The Sin of Omission

It isn't the thing you do, dear,
　It's the thing you leave undone,
Which gives you a bit of a heart-ache
　At the setting of the sun.
The tender word forgotten,
　The letter you did not write,
The flower you might have sent, dear,
　Are your haunting ghosts tonight.

The little acts of kindness,
　So easily out of mind,
Those chances to be angels
　Which everyone may find,
They come in night and silence,
　Each chill reproachful wraith,
When hope is faint and flagging
　And a blight has dropped on faith.

The stone you might have lifted
　Out of a brother's way,
The bit of heartsome counsel
　You were hurried too much to say.
The loving touch of the hand, dear,
　The gentle and winsome tone,
That you had no time nor thought for,
　With troubles enough of your own.

For life is all too short, dear,
　And sorrow is all too great,
To suffer our great compassion
　That tarries until too late;
And it's not the thing you do, dear,
　It's the thing you leave undone,
Which gives you the bit of heartache
　At the setting of the sun.

MARGARET SANGSTER (1838–1912)

Comment

Maybe there is less grandeur in the poetry than in yesterday's verses, but the lesson is pungent and pungently expressed. Our love of God must demonstrate itself in three dimensions – love of self, love of the brotherhood and love of our enemies. We must not demur from the first. We are bidden to 'love our neighbour *as ourself*'. As lovers of God that is our first duty. That means, in effect, that to do something for our neighbour that we know to be morally wrong, would be sinful, however great a service he might regard it. Not to love him – that is, to commit the sins of omission which our poet indicates – would also be to fail in Christian love whether that neighbour be firmly within the brotherhood of the Church or not. But Christian love goes a step further in that it requires that we shall love our enemies. We may not *like* them but we still have to love them in that we may not as Christians be indifferent to their needs. That is what the parable of the Good Samaritan is all about. We must be alert – to our own needs, to the needs of the brotherhood, to the needs even of our enemies. Remember, that so often, 'It's not the thing you do, but the thing you leave undone'.

Prayer　　*God of love, help me to love – to love you and to show my love for you by loving my neighbour as I love myself.*

Commemorating Lancelot Andrews
Bishop of Winchester, 1626

Watch ye and pray always, that ye may be accounted worthy to escape the things that shall come to pass. Love the Lord all thy life and call upon Him for thy salvation. Humble thy soul greatly. A man can receive nothing except it be given. If he that was without sin prayed, how much more ought a sinner to pray, for God is a hearer not of the voice but of the heart.

More is done by groaning than by words: to this end Christ groaned, for to give us an example of groaning. It is not that God desireth us to be suppliant or loveth that we lie prostrate: the profit thereof is ours and it hath regard to our advantage.

Prayer goeth up; pity cometh down. God's grace is richer than prayer: God always giveth more than He is asked. God commandeth that thou ask, and teacheth what to ask, and promiseth what thou dost ask, and it displeaseth him if thou ask not. Dost thou not ask notwithstanding?

Prayer is a summary of faith, an interpreter of hope. It is not by paces but by prayer that God is come at. Faith poureth out prayer and is grounded in prayer. Therefore go on to labour permanently in prayers, always to pray and not to faint in spirit and in truth. Faith is the foundation and basis of prayer: the foundation of faith is the promise of God. He that made us to live, the same taught us withal to pray.

Lift up your hearts! Prayer is colloquy with God.

BISHOP LANCELOT ANDREWES (1555–1626)

Comment

Lancelot Andrewes, a saintly man who has left his imprint upon the Church which he served so faithfully throughout his life, was ordained when he was 25. Nine years later he became a Prebendary of St Paul's Cathedral, and subsequently Dean of Westminster and Bishop successively of Chichester, of Ely, and of Winchester. Many of his sermons are extant but the work which has probably exercised the greatest influence on the spiritual lives of the greatest number is his *Preces Privatae* which sets out the manner and content of his own private prayers and devotional exercises. The young George Herbert, who was at Westminster School when Andrewes was Dean, was so impressed by his holiness that he himself made a solemn resolution 'to attain such whiteness of soul' as he saw in Andrewes, whose habit it was to take 'a brace of this young fry' for occasional walks, in the course of which he would not only interpret the scenes about him but speak to them about their faith and its sustenance by prayer, by reception of the Holy Sacrament and by Christian action. He earned a reputation as a lively if lengthy preacher. He resisted the 'tyrannous narrowness of Puritanism' and demanded that there be dignity and solemnity in worship.

Prayer

O Thou which makest the outgoings of the morning and evening to praise Thee, which givest thy beloved wholesome sleep, let me think upon Thy Name in the night season, and keep thy law. Let my evening prayer go up unto Thee, and Thy pity come down unto us.

FROM LANCELOT ANDREWES' PRIVATE PRAYERS

Love of God

The beginning and the End

All that I am to do is reduced to one word only and that is, love; this is the first and great command which comprehends all others, the proper evangelical grace; and eternal truth has assured me, 'this do and thou shalt live', so that if I truly love God, I shall be loved by God for all eternity.

The love of God is a grace rather to be felt than defined, so that I can do no more than rudely describe it; it is the general inclination and tendency of the whole man, of all his heart, and soul, and strength, of all his powers and affections, and of the utmost strength of them all, to God, as his chief, and only, and perfect and infinite good.

If I seriously desire the love of God, I must first expel all contrary loves out of my heart, and then consider the motives and causes that excite it; the former is taught in the vow of baptism, the latter in the creed.

When divine love is once produced, my next care is to put into practice; and that is, by bringing forth the fruits or effects of love, which are all contained in the ten commandments.

When the love of God is produced in my heart, and is set on work, my last concern is to preserve, and ensure, and quicken it; it is preserved by prayer, the pattern of which is the Lord's Prayer; it is ensured to us by the sacraments which are the pledges of love; and more particularly, it is quickened by the Holy Eucharist which is the feast of love.

BISHOP THOMAS KEN (1637–1711)

Comment

The saintly Thomas Ken, who was Bishop of Bath & Wells, and is remembered frequently since his morning and evening hymns are sung throughout Christendom, sums up our thoughts about love, reminding us that it has its origin in God – God is love – that the love we have for him is the beginning of all the love which it is our duty and our joy to pass on to our neighbours. He then explains, with a clarity which he doubtless practised as he taught the boys of Winchester College three centuries ago, that love had to be preserved, assured and quickened. Regular prayer would preserve it; the use of the sacraments would ensure it, and regular reception of the Blessed Sacrament in the Eucharist would quicken it. As we go about our daily lives the reality and strength of our love of God is tested in all manner of ways and of differing circumstances, many of them demanding illimitable patience, understanding and sympathy. The love of neighbour which derives from our love of God is a tender plant which has to withstand severe trials. Bishop Ken points us to the sure way in which it can become sturdy and enduring.

Prayer   *Lord Jesus, grant us daily grace for daily need; daily patience for a daily cross so that when the tests of our love of you and of our neighbour come to us, we may rise to them with courage and bear a faithful witness.*

If –

If you can keep your head when all about you
    Are losing theirs and blaming it on you,
If you can trust yourself when all men doubt you,
    But make allowance for their doubting too;
If you can wait and not be tired of waiting,
    Or being lied about, don't deal in lies,
Or being hated don't give way to hating,
    And yet don't look too good, or talk too wise

If you can dream and not make dreams your master;
    If you can think – and not make thoughts your aim,
If you can meet with Triumph and Disaster
    And treat those two impostors just the same;
If you can bear to hear the truth you've spoken
    Twisted by knaves to make a trap for fools,
Or watch the things you gave your life to, broken,
    And stoop and build 'em up with worn-out tools;

If you can make one heap of all your winnings;
    And risk it on one turn of pitch and toss,
And lose, and start again at your beginnings
    And never breathe a word about your loss;
If you can force your heart and nerve and sinew
    To serve your turn long after they are gone,
And so hold on where there is nothing in you
    Except the Will which says to them: 'Hold on!'

If you can talk with crowds and keep your virtue,
    Or walk with kings – nor lose the common touch,
If neither foes nor loving friends can hurt you,
    If all men count with you, but none too much;
If you can fill the unforgiven minute
    With sixty seconds' worth of distance run,
Yours is the Earth and everything that's in it,
    And – which is more – you'll be a Man, my son!

RUDYARD KIPLING (1865–1936)

Comment

Turning once more to the four so-named 'cardinal' virtues – prudence, justice, temperance and fortitude – we must remind ourselves that these are pre-Christian – values which reached the Christian world via Greece and Rome. we must not suppose that everything which was pre-Christian was evil. These virtues were, as it were, the minimum qualifications for good citizenship. Kipling's very popular poem covers them all admirably and it could well have been written in ancient Rome. But it smacks of what has been called 'the British heresy' and that is that a man can achieve all these virtues and more by his own efforts – that he has no need of Divine Grace. (The heresy is called Pelagianism). The Christian Church had its own touchstones of conduct – Faith, Hope and Charity – but seeing the good in the pagan values, it took them over, baptised them and interpreted them in the light of the Gospel. We shall see what that means for us as we think of them in turn. Meanwhile we can go on enjoying 'If'!

Prayer   *Grant us, O Lord, the will and the grace to discharge our duties as citizens of this earthly kingdom that it may be the nobler for our lives in it, through Jesus Christ our Lord.*

Commemorating Vincent de Paul
Founder of the Vincentian Order, 1660

The Poor Children

Take heed of this small child of earth;
  He is great; he hath in him God most high.
Children before their fleshly birth
  Are lights alive in the blue sky.

In our dark bitter world of wrong
  They come; God gives us them awhile.
His speech is in their stammering tongue,
  And his forgiveness in their smile.

Their sweet light rests upon our eyes.
  Alas! their right to joy is plain.
If they are hungry, Paradise
  Weeps, and if cold, Heaven thrills with pain.

The want that saps their sinless flower
  Speaks judgment on sin's ministers.
Man holds an angel in his power.
  Ah! deep in Heaven what thunder stirs,

When God seeks out these tender things
  Whom in the shadow where we sleep
He sends us clothed about with wings
  And finds them ragged babes that weep.

VICTOR HUGO (1802–1885)
TRANS. A.G. SWINBURNE (1837–1909)

Comment

Just about the time when the author of this poem about the poor children died, the Pope declared Vincent de Paul to be the Patron of Charitable Works through the world. Vincent, son of a peasant family, was ordained in 1600 and about thirteen years later he became chaplain to one of the richest and most influential families in Paris. In this devoutly Christian household he remained for seventeen years, not only serving the family but also directing from their home parochial missions through which he himself became well known as one who was deeply concerned about the poor. He founded the first Order of Sisters of Mercy whose concern was to be the care of the poor by teaching, by visiting and by nursing. He founded too a Confraternity of Charity into which he drew the rich and influential to give of their time and substance for the relief of poverty and for their care in sickness. He founded too the Vincentian Order which undertook missions in the parishes and the training of clergy to conduct them. It is estimated that in his day many hundred babies were deserted by their parents and exposed to die. Night after night Vincent roamed the streets looking for the abandoned children and taking them into his Foundling Hospital. Later he provided a similar hospice for the destitute, the beggars and aged sick. He can be regarded with justice as the father of the world's philanthropic activities – the man who directed the world's attention to the plight of those whom the world was content to ignore.

Prayer

Lord, you have taught us that whatever we do for the least of your brethren we do for you: Give us grace to see you in all who are poor and needy both here at home or overseas. Melt our hearts and move our wills to be ready and willing to serve these our brothers and sisters in your family for the relief of their need and the glory of your name.

St Michael and All Angels

Michael, Archangel

Michael, Archangel
Of the King of Kings,
Give ear to our voices.

Thou wert seen in the Temple of God,
A censer of gold in thy hands,
And the smoke of it, fragrant with spices
Rose up till it came before God.

Thou with strong hands didst smite the cruel dragon,
And many souls didst rescue from his jaws.
Then was there a great silence in heaven,
And a thousand, thousand saying 'Glory to the Lord'.

Hear us. Michael,
Greatest angel,
Come down a little from thy seat,
To bring us the strength of God
And the lightening of His mercy.

And so thou, Gabriel,
Lay low our foes,
And thou, Raphael,
Heal our sick,
Purge our disease, ease thou our pain,
And give us to share
In the joys of the blessed.

ALCUIN (735–804)
TRANS. HELEN WADDELL

Comment

A belief in angels is amply attested in Holy Scripture where they are seen as ministering spirits. It is significant that our Lord sanctioned this belief and in the New Testament we are told that he was surrounded by angels at the specially important moments of his ministry. They announced his Incarnation and were present at his Birth. They sustained him in the desert and through his agony on the Mount of Olives. In the Book of Revelation they are seen caught up in the worship of God. Michael the Archangel, and Gabriel, get special mention and in Christian literature Raphael appears too as an archangel. They are spirits, not human beings – and there is no evidence that when a good little child dies he becomes an angel! We live today in an age which is gripped in an arid materialism and in which millions have no sense of a spiritual dimension of life. Such people find belief in anything but human flesh to be impossible. But even one such, receiving a particular kindness from another, will say 'O you are an angel!' I sense that neither the Vatican Council, nor the General Synod, nor any other ecclesiastical body would dare to eliminate the angels from the spiritual arena. Their spiritual existence is attested in the Bible, embedded in literature and for many in personal experience. Maybe as children we prayed – and can pray again:

Prayer *Matthew, Mark, Luke and John; the bed be blest that I lie on,*
Four angels to my bed; Four angels round my head,
One to watch and one to pray, and two to bear my soul away!

THOMAS ADY (C. '655)

The Golden Mean

Receive, dear friend, the truths I teach,
So shalt thou live beyond the reach
   Of adverse fortune's power;
Not always tempt the distant deep,
Not always timorously creep
   Along the treacherous shore.

He that holds fast the golden mean,
And lives contentedly between
   The little and the great,
Feels not the wants that pinch the poor,
Nor plagues that haunt the rich man's
   door,
   Embittering all his state.

The tallest pines feel most the power
Of wintry blasts; the loftiest tower
   Comes heaviest to the ground.
The bolts that spare the mountain's
   side,
His cloud-capped eminence divide,
   And spread the ruin round.

The well-informed philosopher
Rejoices with a wholesome fear,
   And hopes in spite of pain;
If Winter bellow from the north
Soon the sweet Spring comes dancing
   forth,
   And Nature laughs again.

If hindrances obstruct thy way,
Thy magnanimity display,
   And let thy strength be seen;
But O! if fortune fill thy sail
With more than a propitious gale,
   Take half thy canvas in.

Horace (65–8 BC)
trans. William Cowper (1731–1800)

Comment

The poem is pre-Christian but the translation is, or course, by a devout Christian whom we have met before in this anthology. This choice is apt as an introduction to our thoughts on Prudence since the Christian approach to our moral choices does not regard the Mean as *invariably* the right course to take. It might be said that Caiaphas was moved by the classical virtue of prudence when he judged it to be expedient that one man should die rather than that the whole nation should perish. Bishop Robert Mortimer, sometime Bishop of Exeter and a moral theologian of stature, in his book on moral theology said: 'It is prudence which informs the conscience. When the conscience gives a correct judgment, ordering us to do this particular action, that is an act of prudence'. Jesus stresses the need of the Christian for this virtue in such parables as the wise and foolish virgins, the king who must count the cost of the operation he contemplated, and in the warning that whilst Christians must be 'as harmless as doves', they must also be as 'wise as serpents'.

Prayer   *O Lord from whom all good things do come; grant to us, your humble servants, that by your holy inspiration we may think those things that are good and by your merciful guidance may perform the same, through Jesus Christ our Lord.*

Gelasian Sacramentary

'O World'

O world, thou choosest not the better part!
It is not wisdom to be only wise,
And on the inward vision close the eyes,
But it is wisdom to believe the heart.
Columbus found a world and had no chart,
Save one that faith deciphered in the skies;
To trust the soul's invincible surmise
Was all his science and his only art.
Our knowledge is a torch of smoky pine
That lights the pathway but one step ahead
Across a void of mystery and dread.
Bid, then, the tender light of faith to shine
By which alone the mortal heart is led
Unto the thinking of the thought divine.

GEORGE SANTAYANA (1863–1952)

Comment

Our lives are full of choices, and our hope is always that we shall choose aright. Our poet makes it clear that something more than worldly wisdom is necessary to ensure this. The 'inward vision' must be penetrated; faith must come into our reckoning and, in the end, 'the soul's invincible surmise'. The poet is talking about Christian prudence. There is, for example, the prudence of the unjust steward (St Luke, ch. 16) who, realising that he was about to be sacked by his lord and master for 'fiddling the books', conceived a dishonest scheme which might ensure some future for him even though it might involve blackmail. His lord, we are told commended him because he had behaved astutely, prudently indeed! The steward had fitted his means to a bad end. This was false prudence – evil prudence. There is another sort of prudence which fits the means to a good end for the person who has to make the choice but which, nevertheless is not an end for the common good. This is the prudence of the children of light! If it offers an opportunity of moving towards the common good, it can be a step towards Christian prudence. The third kind of prudence – Christian prudence – takes account of all the circumstances, seeks the counsel of conscience, which must be awake and alert, and by grace moves to a decision. This Christian prudence is not a gift of nature – our poet makes that clear. It is a gift of grace. We may be sure that this virtue like all the others 'attracts' its own vices. The sure protection against these is the grace of God.

Prayer   *Lord God, let me depend on you alone, you who know what is best for me. Guide me in the choices which confront me, enlighten my mind and give me the will to follow the way you direct, in the faith that that way will be both wise and beneficent.*

AFTER ERIC MILNER-WHITE

Aristides the Just

Coming together from all parts of Athens they banished Aristides the Just. Everyone taking a sherd – a piece of earthenware – wrote upon it the name of the citizen he would have banished. It is reported that, as they were writing the names, an illiterate clownish fellow, handing his sherd to Aristides himself, supposing him to be a common citizen, begged him to write *Aristides* upon it. Aristides being surprised, asked: 'Has Aristides ever done you any injury?' 'None at all', said the illiterate man, 'neither know I the man, but I am tired of hearing him everywhere called "the Just" '. Aristides, hearing this, is said to have made no reply, but returned the sherd to the man, with his own name inscribed upon it.

FROM PLUTARCH (46–120 AD)

Comment

We turn to Justice – the second of the so-named cardinal virtues. This incident is a further indication that Justice, which again the Christian Church 'baptised' so that it became a Christian virtue, was itself a pre-Christian principle of civic responsibility. Aristides was a statesman and general of ancient Greece (530–468 BC). He covered himself with glory at the battle of Marathon. Subsequently, as the Archon – chief magistrate – of Athens, he became so highly respected for his impartiality and integrity that he was titled 'Aristides the Just'. His popularity excited the jealousy of Themistocles who engineered his banishment by ostracism. Citizens were entitled to vote, each on an *ostracon* – i.e. a piece of earthenware – for the banishment of anyone who seemed to be becoming too powerful. The 'lay-about' did not understand this example of early democracy! He was prepared to cast his vote against the man whose name was on everybody's lips, namely Aristides. The great man could have inscribed the man's *Ostracon* with the name Themistocles without the illiterate man knowing any difference. Justice was clearly a virtue which the Grecians understood and appreciated when they saw it demonstrated in a statesman's life. It was clearly too a virtue which Aristides himself cherished, or he would at that moment have sacrificed integrity and honour to his own disadvantage. How nearly this one of the four so-named cardinal virtues moves towards the subsequent Christian virtue can be seen in Artistotle's dictum that 'Justice of all the virtues is thought to be a good for others because it has an immediate relation to some other person, inasmuch as the just man does what is advantageous to another, either to his ruler or fellow subject . . . 'He rewarded Justice as in a special sense the perfect Virtue. We shall see how that works out in the Christian context.

Prayer   *Almighty God, who has created man in thine own image, grant us grace fearlessly to contend against evil, and to make no peace with oppression; and, that we may readily use our freedom, help us to employ it in the maintenance of justice among men and nations, to the glory of thy holy name, through Jesus Christ our Lord.*

AMERICAN PRAYER BOOK

I have a Room

But art Thou come, dear Saviour? Hath Thy love
Thus made Thee stoop, and leave Thy throne above
The lofty heavens, and thus Thyself to dress
In dust to visit mortals? Could not less
A condescension serve? And after all,
The mean reception of a cratch and stall?
Dear Lord, I'll fetch Thee thence; I have a room.
'Tis poor but 'tis my best, if Thou wilt come
Within so small a cell, where I would fain
Mine and the world's Redeemer entertain.
I mean my heart; 'tis sluttish, I confess,
And will not mend my lodging, Lord, unless
Thou send before Thy harbinger, I mean
Thy pure and purging grace, to make it clean
And sweep its nasty corners; then I'll try
To wash it also with a weeping eye;
And when 'tis swept and washed, I then will go
And, with thy leave, I'll fetch some flowers that grow
In thine own garden, faith and love to Thee;
With those I'll dress it up ; and these shall be
My rosemary and bays; yet when my best
Is done, the room's not fit for such a guest.
    But here's the cure; Thy presence, Lord, alone
    Will make a stall a court, a cratch a throne.

SIR MATTHEW HALE (1609–1676)

Comment

Justice is a virtue which concerns our relations to others and the first of the others is, for the Christian, the Living God. Christian justice means rendering to God his due, and as a natural consequence of that, rendering to all the children of God, whom we embrace within his family every time we say 'Our Father', everything which is due to them as our brothers and sisters. When the Christian tries to fulfil the first aspect of Christian justice – that is, to give God his due, he realises at once the impossibility of the task. However humbly he tries – as our poet expresses so well – he realises that he falls short of what is due from himself to God. Nevertheless it remains true that Christian justice is first of all the virtue which prompts us to give God his due in worship, in honour and in reverence. For the man who sincerely believes in God as the Creator and Father of all mankind, the exercises of religion – devotion, private prayer, public worship – are his necessary, if humble, efforts to give God his due. In very truth so far has man fallen that in them he cannot but adore and throw himself on to God's mercy. This he must do in public and in private. Christian justice to the living God demands that. It is not by chance that the first clauses of the Lord's Prayer are directed to God's holiness not to man's needs. So it is that having given God his due, Christian justice then turns us naturally to thoughts of forgiveness, compassion and benevolence towards those who are one with us in God's family.

Prayer   *God, whom it belongeth only to adore, teach me, inspire me, assist me to adore.*
Let my adoration be pure and deep, whole and thankful, joyous and silent,
and do thou pardon and accept both it and me, O most pitiful Lord and most
high God.

ERIC MILNER-WHITE

Commemorating Francis of Assisi, Friar, 1226

O Most High, almighty, good Lord God, to Thee belong praise, glory, honour, and all blessing!

Praised be my Lord and God with all His creatures, and especially our brother the sun, who brings us the day, and who brings us the light; fair is he and shining with a very great splendour: O Lord, to us he signifies Thee!

Praised be my Lord for our sister the moon, and for the stars, the which He has set clear and lovely in heaven.

Praised be my Lord for our brother the wind, and for air and cloud, calm and all weather, by the which Thou upholdest in life all creatures.

Praised be my Lord for our sister water, who is very serviceable unto us, and humble, and precious, and clean.

Praised be my Lord for our brother fire, through whom Thou givest us light in the darkness; and he is bright, and pleasant, and very mighty, and strong.

Praised be my Lord for our mother the earth, the which doth sustain and keep us, and bringeth forth divers fruits, and flowers of many colours, and grass.

Praised be my Lord for all those who pardon one another for his love's sake, and who endure weakness and tribulation; blessed are they who peaceably shall endure, for Thou, O most Highest, shall give them a crown.

Praised be my Lord for our sister the death of the body, from whom no man escapeth. Woe to him who dieth in mortal sin! Blessed are they who are found walking by thy most holy will, for the second death shall have no power to do them harm.

Praise ye, and bless ye the Lord, and give thanks unto Him, and serve Him with great humility.

FRANCIS OF ASSISI (1182–1226)

Comment

Our various commemorations have, hitherto, interrupted the flow of our themes. Not so with St Francis in his lovely *Canticle of the Creatures!* As, yesterday, we were thinking of Christian justice which begins by giving God his due, here is St Francis doing just that in his well-known song of praise. So greatly beloved and venerated is this humble man of God that no sustained story of his life is called for here. Suffice it to say that it was his life of poverty and self-denial, his total dedication to God in Christ, and the joy with which he proclaimed Christ's gospel of love by word and deed, that evoked emulation. So there were founded two religious Orders, namely the *Society of St Francis* for the Friars and the *Poor Clares* for the Sisters. Their worship and their work has continued from that day to this – and the world over.

Prayer   *St Francis' Prayer of Praise needs only your 'Amen' to make it yours!*

Huswifery

Make me, O Lord, thy spinning wheel complete,
  Thy holy word my distaff make for me,
Make mine affections thy swift flyers neat,
  And make my soul thy holy spool to be.
  My conversation make to be thy reel,
  And reel the yarn thereon spun off thy wheel.

Make me thy loom then, knit therein this twine;
  And make thy Holy Spirit, Lord, wind quills;
Then weave the web thyself. The yarn is fine.
  Thine ordinances make my fulling mills.
  Then dye the same in heavenly colors choice,
  All pinked with varnished flowers of paradise.

Then clothe therewith mine understanding, will,
  Affections, judgment, conscience, memory,
My words and actions that their shine may fill
  My ways with glory, and thee glorify.
  Then mine apparel shall display before ye
  That I am clothed in holy robes for glory.

EDWARD TAYLOR (1645–1729)

Comment

The poet emigrated to America when he was a young man and after graduating at Harvard he practised medicine in Massachusetts. But he was not only the doctor for the village near Boston where he settled; he was also the people's pastor. He was a strict Puritan deeply concerned for his flock's souls as for their bodies. He despised his own poems, some of which, so metaphysical are they, would need him at hand to interpret. Further he refused to publish any of his verses and the United States knew nothing of the poems until 1937 when a descendant published them. He called his poems 'ragged rhymes' but in this, as in others, he betrays something of his strong faith in God. In this one he is concerned to give God what he conceives to be due to him, namely *glory* spelt out in a complete surrender of himself and his gifts and his work to the Lord. But as filial piety is an imperfect expression of Christian justice, since children can never recompense their parent fully for all they owe to them, so the poet recognises that even though he offers everything he has in the way of talents and gifts, 'affections, judgment, conscience, memory', he is aware that all these come to him from God himself, that these are but the robes in which he is clothed – robes already holy in the light of their Divine source. We may surmise from this dedication of himself that he was to his patients a man whom they could regard as one who 'went about doing good' – an instrument in the hand of God for the healing of body, soul and spirit. Here is someone whom we can emulate!

Prayer   *Make me, O Lord, what you would have me be. Grant me grace to subject my will to your will, that giving you the glory I may serve you ever with a pure mind, through Jesus Christ our Lord.*

Commemorating William Tyndale
Translator of the Bible, 1536

Let it not make thee despair, neither yet discourage thee, O reader, that it is forbidden thee in pain of life and goods, or that it is made breaking of the king's peace, or treason unto his highest, to read the word of thy soul's health; but much rather to be bold in the Lord, and comfort thy soul. Christ is with us unto the world's end. Let his little flock be bold therefore; for if God be on our side what matter maketh it who be against us, be they bishops, cardinals, popes of whatsoever names they will.

They tell you that scripture ought not to be in the mother tongue, but that is only because they fear the light, and desire to lead you blindfold and in captivity. The Old Testament was in the mother tongue; yet those ages were in twilight, while we walk in the noonday; did Christ come to make the world more blind? At that rate he is not the light of the world, but its darkness. They say that laymen would interpret it each after his own way. Why then do the curates not teach people the right way? The scripture would be a basis for such teaching and a test of it. We do not wish to abolish teaching and to make every man his own master; but if the curates will not teach the gospel, the layman must have the scripture and read it for himself, taking God for his teacher.

A thousand more reasons might be given... But I hope that these are sufficient unto them that thirst for the truth. God for his mercy and truth shall well open them more, yea and other secrets of his godly wisdom, if they be diligent to cry unto him; which grace grant God.

WILLIAM TYNDALE (1490–1536)

Comment

The world's debt to William Tyndale is immeasureable. Tyndale was a Gloucester-shire man who whilst he was at Cambridge came under the influence of Erasmus who was his Professor of Greek and Divinity. It was in 1522 that Tyndale decided that he would translate the Bible so that its treasures could be shared by everyone. The Bishop of London refused to support him in such a project, and from high and low came words of vigorous opposition. Undaunted, Tyndale left England and settled in Germany, and it was there that he achieved his aim, though the printing of his translation of the New Testament was halted by the magistrates. At length, however, he completed the New Testament, but when his translation reached England it was bitterly attacked by Archbishop Warham and others. Once more Tyndale ignored the opposition and began his work on the Old Testament and although this too was interrupted, none can deny that our Bible as we have it, both Authorised and Revised versions, differs little from the great work which Tyndale accomplished. He was arrested in 1535 and burnt at the stake on this day in 1536. Undoubtedly he did a great work. We ask ourselves: 'How much does the Bible mean to me?'

Prayer   *Your Word, Lord, is a lamp unto my feet and a light unto my path. Help me to search its secrets diligently, to treasure its truths watchfully and to walk its way faithfully.*

Intolerance

When the white glug contemptuously
Says 'nigger', it is plain to me
He is of lower grade than we.

When the dark stockman, used to hate,
Is not accepted as a mate,
Democracy is empty prate.

When we hear from the white élite,
'We won't have abos in our street',
Their Christianity's a cheat.

When blacks are banned as we know well
From city, café and hotel,
The stink of Little Rock we smell.

Dark children coming home in tears,
Hurt and bewildered by their jeers –
I think Christ weeps with you, my dears.

People who say, by bias driven,
That colour must not be forgiven,
Would snub the Carpenter in heaven.

KATHLEEN WALKER (CONTEMPORARY)

Comment

Kathleen Walker is an Australian poet. She is herself an aboriginal and this poem is one of a collection she has published under the title *My People*. She harbours no bitterness and is very conscious of the way in which things have changed and are changing still for the aboriginals of Australia. Indeed in her subsequent poem entitled *Let us not be bitter*, she wrote, obviously with great satisfaction:

> Away with bitterness, my own dark people,
> Come stand with me, look forward, not back,
> For a new time has come for us. . .
> The past is gone like our childhood days of old
> The future comes like dawn after the dark,
> Bringing fulfilment.

But there are parts of the world where this is far from true and even in our own country there are examples of intolerance. The blacks of South Africa still smart beneath the vicious policy of apartheid which diminishes and deprives thousands. It is not charity the coloured people ask of the white nations. It is justice. Of course we must succour the deprived and the hungry with our charitable gifts. Of course we must help them to help themselves. But we must never suppose that charitable and humanitarian gestures can relieve us of our responsibility to press for Christian justice for them. Every attitude which demeans a fellow human being whose skin happens to be a different colour from our own is an offence against Christian justice. When we pray 'Our Father. . . ' we embrace in our prayer the whole human family in which our black and brown and yellow brothers and sisters are one with us. In our personal contacts with them, in discussions touching their status and welfare, we must speak and act as those who know that they are our neighbours.

Prayer *Lord Jesus, you have taught us that there is no brotherhood of man without the fatherhood of God, help us who pray 'Our Father' to be kindly affectioned one to another in brotherly love.*

Social Justice

1. Every child should find itself a member of a family housed with decency and dignity, so that it may grow up as a member of that basic community in a happy fellowship unspoilt by under-feeding or over-crowding, by dirty and drab surrouundings or by mechanical monotony of employment.

2. Every child should have the opportunity of an education till years of maturity, so planned as to allow for his peculiar aptitudes and make possible their full development. This education should throughout be inspired by God and find its focus in worship.

3. Every citizen should be secure in possession of such income as will enable him to maintain a home and bring up children in such conditions as are described in paragraph 1 above.

4. Every citizen should have a voice in the conduct of the business or industry which is carried on by means of his labour, and the satisfaction of knowing that his labour is directed to the well-being of the community.

5. Every citizen should have sufficient daily leisure, with two days of rest in seven, and, if an employee, an annual holiday with pay, to enable him to enjoy a full personal life with such interests and activities as his tasks and talents may direct.

6. Every citizen should have assured liberty in the forms of freedom of worship, of speech, of assembly, and of association for special purposes.

WILLIAM TEMPLE (1881–1944)

Comment

Here we have Archbishop Temple's summary of what Christian justice demands of society for the highest welfare of its citizens. Some Christians may be tempted to say 'But all these are the responsibilities of economists and politicians, and the Church should keep out of politics'. But the Church cannot keep out of politics because Christianity is concerned with the whole of life and has to be applied to all human relationships. From the days of St Thomas Aquinas, in the thirteenth century, the Church has always claimed a say in everyday affairs and has seen it as its responsibility to speak out against economic, social, or political arrangements which demean or impoverish Man. It was when that claim was muted through the Church's weakness, between the 16th and 19th centuries, that things went awry so far as the highest welfare of Man was concerned. There were years when the Church was merely content to found charities to alleviate the terrible deprivations which so many suffered – content, as Bishop Gore said, 'to go round with an ambulance when it should have been thundering at the gates of hell'. It is not for the Church publicly to ally itself to this or that political party, but it is for the individual Christian to see it as part of the church's mission to denounce whatever affronts the dignity of Man and to press for those which lift the common life to levels consistent with the purpose of God for his people.

Prayer *O God, the King of righteousness, lead us, we pray thee, in the ways of justice and peace; inspire us to break down all tyranny and oppression, to gain for every man his due reward, and from every man his due service; that each may live for all and all may care for each, in the name of Jesus Christ our Lord.*

WILLIAM TEMPLE

Loving, Trusting, Praising

Wilt Love Me? Trust Me? Praise Me?

O thou beloved child of my desire,
Whether I lead thee through green valleys,
> *By still waters,*
> *Or through fire,*
Or lay thee down in silence under snow,
Through any weather, and whatever
> *Clouds may gather,*
> *Wind may blow –*

Wilt love Me? trust Me? praise Me?

No gallant bird, O dearest Lord, am I,
That anywhere, in any weather,
> *Rising singeth;*
> *Low, I lie*
And yet I cannot fear, for I shall soar,
Thy love shall wing me, blessed Saviour;
> *So I answer,*
> *'I adore,*
I love Thee, trust Thee, praise Thee'.

AMY CARMICHAEL (1867–1951)

Comment

It is appropriate that we close our thoughts about Christian justice in the way we began – reminding ourselves that the first expression of Christian justice is that we give God his due. None can pretend that that is always easy, for inwardly we rebel against God, if not in words then in feelings, when we go through a period when everything seems to be going against us. Amy Carmichael first set out on her itinerant missionary work when she was 26. Even before that she had nursed a burning desire to do something for the under-privileged. Motivated by a sense of Christian justice she worked among deprived young people in Belfast and Manchester, did missionary work in Japan for a short spell and in 1895 went to India. It was there that she came up against the pernicious practice of dedicating little girls to Hindu temples – little girls who would ultimately be cult prostitutes, One such infant ran away from the temple where, in effect, she was a prisoner and Amy took care of her. That was the beginning of the Dohnavur Fellowship which has been mentioned in an earlier comment. Amy Carmichael had many frustrations with which to contend and much opposition to counter. Her path of service was not always 'through green valleys'. Clouds gathered and winds blew, but even in the moments when she could not trace the hand of God her faith remained strong. 'There have been times', she wrote in *Things as they are*, 'when I have had to hold on to one text with all my might... "It is required in stewards that a man be found *faithful*". Praise God, it does not say "successful".

Prayer *Almighty God our heavenly Father, you know the needs of your people and you care for them all. Help us to help those who are under-privileged, deprived or forgotten, and in our service ever to turn towards you for strength to carry on.*

Commemorating Paulinus, Bishop, Missionary, 644

Christ and the Pagan

I had no God but these,
The sacerdotal Trees,
And they uplifted me.
'I hung upon a Tree!'

The sun and moon saw,
And reverential awe
Subdued me day and night,
'I am the perfect Light'.

Within a lifeless Stone –
All other gods unknown –
I sought Divinity.
'The Corner-stone am I'

For sacrificial feast,
I slaughtered man and beast,
Red recompense to gain.
'So I, a Lamb, was slain'

'*Yea; such My hungering Grace*
That whereso'er My Face
Is hidden, none may grope
Beyond eternal Hope'.

JOHN BANNISTER TABB (1845–1909)

Comment

The poem is appropriate, for Paulinus met such pagans when he was sent to Northumbria to accompany Ethelburga, daughter of the Christian King of Kent, who was to marry Edwin, the pagan King of Northumbria. With some hesitation Edwin accepted the Christian faith but before he would be baptised he insisted on calling his principal counsellors together – all of them pagans too – to tell them of his conversion to Christianity and to urge them to consider following his example. Coifi, the chief pagan priest, said more or less what the pagan in the poem is saying – that his religion had done nothing for him and that he would try the new religion. Another of the pagan priests declared his intention with words which are memorable. He said 'The life of man, O king, is like the flight of a sparrow through the hall wherein you sit in winter, while outside are storms. The sparrow flies in at one door, but after a short space vanishes out of your sight into the dark winter from which he had emerged. So appears the life of man, and if the new teaching can tell us something more certain of what goes before or what comes after, let us follow it'. Follow it they did, and in their thousands, and because 'oratories and fonts could not be made in the early infancy of the Church in those parts', Paulinus baptised them in the rivers throughout Northumbria. It was Paulinus who began to build York Minster and he also founded Southwell Minster.

Prayer *Almighty God who raised up your servant Paulinus to bring our fathers out of darkness to the splendour of the true light; grant that we who have entered into the fruit of his labour may prove worthy of our inheritance, through Jesus Christ our Lord.*

The Blind Boy

O say! what is that Thing called
* Light,*
* Which I can ne'er enjoy;*
What is the blessing of the sight,
* O tell your poor Blind Boy!*

You talk of wondrous things you see,
* You say the sun shines bright;*
I feel him warm, but how can he
* Then make it Day or Night?*

My Day or Night myself I make,
* When'er I wake or play;*
And could I ever keep awake
* It would be always Day.*

With heavy sighs, I often hear,
* You mourn my hopeless woe;*
But sure, with patience I may bear
* A loss I ne'er can know.*

Then let not what I cannot have
* My cheer of mind destroy;*
Whilst thus I sing, I am a king,
* Although a poor blind boy.*

COLLEY CIBBER (1671–1757)

Comment

Colley Cibber was a poet, dramatist and actor who became Poet Laureate and by his acceptance of that honour drew upon himself the criticism of other poets of the day, including Pope. His moving little poem spells out something of the virtue which we reach in our thoughts about the Christian virtues – namely fortitude. Those around the little lad certainly did not help with their 'heavy sighs' about his hopeless woe. He faced his disability with fortitude and cherished a 'cheer of mind' which probably baffled his associates, but which was so strong that nothing and none could destroy it. His fortitude was not the pre-Christian fortitude which was seen as something which a man needed for, and exhibited in, wars on behalf of the state. His was a fortitude which resided within him and one which, we doubt not, was a gift of the Spirit of God. Perhaps the poem says two things to us. The first, that we do not help one who is disabled in any way by constant references to his disability. We help by fastening upon the ways in which he overcomes it and entering into his 'cheer of mind'. The second is that under any sort of pressure or disability the Christian can call on resources of power which will help him to bear with fortitude his own 'hopeless woe', and that to his own joy and, maybe, to the wonder of those about him.

Prayer   *O Lord Jesus Christ, perfect God and perfect man, we ask that you bless all the work which is being carried out in your name, in this land and elsewhere, on behalf of those who are blind or deaf and dumb. Strengthen and inspire with your Holy Spirit all who are engaged in this work. Endue them with patience, cheerfulness and courage and help them to pass on these gifts so that those whom they serve may be strengthened with the spirit of fortitude – all this to your honour and glory.*

Stanzas on Freedom

Men whose boast it is that ye
Come of fathers brave and free,
If there breathe on earth a slave,
Are ye truly free and brave?
If ye do not feel the chain,
When it works a brother's pain,
Are ye not base slaves indeed,
Slaves unworthy to be freed?
Is true Freedom but to break
Fetters for our own dear sake,
And, with leathern hearts, forget
That we owe mankind a debt?

No! true freedom is to share
All the chains our brothers wear,
And, with heart and hand, to be.
Earnest to make others free!
They are slaves who fear to speak
For the fallen and the weak;
They are slaves who will not choose
Hatred, scoffing and abuse,
Rather than in silence shrink
From the truth they needs must think;
They are slaves who dare not be
In the right with two or three.

J. RUSSELL LOWELL (1819–1891)

Comment

Here is another example of what Christian fortitude demands. The poet, who also wrote a number of hymns, is pleading for his fellow countrymen – he was an American – to have the courage of their own convictions. He was a poet of distinction, a great patriot and a vigorous opponent of slavery. His most well-known hymn is *Once to every man and nation comes the moment to decide* – to decide, that is, between truth and falsehood, good and evil, between freedom and slavery. He was also a diplomat, one time Ambassador in London and in Madrid. Certainly he cherished the virtue of fortitude and by what he wrote and what he said none could doubt that here was a man with convictions which he derived from his Christian faith. There is in our own day not slavery in the sense in which that word was once used, when men, women and children were bought and sold, but there is much exploitation, there is unfairness, there is much that demeans many in the human family. Let us take the poet's challenge to our own hearts:

We see dimly in the present what is small and what is great,
Slow of faith, how weak an arm may turn the iron arm of fate;
But the soul is still prophetic; list amid the market's din
To the ominous stern whisper of the oracle within,
'They enslave their children's children who make compromise with sin'

Prayer   *Heavenly Father, strengthen us to meet all the experiences of daily life with a steadfast and undaunted heart. When we are confronted with evil give us the courage of our convictions that we may stand fast in the path of righteousness to the glory of your holy name.*

Commemorating Edward the Confessor
King of England d.1066

Upon Westminster Bridge

Earth has not anything to show more fair:
Dull would he be of soul who could pass by
A sight so touching in its majesty:
This City now doth, like a garment, wear
The beauty of the morning; silent, bare,
Ships, towers, domes, theatres, and temples lie
Open unto the fields, and to the sky;
All bright and glittering in the smokeless air.
Never did sun more beautifully steep
In his first splendour, valley, rock or hill;
Ne'er saw I, never felt, a calm so deep!
The river glideth at his own sweet will:
Dear God! the very houses seem asleep;
And all that mighty heart is lying still!

WILLIAM WORDSWORTH (1770–1850)

Comment

That was the experience which Wordsworth appreciated on 3rd September 1802. Now he would find it necessary to be up and about very early indeed to find 'a calm so deep'; nor would he see any buildings 'open unto the fields'. The river glides still and the sight is still 'touching in its majesty' for the Palace of Westminster and the Abbey abide. Nor can the eye rest upon the Abbey without remembering Edward the Confessor. He was a godly man who reigned not merely over a country but in the hearts of his people. Butler's *Lives of the Saints* says of him – 'The love, harmony and agreement seen in retrospect between him and the great Council of the Nation became the traditional measures of the people's desires in all succeeding reigns. He was generous to the poor and strangers, and a great encourager of monks . . . and he never omitted to be present at Mass every morning'. During his exile in Normandy he vowed that he would go on a pilgrimage to the tomb of St Peter in Rome but when he became king his counsellors advised him that it would be unwise to leave the country. He asked the Pope to release him from his vow and His Holiness agreed, provided that Edward would donate all the money which the pilgrimage would have cost him towards the endowment of a monastery in honour of St Peter. Thus was Westminster Abbey built on the site of a smaller abbey-church. It was consecrated on Holy Innocents' Day 1065 by which time the king was too ill to be present. He died a week later and lies buried in the Abbey. He had been conspicuous for his piety, his gentleness and sheer goodness. He has always been known as 'the Confessor' because, although he was not called to martyrdom, he went through periods of acute suffering for the Faith which he confessed so bravely. Other kings of England have other memorials. None has a finer than Edward the Confessor, and if we knew no more about him than that he built the Abbey his name can never be omitted from the calendar of our Church.

Prayer

Almighty Father, who set your servant Edward upon the throne of an earthly kingdom and, by the grace of your spirit, inspired him with zeal for the kingdom of your dear Son. Grant us so faithfully to love and serve you in this life, that with him we may inherit the kingdom of your glory, through Jesus Christ our Lord.

Say not the Struggle

Say not the struggle naught availeth,
The labour and the wounds are vain,
The enemy faints not, nor faileth,
And as things have been, things remain.

If hopes were dupes, fears may be liars;
It may be, in yon smoke concealed,
Your comrades chase e'en now the fliers,
And, but for you, possess the field.

For while the tired waves, vainly breaking,
Seem here no painful inch to gain,
Far back, through creeks, and inlets making,
Come silent, flooding in, the main.

And not by eastern windows only,
When daylight comes, comes in the light,
In front the sun climbs slow, how slowly,
But westward, look the land is bright.

ARTHUR HUGH CLOUGH (1819–1861)

Comment

Here is the poet who was at Rugby School when Thomas Arnold was its head-master. He was a man of intellectual stature and many of his longer poems are perhaps the more well known. Doubtless he faced, as do all of us, struggles which momentarily defy resolution – struggles touching our work, our hobbies, our personal relationships, our faith. There comes the moment when we are tempted to surrender and 'as things have been, things remain'. But our poet is urging us not to give way. He is counselling us to grasp the virtue of fortitude. The task has to be accomplished, the problem has to be resolved, the doubts have to be discounted, the struggle will not be in vain. Our thoughts about the Christian virtue of fortitude began by our differentiating Christian fortitude from the pre-Christian virtue which saw it only in relation to wars and a man's civic responsibility. Physical discipline and self-imposed trials of endurance were the order of the day. It is interesting that the word *courage* occurs only once in the New Testament. Christian fortitude is the quality which sustains a man in his contest with his lower nature, in his meeting with his inner struggles, in his attitude to his misfortunes, in his tenacious holding on to his faith when things seem to conspire against him. Christian fortitude is concerned with meeting dangers to the soul, as well as meeting 'the slings and arrows of outrageous fortune'. Either way, the Christian can take up spiritual arms against any 'sea of troubles' and know that his Lord's promise remains for ever true: 'I am with you always'.

Prayer

Look upon us and hear us, O Lord our God; assist those endeavours to please you which you yourself have granted to us; as you have given us the first act of will, so give the completion of the work; grant that by perseverance we may be able to finish what you have granted us the wish to begin; through Jesus Christ our Lord.

MOZARABIC LITURGY

Commemorating Teresa of Avila, Mystic, 1582

The Teresian Contemplative

She moves in tumult; round her lies
The silence of the world of grace;
The twilight of our mysteries
Shines like high noonday on her face;
Our piteous guesses, dim with fears,
She touches, handles, sees and hears.

In her all longings mix and meet;
Dumb souls through her are eloquent;
She feels the world beneath her feet
Thrill in a passionate intent;
Through her our tides of feeling roll
And find their God within her soul.

Her face the awful Face of God
Brightens and blinds with utter light;
Her footsteps fall where late He trod;
She sinks in roaring voids of night;
Cries to her Lord in black despair,
And knows, yet knows not, He is there.

A willing sacrifice she takes
The burden of our fall within;
Holy she stands; while on her breaks
The lightning of the wrath of sin;
She drinks her Saviour's cup of pain,
And, one with Jesus, thirsts again.

ROBERT HUGH BENSON (1871–1914)

Comment

Teresa, the Spanish Carmelite nun and mystic, was born in 1515. She had three brothers and nine sisters and all of them from time to time played at being monks and nuns! Following the death of her mother, Teresa went through a period of 'teenage indiscipline'; but a short time in a convent under Augustine rule transformed her life and thinking, and it was during her time there that she began to think seriously of becoming a nun. However, a severe illness prevented this for the time being and it was on her complete recovery at the age of 18 that she decided to enter the Convent of the Incarnation at Avila. It was then that her life of prayer and mysticism began. It is recorded that 'in twenty years she had filled Spain with monasteries, in which more than a thousand religious praised God'. The way had not been easy for her and she frequently found herself moving 'in tumult' in her efforts to reform the Carmelite Order. She wrote several substantial books about the spiritual life, notably: *The Way of Perfection, Foundations* and *The Interior Castle.* She might be described as a 'Martha-Mary' saint for she demonstrated that ceaseless activity for Christ's work and constant pursuit of the way of perfection through prayer were both necessary elements of Christian commitment. Some lines written in her Breviary confirm this and they can easily be adapted as our Prayer

Prayer   *Let nothing disturb thee,*
Nothing affright thee;
All things are passing
God never changeth;
Patient endurance
Attaineth to all things;
Who God possesseth
In nothing is wanting;
Alone God sufficeth.

The Ten Commandments

I	*Have thou no other gods but me,*
II	*And to no image bow thy knee.*
III	*Take not the name of God in vain:*
IV	*The Sabbath day do not profane.*
V	*Honour thy father and mother too;*
VI	*And see that thou no murder do.*
VII	*Abstain from words and deeds unclean;*
VIII	*Nor steal, though thou art poor and mean.*
IX	*Bear not false witness, shun that blot;*
X	*What is thy neighbour's covet not.*

ANONYMOUS (1731)

Comment

Would that the Ten Commandments revealed to Moses on Mount Sinai had been as brief and succinct as the eighteenth-century rhymester has made them. Life would have been so much easier for those who were young when I was and who were expected to know them by heart before Confirmation. And how much less irksome it would have been for those whose task it was to engrave them on stone! The rhymester has everything in his summary which really matters, remembering, of course, that the Commandments were based on the Hebrew monotheistic conception of God. They are rarely heard in our churches nowadays nor can they be seen boldly and often artistically displayed on the interior walls of the church as was once the case. Tertullian, the Great Christian theologian of the third century regarded them as having been engraven on human hearts long before they were engraven on stone. They were part of the 'Natural Law' and demanded acceptance from all God's people. Other great Christian teachers, Augustine and Thomas Aquinas for example, treated them with great respect and, like the Church of England later, they used them for instructing young catechumens. They were inserted into the Church's 1552 prayer book as part of the Holy Communion service and so they remained until 1928 when a revised prayer book contained an abbreviated version of them. The Alternative Services Book has omitted them and inserted in their place a reading from the New Testament, and of course the *Kyrie Eleison*: (Lord, have mercy). Some people have complained that these stern reminders of the moral law are no longer heard in an age when so much that they condemn fills our papers day by day. It may well be true that we do need in our day more explicit 'Thou shalt NOT's. The same sort of complaints reached our Lord's ears – complaints that the Law was being not merely defied but destroyed. This is what prompted his: 'I came not to destroy the Law but to fulfil it' – that was to fill it full of its deepest meaning. That He did, and we can in the coming days think of the Commandments one by one to consider how our Lord did just that and what it demands of us.

Prayer *Almighty God, we know that by your servant Moses you gave your people the Law; we know that by your Son our Saviour Jesus Christ the Law was fulfilled in his new commandment of Love. Give us grace that it may be fulfilled in our lives day by day, through the same Jesus Christ our Lord.*

Commemorating Ignatius, Bishop of Antioch, Martyr, c. 107

From Ignatius, whose other name is Theophorus... Greeting, in the name of Jesus Christ the Father's Son. All perfect happiness in Jesus Christ our Lord, to you who are bodily and spiritually at one with all his commandments, wholeheartedly filled with the grace of God, and purified from every alien and discolouring stain.

My prayers that I might live to see your beloved community face to face have been answered; since I can now hope to greet you in the very chains of a prisoner of Jesus Christ, if his will permits me to reach my journey's end. So far, things have made an admirable beginning; and all now depends on whether I can reach the goal and secure my inheritance without hindrance. But what fills me with fear is your own kindly feeling for me, and the disservice it may do me. What you are bent on doing will certainly present no difficulties to yourselves, but for me it is going to be very hard to get to God unless you spare me your intervention.

It is not men that I want you to gratify, but God just as you habitually do... By staying silent and letting me alone you can turn me into an intelligible utterance of God; but if your affections are only concerned with my poor human life, then I become a meaningless cry once more. This favour only I beg of you, suffer me to be a libation poured out to God while there is still an altar ready for me... How good it is to be sinking down before the world's horizon towards God, to rise again later into the dawn of his presence!

St Ignatius (35–107)

Comment

Before his conversion Ignatius was a pagan and an active one in that he played a part in the persecution of the Christians. Ultimately he became as ardent winning people for Christ as he had been in turning them from Christ. He became Bishop of Antioch in Syria. All we know about his life and work is what is contained in a series of Pauline-type letters which he wrote to different Churches, for example to the Church in Rome, in Smyrna and in Philadelphia. These reveal how passionately he believed in the Divinity and the Humanity of Christ and in the Church as the Body of Christ. He exalts too the office of the bishop as in some sense standing in for Christ in the shepherding and feeding of the flock through the Eucharist. It was on his way to Rome, where he knew that he was to meet his death at the hands of Trajan's officers, that he wrote the letter from which the above quotation is an extract. He pleads with the Roman Christians to make no excuses for him, for he had no intention of rendering to Caesar what belonged only to God. He was martyred in the year 107. His second name, Theophorus, means 'one who carries God in his heart'. Can there be a more appropriate prayer for us to offer today than a prayer which asks that we may do just that:

Prayer   *God be in my head, and in my understanding;*
God be in mine eyes, and in my looking;
God be in my mouth, and in my speaking;
God be in my heart, and in my thinking;
God be at mine end, and at my departing.
AMEN

St Patrick's Breastplate

St Luke the Evangelist

Saint Luke the Painter

Give honour unto Luke Evangelist;
For he it was (the aged legends say)
Who first taught Art to fold her hands and pray.
Scarcely at once she dared to rend the mist
Of devious symbols; but soon having wist
How sky-breadth and field-silence and this day
Are symbols also in some deeper way,
She looked through these to God and was God's priest.

And if, past noon, her toil began to irk,
And she sought talismans and turned in vain
To soulless self-reflections of man's skill –
Yet now, in this the twilight, she might still
Kneel in the latter grass to pray again,
Ere the night cometh and she may not work.

DANTE GABRIEL ROSSETTI (1828–1882)

Comment

Our author was a Pre-Raphaelite poet and painter. In all his early poetry Christian themes are dominant. St Luke, who is the patron saint of doctors (Luke, the beloved physician) and the patron saint of artists, is seen by Rossetti as one who brought to the field of art a sensitivity to holy things which it sometimes lacked. Scripture attests that Luke was trained in the science of medicine but there is no such evidence that he was also a painter though there is to this day, in one of Spain's cathedrals, a painting of Our Lady which is attributed to St Luke. An artist Luke certainly was, for no one who could write such a beautiful book as the Gospel which bears his name could be other than a man with a rich artistic temperament. Luke was also the author of the *Acts of the Apostles* and that, too, has such careful documentation and detail in it that Luke could claim the title of historian. Unlike all the other authors of New Testament books Luke was a Gentile. He addresses his Gospel to one Theophilus and, since he calls him 'Most Excellent', it would appear that Luke had, as it were, friends at court whom he wished to win for Christ. St Luke accompanied St Paul on his second and third missionary journeys and it is clear that they became bosom friends. Furthermore he was with Paul for some of his time in prison and indeed in Paul's second letter to Timothy, written not long before his execution, he added the pathetic note: 'Only Luke is with me'. Luke's Gospel has been described as especially the gospel of prayer and of praise – he it is who gives us the *Magnificat*, the *Benedictus* and the *Nunc Dimittis* – and it is the gospel of women. Women were very much the 'underdogs', and Luke makes much of all Christ's contacts with women, determined as he was to stress that in Christ's new order women were equal in stature with men within the family of God. There were to be no second class citizens within the kingdom of God.

Prayer *Almighty God, who inspired Luke the physician to proclaim the love and healing power of your Son; give your Church, by the grace of the Spirit and through the medicine of the gospel, the same love and power to heal; through Jesus Christ our Lord.*

Elevation

Above the pools, above the valley of fears,
Above the woods, the clouds, the hills, the trees,
Beyond the sun's and the moon's mad mysteries,
Beyond the confines of the starry spheres,

My spirit, you move with a pure ardency,
And, as one who swoons in the senses of sound,
You furrow furiously the immensity profound
With an indictable and male sensuality.

Fly from those morbid miasmas and their mire;
Purify your own self in the mid air malign,
And there drink, as a delicious and rare wine,
The enormity and the intensity of fire.

Beyond the universe and the vast chagrins
Which load the smoky air with their existence,
Joyous is he who can with a bird's persistence
Rush toward the heavens not fashioned by our sins!

He whose thoughts, like the lark that sings and wings
Its way at dawn toward the sky in a higher flight,
Wandering over the immensity of the night,
Knows the flowers' speech and the speech of silent things!

CHARLES BAUDELAIRE (1821–1867)
TRANS. ARTHUR SYMONS 1865–1945)

Comment

Turning to the rhyme about the Ten Commandments (October 16th) and reading the first line: 'Have thou none other gods but me', we know that that was God, through Moses, telling his people to run away from their many gods to the Living God. They were being summoned to turn away from polytheism – the worship of many gods – to monotheism, the worship of the one personal and transcendent God. But we must not dismiss the commandment as though it is now irrelevant to ourselves since we do worship that one personal transcendent God. Charles Baudelaire was a Christian but one has only to read his poem to see that he was ever fearful that he would be worshipping other gods – and he was for ever trying to lift himself above them towards the Living God. The translator of his poem – himself a Welsh poet – describes him as a 'man with a passionate devotion to passions' and in his poems there is 'a deliberate science of sensual and sexual perversity'. Yet Baudelaire was a professing Christian – a Christian who had 'other gods', but a Christian who could still write in one of his works: 'The man who says his prayers in the evening is a captain posting his sentries. After that, he can sleep'. The truth is, of course, that all of us are tempted to worship 'other gods'. A man's god is that to which, or to whom, he yields himself totally. It may be money, leisure or that 'sensual and sexual perversity' which dogged Baudelaire. Our Lord's last word on the Cross was 'Father into your hands I commend my spirit'. He to whom, or that to which, a man commends his spirit is the decisive test. Is our commendation to God, or to a god?

Prayer *O God, Creator of all things and lover of all your children, shed forth continual day upon us who watch and look for you, that our lips may praise you, our lives may bless you, and our meditations may glorify you, our One True God.*

Essay on Man

What if the foot, ordained the dust to tread,
Or hand to toil, aspired to be the head?
What if the head, the eye, or ear repined
To serve mere engines to the ruling mind?
Just as absurd for any part to claim
To be another, in this general frame;
Just as absurd to mourn the tasks or pains
The great Directing Mind of all ordains.

All are but parts of one stupendous whole,
Whose body Nature is, and God the soul;
That, changed through all, and yet in all the same;
Great in the earth, as in the ethereal frame;
Warms in the sun, refreshes in the breeze,
Glows in the stars, and blossoms in the trees;
Lives through all life, extends through all extent;
Spreads undivided, operates unspent!
Breathes in our soul, informs our mortal part,
As full, as perfect in a hair as heart;
As full, as perfect in vile Man that mourns,
As the rapt Seraph that adores and burns;
To him no high, no low, no great, no small;
He fills, He bounds, connects, and equals all.

ALEXANDER POPE (1688–1744)

Comment

The lines are from Pope's *The Essay on Man*. 'To no image bow thy knee', said the second line of our Commandments' rhyme, summarising the second commandment. There are, as our Book of Common Prayer reminds us, 'all sorts and conditions of men'. Man oscillates between heaven and hell, between good and evil. Sometimes he makes his own gods as we were reminding ourselves yesterday, sometimes he makes God's creatures his god. He does not in these enlightened days sit down to construct idols of wood or stone but by his attitude he sets himself above 'the great Directing Mind', or sets God's creatures above God himself, or equates God's creations with God, as does the pantheist. Man stands in ever present danger of making an idol of himself or of others or of God's creation. As Cardinal Newman puts it in *The Dream of Gerontius*

> *O Man, strange composite of Heaven and Earth!*
> *Majesty dwarfed to baseness! fragrant flower*
> *Running to poisonous seed! and seeming worth*
> *Cloaking corruption! weakness mastering power!*

Putting his ultimate trust in himself Man is soon deceived. Oscar Wilde once quipped that he sometimes thought that God in creating Man 'somewhat over-estimated his ability'. He was wrong, for there is such a thing as Grace which has made Man and can make Man 'Heaven's masterpiece'.

Prayer

The dearest idol I have known,
Whate'er that idol be,
Help me to tear it from thy throne,
And worship only Thee.

WILLIAM COWPER (1731–1800)

Evening

It is the silent hour when they who roam,
  Seek shelter, on the earth, or ocean's
breast;
It is the hour when travel finds a home,
  On deserts, or within the cot to rest.
  It is the hour when joy or grief are blest
And Nature finds repose where'er she roves;
  It is the hour that lovers like the best,
When in the twilight shades, or darker
groves,
The maiden wanders with the swain she
loves.

The balmy hour when fond hearts fondly
meet;
  The hour when dew like welcome rest descends
On wild flowers, shedding forth their odours
sweet;

  The hour when sleep lays foes as quiet
friends; –
The hour when labour's toilworn journey
ends.
And seeks the cot for sweet repose till morn;
  The hour when prayer from all to God as-
cends; –
At twilights's hour love's softest sighs are
born,
When lovers linger neath the flowering thorn.

Oh! at this hour I love to be abroad,
  Gazing upon the moonlit scene around,
Looking through Nature up to Nature's God.
  Regarding all with reverence profound!
  The wild flowers studding every inch of
ground,
And trees, with dews bespangled, looking
bright
  As burnished silver; – while the entranc-
ing sound
Of melody, from the sweet bird of night,
Fills my whole soul with rapture of delight.

JOHN CLARE (1793–1864)

Comment

'Take not the name of God in vain' says our rhymester summing up the third commandment. Here is the commandment which bids us to shun profanity whether in the use of God's name, God's purpose, God's creation. It is a call for reverence which is, in fact, the first element of religion. John Clare's poem reveals his own reverent approach to the whole of life. He saw it as something which touched the behaviour of the 'younger lovers in the twilight shades'. He saw it as something due to all created things – the flowers, the trees, the birds – and that because he could look through these 'up to Nature's God.' Writing specifically to young people in the seventeenth century, Francis Hawkins counselled them: 'Let thy speeches be seriously reverent when thou speakest of God or his attributes; for to jest or utter thyself lightly in matters divine is an unhappy impiety, provoking heaven to justice, and urging all men to suspect thy belief'. He could with profit say the same to people today and not merely the young. But I fancy that he would say something to the young of even greater urgency, something such as 'Reverence your body. It is the dwelling place of your self. To do anything to harm it is blasphemy against God and injurious to his greatest gift to you. Say, 'No' to drugs'.

Prayer   *O God, most holy, most loving, infinite in wisdom and power: Teach us to reverence you in all the works of your hands, and to hallow your name both in our lives and in our worship: through Jesus Christ our Lord.*

Sir Roger de Coverley at Church

I am always very well pleased with a country Sunday, and think if keeping holy the seventh day were only a human institution, it would have been the best method that could have been thought of for the polishing and civilising of mankind... and for joining together in adoration of the Supreme Being... Sunday clears away the rust of the whole week, not only as it refreshes in their minds the notions of religion, but as it puts both the sexes upon appearing in their most agreeable forms and exerting all such qualities as are apt to give them a figure in the eye of the village ..

My friend Sir Roger being a good churchman, has beautified the inside of his church with several texts of his own choosing; he has likewise given a handsome pulpit cloth, and railed in the communion table at this own expense. He has often told me, that at his coming to his estate he found his parishioners very irregular; and that in order to make them kneel and join in the responses, he gave every one of them a hassock and a common-prayer book; and at the same time employed an itinerant singing master, who goes about the country for that purpose, to instruct them rightly in the tunes of the psalms; upon which they now very much value themselves, and indeed outdo most of the country churches I have heard.

Joseph Addison (1672–1719)

Comment

'The Sabbath day do not profane', says the rhyme. The Sabbath day was, of course, the seventh day of the week and Sunday, the day of the Resurrection, was the first. Given that amendment Christians can and should accept the command that they should keep it holy! 'But should they not keep all days holy?' retorts the purist. The answer is indubitably 'Yes'. But as the ancient people of God believed it to be right that there should be a 'day of rest' which should be hedged about by restrictions to ensure that everyone should enjoy it, and everyone should have opportunity to worship, so from the beginning the Church celebrated the Resurrection by instituting Sunday as its 'special' day for worship and for rest. In the days when Puritanism held sway in our country the rigid 'Thou shalt not's of the Jewish Sabbath were imposed upon Christians, and an oppressive Sabbatarianism wrung all the joy out of the Day of Resurrection. Things are not easy for the Christian today since the trend has for long been to deprive Sunday of its special character. God forbid that we should become dogmatically sabbatarian, but God forbid too that Sunday should become precisely the same as other days! Sir Roger apparently knew what was the first duty on a Sunday – that of joining in public worship. It remains so, but that does not rule out opportunities for rest and recreation.

Comment

Teach us, good Lord, to use our Sundays for the worship of your holy name and the refreshment of our souls and bodies. Prosper the efforts of all those whose resolve it is to preserve the sanctity of this holy day to your glory and the welfare of your people, through Jesus Christ our Lord.

The Family

The Englishman's home used to be his castle. In modern life it is coming to be regarded as somewhere to sleep next to the garage. How can it be made into a home again? This is the most searching moral issue that Christianity today has to face... The weakening of the Christian belief and the disintegration of the family seem to be mutually involved together. Here the Christian faith is on trial at the very heart and nerve centre of the world's ethical and religious problem. For it is probably true on the whole that the religious and moral scepticism which is paralysing our contemporaries is due less to intellectual solvents than to the seeming failure of home life. The modern man thinks he has been betrayed in the citadel of his inmost intimacies. Bertrand Russell no doubt exaggerates when he asserts that in nine cases out of ten the relations between children and parents are a source of unhappiness to both parties. He must have moved and formed his social judgments in a sombrely monochrome environment. But he is, I believe, profoundly right in saying that 'the failure of the family to provide the fundamental satisfactions which in principle it is capable of yielding is one of the most deep-seated causes of the discontent prevalent in our age'. If the world is to recover moral mastery it is here that Christianity must help it.

BISHOP RUSSELL BARRY (1890–1976)

Comment

> Christ is the Head of this House
> The Unseen Guest at every meal
> The Silent Listener to every conversation.

I recall that in my boyhood days I never sat down to a meal without looking at the sampler hanging on the wall opposite me which bore those words. They exercised a profound effect on me as I doubt not they did on every member of the family.

The quotation from Bishop Barry's book *The Relevance of Chritianity*, which was written in 1951, is itself sad reading, but none alas! would dispute the contention that the quality of family life has deteriorated vastly since then. The Commandment, summed up by our anonymous rhymester in six words – 'Honour thy father and mother too' – was much more than an exhortation to children. Looked at through Christian spectacles the commandment calls for the santification of family life, and that is something which parents and children alike can either nurture or destroy. For thousands there is no no such thing as 'Home, sweet home'. Divorce, unemployment, poor housing, licentiousness, lack of parental guidance or the refusal of the young to accept it – all these and more contribute to the breakdowns and increase the misery of all concerned. Whatever as individuals we can do to mend what is broken and to heal what is sick will be blessed by God. The Commandment, in effect, calls on Christians to regard the home as a sanctuary with Christ as the Head of the House. There may still be differences and discords, strains and stresses, but with Christ as Lord 'all shall be well and all manner of thing shall be well'.

Prayer *Give us of your goodness, Lord; inspire us with your love; guide us by your Spirit; protect us by your power, and let your blessing rest upon our house and home.*

The Tree of Life

The Master said:
  'I have planted the Seed of a Tree,
It shall be strangely fed,
With white dew and with red,
  And the Gardeners shall be three –
  Regret, Hope, Memory!'

The Master smiled:
  For the seed which he had set
Broke presently through the mould,
With a glimmer of green and gold.
  And the Angels' eyes were wet –
  Hope, Memory, Regret.

The Master said:
  'It liveth – breatheth – see!
Its soft lids open wide –
It looks from side to side –
  How strange they gleam on me,
  The little dim eyes of the Tree!'

The Master said:
  'After a million years,
The seed I set and fed
To itself hath gathered
  All the world's smiles and tears –
How mighty it appears!'

ROBERT BUCHANAN (1841–1901)

Comment

Our poet, a master of the mystical verse, included in his *Ballads of Life, Love and Humour* a long poem under the above title. The poem is concerned with the sanctity of life and moves in its subsequent verses to see that Sanctity in perfection in our Lord. The sixth commandment may well have meant no more than what it says – 'Thou shalt no murder do' – in its Hebrew context, but again through Christian eyes its concern is with the sanctity of human life. It is interesting to note that the last five of the Commandments are all concerned with injuries to others – that is, with offences against human life, against chastity, against property and against character. In the context of this Commandment the Christian must know where he stands in discussions and debates concerned with human life. The wanton destruction of human life, capital punishment, euthanasia, drug abuse – everything which conspires to destroy what only God can create, must arouse Christians to very serious consideration of what is at stake. Conversely we must applaud all that is done to preserve life in, for example, humanitarian work at home and overseas, and all that is done in the world of medicine and surgery in our hospitals here at home.

Prayer   *Merciful Father, you have wonderfully fashioned man in your own image, making his body to be a temple of the Holy Spirit, we ask you to sanctify all those who have dedicated their lives to the healing of the sick and the preservation of life. Bless them in their work, and those whom they serve in their need, that all things may be to your honour and glory, through Jesus Christ our Lords.*

The Character of a Happy Life

How happy is he born and taught
That serveth not another's will;
Whose armour is his honest thought,
And simple truth his utmost skill!

Whose passions not his masters are;
Whose soul is still prepared for death,
Not tied unto the world by care
Of public fame or private breath;
Who envies none that chance doth raise,
Nor vice; who never understood
How deepest wounds are given by praise;
Not rules of state, but rules of good;

Who hath this life from rumours freed;
Whose conscience is his strong retreat;
Whose state can neither flatterers feed,
Nor ruin make oppressors great;

Who God doth late and early pray
More of His grace than gifts to lend;
And entertains the harmless day
With a religious book or friend; –
This man is freed from servile bands
Of hope to rise or fear to fall:
Lord of himself, though not of lands,
And having nothing, yet hath all.

HENRY WOOTTON (1568–1639)

Comment

Our Commandments' rhyme deals with the seventh Commandment somewhat delicately by summarising it thus: 'Abstain from words and deeds unclean'. The Bible does not shrink from the word adultery and we recall that our Lord was once confronted with the woman 'taken in adultery', an offence which, under the Rabbinic law, was punishable by death (St John ch.7 v.53). As the Commandment reads, it condemns adultery. As the Christian reads it, it calls for chastity and the control of the passions. In his poem Sir Henry Wooton describes the man as happy 'whose passions not his masters are' and the man who has his passions well controlled as 'freed from servile bands'. Chastity is not concerned merely with physical purity. It is one aspect of that love of neighbour by which the Christian is bound. The catechism in the Book of Common Prayer teaches 'every person before he be brought to be confirmed by the bishop' that it is part of his duty to his neighbour to keep his body 'in temperance, soberness and chastity'. Uncontrolled passions can wreak uncontrollable havoc in human lives. When the storm threatens within us we should do well to turn to our Lord as did the disciples when they were threatened with shipwreck and to plead in an 'arrow prayer' – 'Lord, save us, we perish'.

Prayer   *O Lord God, King of Heaven and earth, may it please you to order and to hallow, to rule and to govern, our hearts and bodies, our thoughts and our works and our words, that we being helped by you, may not bring suffering to others, and in your service may glorify your holy Name.*

Integer Vitae

The man of life upright,
    Whose guileless heart is free
From all dishonest deeds,
    Or thought of vanity.

The man whose silent days
    In harmless joys are spent
Whom hope cannot delude
    Nor sorrows discontent;

That man needs neither towers
    Nor armour for defence,
Nor secret vaults to fly
    From thunder's violence;

He only can behold
    With unaffrighted eyes
The horrors of the deep
    And terrors of the skies.

Thus, scorning all the cares
    That fate or fortune brings
He makes the heaven his book,
    His wisdom heavenly things.

Good thoughts his only friends,
    His wealth a well-spent age,
The earth his sober inn
    And quiet pilgrimage.

HORACE (65–8 BC)
TRANS. THOMAS CAMPION (1565–1620)

Comment

Quintus Horatius Flaccus has been described as the Poet Laureate of his day such was the quality and quantity of his poems. This poem – its title is roughly translated in its first line – reveals him as an honest and upright man. He was apparently a jolly sort of fellow who could write amusingly about his not very distinguished days as a soldier. So here we have a godly pagan translated by a Christian poet. Honesty was not a 'Christian invention' and 'Thou shalt not steal' was not a Commandment which struck an entirely new ethical principle. But here again there is more in this Commandment than meets the eye. Theft is the taking in secret of what belongs to another – an act which is always a sin, first because it flies in the face of justice and secondly because of the guile which motivates the thief. But we cannot dismiss this Commandment summarily as one which bears no reference to ourselves. Our poet began his verses by his assertion that 'the man of life upright' was the man who was 'free of all dishonest deeds'. Pagan though he was he would doubtless have accepted the Christian principle which extends this Commandment to embrace honesty in thought, in word and in deed. It needs no extended thesis to demonstrate what this means in our relationship with each other, and in the world of industry and economics, of journalism and the media. The highest integrity is demanded of Christians in all these fields and all of us need constantly to be on our guard.

Prayer   *Lord God, inspire us with such love for our neighbour that we may in all our relationships be straightforward and true. Guide the thoughts and words of all who speak where many hear and all who write what many read, that all things may work together for the good of your people and to the glory of your name; through Jesus Christ our Lord.*

Make sure of truth

Make sure of truth,
And truth will make thee sure;
It will not shift nor fade nor die,
But like the heavens endure.

Man and his earth
Are varying day by day;
Truth cannot change, nor ever grow
Feeble and old and grey.

God's Thoughts, not man's
Be these thy heritage;
They, like himself, are ever young,
Untouched by time or age.

With God alone
Is truth, and joy, and light;
Walk thou with him in peace and love,
Hold fast the good and right.

HORATIUS BONAR (1808–1889)

Comment

Horatius Bonar was a Presbyterian minister and is perhaps best known for some of his hymns – for example, 'I heard the voice of Jesus say', and 'Fill thou my life, O Lord my God'. Here he exalts truth, thus giving the Christian version of the ninth Commandment, summed up by our rhymester with the line 'Bear not false witness, shun that blot'. Falsehood may transcend the truth or fall short of the truth, but whenever another person's harm is intended, falsehood is sinful. St Paul, reminding the Christians in Ephesus that they must 'put on the new nature after the likeness of God in true righteousness and holiness' then lists the qualities they must cherish to the end, and the first is 'putting away falsehood, let every man speak truth with his neighbour, for we are members one of another'. We remember that Pilate asked – I suspect with a shrug of the shoulder – 'What is truth?' and then went on his way caring nothing for the answer. The Christian must learn that truth is not merely something that he speaks. It is something that he *is* if the Spirit of God is within him. Pilate did not stay for an answer to his question. Plato in his *Laws* had given him one worth consideration: 'Truth is the beginning of every good thing in heaven and earth; he who would be blessed and happy should be from the first a partaker of the truth for then he could be trusted'. Jesus would have given him another answer: 'I am the Way, the Truth and the Life'. In another of his works our poet sums up the lesson admirably:

Sow truth, if thou the truth would reap:
    Who sows the false shall reap the vain;
Erect and sound thy conscience keep;
    From hollow words and deeds refrain'.

Prayer   Light of the world, shine upon our minds and hearts. Spirit of truth, guide us into all truth. Holy Father, sanctify us through your truth, and make us wise unto salvation, through Jesus Christ our Lord.

THE REV. L. TUTTIETT (19TH CENTURY)

St Simon and St Jude, Apostles

Dover Beach

The sea is calm to-night.
The tide is full, the moon lies fair
Upon the straits; – on the French coast the
*   light*
Gleams and is gone; the cliffs of England
*   stand,*
Glimmering and vast, but in the tranquil
*   bay.*
Come to the window, sweet is the night-air!
Only, from the long line of spray
Where the sea meets the moon-blanched land,

Listen! you hear the grating roar
Of pebbles which the waves draw back, and
*   fling,*
At their return, up the high strand,
Begin, and cease, and then again begin,
With tremulous cadence slow, and bring
The eternal note of sadness in.

The sea of faith
Was once, too, at the full, and round earth's
*   shore*
Lay like the folds of a bright girdle furled.
But now I only hear
Its melancholy, long, withdrawing roar,
Retreating, to the breath
Of the night-wind, down the vast edges drear
And naked shingles of the world.

Ah, love, let us be true
To one another! for the world which seems
To lie before us like a land of dreams,
So various, so beautiful, so new,
Hath really neither joy, nor love, nor light
Nor certitude for peace, nor help for pain;
And we are here as on a darkling plain
Swept with confused alarms of struggle and
*   flight,*
Where ignorant armies clash by night.

MATTHEW ARNOLD (1822–1888)

Comment

Very little is known about Simon and Jude save that they were both apostles. Simon is referred to as 'Simon the Zealot, which means no more than that before his call to the apostleship he was regarded as a man who was very zealous for the Jewish law. Jude is referred to in St John ch.14 v.22 as 'Judas – not Iscariot'. From about the 2nd century the Epistle of Jude was regarded as the work of Jude the Apostle. Accepting it as such prompted the quotation of Arnold's poem with its reference to the receding tide of faith. Jude's claim to distinction is that the epistle which bears his name is largely concerned with an attack on renegade Christians, 'grumblers, malcontents, loud-mouthed boasters, flattering people to gain advantage'. Jude begins his letter: 'I found it necessary to write, appealing to you to contend for the faith once delivered to the saints', and because so many Christians were slipping away from it. Arnold heard a 'melancholy, long, withdrawing roar' of heresy and infidelity which he was at pains to challenge. How do *we* view the situation? Is the tide of faith receding? If it is, what are *we* doing about it?

Prayer   *Lord, increase our faith and help us to strengthen the faith of others,*
for their good and for your glory.

Commemorating James Hannington, Bishop of East Equatorial Africa, Missionary, Martyr, 1885

The 'Little' Martyrs

For all Christ's little martyrs, God be
praised!
Men, women, aye – and children too –
Their names unknown, their deeds unsung
Save in the Book of Life, where all are raised
To high degree. With status new
They stand with those who died when
Christ was young.

For all Christ's little martyrs, God be
praised!
'Gainst fierce antagonistic powers
They stood four-square by Christ their Lord,
What time the weaker, fearful, watched
amazed
As they displayed a faith that cowers
At naught – so strong its binding cord.

For all Christ's little martyrs, God be
praised!
Baited, imprisoned, tortured, killed --
Witnesses all, whate'er their fate.
Each one possessed a virile faith which
blazed
With fire divine – by Spirit filled;
Each was received at heaven's gate.

For all Christ's little martyrs, God be
praised!
In concert with the great they sing
Unending songs of praise and joy.
Around the throne of God with hands
upraised
They make the courts of heaven ring
With all that hearts and souls employ.

For all Christ's little martyrs, God be
praised!
Remark them there! – among the great –
With Matthew, Mark, and Luke, and
John,
Those brave young lads whom holy
parents raised –
Those dusky ones arrived of late –
See! Peter, there to wave them on
Records these nameless, one by one:
'Anon', 'Anon', 'Anon', 'Anon'.

BISHOP CYRIL BULLEY

Comment

The commemoration of the death of James Hannington cannot but remind us that he was murdered by the pagan king of Uganda along with many hundreds of Christians, including young lads, because they refused to renounce their faith. Similar things have happened in the Uganda of today, for no one doubts that Archbishop Janani Luwum was murdered by President Amin. Nor is Uganda the only country where men and women die for the Faith. The word martyr means a witness – and there are thousands who bear witness to the faith in Christ, who suffer torture and imprisonment. The great are known by name. The 'little' martyrs are not – save by God himself who receives them into eternal life. We can commend their souls to his loving care, and pray that the wicked who condemn them may themselves be brought to penitence.

Prayer *O God, we praise you that from the day when your church was young to the present, there have been those who have borne their witness faithfully even unto death. As they have entered into the joy of eternal life, so strengthen all whose witness is severely tested, that they too may be faithful unto death, through Jesus Christ our Lord.*

A Contented Mind

I weigh not fortune's frown or smile;
I joy not much in earthly joys;
I seek not state, I reck not style;
I am not fond of fancy's toys:
I rest so pleased with what I have,
I wish no more, nor more I crave.

I quake not at the thunder's crack;
I tremble not at news of war;
I swound not at the news of wrack:
I shrink not at a blazing star;
I fear not loss, I hope not gain,
I envy none, I none disdain.

I see ambition never pleased;
I see some Tantals starved in store;
I see gold's dropsy seldom eased;
I see e'en Midas gape for more;
I neither want nor yet abound –
Enough's a feast, content is crowned.

I fain not friendship where I hate;
I fawn not on the great (in show);
I prize, I praise a mean estate –
Neither too lofty nor too low;
This, this is all my choice, my cheer, –
A mind content, a conscience clear.

JOSHUA SYLVESTER (1562–1618)

Comment

A happy picture of a contented man – one who doubtless knew his Bible well. 'Take heed', said Jesus, 'and beware of covetousness, for a man's life consisteth not in the abundance of the things which he possesseth'. The last line of our Commandments' rhyme reads: 'What is thy neighbour's covet not'. In St Mark's gospel we find a further warning which our Lord gave, a warning indeed touching all the sins which our thoughts about the Commandments have high-lighted. 'From within', he said, 'out of the heart of man proceed evil thoughts, adulteries, fornication, murders, thefts, covetousness, wickedness, deceit, lasciviousness, an evil eye, blasphemy, pride, foolishness: all these things come from within and defile a man' (St Mark ch.7 vv.21–23). There is, however, a warning about the warning – at least as it concerns coveting – Shakespeare in *Henry V*, says:

> *'I am not covetous for gold,*
> *Nor care I who doth feed upon my cost;*
> *It yearns me not if men my garments wear;*
> *Such outward things dwell not in my desires:*
> *But if it be a sin to covet honour,*
> *I am the most offending soul alive'.*

Is it a sin to covet? St Paul would answer 'That depends on what you covet'. In his letter to the Corinthians he exhorts Christians to 'covet earnestly the best gifts', and that verse is followed by 1 Corinthians ch.13 which sets out a list of those gifts and 'the greatest of these is charity'.

Prayer   *Lord, help me to be contented with what I have but not with what I am – to covet nothing save the best gifts of your Spirit.*

Commemorating the Saints and Martyrs of the Reformation Era

The Supplication of the Beggars

'In the times of your noble predecessors past, craftily crept into this your realm another sort (not of impotent but) of strong, puissant and counterfeit, holy and idle beggars and vagabonds... the Bishops, Abbots, Priors, Deacons, Archdeacons, Suffragans, Priests, Monks, Canons, Friars, Pardoners and Summoners. And who is able to number this idle, ruinous sort, which (setting all labour aside) have begged so importunately that they have gotten into their hands more than a third part of your Realm? The goodliest lordships, manors, lands and territories, are theirs. Besides this they have the tenth part of all corn, meadow, pasture, grass, wool, colts, calves, lambs, pigs, beef and chickens... Yea, and they look so narrowly upon their profits, that the poor wives must be countable to them of every tenth egg, or else she getteth not her rights at Easter... How much money get the Commoners by extortion in a year, by citing the people to the Commissaries' Court, and afterwards releasing their appearance for money?... Who is she that will wet her hand to work for 3d a day, and may have at least 20d a day to sleep with a friar, a monk, or a priest?'

SIMON FISH (16TH CENTURY PAMPHLETEER)

Comment

I doubt not that Henry the Eighth read this pamphlet without a blush! As a race, pamphleteers tend to exaggerate, but there was enough truth in these allegations to suggest that all was far from well in the Church or in the State. But this was the rumble of the distant thunder. The storm which was the Reformation had yet to break. There was a religous, a political and a social malaise and the ultimate remedy lay with the Church. For the Church there had to be a Re-formation that it should become again what Christ meant it to be – the salt of the earth, the leaven to lift the whole of society, and to that end the mighty rushing wind of the Spirit blew through the land. It was indeed a storm, and in a storm many are liable to be hurt. To quote the historian G.M. Trevelyan, 'the Anglican vessel slipped safely on between the clashing rocks of Romanism and Puritanism' and there emerged the Church of England, still part of the One Holy Catholic Church though turning aside the claims of Rome and counting among its clergy saints as Richard Hooker and George Herbert. Martyrs there were, known and unknown, and too many to enumerate. But from this Re-formation of Christ's Church the whole of Christendom was the purer. Maybe our best praise for those who suffered and died for what they believed to be right in the sight of God, could be best expressed in continuing efforts toward the Unity of Christendom.

Prayer   *O God, who biddest us dwell with one mind in Thine house, of thy mercy put away from us all that causeth us to differ, that through thy bountiful goodness we may keep the unity of the Spirit in the bond of peace: through Jesus Christ our Lord.*

E.B. PUSEY (1800)

All Saints' Day

The differentia of the Saints

We may allow that the saints are specialists but they are specialists in a career to which all Christians are called. They have achieved the classic status. They are the advanced guard of the army; but we, after all, are marching in the same ranks. The whole army is dedicated to the same supernatural cause and we ought to envisage it as a whole, and to remember that everyone of us wears the same uniform as the saints, has access to the same privileges, is taught the same drill, and fed with the same food. The difference between them and us is a difference in degree, not in kind. They possess, and we most conspicuously lack, a certain maturity and depth of soul, caused by the perfect flowering in them of self-oblivious love, joy and peace. We recognise in them a finished product, a genuine work of God. But this power and beauty of the saints is, on the human side, simply the result of their faithful life and is something to which every Christian worker can attain. Therefore we ought all to be a little bit like them; to have a sort of family likeness and to share the family point of view...

Nothing in all nature is so lovely and so vigorous, so perfectly at home in its environment, as a fish in the sea. Its surroundings give to it a beauty, quality and power which is not its own. We take it out and at once a poor, limp, dull thing, fit for nothing, is gasping away its life. So the soul sunk in God, living the life of prayer, is supported, filled, transformed in beauty, by a vitality and a power which are not its own. The souls of the saints are so powerful because they are are thus utterly immersed in the Spirit; their whole life is a prayer.

EVELYN UNDERHILL (1875–1941)

Comment

All Saints' Day is one of the Church's 'red letter days' when we remember all those who have striven to live their lives in the way which Evelyn Underhill describes. The fact that there is this commemoration in the Church's calendar – that is, in addition to the days when a particular saint is commemorated – is, too, a reminder that the Church is aware that *many* Christians have aspired to live their lives 'utterly immersed in the Spirit'. Their names do not appear in any earthly roll of honour, but we may be assured that they do appear in the Book of Life. St Paul in his letters refers to those to whom he is writing as saints – reminds them that they are 'called to be saints' (1 Cor. 1 v.1). The translations of the New Testament subsequent to the Authorised version probably make his meaning clearer when the Greek word is translated 'holy ones', or 'dedicated'. Each of us is a dedicated person, for that is what our Christian commitment makes us. This means that our lives must be lives of prayer, and that in turn means that they will be marked by a Christian activity which is motivated and sustained by prayer. In other words it will be recognised as having an element of 'Martha service' and 'Mary devotion' (St Luke ch.10).

Prayer   *Almighty and Everlasting God, Who dost enkindle the flame of Thy love in the hearts of the Saints, grant to our minds the same faith and power of love, that as we rejoice in their triumphs, we may profit by their examples, through Jesus Christ our Lord.*

GOTHIC MISSAL (17TH C.)

All Souls' Day

On All Soul's Day

Last night they lit your glass with wine
And brought for you the sweet soul-cake,
And blessed the room with candle shine
For the grave journey you would make.

They told me not to stir between
The midnight strokes of one and two,
And I should see you come again
To view the scene that once you knew.

'Good night', they said, and journeyed on.
I turned the key, and – turning – smiled,
And in the quiet house along
I slept serenely as a child.

Innocent was that sleep, and free,
And when the first of morning shone
I had no need to gaze and see
If crumb, or bead of wine, had gone.

My heart was easy as this bloom
Of waters rising by the bay.
I did not watch where you might come,
For you had never been away,
For you have never been away.

CHARLES CAUSLEY (CONTEMPORARY)

Comment

All Soul's Day is one of the oldest commemorations in the Church. A certain St Odilo, who lived from 962 to 1048 and was Abbot of Cluny, exercised a profound influence on the life and work of the Church in France and Italy. It was he who introduced to the Church in his diocese the commemoration of the departed on November 2nd and although he regarded it as a local observance it gradually captured the imagination of the whole Church. In one sense it was a natural development of the Christian hope of life eternal for which hope we have our Lord's teaching in St Mark's Gospel (ch.12 vv.18–27), but that apart it is inconceivable that those who are in active communion with the Living God in this life should not continue to enjoy that communion in the life beyond the grave. To contemplate the snuffing out of the human personality which God himself made, and which is temporarily wrapped in flesh, is to deny an essential element of the Christian faith. Our Lord's own words: 'He is not the God of the dead but of the living', are all the Christian needs to assure him that the death of a body is not the death of the self in which the person has lived. This has nothing to do with psychical research, nor can it be sustained or disproved by empirical observation. Of the life beyond the grave we can speak only in symbols, but of its reality we can speak with conviction. Inevitably man in his ingenuity has invented all sorts of legends and created all sorts of symbols – our contemporary poet has one in mind – but the essential truth 'YOU have never been away' stands firm, for the 'you' is the real 'you' which can never die.

Prayer   *Give rest, O Christ, to thy servants with thy saints, where sorrow and pain are no more, neither sighing but life everlasting.*

THE RUSSIAN CONTAKION OF THE DEPARTED

Commemorating Richard Hooker, Teacher of the Faith, 1600

Man – and associate with God

We have right to the same inheritance with Christ, but not the same right which he hath, his being such as we cannot reach, and ours such as he cannot stoop unto.

To be the way, the truth and the life; to be the wisdom, righteousness, sanctification, resurrection; to be the peace of the whole world, the hope of the righteous, the heir of all things; to be that supreme head whereunto all power both in heaven and earth is given: these are not honours common unto Christ with other men; they are titles above the dignity and worth of any which were but a mere man, yet truer of Christ even than that he is man, but man with whom deity is personally joined, and unto whom it hath added those excellencies which make him more than worthy thereof.

Since God hath deified our nature, though not by turning it into himself, yet by making it his own inseparable habitation, we cannot now conceive how God should without man either exercise divine power, or receive the glory of divine praise. For man is in both an associate of deity.

RICHARD HOOKER (1554–1600)

Comment

Richard Hooker has an honoured place among Anglican clergy and that despite the fact that he has been described as 'a poor obscure English priest'. He may well have been that in his early days, but he became the greatest advocate that Anglicanism has ever had. The Elizabethan Settlement can be regarded as the fruit of his wise guidance and great learning, and what he was able to accomplish resulted in the Church of England being able to preserve its continuity with the mediaeval Church whilst at the same time accepting necessary reforms. His great literary work, from which our quotation is extracted, *The Treaties on the Laws of Ecclesiastical Polity*, embraced his teaching, in which there is criticism of the Puritan position with regard to the Bible, commendation for the Anglican form of Church order and clear guidance about Church government. The comprehensiveness of the work can be surmised in that it is in eight books, four of which were published in Hooker's lifetime and the others within fifty years of his death. Undoubtedly Hooker prepared the way for some of the greatest of the Church of England's parish priests, among them Lancelot Andrewes, William Laud and George Herbert. The passage quoted is a reminder to us that we are those whom God has deified and we therefore bear the responsibility of co-operating with him in his purposes for his world. Expressed simply the passage means that God achieves his purpose for his people through his people. Nothing less than that solemn responsibility rests on us.

Prayer   *Almighty God, fount of all knowledge, who raised up your servant Richard Hooker to expound divine truth to your people; grant that all those who seek to know your mind and understand your will, may be enlightened by the gracious visitation of your Spirit; through Jesus Christ our Lord.*

More Beyond

Pierce the cloud and there is more beyond,
More such that man cannot comprehend
The infinity of space –
Ever, ever, ever more.
Read the tiny puzzled face
Of the child upon the shore,
Gazing seawards towards the place
Which to him says, 'Stop! No more!'
Of his world horizon marks the end.
'No, No' his father says, 'there's more beyond'.

Strong men and women of life so fond,
Pond'ring deeply what death may portend:
Darker than the darkest night?
Colder than the coldest morn?
Loveless, neither joy nor light?
Silent as a bird-less dawn?
Nothingness – man's final blight?
Is it for this that man was born?
Is death but life's ignoble end?
'No! No!', the Father says, 'there's more beyond'.

BISHOP CYRIL BULLEY

Comment

With the month of November beginning with All Saints' Day and All Souls' Day our thoughts turn to that 'Beyond' and that, for Christians, is not to immerse ourselves in the morbid and melancholy. It is to face a reality which is not grim but gracious. Juliette Adam, who wrote early in this century under the pseudonym Comte Paul Vasili, expressed this move from the 'here' to the 'beyond' very finely when she said: 'Death is the opening of a more subtle life. In the flower it sets free the perfume; in the chrysalis, the butterfly; in man, the soul'. A body dies; its lifelong tenant, the person, the soul, leaves the corruptible for the incorruptible. Quite apart from the New Testament itself, where one would naturally anticipate assurance that at death we pass from the narrow isthmus of time into the vastness of eternity – that is from death unto life (St John ch.5 v.24) – the pages of literature are rich with expressions in prose and poetry of the convictions of men and women throughout the ages, that death is but the horizon, the limit of our mortal sight. St Bernard of Clairvaux would have the support of all the great saints when he describes death as 'the gate of life'. Tennyson is but one of the great poets who would say with him, 'Death's truer name is *Onward*'. William Penn, the Quaker founder of Pennsylvania, wrote in his *Fruits of Solitude*: 'They that love *beyond* the *world*, cannot be separated. Death cannot kill what *never* dies... Death is but *crossing* the *world*, as Friends do the Seas, they live in one another still'.

Prayer

O Lord, by whom all souls live, we thank you for those near and dear to us whom you have called from the life here to the life beyond the veil of death. We trust them to your care, and we pray that by your grace we may be brought to enjoy with them the endless life of glory, through Jesus Christ our Lord.

The Way of Blessedness

Holy purity of heart sees God, and true devotion enjoys Him.
If thou lovest, thou shalt be loved.
If thou servest, thou shalt be served.
If thou fearest, thou shalt be feared.
If thou doest good to others, fitting is it that others should do good to thee.
Blessed is he who truly loves and desires not to be loved again.
Blessed is he who serves and desires not to be served.
Blessed is he who fears and desires not to be feared.
Blessed is he who does good to others and desires not that others should do good to
*   him.*
But because these things are very sublime and of high perfection,
*   therefore they that are foolish can neither understand them nor attain unto*
*   them.*
There are three things that are very sublime and very profitable,
*   which he who has once acquired shall never fail.*
The first is that thou bear willingly and gladly, for the love
*   of Christ, every affliction that shall befall thee.*
The second is that thou daily humble thyself, in everything thou
*   doest, and in everything thou seest.*
The third is that thou love faithfully with all thy heart that
*   invisible and supreme Good which thou canst not behold with*
*   thy bodily eyes.*

BROTHER GILES (D. 1251)

Comment

The Little Flowers of Saint Francis has within it 'some chapters of sundry good sayings and of the teaching of Brother Giles', who died twenty-six years after St Francis, having been one of the saint's close companions. Giles appears to have been a valued counsellor of the spiritual life, believing that to be one of the duties and privileges of the Friars Minor, and whilst he set out this Way of Blessedness in great detail 'for the profit and abundant edifying of the people and for their present happiness and joy', he saw it too as the right preparation for a holy death. 'If a man had always before his mind the remembrance of death and of the last judgment . . . sure it is that nevermore would desire or sin or fear of offending God assail him'. There was indeed a 'beyond', but it was in the here and now that all should learn the language and the code of ethics of that life to come. 'I tell thee that the man who leadeth a good life after the mind of God, and guardeth himself from offending God, will surely receive of God the highest blessings, and an infinite reward for ever'. Brother Giles' three ways set us a high ideal, but the Way has been set before us by Christ himself and we have his promise to be with us always in our endeavour.

Prayer   *Look upon us and hear us, O Lord our God; assist our endeavours to*
follow the path of Christ who is the Way, the Truth and the Life. As
you have given the first act of will, so give the completion of our good
intentions, through the same Christ our Lord.

Death

Death, be not proud, though some have called thee
Mighty and dreadful, for thou are not so;
For those whom thou thinkst thou dost overthrow
Die not, poor Death; nor yet canst thou kill me.
From Rest and Sleep, which but thy picture be,
Much pleasure, then from thee much more must flow;
And soonest our best men with thee do go –
Rest of their bones and souls' delivery!
Thou'rt slave to fate, chance, kings, and desperate men,
And dost with poison, war and sickness dwell;
And poppy or charms can make us sleep as well
And better than thy stroke. Why swell'st thou then?
One short sleep past, we wake eternally,
And Death shall be no more; Death, thou shalt die!

JOHN DONNE (1573–1631)

Comment

It would be strange indeed if any book which contained religious poetry should be without some of Donne's compositions. We have met him before in this book. In this poem he reveals himself as one of the finest poets of the so-called 'metaphysical' school. This is one of his *Divine Meditations* in which he reflects upon the impotence of death. He begins by diminishing it. 'Mighty and dreadful' it is certainly not, and if rest and sleep are seen as symbols of Death, as they generally are, he argues that as they give pleasure, so Death itself must do the same. He suggests that as the poppy, which contains opium, or the 'charms' – sleep-inducing drugs – can send people to sleep better than death's stroke, death has nothing to boast about. It cannot claim the final victory. A sonnet which begins by diminishing Death, ends triumphantly by declaring the death of Death!

Another writer of religious poetry, Francis Quarles, a contemporary of Donne who, like Donne, wrote poems and prose about the transitoriness of human life, closes one of his essays with the words: 'If thou expect Death as a friend, prepare to entertain him; if as an enemy, prepare to overcome him. Death has no advantage except when he comes as a stranger'. Both poets are ready to meet Death with equanimity for each sees it as impotent over life. We can follow this with a prayer of Donne's composition:

Prayer   *Eternal and most glorious God, suffer me not so to under-value myself as to give away my soul, Thy soul, Thy dear and precious soul, for nothing; and all the world is nothing if the soul must be given for it. Preserve therefore my soul, O Lord, because it belongs to Thee, and preserve my body because it belongs to my soul. Thou alone dost steer my boat through all its voyage, but hast a more special care of it, when it comes to a narrow current, or to a dangerous fall of waters. Thou hast a care of the preservation of my body in all the ways of my life; but, in the straits of death, open Thine eyes wider, and enlarge Thy providence towards me, that no illness or agony may shake or benumb the soul. Do Thou so make my bed in all my sickness, that, being used to Thy hand, I may ever be content with any bed of Thy making. Amen.*

JOHN DONNE

Last Lines

No coward soul is mine,
No trembler in the world's storm-troubled
    sphere,
    I see Heaven's glories shine,
And faith shines equal, arming me from
    fear.

    O God within my breast
Almighty, every-present Deity!
    Life – that in me has rest
As I – undying Life – have power in
    Thee!

    Vain are the thousand creeds
That move men's hearts, unutterably vain,
    Worthless as withered weeds,
Or idle froth amid the boundless main.

    To waken doubt in one
Holding so fast by Thine infinity:
    So surely anchored on
The steadfast rock of immortality.

    With wide-embracing love
Thy spirit animates eternal years,
    Pervades and broods above,
Changes, sustains, dissolves, creates and
    rears.

    Though earth and man were gone
And suns and universes ceased to be
    And Thou wert left alone,
Every existence would exist in Thee.

    There is not room for Death,
Nor atom that his might could render void:
    Thou – Thou art Being and Breath,
And what Thou art may never be
    destroyed.

EMILY BRONTE (1818–1848)

Comment

The Bronte sisters – Charlotte, Emily and Anne – daughters of the Rector of Haworth in Yorkshire, were all distinguished in the field of literature, Charlotte and Emily in particular as novelist and poet respectively. *Jane Eyre* and *Wuthering Heights* are novels which reveal genius in their penetration of human nature and in gripping the attention of their readers. It is fair to say that Emily was the better poet and as such has always received more attention in anthologies of poetry. Through all her verses the faith in which she was brought up by her devout father shines brilliantly and in this poem – the last she ever wrote, so Charlotte has recorded – it is clear that she approached her death fearlessly and with an unshakable confidence that, far from being an end, it was a natural step towards a closer relationship with the Living God in whose 'wide-embracing love' she would be caught up in a new way. As what God is – 'the steadfast rock of immortality' – may never be destroyed, so she – her soul, the real self – would live too in Him. That, she declared, was her faith – a faith so strong that at that moment it was arming her from fear. She died as she lived and, in another of her poems, she affirms 'I trust Thy might', and pleads 'Trust Thou my constancy'.

Prayer   *Lord, grant me a like constancy to walk in your Way, to hold fast to your Truth and to share your Life here and hereafter.*

Commemorating the Saints and Martyrs of England

Qua Cursum Ventus

As ships, becalmed at eve, that lay
With canvas drooping, side by side,
The towers of sail at dawn of day
Are scarce long leagues apart descried;

When fell the night, unstrung the breeze,
And all the darkling hours they plied,
Nor dreamt but each the self-same seas
By each was cleaving, side by side:

E'en so – but why the tale reveal
Of those, whom year by year unchanged,
Brief absence joined anew to feel,
Astounded, soul from soul estranged?

At dead of night their sails were filled,
And onward each rejoicing steered –
Ah, neither blame, for neither willed,
Or wist, what first with dawn
appeared!

To veer, how vain! On, onward strain,
Brave barks! In light, in darkness too,
Through winds and tides one compass guides
To that, and your own selves, be true.

But O blithe breeze! and O great seas
Though ne'er, that earliest parting past,
On your wide plain they join again,
Together lead them home at last.

One port, methought, alike they sought,
One purpose hold where'er they fare, –
O boundless breeze, O rushing seas!
At last, at last, unite them there!

ARTHUR HUGH CLOUGH 1819–1861)

Comment

Alban we have all heard of as England's first martyr, and a few others who have their names in the calendar of those whose life and work should be remembered. But who has heard of Birinus, of Cadoc, of Deusdedit, of Honorius, of Enedoc, of Odo, of Mungo and dozens more about whom something of their witness, and in some cases of their martyrdom, is known? Add to the list of those whose names are known, the countless other holy men and women in our land who have carried their witness to the point of persecution and suffering of mind or body if not to martyrdom, and we have an impressive record of Christian witness in our own land through the ages. But the method of their witness, and the factors which prompted it, may never be known. Our poet's theme is a familiar one in that he sees life as a voyage, and he knows that, whatever may befall those who are living it to the full, they are heading for 'One port' and 'One purpose'. Sometimes they will feel that they are making no progress in their witness for Christ. They will be 'becalmed'. At other times, pressing on 'in light, in darkness too, through winds and tides' they encounter difficulties unforeseen when they made their commitment to Christ's Way. But with the 'one port' in mind they press on and 'at last, at last' they are united with those who have sailed the seas of life before them and reached 'the haven where they would be.'

Prayer   *Praise be to God for all the saints and martyrs of our own land, known and unknown! God grant us grace to be faithful as were they.*

The Faces of the Dead

I have seen upon the faces of the dead
A grave and quiet dignity;
As if the spirit now released
Had caught a glimpse of majesty divine
Which left its trace
Upon the still and lifeless face.

And I have seen upon the faces of the dead
A look of happy mirth;
As if the spirit now released
Had heard the laughter of God's saints,
And left a message
Saying – 'All is well!'

But I have seen upon the faces of the dead
A look of radiant ecstasy;
As if the spirit now released
Had soared untramelled up to God
And left behind a token of His love.

SISTER ISOBEL EVERILD C.S.M.V

Comment

Many have looked upon the faces of the dead – parish priests, doctors, nurses, relatives – and many have sensed a similar calm and peace, but none could express the experience which was theirs more beautifully than has Sister Isobel. Her poem was written out of long experience of service as a nurse in England, Japan and South Africa and in all those countries she has looked 'upon the faces of the dead' – the faces of those with whom she had had that intimate contact of nurse with patient which at its noblest is Christlike. The great Dr Samuel Johnson, who is probably the best-known figure in the whole realm of English literature, suffered from a morbid fear of death and when advised by a much humbler person that he should not cherish a horror for that which was the gate of life, he replied that he never had a moment in which the thought of death was not terrible to him. Maybe he had in mind the 'sting' of death. 'O death where is thy sting? . . . The sting of death is sin, and the strength of sin is the law'. William Barclay expresses the Christian answer to that in fine language when he says: 'So long as a man sees in God only the law of righteousness, he must forever be in the position of a criminal before the bar of God with no hope of acquittal and with the certainty of condemnation. But it is precisely that, that Jesus came to abolish. He came to tell us that God is not law, but love; that the centre of God's being is not legalism but grace; that we go out not to a judge, but to a Father. . . The fear of death is banished in the wonder of the love of God'. Is this the truth which leaves on the faces of the dead 'a glimpse of majesty divine', 'a look of happy mirth', a 'radiant ecstasy'?

Prayer *Remember, O Lord, our loved ones who have passed beyond this world of time and stand now in your nearer presence. Grant them eternal rest and peace in your kingdom, and give to us each a measure of communion with them as is best for us, through Jesus Christ our Lord.*

Do not go gentle...

Do not go gentle into that good night;
Old age should burn and rage at close of day,
Rage, rage, against the dying of the light.

The wise men at their end know dark is right,
Because their words had forked no lightning they
Do not go gentle into that good night.

Good men, the last wave by, crying how bright
Their frail deeds might have danced in a green bay,
Rage, rage, against the dying of the light.

Wild men who caught and sang the sun, in flight
And learn, too late, they grieve it on its way,
Do not go gentle into that good night.

Grave men, near death, who see with blinding sight
Blind eyes could blaze like meteors and be gay,
Rage, rage against the dying of the light.

And you, my father, there on the sad height,
Curse, bless me now with your fierce tears, I pray.
Do not go gentle into that good night.
Rage, rage against the dying of the light.

DYLAN THOMAS (1914–1955)

Comment

The English-speaking world everywhere knows and delights in this poet's *Under Milk Wood*, and those who have heard the poet himself recite it in his rich lilting voice as he wanders to and fro in the Welsh village are not likely to forget it. But the poem above is surely the sad lament of a tortured soul. It has a beauty in its very pathos, but it is as far removed from Christian thought about death and the Christian approach to death as one can imagine. Here at the bedside of his dying father the poet bids him 'rage' against death as though it were some ignoble end. He speaks of it as 'that good night', yet he bids his father approach it not with serenity but with 'rage'. In the closing lines, conscious – maybe – of his own waywardness as a son, he appears not to know whether to anticipate a 'curse', or a blessing from his father's lips. As we read this pathetic poem, admiring as we may its literary beauty, we might recall Paul's words to the Corinthian Christians: 'Now we see through a glass darkly, but then shall we see face to face'. The glass which Paul had in mind was not, of course, the mirror which we know, which did not appear until the thirteenth century, but a mirror of polished steel which could give only an imperfect reflection. On the other hand it could mean 'looking through a clouded glass'. Here we look into the glass of death and our perception is inevitably far from perfect. But looking at death through the eyes of Christ we shall indeed be able 'to go gentle into that good night'. Mother Julian has the appropriate word: 'All shall be well and all manner of thing shall be well'.

Prayer

O Heavenly Father, in whose hands are the hearts of all thy children: Grant us the faith that commits all to thee, without question and without reserve; that trusting ourselves wholly to thy love and wisdom, we may meet all that life may bring, and death itself at last, with serenity and courage; through Jesus Christ our Lord.

CANON FRANK COLQUHOUN

Commemorating Martin, Bishop of Tours, d.397

Looking at Heaven

Martin called his brethren to his death-bed and told them that he was dying. Great sorrow gripped his hearers, and there was only one cry in the midst of all their tears. 'Father, why are you deserting us? To whose care are you leaving us in our grief? The wolves in their savagery will fall on your flock! When you, our shepherd are dead, who will save us from their teeth? Oh, we know you are weary for Christ, but that reward of yours is sure and it will not grow less for the waiting. Oh, pity us whom you are leaving desolate'.

Martin was deeply moved by their tears, which stirred the life-long sympathy in him that flowed from the heart of God's mercy. He too wept, we are told, then turned to God and, as his answer to their pleading, he made this prayer: 'Lord, if I am still needed by your people, I will not refuse the work. Your will be done'.

The wonder of the man! Neither toil nor death could defeat him. Indifferent alike to life or death he would not refuse the one or fear the other. He lay, with all his being intent on heaven, holding his unconquered soul fast to its prayer. The priests around his bed wished to turn him over on his side to ease his poor body but he stopped them: 'Brothers, let me go on looking at heaven, not at the earth; my soul will be pointing to God when its moment of departure comes'.

SULPICIUS SEVERUS (c.363–420)

Comment

Our author wrote his *Life of St Martin* during the lifetime of the saint under whose influence he had become first a priest and later a monk. Mention was made earlier about the many saints of whom little or nothing is known. Much is known about St Martin and perhaps the incident in his life which is imprinted on so many memories is one which occurred whilst he was still a catechumen, when he gave half his cloak to a beggar. At that time he was a soldier but on being baptised he sought to be relieved from military service. His request was refused but at the end of the war he was ordained and soon founded a monastery. When the Bishopric of Tours fell vacant the people decided to have him as their bishop. Very reluctantly he acceded to their pleas, and as the vast majority of the people in his diocese were pagans he set to work for their conversion, pulled down heathen temples and built many churches. He was a man of great compassion and one who pleaded more than once with the secular power to show mercy to prisoners. It was to his great grief that certain Christians who had been preaching heresy were condemned to death by the emperor Maximus, and despite Martin's protest and appeals, and for the first time in history, Christians were condemned to death by Christians for heresy. The keynotes of Martin's life were charity, humility, compassion and mercy – all of them facets of Christian love and all of them virtues which should adorn our lives.

Prayer   *Almighty God, we praise you for the life and witness of your servant Martin and we pray that we may seek and seize opportunities to serve the poor and needy and to show compassion and mercy on all who are distressed. We ask this in the name and for the sake of Jesus Christ our Lord.*

Saint Cadoc

A flame of rushlight in the cell
On holy walls and holy well
And to the west the thundering bay
With soaking seaweed, sand and
spray,
*   O good St Cadoc, pray for me*
*   Here in your cell beside the sea.*

St Cadoc blessed the woods of ash
Bent landwards by the Western lash,
He loved the veined threshold stones
Where sun might sometimes bleach his
bones;
*   He had no cowering fear of death*
*   For breath of God was Cadoc's*
breath.

St Cadoc when the wind was high,
Saw angels in the Cornish sky
As ocean rollers curled and poured
Their loud Hosannas to the Lord.
*   His little cell was not too small*
*   For that great Lord who made them*
all.

Here where St Cadoc sheltered God
The archaeologist has trod,
Yet death is now the gentle shore
With Land upon the cliffs before
*   And in his cell beside the sea*
*   The Celtic saint has prayed for me.*

JOHN BETJEMAN (1906–1984)

Comment

November is the month when we remind ourselves of the witness of the saints as well as calling to our mind the faithful departed. Here in this jolly little poem the erstwhile Poet Laureate, himself a deeply dedicated Christian, calls to mind a little known saint who is believed to have visited Cornwall to which part of England Betjeman went regularly to his holiday home near Trebetherick. St Cadoc, who finds no place in our church calendar, was a sixth-century Welsh missionary who saw it as part of his duty to visit Cornwall in an attempt to win the Cornish folk for Christ. Not far from Harlyn Bay on the Cornish coast there is a site which is said to be the place where Cadoc built a little chapel as the base for his mission. Cadoc is one of a vast number of saints of old whose praises are unsung and about whose work very little is known. Even so they have left their mark on our nation's history, modest though that mark may be. In the last two lines of the second verse Betjeman embraces in a few words the way in which the Spirit of God – 'the breath of God' – filled the mind and possessed the soul of Cadoc, thus rendering him immune from any fear of death even though his missionary task could have been hazardous. In the last two lines of the fourth verse there is the thought that the saints remember in their worship and prayers the needs of the faithful on earth. One further thought is relevant. It is that a place made holy by holiness tends itself to preserve an atmosphere of holiness. John Betjeman is not the only one who has experienced that.

Prayer   *Praise be to you, our God, who didst enkindle the flame of love in the hearts of the saints. Help us, as we rejoice in their triumphs, to profit by their witness, through Jesus Christ our Lord.*

Commemorating Charles Simeon, Pastor, Preacher, 1836

If I Him but have

If I Him but have,
  If He be but mine,
If my heart hence to the grave,
  Ne'er forgets His love divine –
Know I nought of sadness,
Feel I naught but worship, love, and
    gladness.

If I Him but have,
  Pleased from all I part;
Follow, on my pilgrim staff,
  None but Him, with honest heart;
Let the rest, naught saying,
On broad, bright and crowded streets
    go straying.

If I Him but have
  Glad to sleep I sink;
From His heart the flood He gave
  Shall to me be food and drink;
And – oh, soft compelling! –
All shall mollify with deep indwelling.

If I Him but have,
  Mine the world I hail;
Happy, like a cherub grave
  Holding back the Virgin's veil;
I deep sunk in gazing,
Earth's distastes are lost in heavenly
    praising.

Where I have but Him,
  Is my gatherland,
Where all favours to me come
  As a portion from His hand;
Brothers long deplored –
Lo, in His disciples all restored!

FRIEDRICH VON HARDENBURG (1772–1801)

Comment

Our author, who wrote under the pseudonym *Novalis*, was a German Romantic poet, brought up as a member of the Moravian Church, though gradually he veered towards the principles of Evangelicalism. He was deeply religious, a lover of the Bible with a firm recognition of its inspiration and authority. He was happy in the knowledge that he possessed Christ and Christ possessed him. That spelt out his personal conversion and confidence in Christ's atoning work. The priest whom we commemorate would have been happy to have such a man as his curate! Simeon was an evangelical churchman of great piety who exercised a profound influence as Vicar of Holy Trinity, Cambridge, for over 50 years. He with others founded the Church Missionary Society in 1797 and, to ensure that there should always be available for the parishes clergy of his evangelical persuasion, he created a trust, known as the Simeon Trustees, which has in its patronage a number of benefices throughout the land.

Prayer

Lord Christ, you gave yourself for me; many have given themselves to you. Here am I – I give myself to you. Sustain me by your grace that in word and deed I may be true to my resolve.

(17TH CENTURY – ADAPTED)

A Funny Little Fellow

'Twas a Funny Little fellow
  Of the very purest type,
For he had a heart as mellow
  As an apple over-ripe;
And the brightest little twinkle
  When a funny thing occurred,
And the lightest little tinkle
  Of a laugh you ever heard!

He laughed away the sorrow
  And he laughed away the gloom
We are all so prone to borrow
  From the darkest of the tomb;
And he laughed across the ocean
  Such a happy laugh and passed,
With a laugh of glad emotion,
  Into Paradise at last.

And I think the angels knew him,
  And had gathered to await
His coming, and run unto him
  Through the widely-opened gate,
With their faces gleaming sunny
  For his laughter-loving sake,
And thinking – What a funny
  Little angel he will make!

JAMES WHITCOMBE RILEY (1853–1916)

Comment

I could not resist finding a place in November for this jolly little poem of a Christian poet whose output was limited but sufficient to win him a place in the *Oxford Dictionary of Quotations:*

> *It haint no use to grumble and complain,*
>   *It's just as cheap and easy to rejoice;*
> *When God sorts out the weather and sends rain,*
>   *W'y, rain's my choice.*

Apparently he not only rejoiced in his 'funny little fellow' but himself brought smiles and laughter to the lives of those whom he met. Yes indeed! – to be 'laughter-loving' is not to be irreligious. At its best – and that is often in the laughter of a little child – it is, as a great priest once said, 'the echo of God's life within us'. Let this same poet provide us with our prayer.

Prayer   *Dear Lord! Kind Lord! Gracious Lord! I pray*
Thou wilt look on all I love tenderly to-day.
Weed their hearts of weariness; scatter every care
Down a wake of angel wings winnowing the air.
Bring unto the sorrowing all release from pain;
Let the lips of laughter overflow again.
And with all the needy, O divide I pray
This vast treasure of content that is mine to-day!

Last Thoughts

Believe it, Christians, for a certain truth that, when you come to die, your thoughts will not be: what a figure have I made in the world; how pleasantly have I passed my days; how plentifully have I lived; what pleasures have I enjoyed; what rare friends have I had; what an estate have I gotten; and what wealth do I leave behind?

No, no. But such as these following will be your dying reflections, if you do not stifle them: How have I spent my life; how have I employed my time and my health; how have I improved the talents with which God entrusted me; what good have I done in the world; have I brought up my children in the fear of God; have I been kind and helpful to poor and needy people, according to my ability; have I been true and just in my dealings; have I lived in the fear of God and worshipped Him in public and in private, according to my ability; and lastly have I taken pains to be doing something good all my life? . . .

These, I say again, will be the thoughts of such as die in their right mind. And to such whose consciences cannot answer for them that something like this has been the tenor of their past life, to such as have led an unthoughtful, fearless, useless, sinful life, and are just going into eternity, what arguments can be brought in to comfort them?

BISHOP THOMAS WILSON (1663–1755)

Comment

Thomas Wilson was Bishop of Sodor and Man for 57 years. Those were the days when it was possible for a bishop to inflict penance on people who committed perjury and a number of other offences. The bishop did just that against the Governor's wife! Later he dismissed his archdeacon for heresy and for this the governor clapped him into the island gaol; but he was subsequently over-ruled and the bishop was released. Thereupon he was offered the bishopric of Exeter as a recognition that he was without guilt in this matter. He refused and continued to serve his diocese faithfully as a pastor and a teacher.

These 'last thoughts' quoted from one of his many sermons which were published, are salutary indeed. They can be our closing thoughts on death which we have been following throughout November. With the approach of Advent we shall be turning our minds towards its stern warnings. Bishop Wilson wrote a great many books of prayers and it will be appropriate if we offer one of his prayers which bears reference to the sermon from which the quotation was extracted.

Prayer *Forgive us our sins, O Lord; the sins of our present and the sins of our past; the sins of our souls and the sins of our bodies; the sins which we have done to please ourselves and the sins we have done to please others. Forgive us our casual sins and our deliberate sins, and those which we have laboured so to hide that we have hidden them even from ourselves. Forgive us, O Lord, forgive us all our sins, for the sake of thy Son our Saviour Jesus Christ.*

Commemorating Margaret of Scotland, Queen, Wife, Mother, 1093

The Cotter's Saturday Night

They chant their artless notes in simple guise;
  They tune their hearts, by far the noblest
    aim:
From 'Dundee's' wild-warbling measures rise,
  Or plaintive 'Martyrs' worthy of the name.
Or noble 'Elgin' beats the heavenward flame,
The sweetest far of Scotia's holy lays:
  Compared with these, Italian trills are tame;
The tickled ear no heartfelt raptures raise;
Nae unison hae they with our Creator's praise.

The priest-like father reads the sacred page, –
  How Abram was the friend of God on high;
Or Moses bade eternal warfare wage
  With Amalek's ungracious progeny
  Or how the royal bard did groaning lie
Beneath the stroke of Heavens avenging ire;
  Or Job's pathetic plaint, and wailing cry;
Or rapt Isaiah's wild, seraphic fire;
Or other holy seers that tune the sacred lyre.
Perhaps the Christian volume is the theme, –
  How guiltless blood for guilty men was
    shed;

How He, who bore in heaven the second name,
  Had not on earth whereon to lay his head;
  How his first followers and servants sped;
The precepts sage they wrote to many a land;
  How he, who lone in Patmos banished,
Saw in the sun a mighty angel stand,
And heard great Babylon's doom pronounced by
Heaven's command.
Then kneeling down to Heaven's Eternal King,

  The saint, the father, and the husband
    prays:
Hope 'springs exulting on triumphant wing'.
  That thus they all shall meet in future days:
  There ever bask in uncreated rays,
No more to sigh or shed the bitter tear,
  Together hymning their Creator's praise,
In such society, yet still more dear;
While circling Time moves round in an eternal
    sphere.

ROBERT BURNS (1559–1796)

Comment

The verses form part of the Scottish poet's long poem which pictures the simple piety which marked the cottager's Saturday night – a piety which stretched back to the work and witness of Margaret, who became Queen of Scotland on marrying its king, Malcolm, in 1070. She exercised an immediate influence over her husband, who became as enthusiastic as was she in winning the country for Christ and in ensuring that education should be aimed to that end. Together they founded many churches, brought up a family of eight children, Margaret herself ensuring that they were grounded in the Christian faith, and by the pattern of their own lives they set a good example to all the citizens.

Prayer   *Look in your mercy and love, O God, upon Scotland and her people; May they be true and upright, loyal and unselfish, fearing thee and serving one another in the faith of Jesus Christ our Saviour.*

Commemorating Hilda, Abbess of Whitby, 680, and Hugh, Bishop of Lincoln, 1200

I Took Love to Task

I took Love to task:
'Behold', I said
'How many a weary one
Hath only straw to lie upon?'
'There will I lay my head',
Said Love, 'tis straw I ask'.

I took Love to task:
'Behold', I said.
'How many thorns there be,
To rend and pierce with treachery
Our lives?' Love bent Him down
And took the thorns and made
A Crown!

I took Love to task:
'Behold', I said,
'Yon gibbet with its burden dread!
Hate reigns!' Love answered me,
'I found a throne like that
On Calvary'.

I said to Love:
'Thy law is much too hard,
I cannot follow Thee'.
Love stretched forth mighty arms
And said, 'Come child,
I'll carry thee'.

FATHER ANDREW S.D.C. (1869–1946)

Comment

Hilda, a lady of royal birth, was baptised when she was 13. Of her, Bede wrote that she lived 'most nobly in the secular habit; and more nobly dedicated the remaining half of her life to our Lord in a monastic life'. Bede writes of her piety and grace, of her wisdom and ability in training those under her care and in giving advice to kings and princes who came to her. Her monastery at Whitby became famous throughout Europe as a centre of learning and a place where men and women from near and far became deeply versed in the things of God. However, the last six years of her life she was tormented with a lingering disease, and the patience and courage with which she bore her illness became known throughout the Christian world – for no less than five bishops as well as a great number of priests had gone out from her monastery. Bede tells us that in the course of her years of illness 'she never failed either to return thanks to her Maker, or publicly and privately to instruct the flock committed to her charge; for by her own example she admonished all persons to serve God dutifully, and always to return thanks to Him in adversity or bodily infirmity'. She taught by word and example the lesson which Father Andrew expresses so beautifully in his poem. God grant that we may with like faith and courage face any such trial as may come to us.

Prayer   *God our Father, grant us patience under suffering of body or of mind, and so help us to unite our distresses with the sufferings of our Lord and Saviour Jesus Christ that we may experience that serenity of heart and mind which sustained your servant Hilda.*

Hugh of Avalon

Hugh was born in Burgundy where he first became a member of the 'canons regular' of Grenoble and then changed into the Order of the Charter House, where he excelled his fellows in godliness and obedience. Henry the Second, King of England, moved by the fame of his holiness, prevailed upon him to come into England, and afterwards with the consent of the Canons, made him Bishop of Lincoln. But the man of God recoiled from such an action and would not take the See until he had been elected again and that time freely.

His first care after taking possession of his See was to call around him men of knowledge and of wisdom, with whose counsel he manfully discharged the duties of a shepherd of souls. He would not have any to take charge of any of the flock, however they might be distinguished for industry or culture, unless they had the ornament of a quiet and modest spirit. He opposed by church censures the King's officers who practised cruelties upon the people, in regard to the forest laws.

Right often had he to contend with King Richard who strove to scrape money together from all quarters, and calmly disregarded his threats. He toiled much, and not without success, to re-establish peace between the Kings of England and France, and was returned from that work into England, when he fell sick in London, and having received the Sacraments of the Church, died a holy death in the Lord, in the year 1200. All the nobility of England, and the Kings of England and Scotland, attended his funeral at Lincoln.

ADAM – THE BISHOP'S CHAPLAIN.

Comment

Hugh's commemoration day was yesterday but since we thought then only of St Hilda, it seemed right to give this page over to the great Bishop of Lincoln whose life and work is described in his chaplain's *Magna Via*. Like the Psalmist who declared: 'I will speak of thy testimonies also even before kings', Hugh was fearless in his relationships with the kings with whom he had to deal – Henry the Second, Richard and John. With the first he had a happy relationship though he never feared to rebuke him when he believed it to be necessary. To King Richard he said: 'You are my parishioner for whose soul I shall have to answer. Tell how you stand with God'. For his candour as for his advice both Henry and Richard loved him. John, however, refused to receive the Sacrament at his coronation, and on another occasion walked out in the middle of his bishop's sermon. Hugh was a great pastor, ministering not merely to kings and courtiers, but the needy, the sick and even to the lepers. A great man of God indeed – one who could talk and walk with kings but one who mixed and was known and loved by the poor, the simple and the humblest in his great dioceses.

Prayer   *Almighty God, grant that as we recall the courage, the love and the humility with which your servant Hugh fulfilled his sacred task, we may, by your grace, bring to our tasks and our relationships the same virtues, to your glory and to the joy of all with whom we have to deal.*

Man

Weighing the steadfastness and state
Of some mean things which here before
reside,
Where birds like watchful clocks the
noiseless date
And intercourse of times divide,
Where bees at night get home and hive,
and flowers,
Early as well as late,
Rise with the sun, and set in the same
bowers.

I would (said I) my God would give
The staidness of these things to man! for
these
To his divine appointments ever cleave,
And no new business breaks their peace;
The birds nor sow nor reap, yet sup and
dine,
The flowers without clothes live,
Yet Solomon was never dressed so fine.

Man hath still either toys, or care,
He hath no root, not to one place is tied,
But ever restless and irregular
About this earth doth run and ride,
He knows he hath a home, but scarce
knows where,
He says it is so far
That he hath quite forgot how to go there.

He knocks at all doors, strays and
roams,
Nay, hath not so much wit as some stones
have,
Which in the darkest nights point to their
homes
By some hid sense their Maker gave;
Man is the shuttle, to whose winding
guest
And passage through these looms
God ordered motion, but ordained no rest.

HENRY VAUGHAN (1622–1695)

Comment

Here the mystical poet is contemplating what might be described as the reliability of nature when it is compared with the lack of that in man. In his first verse he compares the 'mean things' – that is 'mean' in the sense that they are low in man's estimation – things such as the bees, the birds, the flowers, the sun, all of which are so steadfast, to the waywardness of man. He says that we know what will happen when the sun sets tonight. It will rise again tomorrow. With man, he complains, one never knows what he is going to do next! He wishes that man could possess the 'staidness' of nature which sticks rigidly to its 'divine appointments'. 'Solomon in all his glory was not arrayed like one of these'. In the last verse he flays into man – and he doubtless indicts himself – for his aimless meanderings through life, often forgetting that he has God with whom to reckon and God whose guidance he should seek. Without God, he is saying, man is without an ordered purpose. Without God man is lost. A salutary word as we approach the Advent season!

Prayer   *Lord, lift thou up the light of thy countenance upon us, that in thy light we may see light: the light of thy grace to-day, and the light of thy glory hereafter; through Jesus Christ our Lord.*

LANCELOT ANDREWES

Commemorating Edmund of East Anglia, King, Martyr, d.870

To the Christians

I give you the end of a golden string;
Only wind it into a ball,
It will lead you in at Heaven's gate,
Built in Jerusalem's wall. . .

England! awake! awake! awake!
Jerusalem thy sister calls!
Why wilt thou sleep the sleep of death
And close her from thy ancient walls?

Thy hills and valleys felt her feet
Gently upon their bosoms move:
Thy gates beheld sweet Zion's ways;
Then was a time of joy and love.

And now the time returns again:
Our souls exult, and London's
towers
Receive the Lamb of God to dwell
In England's green and pleasant
bowers.

For a tear is an intellectual thing.
And a sigh is the sword of an angel
king,
And the bitter groan of a martyr's woe
Is an arrow from the Almighty's
bow.

WILLIAM BLAKE (1757–1827)
FROM *Jerusalem*

Comment

Commemorating one of England's martyr saints it is appropriate to quote from Blake's *Jerusalem* (which might be called England's second national anthem). It was on Christmas Day 885 that Edmund became King of Norfolk when he was a young boy of 14. In the following year Suffolk recognised him as their king. He was a pious lad and virtuous and it is recorded that he learnt to recite all the psalms by heart. Certainly in that part of England the king did exclaim by word and by his behaviour: 'Awake! awake!' and his people responded to his Christian leadership. Then, in the year 866 there came the great Danish invasion about which the *Anglo-Saxon Chronicles* records that 'the Danes came to the land of the Angle king and took up winter quarters among the East Angles who made peace with them'. Later, at Thetford, the Danes began to make unreasonable demands of the king. Following a fierce battle he was summoned to the Danish headquarters where he was told that peace could be restored provided that he would give the Danes half of his treasures and become a vassal prince. He acceded the first request but refused to become a vassal prince unless his overlord became a Christian. He objected to that part of the Dane's demands as he 'had been called to his office by God in order that he might help his people to lead Christian lives and to advance God's Kingdom'. The Danish prince, one Hingmuir, ordered him to be scourged, but he refused to renounce his faith. Edmund could sense the nearness of the arrow of martyrdom but stood firm. He was killed; his body was buried at Hoxne and later translated to Bury St Edmund's.

Prayer   *Heavenly Father, you called your holy martyr Edmund to bear witness to your name even unto death. Mercifully grant that the blood which he shed for you may ever make fruitful for your Church the land over which he was king; through Jesus Christ our Lord.*

Jesus of the Scars

If we have never sought, we seek thee now,
  Thine eyes burn through the dark, our only stars;
We must have sight of thorn-pricks on Thy brow,
  We must have Thee, O Jesus of the scars.

The heavens frighten us; they are too calm;
  In all the universe we have no place.
Our wounds are hurting us; where is the balm?
  Lord Jesus, by Thy scars we claim Thy grace.

If when the doors are shut, Thou drawest near,
  Only reveal those hands, that side of Thine;
We know to-day what wounds are, have no fear,
  Show us the scars, we have no countersign.

The other gods were strong; but Thou wast weak;
  They rode, but Thou didst stumble to a throne;
But to our wounds only God's wounds can speak
  And not a god has wounds, but Thou alone.

EDWARD SHILLITO (1872–1948)

Comment

Very soon the Church begins the season of Advent, a solemn season comparable with Lent in many ways, and having the special significance of being regarded as a prelude to the Christmas festival. Unlike Lent, during which special attention is drawn to the Passion of Christ, terminating in Good Friday, it is to the Second Coming of Christ as Judge at the Last Day that the Church is concerned to turn the thoughts of Christians during the Advent Season, which terminates with the Christmas festival. The familiar Advent hymns sum up its lessons admirably and most are sung throughout Christendom. 'O come, O come, Emmanuel', 'Lo! He comes with clouds descending', and other such hymns with their thrilling choruses: 'Rejoice! Rejoice!' and 'Alleluia', strike the right note, but it should not be forgotten that others balance them with stern warnings to Christians that they must be ready for Christ's coming, and that means more than being ready to celebrate the Christmas festival. Speculations about the *Parousia* (the Second Coming) when this world order will be ended by the coming of Christ in glory to judge the living and the dead, are idle if their only concern is to fix a date for that, after the manner of *Old Moore's Almanac*. But of the belief, amply attested by Holy Scripture, that in God's own time humanity will be confronted and judged by the Christ in His glory, no Christian should shrink. No man knows the hour and the day, but all Christians must know that there is the judgement. Confronted by our 'Jesus of the Scars' we cannot afford not to take seriously the warning note of Advent which is not silenced by the triumphant note. Our 'Rejoice! Rejoice! Emmanuel' has to be balanced by our 'deeply wailing' as 'with what rapture gaze we on those glorious scars'.

Prayer

Make us, we beseech thee, O Lord our God, watchful and heedful in awaiting the coming of thy Son, Christ our Lord; that when he shall come and knock, he shall find us not sleeping in sin, but awake and rejoicing in his praises; through the same Jesus Christ our Lord.

GELASIAN SACRAMENTARY

Door – Opened and Closed

God's respect for the freedom of our affections, thoughts, and purposes is complete. It is part of that respect for our freedom that He never forces upon us His own gifts. He offers them but unless we actively accept them, they remain ineffective as far as we are concerned. 'Behold, I stand at the door and knock' – is always the relation of God our Redeemer to our souls. He has paid the whole price; yet still He waits until we open the door of our hearts to let in His love which will call our love out. He never breaks down the door. He stands and knocks. And this is true not only of His first demand for admission to the mansion of the soul; it is true also of every room within that mansion. There are many of us who have opened the front door to Him, but have only let Him into the corridors and staircases; all the rooms where we work or amuse ourselves are still closed against Him. There are still greater multitudes who have welcomed Him to some rooms, and hope that He will not ask what goes on behind the doors of others. But sooner or later He asks; and if we do not at once take Him to see, He leaves the room where we were so comfortable with Him, and stands knocking at the closed door. And then we can never again have the joy of His presence in the first room until we open the door at which He is now knocking. We can only have Him with us in the room that we choose for Him, if we really give him the freedom of all the house.

ARCHBISHOP WILLIAM TEMPLE (1881–1944)

Comment

Time was when the man of the house was moved to distraction by the zeal of the woman of the house in the operation which was known as spring-cleaning! All the doors were opened and every crevice of every room was swept clean and in the process every piece of furniture was moved to some unfamiliar spot. Nowadays modern technology has provided the instruments which make the cleaning of the house an easier and less disruptive operation. Archbishop William Temple surely had spiritual spring-cleaning in mind as he wrote the above words, quoted from his *Personal Religion and the Life of Fellowship*. It is easy for us as Christians, anchored as we are in fellowship of the Church, to afford to Christ a prominent place in the Sundays of our lives whilst at the same time, either by indolence or reluctance, barring him entry into the working and playing rooms of daily life. Sometimes indeed there are crevices in our characters which we prefer to conceal. Lent and Advent are both seasons of the church's year when we should engage in spiritual spring-cleaning. It can be disturbing; it can be disruptive; but if it makes for spiritual cleanliness we are nearer to Christ's Way and Truth and Life.

Prayer *We confess to thee, O Lord most holy, all the sins which hinder thy purpose for our lives and do harm to the lives of others. Forgive us, Lord, and turn our hearts to seek thee more sincerely and to serve thee and our fellow men more faithfully. We ask it through our Saviour Jesus Christ.*

WILLIAM TEMPLE

The Dawning

Ah! What time wilt thou come? when shall
   that cry,
'The Bridegroom's coming!' fill the sky?
Shall it in the evening run
When our words and works are done?
Or will thy all-surprising light
   Break at midnight. . .
O at what time soever thou
(Unknown to us) the heavens will bow,
And with thy angels in the van,
Descend to judge poor careless man.
Grant, I may not like a puddle lie
In a corrupt security
Where, if a traveller water crave,
He finds it dead, and in a grave.

But as this restless vocal spring
All day and night doth run and sing,
And though here born, yet is acquainted
Elsewhere, and flowing keeps untainted;
So let me all my busy age
In thy free services engage,
And though, while here, of force I must
Have commerce sometimes with poor dust,
And in my flesh though vile and low,
And this doth in her channel flow,
Yet let my course, my aim, my love
And chief acquaintance be above;
So when that day and hour shall come
In which thyself shall be the sun,
Thou'lt find me dressed and on my way
Watching the break of thy great day.

HENRY VAUGHAN (1622–1695)

Comment

This is a part of Henry Vaughan's great Advent poem – the dawning being that of the Second Coming of Christ in glory to judge mankind. The words 'The Bridegroom's coming' refers to the incident in St Matthew ch.5 of the wise and foolish virgins, where the foolish virgins suddenly realised that their lamps were going out and they had to leave to replenish them. They were thus unprepared and in the event missed the Bridegroom's arrival. In his picturesque language Vaughan sees the Angels 'in the van', i.e. leading the procession. When the moment comes he hopes that he will not be found in the 'puddle' of corruption. In this life he feels he will not be able to avoid being tainted with the commerce of dust – the sins of the flesh – but he is resolved to be ready at all costs on that great Day. We must think on these things!

Prayer   *Stir up our hearts, O Lord, we beseech thee, to prepare the Way of thine only begotten Son; so that when he cometh we may be found watching, and serve thee with a pure and ready will; through the same thy Son Jesus Christ our Lord.*

Patience

Sometimes I wish that I might do
  Just one grand deed and die,
And by that one grand deed reach up
  To meet God in the sky.
But such is not Thy way, O God,
  Not such is Thy decree,
But deed by deed, and tear by tear,
  Our souls must climb to Thee,
As climbed the only Son of God
  From manger unto Cross.
Who learned through tears and bloody
  sweat,
  To count this world but loss;

Who left the Virgin Mother's arms
  To seek those arms of shame,
Outstretched upon the lonely hill
  To which the darkness came.
As deed by deed, and tear by tear,
  He climbed up to the height,
Each deed a splendid deed, each tear
  A jewel shining bright,
So grant us, Lord, the patient heart,
  To climb the upward way,
Until we stand upon the height,
  And see the perfect day.

G.A. STUDDERT-KENNEDY (1883–1929)

Comment

Here in a simple but beautiful poem with but one mystical symbol – namely 'To meet God in the sky' – Geoffrey Studdert-Kennedy voices what the ordinary Christian sometimes feels as he strives to be true to the Christ to whom he has committed himself. It is not that we do not know what is demanded of us. It is that knowing we still fail when the moment of testing comes – through indolence, through fear, through selfishness. It was as Advent approached that a French priest distributed to each of his parishioners a card which he asked them to hang in a room where they would see it constantly. It carried this challenging message: 'Understand well the force of these three words: GOD, MOMENT, ETERNITY, the God who sees thee always, the Moment which flees from thee, Eternity which awaits thee. The God whom you serve so ill, the Moment which passes without thought, Eternity which you hazard so rashly'. Progress in the Christian pilgrimage is a process of deed by deed and tear by tear. Over the next three days we can ponder the force of the old priest's three words.

Prayer   *Teach us, O gracious Lord, to begin our works with fear, to go on with obedience, and to finish them in love, and then to wait patiently in hope, and with cheerful confidence to look up to thee whose promises are faithful and rewards infinite; through Jesus Christ our Lord.*

BISHOP GEORGE HICKES

God our Creator

God is the Creator. He is mind, mighty, righteous, unchanging, perfect; and everything that exists depends upon him utterly . . . God is Creator not, however, like a carpenter who makes a box, once for all complete and static; or like a watchmaker who makes a mechanism and leaves it to run of itself and only comes back to mend it when it goes wrong. No, God as Creator is more like an artist who expresses himself within the beauty of his work, or like a dramatist whose drama unfolds itself in the characters he has called into being . . .

If God is the perfection of righteousness and love, he will desire to create something which can fully reflect that perfection and receive his love and return it. Christian tradition asserts that he has done so and finds its belief in the Bible words: 'Let us make Man in our own image after our own likeness'. When we say that 'Man is made in the image of God' we remember indeed that there is a line of utter distinction between Creator and creature which cannot be blurred; yet we say that, despite that line, there is a real affinity between Man and God – for Man has freedom, reason, the power to love, and, above all, the power to love his Creator and to have fellowship with him. That is *you*. What a creature to be: what possibilities to possess! . . .

Our goal is a growing *likeness to God in doing his will, a growing intercourse* with him; but mingled throughout with a growing *dependence* upon him in reverence and awe, for he is our Maker no less than our friend.

ARCHBISHOP MICHAEL RAMSEY (CONTEMPORARY)

Comment

The quotation is from the archbishop's book *Introducing the Christian Faith* – part of the introductory address which he gave in a mission to the undergraduates of Oxford University. He could not, of course, have introduced such a mission in any other way – just as the old French priest put the word GOD as the first of those which he wished his parishioners to contemplate throughout the days of Advent. 'God who sees you always . . . God whom you serve so ill'. *Likeness to, Intercourse with* and *dependence upon* are the duties of the Christian towards God. This means that as we see God in Christ we have God's likeness as our aim. He is the Way, the Truth and the Life which we must follow. We know that for this we need to have intercourse with God in ties of sacrament and prayer. We know too that we are utterly dependent upon God. Francis Quarles, the seventeenth-century poet who became private secretary to the Archbishop of Armagh, summed it up thus: 'God is *alpha* and *omega* in the great world; endeavour to make him thy evening epilogue and thy morning prologue. So shall thy rest be peaceful, thy labours prosperous, thy life pious, and thy death glorious'. Such a life is a life of glory to God.

Prayer   *God – Holy, Holy, Holy; Father, Father, Father; Saviour, Saviour, Saviour; Spirit, Spirit, Spirit. Alleluia!*

The Moment

They do me wrong who say I come no more
    When once I knock and fail to find you in;
For every day I stand outside your door
    And bid you wake, and rise to fight and
    win.

Wail not for precious chances passed away!
    Weep not for golden ages on the wane!
Each night I burn the records of the day –
    At sunrise every soul is born again!

Dost thou behold thy lost youth all aghast?
    Dost reel from righteous Retribution's blow?
Then turn from blotted archives of the past
    And find the future's pages white as snow.

Art thou a mourner? Rouse thee from thy spell!
    Art thou a sinner? Sins may be forgiven;
Each morning gives thee wings to flee from hell,
    Each night a star to guide thy feet to heaven.

Laugh like a boy at splendours that have sped;
    To vanished joys be blind, and deaf and
    dumb;
My judgments seal the dead past with its dead,
    But never bind a moment yet to come.

Though deep in mire, wring not your hands
    and weep;
    I lend my arm to all who say, 'I can!'
No shame-faced outcast ever sank so deep
    But yet might rise and be again a man.

WALTER MALONE (1866–1915)

Comment

'Man never continueth in one stay', says the Psalmist. That means that spiritually there is never for any of us a static position. Every moment of our lives we are moving towards God or away from him. This surely is what the French priest had in mind when he warned his flock about the 'moment which flees from thee' and 'the moment which passes without thought'. This cannot mean, of course, that in every moment of our lives we should be consciously in touch with God in thought or prayer. It means that the force of the word 'moment' is, that it is in the 'here and now' that the direction of our lives is settled – the moments of work, of leisure, of trials, of temptation, of reflection, of conversation, of opportunity, of contact with people. All these have to be consecrated moments, and they can only be just that if we have periods of time in which by our prayer and conscious communion with God we chart our way through life. In the moment of failure it is no use our saying – as did the fool mentioned by the psalmist – 'Tush, the Lord shall not see'. This thought is not one to drive Christians into a mood of gloomy introspection. It is one rather to quicken the Christian conscience and brace the Christian nerve. Moments to fight against temptation! Moments of opportunities to be grasped!

Prayer

Almighty God, you have made all things for man, and man for your glory, sanctify our bodies and souls, our thoughts and our intentions, our words and our actions, that whatsoever we think, or speak or do may be to your glory and to the welfare of those whom we meet day by day. We ask this through Jesus Christ our Lord.

AFTER ST THOMAS À KEMPIS

To-day

So here hath been dawning
　Another blue Day:
Think, wilt thou let it
　Slip useless away?

Out of Eternity
　This new Day is born;
Into Eternity,
　At night, will return.

Behold it aforetime
　No eye ever did:
So soon it for ever
　From all eyes is hid.

Here hath been dawning
　Another blue Day:
Think, wilt thou let it
　Slip useless away?

THOMAS CARLYLE (1795–1881)

Comment

Thomas Carlyle, who was a great essayist and historian, affected to despise theology, but his religious influence was nevertheless profound. He had a firm belief in God himself and he believed that 'the Religious Principle lies unseen in the hearts of all good men'. He can rightly claim to be not only a historian, an essayist and a poet but also a prophet who was unshakeable in his confidence that man's chief purpose is to love God. In this little poem he regards a day as 'useless' if it has passed without a conscious thought of the Eternal and Eternity. He would have been at one with the French priest in his warning to his parishioners: 'Eternity which awaits thee – Eternity which you hazard so rashly'. But he would have wished to make it clear that they should not think of Eternity as something which starts only after the death of the body. The distinction between Time and Eternity is false. As another poet, James Montgomery, says:

Then shall be shown, that but in name
Time and Eternity were both the same;　.
A point which life nor death could sever,
A moment standing still forever.

Time is a mere parenthesis in Eternity, and it is in Time that we learn the language of Eternity, practise the morals of Eternity and discern the grand purpose of Eternity. Here we have no abiding city; our citizenship is in heaven. Our poet is making it crystal clear that our days come from Eternity and return to Eternity and what we do with our days has reference to the hereafter. Here we must keep open the lines of communication between the temporal and the eternal, between earth and heaven, between Time and Eternity.

Prayer

Keep alive in our souls, O God, the vision of Eternity, that here in the parenthesis of Time we may think and do those things which prepare us for our citizenship in Heaven. This we ask in the name of our Lord and Saviour, Jesus Christ.

Morality

We cannot kindle when we will
The fire which in the heart resides.
The Spirit bloweth and is still,
In mystery our soul abides.
    But tasks in hours of insight willed
    Can be through hours of gloom fulfilled.

With aching hands and bleeding feet
We dig and heap, lay stone on stone;
We bear the burden and the heat
Of the long day, and wish 'twere done.
    Not till the hours of light return
    All we have built do we discern.

Then, when the clouds are off the soul,
When thou dost bask in Nature's eye,
Ask, how she viewed thy self-control,
Thy struggling, tasked morality –
    Nature, whose free, light cheerful air,
    Oft made thee, in thy gloom, despair.

And she, whose answer thou dost dread
Whose eye thou wast afraid to seek,
See, on her face a glow is spread,
A strong emotion on her cheek!
    'Ah, child', she cries, 'that strife divine
    When was it, for it is not mine?'

'There is no effort on my brow –
I do not strive, I do not weep;
I rush with the swift spheres and glow
In joy, and when I will, I sleep.
    Yet that severe, that earnest air,
    I saw, I felt it once – but where?

I knew not yet the gauge of time,
Nor wore the manacles of space;
I felt it in some other clime,
I saw it in some other place.
    'Twas when the heavenly house I trod,
    And lay upon the breast of God'.

MATTHEW ARNOLD (1822–1888)

Comment

This fine poem of Matthew Arnold's can be seen as an appropriate sequence to our thoughts about God, Moment and Eternity. In our resolves, intentions and efforts to be true to our commitment as Christians, we experience 'aching hands and bleeding feet' – that is, frustrations, disappointments, failures in self-control, and moments of despair, but when through our prayers, our acts of worship 'the clouds are off the soul', we are enabled to struggle on in our pilgrimage. We do not always realise the source of the renewed burst of enthusiasm and strength with which we start again; we tend sometimes to think of it as a gift from Nature. Arnold shows us that Nature disclaims the credit! The renewed strength is *divine* and it is given, he says, when 'in the heavenly house I trod, and lay upon the breast of God'.

Prayer   O God, you have promised that they who endure to the end shall be saved. Give us grace to persevere in your service all our days, that we may reach the end of our faith, even the salvation of our souls.

Essentials of True Religion

Religion is essentially social *horizontally*; in the sense that each several soul is therefore unique because intended to realise just *this* post, function, joy, effect, within the total organism of all souls. Hence no soul is expected to be a 'jack-of-all-trades', but only to develop fully its own special gifts within and through and for that larger organism of the human family in which other souls are as fully to develop their own differing gifts . . . 'The striving of any one soul can thus be peaceful, since limited in range to what this particular soul, at its best, most really wants and loves.

And religion is essentially social *vertically* – indeed here is its deepest root. It is unchangeable, a faith in God, a love of God, an intercourse with God; and though the soul cannot abidingly abstract itself from its fellows, it can and ought frequently to recollect itself in a simple sense of God's presence. Such moments of direct preoccupation with God alone bring a deep refreshment and simplification to the soul.

And religion, in its fullest development, essentially requires not only this our little span of earthly years but a life beyond. Neither, an eternal life that is already achieved here below, nor an eternal life to be begun and known solely in the beyond, satisfies these requirements. But only an eternal life already begun and truly known in part here, though fully to be understood hereafter, corresponds to the deepest longings of man's spirit as touched by the prevenient Spirit, God.

BARON FRIEDRICH VON HUGEL (1852–1925)

Comment

Baron von Hugel was an eminent philosopher and theologian who despite his Italian origin – he was born in Florence – spent nearly 60 years of his life in England. The quotation is from his book – and he wrote many – entitled *Eternal Life* where, in fact, he pursues a theme parallel with that which must have prompted our French priest to call his people, as the season of Advent opened, to 'understand well the force of three words: God, Moment, Eternity'. One of the Baron's particular interests was to help people to understand the particular relevance and importance of eschatology to the modern world. It should not be thought, however, that von Hugel was so learned a philosopher and theologian that only his peers could understand him. He was a man of prayer who exercised a great spiritual influence among many and a counsellor to whom many went for guidance of a spiritual nature. The keyword of his religion was 'adoration' – adoration of the Living God who is our Father, but who 'transcends' all things and all persons. It will be noted that in the quotation the French priest's three words all occur in these, the Baron's three essentials of religion. We Meet God in this 'little span of our earthly years', a span in which every moment counts, but we meet him too in 'a life beyond' when we must render a good account of our stewardship.

Prayer   *Blessing and honour and thanksgiving and praise, more than we can utter, more than we can conceive, be unto thee, O holiest and glorious Trinity, Father, Son and Holy Spirit, by all angels, all men, all creatures, for ever and ever.*

LANCELOT ANDREWES

St Andrew the Apostle

'He first findeth his own brother'

When brothers part for manhood's race,
  What gift may most endearing prove
To keep fond Memory in her place,
  And certify a brother's love?

'Tis true bright hours together told,
  And blissful dreams in secret shared,
Serene or solemn, gay or bold,
  Shall late in fancy unimpaired.

Who art thou, that would'st grave thy
  name
  Thus deeply in a brother's heart?
Look on this saint and learn to frame
  Thy love-charm with true Christian art.

Then, potent with the spell of heaven,
  Go, and thine erring brother gain,
Entice him home to be forgiven,
  Till, he, too, see his Saviour plain.

Or, if before thee in the race,
  Urge him with thine advancing tread,
Till, like twin stars, with even pace,
  Each lucid course be duly sped.

No fading frail memorial give
  To soothe his soul when thou art gone,
But wreaths of hope for aye to live,
  And thoughts of good together done.

That so, before the judgment seat,
  Though changed and glorified each face,
Not unremembered yet may meet
  For endless ages to embrace.

JOHN KEBLE (1792–1866)

Comment

'He first findeth his own brother. . . and brought him to Jesus'. Andrew frequently brought people to Jesus. Not content merely to accept Christ himself, he was ever eager to introduce others to him – his own brother (St John ch.1 v.35ff), the little lad with the bread and fishes (St John ch.6 v.8ff), the Greek tourists (St John ch.12 v.22). Andrew was the fearless and enthusiastic evangelist resolved to introduce Jesus to the world. No wonder then that the Christian Church has long called on us to turn our thoughts and prayers during St Andrew's Tide to the work of the Church overseas, to sustain by our prayers and alms the work of those who, like Andrew, are bringing Christ to those who are our own brothers and sisters. But there is another challenge within Keble's verses. Many find it hard to bear their witness to their own kith and kin. Committed Christians though they may themselves be, and ready to challenge the unbelief or lukewarmness to the Christian faith of someone in the office or the factory or club, they are often reluctant to challenge an 'erring brother'. Where do we stand in this?

Prayer   *We praise you, Father, for the life and witness of your servant Andrew, who committed himself wholly to our Lord and Saviour Jesus Christ, and brought others to him. Give us, we ask, a like enthusiasm and courage that we may not fear to bear witness both to those near and dear to us and to all our brothers and sisters overseas.*

Advent

High o'er the lonely hills
  Black turns to grey,
Birdsong the valley fills,
  Mists fold away;
Grey wakes to green again,
Beauty is seen again –
Good and serene again
  Dawneth the day.

So o'er the hills of life,
  Stormy, forlorn,
Out of the cloud and strife
  Sunrise is born;
Swift grows the light for us;
Ended is night for us;
Soundless and bright for us
  Breaketh God's morn.

Hear we no beat of drums,
  Fanfare nor cry,
When Christ the herald comes
  Quietly nigh;
Splendour he makes on earth;
Colour awakes on earth;
Suddenly breaks on earth
  Light from the sky.

Bid then farewell to sleep;
  Rise up and run!
What though the hill be steep?
  Strength's in the sun.
Now shall you find at last,
And for mankind at last
  Day has begun!

JAN STRUTHER (1901–1953)

Comment

'Twenty-four shopping days to Christmas', proclaims every store in every High Street! The Church makes proclamation too from Advent Sunday onwards when it bids its members not only to heed the stern warning of the Second Coming, but also to prepare to celebrate the Christmas festival with the solemnity and joy which it demands. Its call, when the moment comes, will be, 'Come, let us adore him; come and worship Christ the new-born king'. Jan Struther is perhaps best known for her hymns which include 'Lord of all hopefulness, ... of all eagerness, ... kindliness, ... gentleness'. In her poem she sees God's coming in Christ as the dispelling of the world's darkness – something to evoke excitement and joy since 'for mankind at last Day had begun'. Think of that, every time you see 'X shopping days to Christmas'.

Prayer   *We beseech thee, O Lord, to purify our consciences by thy daily visitation; that when thy Son our Lord cometh, he may find in us a mansion prepared for himself; through the same Jesus Christ our Lord.*

GELASIAN SCARAMENTARY

Commemorating Nicholas Ferrar, Deacon, Founder of the Little Gidding Community, d.1637

'The guest who had come to discover what this new religious family was like found himself the object of a rather searching analysis. For in the parlour, as he awaited Nicholas' arrival the guest would read on the wall a framed announcement:

JHS

He who by reproof of our errors and remonstrance of that which is more perfect seems to make us better is welcome as an Angel of God,
but
He who in any way goes about to disturb us in that which is or ought to be among Christians, tho' it be not usual in the world, is a burden whilst he stays and shall bear his judgment whoever he be,
and
He who by a cheerful participation and approbation of that which is good, confirms us in the same, is welcome as a Christian friend,
and
He who censures us in absence for that which in presence he made a show to approve of, doth by a double guilt of flattery and slander violate both the bands of friendship and Christianity'.

QUOTED FROM 'FLAME TOUCHES FLAME' BY
MARGARET CROPPER (1886–1980)

Comment

Nicholas Ferrar, son of a London merchant, born into a Christian family in 1593, could have been a great man in the worlds of business and politics. He did indeed become a Member of Parliament. Leaving Cambridge he became a tutor in the Dutch Royal household. But it soon became apparent that his heart was in none of these things. His mind and heart were set upon the things of God which he had literally learnt at his mother's knee, and ever with his father's encouragement. He founded a religious community at Little Gidding, first with his own family around, and ultimately with an extended family of all and sundry who wished to give themselves to an ordered life of prayer and contemplation. The Community flourished under his deeply spiritual leadership. Visitors came from far and near and none entering the House would miss Ferrar's announcement quoted above. Ferrar was strong in his love for the Church of England and although, some years after his death, the Puritans destroyed his community, its spirit lived and it was in effect the pioneer of Religious Community life in our Communion.

Prayer   *Heavenly Father, send your blessing upon all religious communities that the prayers they offer and the work they do may abound to your glory and to the welfare of all whom they serve.*

Commemorating Saints and Martyrs of Asia;
Francis Xavier, 1552

Darest Thou know, O Soul?

Darest thou know, O soul
Walk out toward the unknown region,
Where neither ground is for the feet nor any path to follow?

No map there, nor guide,
Nor voice sounding, nor touch of human hand,
Nor face with blooming flesh, nor lips, nor eyes are in that land.

I know it not, O soul,
Nor dost thou, all is a blank before us –
All waits undreamed of in that region, that inaccessible land.

Till when the ties loosen,
All but the ties eternal, Time and Space,
Nor darkness, gravitation, sense, nor any bounds binding us.

Then we burst forth, we float,
In Time and Space, O soul! prepared for them,
Equal, equipped at last (O joy, O fruit of all) them to fulfil, O soul!

WALT WHITMAN (1819–1892)

Comment

The poet is, of course, thinking of the soul's journey from earth to heaven, but it seemed to me that his poem expresses admirably the experiences of many of the saints and martyrs of Asia, and in particular the adventures for Christ and his Church which St Francis Xavier endured. St Francis went out to many an 'unknown region'; where there was 'no path to follow'. His was pioneer work for Christ in the East Indies, in India, in Japan, in Singapore. From there he intended to preach the gospel in China, but he died on 2nd December 1552, in the ship which was taking him there. Ignatius of Loyola had attended Francis' lectures in the University of Paris and from that contact the two became friends, and with four others they founded the Jesuit Order. On his missionary journeys, his manner of life was austere but his personality was such that both children and adults were attracted to him. It was said of him: 'He is a true father; no one can see him without great consolation; the very sight of him seems to move people to devotion. His very look kindles in men an inexpressible desire to serve God'. He faced opposition with courage. He was 'wounded with arrows, pelted with mud, almost stoned to death, frequently followed by jeering crowds', but he pressed on and wherever he went hundreds were converted and baptised. Certainly we should remember with admiration and joy the accomplishments of missionaries like St Francis Xavier and others who served Christ from age to age in Asia. All of them could have said with our poet: 'All is a blank before us', but they pressed on, often with 'no map there or guide' always in the confidence that they were called to that ministry.. God be praised for them all! As Francis lay dying on the *Santa Cruz* he fixed his eyes on the crucifix and repeated a verse from the *Te Deum*: 'In te Domine speravi, non confundar in aeternam' and we can make that same prayer our own:

Prayer   *O Lord, in Thee have I trusted; let me never be confounded.*

Sometime

Sometime, when all life's lessons have been
   learned,
   And sun and stars for evermore have set,
The things which our weak judgments here
   have spurned,
     The things o'er which we grieved with
       lashes wet
Will flash before us out of life's dark night
   As stars shine most in deeper tints of
     blue,
And we shall see how all God's plans are right,
   And how what seemed reproof was love
     most true.

And we shall see how, while we frown and
   sigh,
   God's plans go on as best for you and me;
How, when we called, He heeded not our cry
   Because His wisdom to the end could see.
And e'en as prudent parents disallow
   Too much of sweet to craving babyhood,
So God, perhaps, is keeping from us now
   Life's sweetest things, because it seemeth
     good.

And if, sometimes, commingled with life's
   wine
   We find the wormwood, and rebel and
     shrink,
Be sure a wiser hand than yours or mine
   Pours out the potion for our lips to drink;
If we could push ajar the gates of life,
   And stand within and all God's workings
     see,
We could interpret all this doubt and strife
   And for each mystery could find a way.

But not to-day. Then be content, poor heart;
   God's plans, like lilies pure and white,
     unfold;
We must not tear the close-shut leaves apart –
   Time will reveal the chalices of gold.
And if, through patient toil, we reach the land
   Where tired feet, with sandals loosed, may
     rest.
When we shall clearly see and understand,
   I think that we shall say, 'God knew the
     best!'

MAY RILEY SMITH (1842–1927)

Comment

A simple poem, by an American poet, which strikes the Advent note and seeks to inspire confidence in the hearts and minds of those whose Christian commitment, though strong, seems sometimes to be tested beyond endurance. 'Life's wine' – the joy of living, the peace, the serenity – is embittered by 'the wormwood' of some deep disappointment or shattering experience which shakes faith and can call forth rebellion. The answer to the 'Why me?' and the 'What have I done to deserve this?', is wrapped in mystery, and our poet is assuring her readers that the mystery may not be resolved this side of Eternity, nor do we serve ourselves any good or any comfort by tearing apart 'the close-shut leaves' of the problem or the experience – that is by indicting ourselves: 'If only I had. . . '. St Augustine warns Christians that they should never despair about themselves. We have to trust God even where we cannot trace him. The Christ who promised 'I go to prepare a place for you' will in that place hand to us 'chalices of gold'.

Prayer   O Lord, Whose way is perfect, help us, we pray thee, always to trust in thy
   goodness; that, walking with thee and following thee in all simplicity, we may
   possess quiet and contented minds, and may cast all our care on thee, for thou
   carest for us through Jesus Christ our Lord.

CHRISTINA ROSSETTI (1830–1894)

A Hymn to God the Father

1.   *Hear me, O God!*
                A broken heart,
                Is my best part:
Use still thy rod
                That I may prove
                Therein, thy Love.

2.   *If thou hadst not*
                Been stern to me,
                But left me free,
I had forgot
                Myself and thee.

3.   *For sin's so sweet,*
                As minds ill bent
                Rarely repent
Until they meet
                Their punishment.

4.   *Who more can crave*
                Than thou hast done?
                Thou gav'st a Son,
To free a slave,
                First made of naught;
                With all since bought.

5.   *Since Death and Hell*
                His glorious Name
                Quite overcame,
Yet I rebel,
                And slight the same.

6.   *But, I'll come in,*
                Before my loss
                Me farther toss,
As sure to win
                Under his Cross.

BEN JOHNSON (1573–1637)

Comment

Ben Jonson – described in the epitaph on his tomb in Westminster Abbey as 'rare Ben Jonson' – was a poet of great distinction and through many of his poems there shines the conviction of strong faith and by the side of it, of the disruptive power of sin which erects a barrier between himself and God. In another of his longer poems he sighs:

> *Good and Great God, can I not think of thee*
> *But it must straight my melancholy be?*
> *Is it interpreted in me disease*
> *That, laden with my sins, I seek for ease?*
> *O be thou witness, that the reins dost know*
> *And hearts of all, if I be sad for show,*
> *And judge me after, if I dare pretend*
> *To aught but grace, or aim at other end.*

He reveals himself in those words, quoted from his poem entitled *To Heaven* as well as in his *Hymn to God the Father* as one who would count himself the sinner of sinners – 'I know my state both full of shame and scorn' – yet he knew too the forgiving and healing power of the love of God. 'Who falls for love of God', he says in another of his poems, 'shall rise a star', yet held up by 'my faith, my hope, my love'. He was not disturbed that God had been stern to him; sin is, after all, often 'so sweet'. He was very conscious (verse 4) that God through Christ could free him from sin's slavish grip, and that the Cross of Christ was to him both a magnet drawing him ever closer and an assurance that, standing beneath it, he, the sinner of sinners, will win.

Prayer   *Lord, for thy tender mercies sake, lay not our sins to our charge, but forgive us all that is past; and give us the grace to amend our lives, to decline from sin and incline to virtue, that we may walk with a perfect heart before thee, now and evermore.*

Commemorating Nicholas, Bishop of Myra, c.326

A Visit from St Nicholas

'Twas the night before Christmas, when all through the house
Not a creature was stirring, not even a mouse;
The stockings were hung by the chimney with care,
In hopes that St Nicholas soon would be there;
The children were nestled all snug in the beds,
While visions of sugar-plums danced in their heads;
And mamma in her kerchief and I in my cap,
Had just settled our brains for a long winter's nap,
When out on the lawn there arose such a clatter,
I sprang from the bed to see what was the matter.
Away to the window I flew like a flash,
Tore open the shutters and threw up the sash.
The moon on the breast of the new fallen snow
Gave the lustre of mid-day to objects below,
When, what to my wondering eye should appear,
But a miniature sleigh, and eight tiny reindeer,
With a little old driver, so lively and quick,
I knew in a moment it must be St Nick . . .
As I drew in my head and was turning around,
Down the chimney St Nicholas came with a bound . . .
He spoke not a word but went straight to his work,
And filled all the stockings and turned with a jerk,
And laying his finger aside of his nose,
And giving a nod, up the chimney he rose;
He sprang to his sleigh, to his team gave a whistle,
And away they all flew like the down of a thistle,
But I heard him exclaim ere he drove out of sight,
'Happy Christmas to all, and to all a good night'.

CLEMENT CLARKE MOORE 1779–1863)

Comment

There are few in the calendar of saints who have so many legends recorded about them as has St Nicholas, and it must be said that there are few too about whom so few historical facts are recorded. Nicholas was certainly Bishop of Myra in the fourth century. He is the patron saint of sailors, of travellers, of merchants and, supremely, of children – and to all and sundry among these he gave generously of his considerable wealth. But it is as a protector and lover of little children and the bestowal on them of gifts at Christmas time that he has been remembered through the years. 'Santa Claus' is but an American corruption of 'St Nicholas' who steals down chimneys on Christmas Eve with all sorts of goodies to fill all sorts of containers – stockings, pillow-cases, etc! The amusing poem which I stumbled across seemed to me to be too good to miss though it was necessary to abbreviate somewhat what the American poet wrote. But does it not put another thought into our minds? Our Lord was a lover of little children. In days when there is so much cruelty and child abuse, Christians should be alert as protectors.

Prayer   *Heavenly Father, we praise you that you put it into the heart of your servant*
Nicholas to be a lover and protector of children. Give us like concern for the
welfare of your little ones, that they may be protected from every danger both
in body and soul.

Commemorating Ambrose, Bishop of Milan, Teacher of the Faith, 397

Loyalty to God

Where a man's heart is, there will be his treasure also, for God is not wont to refuse a good gift to those who ask. So, because God is good and especially good to those who serve him, we must cling to him and be with him with all our soul and with all our heart and with all our strength. This we must do if we are to be in his light, and see his glory, and enjoy the grace of heavenly joy. To this happiness we must lift our minds, we must be in God, and live in him and cling to him, for he is beyond all human thought and understanding, and he dwells in endless peace and tranquillity. This peace passes all understanding, passes all perception.

This is the good which permeates everything. All of us live in it, depend on it. It has nothing above itself, but is divine. No one is good but God alone, because the good is divine, and the divine is good. So the psalmist says: 'When you open your hand all creatures are filled with goodness'. Through God's goodness, all the truly good things are given to us, and among them is no mixture of evil.

These are the good things that scripture promised to the faithful in the words: 'You shall eat the good of the land'. We are dead with Christ; in our bodies we carry the death of Christ, so that the life of Christ also may be manifested in us. We do not, any longer, live our own life, but the life of Christ, the life of innocence, chastity, simplicity, and of every virtue. We have risen with Christ; we must live in Christ; we must ascend in Christ.

ST AMBROSE (340–397)

Comment

Before Augustine of Hippo became a Christian he used to steal into the church to listen to the sermons of Ambrose, the Bishop of Milan. The above is an extract from one of the sermons of Ambrose. In his *Confessions* Augustine says: 'So I came to Milan, where I found Bishop Ambrose, this godly servant, known throughout the world as one of the best of men. That man of God received me as a father, and welcomed the stranger like a true bishop'. It is not too much to say that, under God, the Church owes to Ambrose the great St Augustine whose influence in the Church is alive after sixteen hundred years. Ambrose was not only a great teacher of the Faith but one who also exhibited the impact of the Faith in deeds of compassion and mercy. He appears to have attempted to persuade the Emperor to abolish the death penalty and when his persuasions were rejected, he pleaded with Christian judges to be sparing in death sentences. 'When the guilty is slain, the criminal is destroyed but not the crime. When the criminal is made to turn from the error of his ways, the crime is blotted out and the criminal is saved'.

Prayer   *Grant, O Heavenly Father, to all the bishops and pastors of your flock, the wisdom and the courage to lead your people to the knowledge of your love so that they may be in truth the messengers, the watchmen, and the stewards of your mysteries, to your glory and the welfare of those committed to their care.*

The Holy Bible

Thoughts from Great Minds

1

The Bible? That's the Book!
The Book indeed,
The Book of Books
On which one looks,
As he should do aright,
Shall never need
Wish for a better light,
To guide him in the night.

GEORGE HERBERT
(1593–1633)

2

It is an armoury of light;
Let constant use but keep it bright.
You'll find it yields
To holy hand and humble hearts
More swords and shields
Than sin hath snares –
Than sin hath snares,
Or hell hath darts.

RICHARD CRASHAW
(1613–1649)

3

Within that aweful volume lies
The mystery of mysteries!
Happiest they of human race,
To whom our God has granted grace
To read, to fear, to hope, to pray,
To lift the latch and force the way:
And better had they ne'er been born,
Who read to doubt, or read to scorn.

SIR WALTER SCOTT
(1771–1832)

4

Out from the heart of nature rolled
The burdens of the Bible told.
The word unto the prophets spoken
Was writ on tables yet unbroken:
The word by seers or sibyls told,
In groves of oak, or fanes of gold
Still floats upon the morning wind
Still whispers to the willing mind.

RALPH W. EMERSON
(1803–1882)

Comment

Just about this time of the year the Church turns the attention of her members to the **Holy Bible**, the collect for the second Sunday in Advent being the one in which Christians are bidden to 'read, mark, learn and inwardly digest' the truths which it embraces. So many great poems have been written about the Bible – as many by laymen as by clerics, that I have selected verses from poets born in the sixteenth, seventeenth, eighteenth and nineteenth centuries. The four poets quoted were all devout men of God and that is what enables us to accept their judgements. But it is one thing to appreciate the praises of great men who have valued the Bible and quite another to recognise its relevance to ourselves and to our day. Those who wrote the scriptures wrote them 'as they were told by the Holy Ghost' (2 Peter ch.1). As Christians we see what they wrote fulfilled by and in Jesus Christ. 'All that I am I owe to Jesus Christ, revealed to me in his divine Book' said David Livingstone. For us as for the poets quoted, and as for all who are committed to Christ's Way and Truth and Life, the Holy Bible is 'profitable for doctrine, for reproof, for correction, for instruction in righteousness', that we may be 'perfect, thoroughly furnished unto all good works'(see 2 Tim. ch.3). Tomorrow we can think about how best to use the Bible to that end.

Prayer *Blessed Lord, who has caused all holy Scriptures to be written for our learning: Grant that we may in such wise hear them, read, mark, learn, and inwardly digest them, that by patience and comfort of thy holy Word, we may embrace and ever hold fast the blessed hope of everlasting Life, which thou has given us in our Saviour Jesus Christ.*

BOOK OF COMMON PRAYER

A Heart Strangely Warmed

I think it was about five this morning that I opened my Testament on those words: 'There are given unto us exceeding great and precious promises, even that ye should be partakers of the divine nature'. Just as I went out, I opened it again on those words, 'Thou art not far from the kingdom of God'. In the afternoon I was asked to go to St Paul's. The anthem was: 'Out of the deep have I called unto thee, O Lord, O let thine ears consider well the voice of my complaint. If thou, Lord, wilt be extreme to mark what is done amiss, O Lord who may abide it? For there is mercy with thee; therefore shalt thou be feared. O Israel, trust in the Lord: for with the Lord there is mercy, and with him is plenteous redemption. And he shall redeem Israel from all sins'.

In the evening I went very unwillingly to a society in Aldersgate Street, where one was reading Luther's preface to the Epistle to the Romans. About a quarter before nine, while he was describing the change which God works in the heart through faith in Christ, I felt my heart strangely warmed. I felt that I did trust in Christ, Christ alone, for my salvation; and an assurance was given me that He had taken away my sins, even mine, and saved me from the law of sin and death. I began to pray with all my might for those who had in a more special manner despitefully used me and persecuted me. I then testified openly to all there what I now first felt in my heart.

JOHN WESLEY (1703–1791)

Comment

As we read that extract from John Wesley's *Journal*, we must remember that the seeds of divine truth which the words of the Bible were sowing, were falling on good ground – ground prepared by prayer and worship. The Bible derives its authority from Christ himself. It is a book about Christ – the Old Testament dealing with prophecy and the New Testament dealing with proclamation. Reading the Bible we must, of course, beware of bibliolatry – that is, of interpreting every word literally. Certainly we must read it intelligently, even critically, but all the time we must remember that it has to be read in the light of its interpretation by the mind of the Church. Without God's gift of faith, God's gift of Holy Scripture must remain beyond our understanding. John Wesley believed that, and he was in line with St Thomas Aquinas who lived 500 years before him. Thus Christians can and must be Bible readers – not merely Bible listeners – Bible readers because we need to read under the guidance of those qualified to interpret and because we too can derive from our reading inspiration, guidance, encouragement and spiritual strength. We can say confidently with the Psalmist: 'Thy word is a lantern unto my feet', but we must remember that we have to carry a lantern with us all the way if it is to be 'a light unto my path'.

Prayer   *O Lord, who has given us thy Word for a light to shine upon our path: Grant us to to mediate upon that Word and to follow its teaching that we may find in it the light that shineth more and more unto the perfect day; through Jesus Christ our Lord.*

ST JEROME (340–420)

A mind strangely convinced

How long, how long, will you keep saying: 'To-morrow? Why not now? Why not an end to my shame in this very hour?' This was what I was saying, and with bitter contrition in my heart, when suddenly from a house close by, I heard the voice of a boy or girl, I don't know which, singing and constantly repeating the words: 'Take and read. Take and read'. Instantly my look of sadness changed, and I began to consider intently whether there was any kind of game in which children used to repeat a song with words like that in it, and I could not recall having heard them anywhere at all. Stifling my tears I rose, reckoning that this was nothing less than a command from God to open the book and read the first passage I came upon. I went back to the place where I had put down the book of St Paul's Epistles when I got up. I seized it and read in silence the first passage my eyes fell upon: 'Not in rioting and drunkenness, not in chambering and wantonness, not in strife and envying, but put ye on the Lord Jesus Christ, and make not provision for the flesh, to fulfil the lusts thereof' . . . I had no wish to read further, and there was no need. The moment I came to the end of this sentence, the light of certainty flooded my heart, as it were, and every cloud of hesitation rolled away.

ST AUGUSTINE OF HIPPO (354–430)

Comment

The quotation is from *The Confessions* – a long book in which the saint tells his life story from childhood, when he says that he was 'a great sinner for so small a boy', to his conversion and beyond. He tells of his university days, when the lusts of adolescence led him into a life of pleasure and, much to the grief of his mother, the saintly Monica, he abandons himself to a dissolute life, seemingly turning his back on the Christian faith and being unwilling, as his mother had hoped, to offer himself for baptism. He was appointed as a Professor at Milan University and whilst there began to listen regularly to the sermons of Bishop Ambrose who, among much else taught him that the Bible's words are not invariably to be understood in a literal sense. Gradually he found himself ready to embrace Christian doctrine as it is found in the Scriptures. But he felt unable to go forward to Holy Baptism since, though now intellectually convinced about the Christian faith, he felt that he could not abandon his life-style which he saw to be inconsistent with the mind and teaching of Christ. Some time later in the quietness of his garden he heard the child's voice: 'Take up and read'. He was baptised, to his mother's great joy, and he began his great work for God and his Church. We may note that here again the seed was falling on ground from which the stones of rejection had been thrown away – ground which was good in the sense that it was receptive. Thus a man of vast intellect came to Christ and became one of the pillars of Christ's Church.

Prayer   *O God, eternal light, in whom is no darkness at all; Illuminate our hearts and minds as we read, and grant that thy Holy Spirit, who is the inspirer of all holy scripture, may be to us its interpreter, and may lead us through the written word to him who is the living Word and the Truth incarnate, even thy Son our Lord and Saviour Jesus Christ.*

FRANK COLQUHOUN

Meditation

The world is too much with us; late and soon,
Getting and spending, we lay waste our powers:
Little we see in Nature that is ours;
We have given our hearts away, a sordid boon!
This sea that bares her bosom to the moon,
The winds that will be howling at all hours,
And are up-gathered now like sleeping flowers;
For this, for everything, we are out of tune;
It moves us not, – Great God, I'd rather be
A Pagan suckled in a creed outworn;
So might I, standing on this present lea,
Have glimpses that would make me less forlorn;
Have sight of Proteus rising from the sea;
Or hear old Triton blow his wreathéd horn.

WILLIAM WORDSWORTH (1770–1850)

Comment

The sonnet is one of William Wordsworth's most well-known. The title at its head is not his but mine, for here Wordsworth is, in fact, meditating. He is doing what we do as Christians must do with our Bibles as we read passages from them – maybe daily, certainly frequently. For merely to read a passage and pass to the next task before us, without a moment's contemplation, does not open up to us the treasures of the Bible. Wordsworth was suddenly conscious of the world's unrelenting demands, of the world's pressures and burdens. In the moment he is inclined to think that all is 'a sordid boon'. He realised that allowing the world to press relentlessly down upon us we shall find ourselves 'out of tune' with life as he believes it has to be led. He arrests his thoughts on that truth. Proteus and Triton are Greek mythological gods – Proteus the god who will reveal to humans whatever they wish to know, and Triton who blows his horn to calm the troubled waters. Thus does Wordsworth meditate as, of course, do innumerable poets. They see with their physical eyes; they look into the world of nature with spiritual insight. Being for ever in a hurry in our lives leaves small time for living. Jesus said: 'Consider the lilies of the field, how they grow, they toil not, neither do they spin, yet Solomon in all his glory is not arrayed like one of these' (St Luke ch.12 v.27). There the Greek word translated 'consider' means 'to perceive thoroughly'. All of us frequently feel that 'the world is too much with us'. The remedy is to make 'spaces' in our lives to consider some word of God – to meditate upon it asking not merely 'What does this mean?' but, more importantly, 'What does this mean for me?'

Prayer *Lord, send thy Holy Spirit into my soul to tranquilllize and to stir, to draw and to drive, to enlighten and to inflame, as I study thy Word – and thy grace in thy covenant, and thy goodness in thy grace, and thy glory in thy goodness, and thyself in thy glory, the Almighty, the Eternal, the Lover and Perfecter of souls, the Father, the Son and the Holy Ghost, one God for ever and ever.*

ERIC MILNER-WHITE

A Way out of 'the World'

Often when we are most in earnest to pray, we are tormented by wandering thoughts and distractions of all sorts. I have been reading some old books lately and found that exactly the same things distracted others. 'The noise of a fly', as one says, is enough to distract him. Do not fuss, do not worry, do not spend time wondering why that thought came just then or that other interruption was allowed (for that is playing into the enemy's hands); but as soon as you are conscious that you have been drawn away, peacefully come back again. 'Return unto thy rest, O my soul'.

Faber describes these uncomfortable things as 'unmannerly distractions which come and force my thoughts from Thee'.

There will be times when we forget ourselves and everyone else and everything else, that we are caught up, absorbed; there is no word for what this is. But it will not be so every day. There must be something salutary in the pressing throng which prayer generally means. 'When Thou saidst, Seek ye my face; my heart said unto Thee, Thy face, Lord, will I seek'. There is a seeking; there is no seeing without that seeking. So the best way is to refuse to be entangled and worried and fussed, and as simply as a child would turn to one whom it loves, so turn to Him Whom our soul loveth, and, distractions or no distractions, say to Him, 'Thy face, Lord, will I seek'.

AMY CARMICHAEL (1867–1901)

Comment

These are the words of a mystic, a lady whom we have met before in this book, a lady who was a great spiritual guide and a great lover of souls, a lady who was very much 'in the world' for she was a 'Mother Teresa' of her day, but did not find that the world was 'too much' with her since her times of prayer preserved a balance. Her life of meditation, prayer and fasting replenished her resources for loving service. This extract from her book *Edges of His Ways* reveals how completely she herself was caught up in the seventh heaven of holiness, and how from her moments of transparent vision of God there came the fuel of love which fired the spirit of Christlike service. Thus did she pray:

> Give me the love that leads the way,
> The faith that nothing can dismay,
> The hope no disappointments tire,
> The passions that will burn like fire,
> Let me not sink to be a clod,
> Make me Thy fuel flame of God.

Where is the snag which for us so often defeats such serenity of service? She recognised it in some things of which the world so easily deprives us – namely the stillness, the silence and the solitude in which we can commune with God.

Prayer   *What better than to make Amy Carmichael's prayer – 'Give. . . ' your own, adding your own Amen.*

A Mother finds the Way

In his commentary on St Luke's Gospel, William Barclay speaks of a time to wait on God, and a time to work for God. He quotes part of a poem by Fay Inchfawn – a poem which I have been unable to trace elsewhere – but a poem which underlines his point that Christians need times of 'wise passivity'. The mother's poem runs thus:

I wrestle – how I wrestle! – through the hours,
Nay, not with principalities and powers –
Dark spiritual foes of God's and Man's –
But with antagonistic pots and pans:
With footmarks on the hall,
With smears upon the wall,
With doubtful ears and small unwashen hands,
and with a babe's innumerable demands.

Exhausted maybe, tired, wearied – she sets everything aside for a few moments of wise passivity – a few moments of stillness, of silence, of solitude – moments when she could consciously seek God. She returns to her work –

With leisured feet and idle hands, I sat.
I, foolish, fussy, blind as any bat,
Sat down to listen and to learn. And lo!
My thousand tasks were done the better so.

FAY INCHFAWN ( )

Comment

The slang way of describing the mother's condition is that she had had about as much as she could stand; everything was getting on top of her and she was perhaps beginning to think that she would not get everything done before the author of the footmarks and smears would be awake and fully active again. She might have paused for the morning service on the radio, or to read a passage from the Bible or some book of devotion. Something like that is precisely what she did. She meditated: she listened: she heard; she answered; she started again and her 'thousand tasks were done the better so'. She had seen things invisible, and heard a voice inaudible. She had, in fact, had a vision. It was 'Mr or Mrs Anonymous', who frequently utters some wise words, who said – if I quote him or her correctly:

A vision without a task is a dream;
A task without a vision is drudgery;
A vision and a task is the hope for the world.

Prayer   *O Lord, our Heavenly Father, by whose providence our duties are variously ordered: Grant to us all such a spirit that we may labour heartily to do our work in our several stations, as serving one Master and looking for one reward. Teach us to put to good account whatever talents thou has lent to us, and enable to redeem our time by patience and zeal; through Jesus Christ our Lord.*

BISHOP B.F. WESTCOTT (1825–1901)

Commemorating John of the Cross, Mystic, Teacher of the Faith, 1591

The Flame of Love

Keep your heart in peace; let nothing in this world disturb it; all things have an end. In all circumstances, however hard they may be, we should rejoice rather than be cast down, that we may not lose the greatest good, the peace and tranquillity of our soul . . .

To endure all things with an equable and peaceful mind, not only brings with it many blessings to the soul, but also enables us in the midst of our difficulties, to have a clear judgment about them and to minister the fitting remedy for them.

The 'Our Father'

It is clear that when the disciples besought Jesus that He should teach them to pray, He would tell them all that is necessary in order that the Eternal Father may hear us, since He knew the Father's nature so well. Yet all that He taught them was the Pater Noster (Our Father), with its seven petitions wherein are included all our needs, both spiritual and temporal . . . He told them that when they prayed they ought not to desire to speak much, since our Heavenly Father knows well what is meet for us, He charged them only, but with great insistence that they should persevere in prayer, saying elsewhere: 'It behoves us always to pray and never to fail'.

ST JOHN OF THE CROSS (1542–1591)

Comment

The first of the quotations is from *The Living Flame of Love* and the second is from *The Ascent of Mount Carmel*. St John of the Cross was a great teacher and he is described as a mystic which, briefly, means that he was one who believed in and strove after direct intercourse with God. To express that in simple terms, it is to say that he was a specialist in the spiritual life, and for the most part he wrote for specialists. He was a great counsellor in the things of God and one whose help was sought by others called on to give spiritual counsel and advice. That does not mean that St John of the Cross was so heavenly-minded that he could not come to terms with the sort of problems with which Christians have to grapple in the course of their pilgrimage. He was often 'down to earth' – certainly so in the difficult tasks which he undertook with St Teresa of Avila in reforming the Carmelite order of which he was a member. He was both upright and downright – upright in the sense that in his work of reforming his Order he demonstrated in his own spiritual life the high demands that he made of others; and downright in the sense that he did not hesitate to frame his teaching in words which admitted of no misunderstanding. Indeed this comment can close with a piece of his advice which all of us should do well to heed. 'Never listen to accounts of the frailties of others; and if anyone should complain to you of another, humbly ask him not to speak of him at all'.

Prayer *Almighty God, who taught us through the lips of your Son that through the narrow gate we shall find entrance to the kingdom: grant that by the example of your servant John of the Cross, we may be ready to enter darkness before beholding the light of your glory; through Jesus Christ our Lord.*

FROM *The Cloud of Witnesses*
by Archdeacon G.B. Timms

Contemplation

Stillness: *Be still my body – restless, fretful frame –*
Be still my mind and stem your winding ways –
Be still my spirit, languid, lax and lame;
Be still, be still, that I my God may praise.

Lord, in this stillness, I your Word may hear –
Word of indictment of the sins deplored,
Word of your mercy which drives away fear,
Word of forgiveness which rests me assured.

Lord, in the stillness, my spirit renewed,
Steel me with courage for life's stern employ,
Show me the way that with your grace imbued,
I may go forward aglow with your joy.

Silence: *I plead for silence –*
The silence man's busy-ness destroys –
The sparkling silence of the stars at night,
The solemn silence which the moon employs –
Noiseless their work – hushed as a holy rite.

I plead for silence –
The silence which casts an eerie spell
On all the clatter of our sad world's noise,
And, sanctified, assures: 'All shall be well', –
Enfolded thus I shall regain my poise.

Solitude: *Alone, alone – though not the world to shun;*
My solitude's divine.
I sought it freely when my tasks were done,
To meditate on thine.

Cleansed by thy mercy of sin's sultry stain,
Washed clean for service royal,
I stand alert and, at your service, deign
No task of thine as toil.

All glory, Lord, all glory to your name;
Anew I dedicate
Myself, that words and deeds may yet proclaim
Your power to recreate.

Bishop Cyril Bulley

Comment

Meditation and Contemplation are two methods of prayer which are in fact complementary, though contemplation is often regarded as a more advanced form of prayer. Each demands that we carve out periods of stillness, silence and solitude from our busy lives, moments when we set out to meet God person to person, that we may go out to serve him more surely in his world. A friend of mine used to find a poor simple old man sitting in his city church very frequently and one day asked what he did there for so long so often. His answer was: 'I just sits 'ere thinking about God in all 'is glory, of 'ow 'e loves me and of 'ow I must love 'im – and'ow us all must love 'im'. I am sure that the great 'Contemplatives' of the Church would say that that old man was 'not far from the Kingdom of God'.

Prayer   *Maybe today you too can utter the old man's words: 'I just sits 'ere thinking about God in all 'is glory, of 'ow he loves me and of 'ow I must love 'im – and 'ow us all must love 'im'.*

Know the ABC

In this life man is able to stand because of three things; by these same things God is worshipped, and we are helped, kept, and saved. The first is the use of man's natural reason; the second, the everyday teaching of Holy Church; the third, the inner working of grace through the Holy Spirit. All three come from the one God. God is the source of our natural reason; God is the basis of the teaching of Holy Church; and God is the Holy Spirit. Each is a distinct gift which we are meant to treasure and to heed. All of them are continually at work in us leading us Godwards. These are great things, and God's will is that we should know something about them here below: to know the ABC as it were, and have the full understanding in heaven. All this will help us on our way.

We know by our Faith that God alone – and no one else – took our nature; moreover, that Christ alone – and no one else – has done all that is necessary for our salvation. In the same way he alone brings it to its final end. In other words, it is he who dwells with us here, who rules and governs us in this life, and who brings us to his blessedness. And this he will do all the while there is any soul on earth destined for heaven. So much so that if there were only one such soul, he would be with that one soul, alone, till he had brought him to bliss.

MOTHER JULIAN OF NORWICH (1342–1416)

Comment

Julian of Norwich has been described as one of the greatest theologians in our national history. Mystic though she is, the *Revelations of Divine Love* is couched in language which the humblest Christian can understand. These revelations of the mystical experiences of a humble woman of the fourteenth century are such that the reader of them can be led very gradually into depths of profound thought which cannot but result in spiritual enrichment. Who would have thought, for example, of describing our present knowledge of God as but the 'ABC' of faith? By our natural reason, by the teaching of the Church, and by indwelling of the Spirit, we have placed ourselves in the finest 'preparatory school' for heaven. We may stumble and fall frequently in our pilgrimage from earth to heaven by reason of our frailty, but we shall never be on our own. When we know the A B C of holy living, we know that, though through wilfulness of frailty we may turn our backs on God in sin, he will never take his eyes off us. God in Christ will see us through in this life, lifting us when we fall, forgiving us when we repent of our sins. Such is the Divine Love that, holding fast to the A B C we are ready for the Second Coming of Christ in his glory, and meanwhile to his being born anew in our hearts in the Christmas festival.

Prayer *Multiply Love in us, O God, who hast first loved us, who art love, that, best and most we may love thyself; by love, learn of thee, by love, adore thee, and by love, serve thee faithfully through all our days; through Jesus Christ our Lord.*

The Old Man's Comfort

'You are old, Father William', the young man cried;
  'The few locks which are left you are gray;
You are hale, Father William – a hearty old man:
  Now tell me the reason I pray'.
'In the days of my youth', Father William replied,
  'I remembered that youth would fly fast,
And abused not my health and my vigour at first,
  That I never might need them at last'.
'You are old, Father William', the young man cried,
  'And pleasures with youth pass away;
And yet you lament not the days that are gone;
  Now tell me reason, I pray'.
'In the days of my youth', Father William replied,
  'I remembered that youth could not last;
I thought of the future, whatever I did
  That I never might grieve for the past'.
'You are old, Father William', the young man cried,
  'And life must be hastening away;
You are cheerful, and love to converse upon death:
  Now tell me the reason, I pray'.
'I am cheerful, young man', Father William replied,
  'Let the cause thy attention engage;
In the days of my youth, I remembered my God,
  And He hath not forgotten my age'.

ROBERT SOUTHEY (1774–1843)

Comment

Robert Southey, the poet despised by Byron and others, did not write great poetry, but he did write several memorable poems such as *The Battle of Blenheim, The Holly Tree* and his *Father William* – the last being a debate twixt youth and age in which 'age' discloses the basis of a life which enables him to account for the qualities which 'youth' admired in him. There are lessons for 'youth' to take to its heart, as the old man accounts for his 'hale and hearty' physical conditions as the natural result of his having in his youth a healthy respect for his God-given body, which had not suffered abuse of any kind. (What a lesson lies there for young people today, subject as they are to the temptations to engage in excessive drinking or smoking – or worse, in the violent self-abuse of drugs!). But the lines which justify the poem's place amongst our Advent thoughts are in the last two verses. The young man is surprised that the old man can talk about death cheerfully and the old man affirms that he has no fears because through his life as in his youth he remembered his God. The faith of the 'old Man' was Southey's faith reflected in many of his poems. In his *Occasional Pieces* he lays bare his soul, and that can be our prayer:

Prayer   Four things, which are not in thy treasury
          I lay before Thee, Lord with this petition –
            My nothingness, my wants,
            My sins, and my contrition.

Julian's thirteenth Revelation

After this our Lord brought to my mind the longing I had for him earlier.
I now saw that nothing hindered me but sin. And this I saw to be true in
general of us all, and I thought to myself that if there had been no sin we
should all have been clean and like our Lord, as when we were made. In
my foolish way I had often wondered why the foreseeing wisdom of God
could not have prevented the beginning of sin, for then, thought I, all would
have been well. This line of thought ought to have been left well alone; as
it was I grieved and sorrowed over it, with neither cause nor justification.
But Jesus, who in this vision informed me of all I needed, answered, 'Sin
was necessary, but it is all going to be all right; it is going to be all right'.
In this simple word *sin* our Lord reminded me in a general sort of way of
all that is not good; the despicable shame and utter self-denial he endured
for us, both in his life and in his dying. And of all the suffering and pain
of his creation, both spiritual and physical. For all of us have already experienced something of this abnegation and we have to deny ourselves as
we follow our Master, Jesus, until we are wholly cleansed. I mean, until
this body of death, and our inward affections (which are not very good)
are completely done away. All this, I saw, together with all the suffering
that ever has been or can be. And of all pain I understood that the passion
of Christ was the greatest and most surpassing. All this was shown in a flash,
and quickly passed over into consolation – for our good Lord would not
have the soul frightened by this ugly sight...

In these words was one of God's marvellously deep secrets – a secret which
he will plainly reveal to us in heaven. And when we know it we will see
the reason why he allowed sin to come, and seeing, we shall rejoice in him
for ever.

MOTHER JULIAN OF NORWICH (1342–1516)

Comment

Julian's 'All shall be well' breaks into this vision as into others. How good is this assurance
in an age when the world is passing through such agonies of conflict, of hatreds and of natural disasters! It is an assurance that the ultimate control is in the hands of the living God.
The concept of Christ's Second Coming has prompted the most absurd speculations about
dates and descriptions. Of these Christians know nothing. But Christians do know that the
world is God's, that history is going somewhere, that that *somewhere* is God's goal for man
whom God has made in his image. Because God is love, all those who respond to him with
their love here and now, and reflect that same love in their relationship with their fellows,
will indeed find that 'everything is going to be all right'. There is no assurance in the Gospels that Christians will enjoy immunity from the trials and testings and temptations which
are the common lot of man, but there is the assurance that he who trusts in the living God
and expresses that trust in Christian worship, in Christian living, and in Christian service,
will find that he can rejoice in God for ever.

Prayer   *Heavenly Father, we know that you order all things for our eternal good. Give
us a firm and abiding trust in your love and care; help us to resist temptations
and to rise above all our anxieties in the confidence that at your coming all will
be well.*

'Rest is not Here'

What's this vain world to me?
  Rest is not here;
False are the smiles I see,
  The mirth I hear.
Where is youth's joyful glee?
Where all once dear to me?
Gone as the shadows flee –
  Rest is not here.

Why did the morning shine
  Blithely and fair?
Why did those tints so fine
  Vanish in air?
Does not the vision say,
Faint lingering heart, away –
Why in this desert stay –
  Dark land of care!

Where souls angelic soar,
  Thither repair:
Let this vain world no more
  Lull and ensnare.
That heaven I love so well
Still on my heart shall dwell;
All things around me tell
  Rest is found there.

CAROLINA NAIRNE (1766–1845)

Comment

Baroness Nairne, a Perthshire lady, wrote a number of poems expressive of her strong faith in God and his purposes. In this, as in her poem entitled *Heavenward*, which latter she wrote in the evening of her life, she affirms her strong belief in the life beyond this world. For her, heaven was no idle figment of man's imagination. She was one who, having sipped the joys of heaven in this life in worship and Christian fellowship and service, was profoundly convinced that there must in the ultimate be a perfection of these things in the life to come. She knew that the way was ascending, and frequently through a 'dark land of care', tiresome and tiring. In this poem she fastens upon the concept of rest – not, surely, forgetting that there 'they rest not day or night', but remembering that in his heaven 'His servants serve him and see his face'. The rest which the poet has in mind is the rest of serenity, not the rest of inactivity. Here in this world which is the vestibule of Eternity, we prepare for the next not in a bid to save our own souls but to learn the language and to understand the currency of Heaven and thus to feel at home there. Henry van Dyke expresses our task well when he says:

> Who keeps for heaven alone to save his soul
> May keep the path, but will not reach the goal.
> While he who walks in love may wander far,
> Yet God will bring him where the blessed are.

Prayer

Our Father, Who art in heaven, help us to love things heavenly, that as we move through things temporal our hearts may be set on things eternal, that coming to your everlasting kingdom we may dwell for ever in the light of your presence.

Paradise

Once in a dream I saw the flowers
  That bud and bloom in Paradise;
  More fair they are than waking eyes
Have seen in all this world of ours.
And faint the perfume-bearing rose,
  And faint the lily on its stem,
And faint the perfect violet,
  Compared with them.

The Tree of Life stood budding there
  Abundant with its twelve-fold fruits;
  Eternal sap sustains its roots,
Its shadowing branches fill the air.
Its leaves are healing for the world,
  Its fruit the hungry world can feed,
Sweeter than honey to the taste,
  And balm indeed.

I saw the Gate called Beautiful;
  And looked, but scarce could look
    within;
  I saw the golden streets begin,
And outskirts of the glassy pool.
Oh harps, oh crown, oh plenteous
    stars,
  Oh green palm-branches, many-
    leaved –
Eye hath not seen, nor ear hath heard,
  Nor heart conceived.

I hope to see these things again,
  But not as once in dreams by night;
  To see them with my very sight,
And touch and handle and attain:
To have all heaven beneath my feet
  For narrow way that once they trod
To have my part with all the saints,
  And with my God.

CHRISTINA ROSSETTI (1830–1894)

Comment

Seldom does a collection of Christian verse appear without one or more of the poems of Christina Rossetti, sister of Dante Gabriel Rossetti whose poems and pictures often reflected the mediaeval mysticism which occasionally marks some of his young sister's verses. A poem entitled *Paradise* could hardly avoid this. Nevertheless Christina's intention is clear. She accepts her dream as a vision of the life after death, where all that is beautiful here is exceeded in beauty there, and all that is hurtful here finds no place there. Paradise is a Persian word meaning a beautiful enclosed garden. It is the word our Lord used in answering the request of the penitent thief that he should be remembered when Christ came to his kingdom. 'To-day', said our Lord, 'thou shalt be with me in paradise'. In popular use, the word means a state of unsullied bliss – a synonym indeed for that heaven to which the poet aspires and in which she will have her 'part with all the saints' and where she will be with God.

Prayer

Grant us, O Lord, not to set our minds on earthly things, but to love things heavenly; and even now, while we are placed among things that are passing away, to cleave to those that shall abide; through Jesus Christ our Lord.

LEONINE SACRAMENTARY

The 'Great O's' of Advent

O WISDOM, that camest out of the mouth of the Most High, reaching from one end to another, firmly and gently ordering all things: COME and teach us the way of understanding.

O ADONAI, Captain of the House of Israel, who didst appear to Moses in the flame of the burning bush, and gavest him the law on Sinai: COME and deliver us with thine outstretched arm.

O ROOT OF JESSE, who standest for an ensign of the people, before whom kings shall shut their mouths, to whom the nations shall seek. COME and deliver us and tarry not.

O KEY OF DAVID, Sceptre of the House of Israel, who openest and no man shutteth, and shuttest and no man openeth: COME and bring forth out of the prison-house him that is bound.

O DAY-SPRING from on high, Brightness of Eternal Light, and Sun of righteousness: COME and enlighten those who sit in darkness and the shadow of death.

O KING of nations, thou for whom they long, the Cornerstone that makest both one: COME and save thy creatures whom thou didst fashion from the dust of the earth.

O EMMANUEL, our King and Lawgiver, the Desire of all nations and their Saviour, COME and save us, O Lord our God.

Comment

Our quotation today is an act of devotion which was already in use in the Christian Church by the 8th century. It was customary to use these prayers as antiphons before the singing of the *Magnificat* on the days immediately before Christmas. Their inclusion on this day is therefore appropriate and our quotation can become our prayer.

The names by which we address God have all a Biblical origin and each is significant in its reference to our Lord. St Paul calls Christ 'the wisdom of God' and in his letter to the Colossians (ch.2) speaks of Jesus as the one 'in whom are all the treasures of wisdom hidden'. The title 'Adonai' applied to our Lord, is again a Divine title derived from the Old Testament, and means 'master' or 'Lord'. Jesus is addressed as 'Root of Jesse' to indicate his human descent from the royal line of David, a descent which is depicted in the 'Jesse' windows in Wells Cathedral and in Dorchester Abbey in Oxfordshire. To call Jesus the 'Day-spring from on high' is again to use a New Testament title. The title 'King' calls for no explanation, and the title with which we are so familiar in the great Advent hymns namely 'Emmanuel', means 'God with us'.

Thus, as we enter the Christmas season we remind ourselves of its real meaning – namely that the historical Christ is at once fully God and fully man. He is Lord, he is King. In him is all the wisdom of God. Thus when we hear his words, and when we discern his purpose – we hear the words and discern the purpose of the Living God. He is the Day-spring on High, so that we need no longer 'sit in darkness and the shadow of death'. he is Emmanuel – God with us. In him we see the wisdom and the truth of God and he it is who spells out for us both by his teaching and by his death on the cross the love of God for us. So, join your *Prayer* with Christians who for at least twelve hundred years have prepared themselves for Christmas by reminding themselves that He whom we adore is Emmanuel, 'Very God, Begotten, not created'.

The First Crib

Now three years before his death it beheld that he was minded, at the town of Greccio, to celebrate the memory of the Birth of the Child Jesus, with all the added solemnity that he might for the kindling of devotion. That this might not seem an innovation, he sought and obtained licence that a little child together with an ox and an ass, be brought unto the place. The Brethren were called together, the folk assembled, the wood echoed with their voices, and that august night was made radiant and solemn with many bright lights, and with tuneful and sonorous praises. The man of God, filled with tender love, stood before the manger bathed in tears, and overflowing with joy. Solemn Masses were celebrated over the manger, Francis, the Levite of Christ, chanting the Holy Gospel. Then he preached unto the folk standing round, the Birth of the King in poverty, called Him, when he wished to name Him, the Child of Bethlehem, by reason of his tender love for Him . . . The example of Francis, if meditated upon by the world, must needs stir up sluggish hearts unto the faith of Christ, and the hay that was kept back from the manger proved a marvellous remedy for Sick beasts, and a prophylactic against divers other plagues, God magnifying by all means His servant, and making manifest by clear and miraculous portents the efficacy of his holy prayers.

ST BONAVENTURE (1221–1274)

Comment

This quotation is from the saint's *Life of St Francis of Assisi*. Many churches throughout Christendom will be following the example of Francis and setting up a Crib just now as an aid to devotion. This is a practice which should be encouraged, remembering that we learn through our eyes as well as through our ears, and that pictures as well as words can stimulate our thoughts about holy things. As in the home great preparations are being made for Christmas – decorations, greeting cards, Christmas trees, lights and maybe, especially where there are children, a modest little crib, hidden presents ready for Christmas morning – everything to ensure that Christmas is a happy, jolly, merry time. All this is splendid, but it touches but the surface of the great mystery. There must be, in addition to all the material planning, a spiritual planning too so that there is time for joining in public worship, and most of all there must be the preparation of that crib which is the heart – the heart in which Christ can be born anew.

Prayer
Thou didst leave thy throne and thy kingly crown
When thou camest to earth for me,
But in Bethlehem's home was there found no room
For thy holy nativity.
O, come to my heart, Lord Jesus
There is room in my heart for thee.

EMILY E.S. ELLIOTT (1835–1897)

The Nativity

A little Boy of heavenly birth,
　But far from home to-day,
Comes down to find His ball, the earth,
　That sin has cast away.
O comrades, let us one and all
　Join in to get Him back His ball!

. . . . .

The Father speaking to the Son,
In all the multitude was none
　That caught the meaning true.
And yet 'This Word from heaven', said He
Was spoken not because of Me –
　But came because of you'.

Thus through the Son of Man alone
The mysteries of God are known;
　Thus to the chosen few,
With eye and ear attentive found,
He speaks in every sense and sound,
　The old becoming new.

. . . . .

Let my heart the cradle be
Of Thy bleak Nativity!
Tossed by wintry tempests wild,
If it rock Thee, Holy Child,
Then as grows the outer din,
Greater peace shall reign within.

JOHN BANISTER TABB (1845–1909)

Comment

The verses come from the pen of an American priest-poet, Father John Tabb, and are contained in his *Collected Poems*. Lent is preparatory to Easter, and Advent to Christmas. Easter, on the other hand, has what might be called a week of intense preparation in Holy Week. Christmas demands something similar, the more so since Christmas calls for so much by way of preparation in the home and family. No Christian would tolerate a Scrooge-like Christmas. Tiny Tim's wish: 'A merry Christmas to us all, my dears. God bless us every one!' is valid from the Christian angle in both particulars – the merriment and the blessing. But every Christian will be at one with Wilfred Peterson in his poem *The Art of Living* where he reminds us all that

> Christmas is not in tinsel and lights and outward show. . .
> The secret lies in an inner glow.
> It's lighting a fire inside the heart. . .
> Goodwill and Joy a vital part.
> It's higher thought and a greater plan,
> It's glorious dream in the soul of a man.
> Christmas begins deep down inside. . .
> Then engulfs the world like a mighty tide.

Prayer　Come, O Lord, abide in us that we also may abide in you and as with hearts and voices we join in the praises of shepherds, wise men and angels, we may in our own worship and in our own service be channels of your love and beacons of your light in the world about us.

No Room at the Inn

No room, no room, no room for Christ in Bethlehem that night,
No room for Beauty, Goodness, Truth, no room for Love and Light.
But 'twas no calculated bar of colour, class or creed,
No cryptic, callous, cautious, cold premeditated deed –
It was not these which kept him out, nor sophistry, nor pride,
It was in fact in ignorance they pushed the Christ aside.

So huddling in that stable mean there lay the pregnant maid,
And jostling in that lively inn the happy revellers played.
Within, all noise and busy-ness, with drink and talk and fun,
Without, a mystic silence reigned as God's great deed was done.
A woman groaned, a baby cried, Eternity pierced Time,
And Christendom began its life in backyard muck and grime.

Though entry on the stage of life was simple, poor and mean,
He moved among men, rich and poor, commanding and serene.
He talked of human rights and worth and love was his refrain,
He demonstrated selflessness, shared sorrow, suffering, pain.
Though great crowds listened eagerly, few took him as their guide;
Once more, and this time wilfully, the Christ was pushed aside.

Rejected yes, but still he lives, his message spans the world,
In every continent and clime his banner stands unfurled,
His stigmata illuminate our history's darkest page,
His law of love draws golden deeds from dross in every age.
He's Christ the King, the Way, the Truth, the Life, the Living Lord,
The man for Others, vocal still, who may not be ignored.

He looked upon a city once, discerning its malaise,
He touched the core of crisis there and blamed its selfish ways.
Come quickly, Lord, and save us from our crass stupidity,
Our selfishness, our turpitude, our cruel cupidity.
Our blindness, our indiscipline, our hatreds and our pride,
Speak now to our condition Lord, come quickly, come inside.

BISHOP CYRIL BULLEY

Comment

There is both a solemnity and an excitement on Christmas Eve and the two are complementary. The solemnity derives from the fact that we are about to celebrate again the world's new beginning in the birth of Christ, the Incarnate Son of God. We may not be able to comprehend the mystery of the Incarnation but facing Jesus we can apprehend the fact. The world acknowledged the new beginning – events are B.C. (before Christ) or A.D. (Anno Domini – in the Year of Our Lord). From its very nature the celebration of that new beginning both kindles and justifies excitement. But we must get our priorities right. We cannot celebrate Christ's birthday and leave him out of the party. We cannot 'keep Christmas' if there is no room for him in the Inn of our hearts. Hands must be uplifted to receive him in the Blessed Sacrament. Voices must be raised to join with others in adoration. Come then, Let us adore him!

Prayer *Almighty God, who by the Incarnation of thy only begotten Son banished the darkness of this world, and by his glorious birth didst enlighten this most holy night: Drive away from us the darkness of sin, and illuminate our hearts with the glory of thy grace, through Jesus Christ our Lord.*

Christmas Day

Rejoice and be Merry

Rejoice and be merry in songs and in
*   mirth!*
O praise our Redeemer, all mortals on
*   earth!*
For this is the birthday of Jesus our
*   King,*
Who brought us salvation – his praises
*   we sing.*

A heavenly vision appeared in the sky,
Vast numbers of angels the shepherds
*   did spy,*
Proclaiming the birthday of Jesus our
*   King,*
Who brought us salvation – his praises
*   we'll sing!*

Likewise a bright star in the sky did
*   appear,*
Which led the Wise Men from the east
*   to draw near:*
They found the Messiah, sweet Jesus
*   our King,*
Who brought us salvation – his praises
*   we'll sing!*

And when they were come, they their
*   treasure unfold,*
And unto him offered myrrh, incense
*   and gold:*
So blessed for ever be Jesus our King,
Who brought us salvation – his praises
*   we'll sing.*

ANONYMOUS

Comment

Poets all over the world have sought to express something of the mystery, the joy, the happiness and – yes! – the merriment of Christmas. I searched among them to find the simplest Christmas poem I could which expressed what lies at the heart of the festival. I think that the heart of Christmas, the wonder of Christmas, the hope of Christmas is contained in the last line of each of the verses of this poem of which no one knows the author. 'O praise our Redeemer... who brought us salvation, his praise we'll sing'. Whoever he was the poet had it right. He turns our eyes away from the angels, away from the shepherds, away from the wise men, away from our Lady and Saint Joseph – and fastens them firmly upon the Babe in the Manger, Jesus our King,

> *Who for us men, and for our salvation*
>   *Came down from Heaven*
> *and was incarnate by the Holy Ghost*
>   *Of the Virgin Mary*
> *and was made man.*

That is the tremendous truth which the Church proclaims again on Christmas Day, namely that the Eternal Son of God took upon himself human flesh of a human mother; that the Babe in the manger is at once truly God and truly Man, and that it is he who in his life and ministry gives to mankind the answer to the question which has teased men's minds through the ages: 'What is God like?' Here is not mere theophany – that is, a passing picture of God – here is One who evoked from the shepherds and the wise men what belongs only to God, namely worship. 'His Name shall be called Wonderful, Counsellor, The Mighty God, the Everlasting Father, the Prince of Peace' (St Luke ch.2 v, 15; Isaiah ch.9 v.6).

Prayer   *All praise to you, Almighty God and Heavenly King, who sent your Son into the world to take our nature upon him and to be born of a pure virgin. Grant that, as we are born again in him, so he may continually dwell in us and reign on earth as he reigns in heaven with you and the Holy Spirit, now and for ever.*

St Stephen the First Martyr

St Stephen

As rays around the source of light
Stream upward ere he glow in sight,
And watching by his future flight
   Set the clear heavens on fire;
So on the King of Martyrs wait
Three chosen bands in royal state,
And all earth owns, of good and great,
  Is gathered in that choir.

Foremost and nearest to His throne,
By perfect robes of triumph known,
And likest Him in look and tone,
   The holy Stephen kneels,
With steadfast gaze, as when the sky
Flew open to his fainting eye,
Which, like a fading lamp, flashed high,
  Seeing what death conceals.

Well might you guess what vision bright,
Was present to his raptured sight,
E'en as reflected streams of light
   Their solar source betray –
The glory which our God surrounds,
The Son of Man, th' atoning wounds –
He sees them all; and earth's dull bounds
  Are melting fast away.

He sees them all – no other view
Could stamp the Saviour's likeness true,
Or with His love so deep embrue
   Man's sullen heart and gross –
'Jesu, do Thou my soul receive:
Jesu, do Thou my foes forgive':
He who would learn that prayer must live
  Under the Holy Cross.

JOHN KEBLE (1792–1866)

Comment

St Stephen stands first in the long line of martyrs, men, women and children – who have borne their witness to their Faith from the earliest days of the Church to the present day. The story about his stand for Christ is told in full in chapter seven of *The Acts of the Apostles*. Appointed as one of the seven deacons whose task it was to be assistants to the apostles in the Christ-appointed task, Stephen put up a vigorous defence before the high priest for his own conversion and for the Faith which he had embraced. That resulted in his being stoned to death and, as Keble's poem expresses so sensitively, his last two prayers were first to commend his spirit to the Lord Jesus and then to pray that his murderers should be forgiven. Keble's line 'Three chosen bands in royal state' needs an explanation which can be set aside until tomorrow.

Prayer   *Almighty God, you filled your servant Stephen with such courage and constancy in faith and truth that he was faithful to the end. Give us a like courage that we may stand firm in the days of testing.*

St John the Evangelist

St John – Martyr?

'As there are three kinds of martyrdom, the first both in will and deed, which is the highest; the second in will but not in deed; the third in deed but not in will; so the Church commemorates these martyrs in the same order: St Stephen first, who suffered death both in will and deed; St John the Evangelist next, who suffered martyrdom in will but not in deed; the Holy Innocents last who suffered in deed but not in will'.

CHARLES WHEATLEY (1686–1742)

Comment

The quotation is from Wheatley's commentary on the Book of Common Prayer with his interesting suggestion that the three days after Christmas are in their different ways all days on which the Church remembers those who suffered for their faith. Keble's lines on the martyrdom of Stephen are recalled:

> *So on the King of Martyrs wait*
> *Three chosen bands in royal state,*
> *And all earth owns of good and great*
> *Is gathered in that choir.*

It is as one of the intimate trio of apostles who were very near to Jesus in the climacterics of his ministry that we remember St John the Divine. Tradition makes him the author of the Gospel which bears his name, along with the short epistles and the Revelation. Beyond what the Bible tells us, little is known save that he lived to a very great age. Wheatley's description of him as one who suffered martyrdom in will but not in deed is a reference to the fact that John stuck to Jesus through thick and thin even to the point of the Cross beneath which he stood as Christ offered himself for our salvation. 'Woman, behold thy son', said Jesus as John stood near to his mother, and 'John, behold thy mother' as he commended his mother to the care of John. Tertullian of the second century and Eusebius, the fourth-century father of ecclesiastical history, both mention St John in their writings, Eusebius reporting that he was sent into exile on the island of Patmos by the Emperor Domitian but was released on that emperor's death. In some verses about the Apostle, John Keble poses Peter's question to Jesus: 'Lord, and what shall this man do?', and has in mind Christ's enigmatic answer: 'If I will that he tarry till I come, what is that to thee? Follow thou me'. Keble's verse suggests that Peter's question about his friend, might on occasion be ours for our friend.

> *'Lord, and what shall this man do?'*
> *Ask'st thou, Christian, for thy friend?*
> *If his love for Christ be true*
> *Christ has told thee of his end;*
> *This is he whom God approves,*
> *This is he whom Jesus loves.*

Prayer   *Pray in your own words for a friend of yours whom you would wish to see standing nearer to Christ and ready to respond to his love.*

The Holy Innocents

Carol for Holy Innocents' Day

*The cat was let out of the bag by an angel
  Who warned them and planned their
    get-away,
And told how Herod would make holy
  with death
    The day that a birth made a holy day.*

*Herod's men were searching the back
  alleys,
  They did not see the refugees go,
Nor how when the child's hands fluttered
  like sparrows,
    His fingers blessed the casual snow.*

*The boy saw sand white as snow in the
  desert,
  And watched it thaw to husks of corn;
And perhaps his merchant uncle showed
  him
    The first white blossoms of the
    Glastonbury thorn.*

*We have hurried the children from a
  German Herod,
  Whose bombs stretch further than a
    city's roofs;
We have brought them westward across the
  Pennines
    To where the sea like a squadron moves.*

*They will see the bracken retard and turn
  rusty,
  And new fronds like clock-springs coil
    into gear;
Many times they will watch the seas'
  renewal,
  And oftener than we know the renewal
    of the year.*

*In farms among the hills, in small mining
  towns,
  Safe the unmartyred innocents lie;
But on the frozen cradle of Europe
  The infant Jesus is left to die.*

NORMAN NICHOLSON (1914–1987)

Comment

A dated poem, do you say? True there is no 'German Herod' hurling bombs now as when the poet penned his lines and Cumbria was giving homes to little refugee children from London and the great cities. But there are alas! still 'Herods' whose care for little children is no more than that of Herod the Great. There are the 'Herods' in different parts of the world, some near to our own land, who murder indiscriminately with lethal devices. There are 'Herods' who for love of money entice children into drug abuse and seemingly care nothing for the ultimate consequences. There are 'Herods' who bring suffering upon children through neglect, through thoughtlessness, through unkindness and – worst of all – through a vicious abuse of young children to satisfy their own unbridled passions. It is our duty as Christians not only to give of our charity to alleviate suffering whether caused by famine or human stupidity, but also to alert those responsible for child welfare to any instances of child abuse or child neglect of which we become aware.

Prayer   *Grant to our children, O God, this gift above all, that as they grow in body and in mind they may grow also in grace. Inspire in us the will to do everything within our power to alleviate suffering and deprivation among the children of our own and other lands: we ask this for the sake of him who suffered little children to come unto him, even Jesus our Lord.*

Commemorating Thomas Becket
Archbishop of Canterbury, Martyr, 1170

Bar the Door

Priests: *Bar the door. Bar the door.*
        The door is barred. We are safe. We are safe . ..
Thomas: *Unbar the door! throw open the doors!*
        I will not have the house of prayer, the church of Christ,
        the sanctuary, turned into a fortress. . . The church shall be open even to our
        enemies. Open the door!
Priests: *My Lord, these are not men. . . who respect the Sanctuary, who kneel to the Body*
        of Christ, but like beasts.
Thomas: *You think me reckless, desperate, and mad.*
        You argue by results as this world does,
        To settle if an act be good or bad.
        You defer to the fact. For every life and every act
        Consequence of good and evil can be shown.
        And as in time results of many deeds are blended
        So good and evil in the end become confounded.
        It is not in time that my death shall be known;
        It is out of time that my decision is taken,
        If you call that decision
        To which my whole being gives entire consent
        To the Law of God above the Law of Man,
        Unbar the door! Unbar the door!
        We are not here to triumph by fighting, by stratagem, or resistance
        Not to fight with beasts as men. We have fought the beast
        And have conquered. We have only to conquer now, by suffering.
        This is the easier victory. Now is the triumph of the Cross.
        Open the door! I command it. OPEN THE DOOR!

T.S. ELIOT (1888–1965)

Comment

And of course the door was opened. The knights rushed in and the Archbishop was murdered. Eliot envisages the scene – its tragedy and its grandeur, for both must have been apparent to all but the blind on that tragic day. The extract is from T.S. Eliot's *Murder in the Cathedral*, and in that same drama Eliot puts into the mouth of Becket thoughts about martyrdom. 'A Christian martyrdom is never an accident, for saints are not made by accident. Still less is a Christian martyrdom the effect of man's will to become a saint, as a man by willing and contriving may become a ruler of men. A martyrdom is always the design of God, for His love of men, to warn them and to lead them, to bring them back to his ways. It is never the design of man; for the true martyr is he who has become the instrument of God, who has lost his will in the will of God, and who no longer desires anything for himself, not even the glory of being a martyr. So thus as on earth the Church mourns and rejoices at once, in a fashion that the world cannot understand: so in Heaven the Saints are most high, having made themselves most low, and are seen, not as we see them, but in the light of the Godhead from which they draw their being'. There can be no finer definition of Christian martyrdom!

Prayer   *Preserve your Church, O Lord, from the hands of evil men: and as your holy martyr Thomas of Canterbury died in her defence, give her always the protection of faithful leaders, who shall guard her freedom and guide your people in the way of holiness, through Jesus Christ our Lord.*

Commemorating Josephine Butler
Social reformer, Wife, Mother. d.1906

Little and Great

A little spring had lost its way
Amid the grass and fern;
A passing stranger scooped a well
Where weary men might turn;
He walled it in, and hung with care
A ladle at the brink;
He thought not of the deed he did,
But judged that Toil might drink.
He passed again; and lo! the well,
By summer never dried,
Had cooled then thousand parchèd
tongues,
And saved a life beside.

A dreamer dropped a random thought;
'Twas old, and yet 'twas new;
A simple fancy of the brain,
But strong in being true.
It shone upon a genial mind,
And lo its light became
A lamp of fire, a beacon ray,
A monitory flame:
The thought was small; its issue great;
A watch-fire on the hill,
It shed its radiance far adown,
And cheers the valley still.

A nameless man, amid the crowd
That thronged the daily mart,
Let fall a word of hope and love,
Unstudied from the heart; –
A whisper on the tumult thrown,
A transitory breath, –
It raised a brother from the dust,
It saved a soul from death.
O germ! O fount! O word of love!
O thought at random cast!
Ye were but little at the first,
But mighty at the last.

CHARLES MACKAY (1814–1889)

Comment

This poem, the work of a Scottish poet, might be seen as indicating the starting point of the great work which Josephine Butler accomplished in the field of social welfare. First, let it be said of her that she was a woman of prayer and it was that which made her 'a lamp of fire, a beacon ray, a monitory flame'. Her heroine was St Catherine of Siena, whose devotion to the care of the sick, in mind as in body, was her great inspiration. Her social work began with attempts to reclaim prostitutes and to fight the 'white slave' trade. To begin with, hers was but 'a whisper on the tumult', but she pressed on and her achievements in the field of social welfare were massive.

Prayer

O God, you have taught us that we are members one of another, help us all to help each other and enable us to be the channels of your love to the fallen, to the lost, to the needy, to the lonely and to the anxious.

Commemorating John Wyclif, Theologian, Reformer, 1384

Grace and Doors

There was a gentle hostler
  (And blessèd be his name!)
He opened up the stable
  The night Our Lady came
Our Lady and St Joseph,
  He gave them food and bed,
And Jesus Christ has given him
  A glory round his head.

There was a courteous hostler
  (He is in Heaven to-night)
He held Our Lady's bridle,
  And helped her to alight.
He spread clean straw before her
  Whereon she might lie down,
And Jesus Christ has given him
  An everlasting crown.

There was a joyous hostler,
  Who knelt on Christmas morn
Beside the radiant manger
  Wherein his Lord was born,
His heart was full of laughter,
  His soul was full of bliss,
When Jesus, on His Mother's lap,
  Gave him his hand to kiss.

So let the gate swing open
  However poor the yard,
Lest weary people visit you
  And find their passage barred.
Unlock the door at midnight,
  And let your lantern's glow
Shine out to guide the traveller's feet
  To you across the snow.

Unlock the door this evening
  And let your gate swing wide,
Let all who ask for shelter
  Come speedily inside.
What if your yard be narrow
What if your house be small?
The Guest who is a'coming
  Will glorify it all.

Unbar your heart this evening
  And keep no stranger out,
Take from your soul's great portal
  The barrier of doubt.
To humble folk and weary
  Give hearty welcoming,
Your breast shall be tomorrow
  The cradle of a King.

JOYCE KILMER (1886–1918)

Comment

First, an apology to John Wyclif if the quotation appears to bear no relevance to his works! The last day of the year could not pass without a reference to the Christmas Feast in the octave of which the Church continues to rejoice. The poem is by an American who was killed in action in the First World War. Wyclif, who was devoted to the theology of St Augustine, and who showed himself to be one who understood the needs of simple people, would appreciate the lesson which the poet is teaching. John Wyclif gave us the first English translation of the whole Bible so that it could be read and understood by all – the simple as well as the lettered. He has been called the 'Morning Star of the Reformation' and whilst it is true that his star shone brightly and led the way in which the Church should move to rid itself of abuses, his fierce language was not universally admired. He attacked the monasteries and monks, but himself started what he called his 'Poor Priests' who could scarcely be distinguished from Friars. His contribution to the renewal of the Church's witness, life and order merits our remembrance of him in our calendar.

Prayer   *Almighty Father, who raised up your servant John Wyclif to be a herald of renewal in the Church; Give your people ears to hear the voice of the prophet and power to discern the true from the false; through him who is the Way, the Truth, and the Life, your Son Jesus Christ our Lord.*

PRAYER FROM *The Cloud of Witnesses*
BY ARCHDEACON G.B. TIMMS

The Kingdom of God

O World invisible we view thee.
O world intangible we touch thee,
O world unknowable we know thee,
Inapprehensible, we clutch thee!

Does the fish soar to find the ocean,
The eagle plunge to find the air
That we ask of the stars in motion
If they have rumour of these there?

Not where the wheeling systems darken,
And our benumbed conceiving soars!
The drift of pinions would we hearken,
Beats at our own clay-shuttered doors.

The angels keep their ancient places;
Turn but a stone, and start a wing!
'Tis ye, 'tis your estranged faces,
That miss the many-splendoured thing.

But (when so sad thou canst not sadder)
Cry; and upon thy so sore loss
Shall shine the traffic of Jacob's ladder
Pitched betwixt Heaven and Charing Cross.

Yea, in the night, my soul, my daughter,
Cry; – clinging Heaven by the hems;
And lo, Christ walking on the water
Not of Gennesareth, but Thames!

FRANCIS THOMPSON (1859–1907)

Comment

This is another of the mystical poems of Francis Thompson who wrote *The Hound of Heaven*. What in effect his imagery is doing here is bringing God down to earth! The Living God did just that. Mrs. Alexander was indeed writing for children when in her great hymn she wrote: 'He came down to earth from heaven, Who is God and Lord of all', but those two simple lines embrace the great truth of the Incarnation. It is not surprising therefore that in the Church's year the great moments of the life and ministry of our Lord have special significance in the Christian calendar. However, since the date of Easter varies from year to year, those significant Fasts and Feasts cannot be assigned to unmovable dates in the calendar. These six – Ash Wednesday, Maundy Thursday, Good Friday, Easter Day, Ascension Day and Whit Sunday (Pentecost) – follow our meditations now in their order. The ancient Celtic Blessing with which the book closes will be wholesome reading on any day and can be used as a prayer, more especially perhaps when we wish to call down a blessing on someone who to our knowledge stands in special need.

To keep a good Lent

Is this a Fast –
The Larder lean
and clean?

Is it to quit the dish
Of flesh, yet still
to fill
The platter high with Fish?

Is it to fast an hour
Or rage to go
or show
A downcast look, and sour?

No! 'tis a Fast, to dole
Thy sheaf of wheat
and meat
Unto the hungry soul.

It is to fast from strife,
From old Debate
and hate;
To circumcise thy life.

To show a heart grief-rent
To starve the sin,
not Bin;
And that's to keep thy Lent.

ROBERT HERRICK (1591–1674)

Comment

Robert Herrick's poem would suggest that the misconceptions of the Lenten Fast were as common in his day as in ours. In the last three verses he seeks to educate his parishioners about the true demands of Lent. The length of the Lenten Fast dates from the fourth century when it was decided that the Fast should begin on Ash Wednesday and cover forty days. Through the centuries the severity of the Fast was gradually relaxed though its observance was retained by the Church of England following the Reformation. But it seems from Herrick's poem that his parishioners asked themselves the same sort of question as we hear today: 'What shall I give up for Lent?'. The first three of his verses give what may be called the 'negative answer' heard now as, apparently, then; the last three verses give the positive answer. There is, of course, a disciplinary merit in 'giving up' for example, some 'goodies' – sweetmeats, alcohol, a TV programme or two – but there is a greater merit in passing the money saved to the needy, and using the time saved in some spiritual discipline – reading, meditation, worship. Lent has something to do with the 'Bin' - food, but much more to do with feeding the hungry (verse 4), healing broken relationships (verse 5), and repenting of sin (verse 6).

Prayer   *O God, Who by Thy Word dost marvellously work out the reconcilia-*
tion of mankind, grant, we beseech Thee, that by this holy Fast we may
both be subjected to Thee with all our hearts, and be united to each other
in prayer to Thee, through Jesus Christ our Lord.

GELASIAN SACRAMENTARY

Holy Thursday

'Twas on a Holy Thursday, their innocent faces clean,
Came children walking two and two, in red, and blue, and green;
Grey-headed beadles walked before, with wands as white as snow.
Till into the high dome of Paul's they like Thames waters flow.

O what a multitude they seemed, these flowers of London town!
Seated in companies they sit, with radiance all their own.
The hum of multitude was there, but, multitude of lambs,
Thousands of little boys and girls raising their innocent hands.

Now like a mighty wind they raise to heaven the voice of song
Or like the harmonious thunderings the seats of heaven among;
Beneath them sit the aged men, wise guardians of the poor.
Then cherish pity, lest you drive an angel from your door.

WILLIAM BLAKE (1757–1827)

Comment

Here is a holy day of which the general public is made aware each year by the distribution by the monarch of the Maundy Pence to impecunious aged people. This happens annually in one of England's cathedrals. Pictures of the ceremony appear in the papers but not all who see them know the origin of the ceremony and the day. Since the year 391 this Thursday before Easter has been a day of commemoration of our Lord's Institution of the Eucharist. Thus the Eucharist is the Lord's Own Service – the only formal act of worship which he instituted – and is thus central in the Church's worship. It was on Maundy Thursday too, and in the course of the Eucharist, that the Holy Oils were blessed for subsequent use by the clergy in anointing the sick – see Epistle of James ch.5 v.14 – and in the Sacraments of Initiation, namely Holy Baptism and Confirmation. These sacramental uses of Holy Oil have happily been restored to our Church in recent years. There is yet another ceremony, and the monarch's distribution of the Maundy Pence is an abbreviated version of it. It is the ceremony of the 'feet washing', during which the bishop – sometimes the monarch – following our Lord's example (see St John ch.13 vv.4–10) ceremonially washed the feet of worshippers. The name 'Maundy' derives from one of the Latin prayers which accompanied the feet washing – namely *mandatum novum*. In some parts of the Christian Church the day is known as *Green Thursday* or *Sheer Thursday*, both names connected with cleansing from sin and probably with the washing of the church's altars on this day before Good Friday. It is a happy thing that these ceremonies, so closely connected with the words and actions of Jesus immediately before his Crucifixion, are being brought back into the worship of the Church. As we learn through the eye as well as through the ear, such symbolic acts cannot but increase devotion. William Blake is clearly calling to mind a Maundy Thursday service which he had attended in St Paul's Cathedral. Certainly on this day we should praise God for the wonderful Sacrament of the Altar and, recalling the humility of Christ in washing the feet of his disciples, we should remind ourselves that there is nothing menial in acts of service to our fellows be they never so humble.

Prayer   *Almighty Father, whose Son Jesus Christ has taught us that what we do for the least of our brethren, we do also for him; give us the will to be the servant of others as he was the servant of all, who gave up his life and died for us, yet is alive and reigns with you and the Holy Spirit, one God now and for ever.*

THE ALTERNATIVE SERVICE BOOK

The Darkest Hour

Is it not strange, the darkest hour
That ever dawned on sinful earth
Should touch the heart with softer power
For comfort, than an Angel's mirth?
That to the Cross the mourner's eye should turn
Sooner than where the stars of Christmas burn,

Sooner than where the Easter sun
Shines glorious on yon open grave,
And to and fro the tidings run,
'Who died to heal, is risen to save'.
Sooner than where upon the Saviour's friends,
The very Comforter in light and love descends.

Yes so it is; for duly there
The bitter herbs of earth are set,
Till tempered by the Saviour's prayer,
And with the Saviour's life-blood wet,
They turn to sweetness, and drop holy balm,
Soft as imprisoned martyr's death-bed calm.

Lord of my heart, by Thy last cry,
Let not Thy blood on earth be spent –
Lo, at Thy feet I fainting lie,
Mine eyes upon Thy wounds are bent,
Upon Thy streaming wounds my weary eyes,
Wait like the parched earth on April skies.

Wash me, and dry these bitter tears,
O let my heart nor further roam,
'Tis Thine by vows, and hopes and fears,
Long since – O call Thy wanderer home;
To that dear home, safe in Thy wounded side,
Where only broken hearts their sin and shame
may hide.

JOHN KEBLE (1792–1866)

Comment

The verses are from Keble's *The Christian Year* – a book in which Keble follows through the year, covering all its Sundays, its Fasts and Festivals and drawing out the particular message of each. His phrase 'touch the heart with softer power for comfort' is his way of expressing the impact of the Cross on the history of the world. What was once an instrument of torture became at a moment in history the symbol of love. It is both the measure of man's sin – the depths to which man may sink – and the measure of God's love, the height to which Christ went for us men and our salvation. Kneeling before the Cross of Christ we learn how we can be forgiven, but we must learn too how we should ourselves forgive. Samuel Rutherford summed that truth up admirably when he wrote: 'The cross of Christ is the sweetest burden that I ever bore. . . It points, in the length of it, to heaven and earth, reconciling them together; and in the breadth of it, to former and following ages, as being equally salvation to both'.

Prayer   *Almighty and everlasting God, by whose Spirit the whole body of the Church is governed and sanctified: hear our prayer which we offer for all your faithful people; that each in his vocation and ministry may serve you in holiness and truth to the glory of your Name; through our Lord and Saviour Jesus Christ.*

THE ALTERNATIVE SERVICE BOOK

Christ's Triumph

Most glorious Lord of life! that, on this day,
Didst make thy triumph over death and sin;
And, having harrowed hell, didst bring away
Captivity, thence captive, us to win;
This joyous day, dear Lord, with joy begin;
And grant that we, for whom thou didest die
Being with thy dear blood clean washed from sin,
May live for ever in felicity!
And that thy love we, weighing worthily,
May likewise love thee for the same again;
And for thy sake, that all like dear didst buy,
With love may one another entertain.
So let us love, dear Love, like as we ought;
Love is the lesson which the Lord us taught.

EDMUND SPENSER (1552–1599)

Comment

Easter is the queen of the Church's festivals because it was the resurrection of Christ which called the Church into being. It is perhaps significant that on the first Easter morning the apostles showed no particular concern for the 'how' or the 'when' of the resurrection. Their urgent concern was to declare that 'The Lord is risen indeed and has appeared to Simon' – that is, Peter. From that moment what they had seen on Calvary's hill as a disastrous end to all their hopes and an obscene nullifying of all Christ's promises, became the beginning of that Church which Christ had promised both to found and to sustain against 'the gates of hell'. Those gates of hell have, as it were, conspired throughout history in virulent opposition of the Church from without and in tragic infidelity of the Church from within. But through all the opposition and despite all the infidelity the Church lives still and that because Christ lives in it. Let's do more on this day than merely greeting our friends with 'A happy Easter'; let us proclaim the Easter truth as the Orthodox Christians do. Let the greeting be: 'Christ is risen!', and let our reply to the greeting be, 'He is risen indeed'.

Some years ago, an editorial in the American journal *Life* summed up the writer's thoughts thus: 'The Resurrection cannot be tamed or tethered by any utilitarian test. It is a vast watershed in history, or it is nothing. It cannot be tested for truth, for it is the test of lesser truths. No light can be thrown on it; its own light blinds the investigator. Once accepted, it tells more about the universe, about history, and about man's state and fate than all the mountains of other facts in the human accumulation'. Yes, 'watershed' – dividing line – it is. No Christian Church could have emerged from Calvary's Hill had that indeed been the end. No Church could have survived what the Church has survived in fierce persecution and grievous infidelity were it not the Church of a Living Lord. So, with Martin Luther,

Wherefore let us all rejoice
Singing loud with cheerful voice,
Alleluia!

Prayer *Lord of all life and power, who through the mighty resurrection of your Son overcame the old order of sin and death to make all things new in him: grant that we, being dead to sin and alive to you in Jesus Christ, may reign with him in glory; to whom with you and the Holy Spirit be praise and honour, glory and might, now and in all eternity.*

THE ALTERNATIVE SERVICE BOOK

Ascension Day

Lift up your heads great gates and sing
Now Glory comes and Glory's King;
Now by your high all-golden way
The fairer Heaven comes home to-day.
Hark! now the gates are ope, and hear
The tone of each triumphant sphere;
Where every angel as he sings
Keeps tune with his applauding wings,
And makes heaven's loftiest roof
rebound
The echoes of the noble sound.

JOSEPH BEAUMONT (1616–1699)

Eternal Light! Eternal Light!
How pure the soul must be
When, placed within Thy searching
sight
it shrinks not but with calm delight
Can live, and look on Thee!

There is a way for man to rise
To that sublime abode, –
An Offering and a Sacrifice
A Holy Spirit's energies
An advocate with God.

These, these prepare us for the sight
Of holiness above;
The sons of ignorance and night
May dwell in the Eternal Light,
Through the Eternal Love.

THOMAS BINNEY (1798–1874)

Comment

Two poets, both Doctors of Divinity, have something to say about our Lord's Ascension into Heaven, Beaumont seeing it as Christ's Coronation. Christ is 'Glory's King' entering into His Kingdom – going up to Heaven – 'up' not spatially but as a child goes 'up' from one form to another, or a teenager goes 'up' to a university. Because Christ is 'in Heaven', He is everywhere in earth. He is no longer merely the Christ of Galilee; He is the Christ of the Universe. For that truth Christians 'hail the day that sees Him rise' and lift their voices in their Alleluias. But our second poet reminds us of a Christian's further duty. He must rise too! Seeing Christ as 'Eternal Light' he must lift up his eyes to Christ who, because He is in Heaven, is everywhere and in every heart save that from which He is barred consciously and deliberately. We must lift up our hearts to Heaven so that 'we may in heart and mind thither ascend and with Him continually dwell'. Thomas Binney, whose chief literary work was entitled significantly *How to Make the Best of Both Worlds*, points the 'way for man to rise' to Eternal Light. It is through Eternal Love, and that reminds us of Christ's Offering and Sacrifice 'for us men and for our salvation' and of our need of the Holy Spirit both to inspire and to sustain our pilgrimage.

Prayer

Almighty God, as we believe your only-begotten Son our Lord Jesus Christ to have ascended into the heavens, so may we also in heart and mind thither ascend and with him continually dwell; who is alive and reigns with you and the Holy Spirit, one God now and for ever.

THE ALTERNATIVE SERVICE BOOK

The Holy Spirit

In the hour of my distress,
When temptations me oppress,
And when I my sins confess,
   Sweet Spirit comfort me.

When I lie within my bed,
Sick in heart and sick in head,
And with doubts discomforted,
   Sweet Spirit, comfort me!

When the house doth sigh and weep,
And the world is downed in sleep,
Yet mine eyes the watch do keep,
   Sweet Spirt, comfort me!

When, God knows, I'm tossed about
Either with despair or doubt,
Yet, before the glass be out,
   Sweet Spirit, comfort me!

When the tempter me pursue'th
With the sins of all my youth,
And half damns me with untruth,
   Sweet Spirit, comfort me!

When the judgment is revealed,
And that opened which is sealed,
When to Thee I have appealed,
   Spirit Spirit, comfort me!

ROBERT HERRICK (1591–1674)

Comment

The verses form part of a somewhat longer Litany to the Holy Spirit. The poet was the parish priest of Dean Prior in Devon, who in his time there, and during a period when he was, as a Royalist, ejected from his benefice, he wrote a great number of poems and some hymns. In this Litany to the Holy Spirit he recognises the power of the Holy Spirit to effect a change within him. As he wrote it he must have been recalling the effect of the Holy Spirit on the first Apostles on the day of Pentecost. In the privacy of the Upper Room, some ten days after the last appearance of Christ to them, they were contemplating, doubtless in prayer, whether they could summon up sufficient courage to obey the Lord's command to go out to the world to preach Christ. Undoubtedly they were conscious of their mission but fearful to set out upon it. It was then, even whilst they prayed, 'all together with one accord in one place' that they were suddenly filled with the Spirit. The Spirit was the Spirit of God and it was therefore the Spirit of Jesus. Commissioned by the Spirit, they were now empowered by the Spirit. There was a transformation from within. They no longer feared the Jews and they rushed from the Upper Room to the market place. At that moment the Church's mission to the world began. Herrick is appealing for the power of the Holy Spirit to help him through his trials, and Christians before Herrick and since have sought the power of the Spirit to set them on Christ's Way, to hold them to Christ's truth, and to empower them to live the Christ life.

Prayer   *Almighty God, who at this time taught the hearts of your faithful people*
by sending to them the light of your Holy Spirit: grant us by the same
Spirit to have a right judgement in all things, and evermore to rejoice
in his holy comfort; through the merits of Christ Jesus our Saviour, who
is alive and reigns with you in the unity of the Spirit, one God, now
and for ever.

ALTERNATIVE SERVICE BOOK

A CELTIC BLESSING

MAY THE BLESSING OF LIGHT
Be on you, light without and light within.

MAY THE BLESSED SUNLIGHT
Shine upon you and warm your heart till it glows
Like a great peat fire, so that the stranger may
Come and warm himself at it, and also a friend, and

MAY THE LIGHT SHINE OUT OF THE EYES OF YOU
Like a candle set in the windows of a house
Bidding the wanderer to come in out of the storm, and

MAY THE BLESSING OF THE RAIN
Be on you – the soft sweet rain. May it fall upon
Your spirit so that the little flowers may spring up
And shed their sweetness on the air.

MAY THE BLESSINGS OF THE GREAT RAINS BE ON YOU
May they beat upon your spirit and wash it fair and clean.
And leave there many a shining pool where the blue
Of Heaven shines, and sometimes a star.

MAY THE BLESSING OF THE EARTH
Be on you – the great round earth;

MAY YOU EVER HAVE A FRIENDLY GREETING
For them you pass as you're going along the roads.

MAY THE EARTH BE SOFT UNDER YOU when
You rest upon it, tired at the end of the day.

MAY IT REST EASY OVER YOU when
At the last you lie out under it.
May it rest so lightly over you that
Your soul may be off from under it quickly
And up and off, and on its way to God.

MAY THE LORD BLESS YOU AND BLESS YOU KINDLY

Index of First Lines of Verses

Index of Authors/Poets and Commemorations*

* *Dates of Commemorations in bold type*

Acknowledgments

The author and publishers acknowledge with thanks the courtesy of a number of authors and publishers who have given their permission for the inclusion of copyright and other material as follows: Jacaranda Riley Ltd. of Queensland, Australia, and Kathleen Walker for *Intolerance* from her book *My People*; Norman Nicholson for his carol *Holy Innocents' Day*. (His permission was given a few weeks before he died); Bishop Oliver Allison for the quotation from his *Memoirs*; Macmillan Publishers Ltd. and Charles Causley for *All Souls' Day* from his *Collection of Poems*; J.M. Dent Ltd. for Dylan Thomas' poem *Do not go gentle into that good night*; A.R. Mowbray Ltd. for (i) Extracts from *The Love of God* by Evelyn Underhill, (ii) poems of the late Father Andrew S.D.C. and (iii) Extracts from *Wantage Poems*; The Mother General of the Community of St. Mary the Virgin, Wantage for poems by the late *Sisters Phoebe, Rosalind Mary* and *Lilian Ailsa*; *Sisters Cyrilla* and *Isobel Everild* for their poems; Faber & Faber for lines from *Murder in the Cathedral* (T.S. Eliot), and *Markings* by Dag Hammarskjöld – the translation by W.H. Auden and Leif Sjöberg; John Murray Publishers Ltd. for (i) some lines from Sir John Betjeman's *Diary of the Church Mouse* and (ii) for *St. Cadoc* from *Collected Poems*; and (iii) for the extracts from *The Faith of Edward Wilson* by George Seaver; The Society of Authors for (i) Richard le Gallienne's *The Second Crucifixion* and (ii) as the literary representatives of the late John Mansfield for his poems *O Little Self* and *Laugh and Be Merry*; Angus & Robertson U.K. Ltd., for *New Guinea* from James McAuley's *Collected Poems* (copyright James McAuley 1971), and for *The Moth* from Judith Wright's *Selected Poems* (copyright Judith Wright 1963); Mr. Gerald Priestland and the St. Andrew Press, Edinburgh for lines quoted from *Who needs the Church?*; Charles Scribner & Sons (New York) for lines from *The Nature and Destiny of Man* by Reinhold Niebuhr; Mr. David Carey and members of the family of the late Archbishop William Temple for quotations from his books and for his prayers; Canon Frank Colquhoun for prayers from his collection *Parish Prayers* including some of his own composition; Archbishop Michael Ramsey for an extract from his *Introducing the Christian Faith*; William Heinmann Ltd. for quotes from *The Prophet* by Kahlil Gibran; The Society for Promoting Christian Knowledge for quotations from the works of Amy Carmichael, namely *Things as They are, Gold by Moonlight* and *Edges of His Ways*, and (ii) prayers from Eric Milner-White's *My God, my Glory*; Jonathan Cape Ltd. for the Executors of the late W.H. Davies Estate for *Leisure* from *The Collected Poems of W.H. Davies*; Collins Harvill Ltd., for some lines from *The Pilgrim's Regress* by C.S. Lewis; Bishop George Appleton for some of his *Prayers*; The Central Board of Finance of the Church of England for prayers from *The Alternative Service Book*; Collins Publishers Ltd., for quotations from Teilhard de Chardin's *Le Milieu Divin*; Hodder & Stoughton Ltd. for lines from Bishop Russell Barry's *Asking the Right Questions*; James Nisbet Ltd., for some lines from Bishop Barry's *The Relevance of Christianity*; Constable & Co. Ltd. for George Santayana's poems *Soon Lovely England* and *O World*;

the representatives of the family of the late Margaret Cropper for an extract from *Flame touches Flame*; The Clarendon Press for lines from S. Radhakrishnan's *Eastern Religions and Western Thought*; Archdeacon G.B. Timms for his prayers from *The Cloud of Witnesses*; Darton, Longman and Todd Ltd., for some lines from *Love is My Meaning* – a quotation from *The Watchword*; Longman Publishers for quotations from the writings of Dean Inge in *Personal Religion*.

Though every effort has been made to trace copyright holders, the author and publishers have in a few instance failed in their efforts to trace original sources. Furthermore there have been instances where letters addressed both to publishers and possibly interested parties have not been answered or have been returned 'gone away'. Any omissions or corrections in this matter will gladly be made in any future edition of this book.